BADGES AND INSIGNIA OF WORLD WAR II AIR FORCE · NAVAL · MARINE

BADGES AND INSIGNIA OF WORLD WAR II AIR FORCE · NAVAL · MARINE

Guido Rosignoli

First published in Great Britain by Blandford Press Ltd as two volumes:
Air Force Badges and Insignia of World War II and
Naval and Marine Badges and Insignia of World War II.

This edition published by Peerage Books
59 Grosvenor Street
London W1

ISBN 0 907408 34 6

Printed in Hong Kong

Book I
Air Force Badges and Insignia

BOOK I
CONTENTS

Acknowledgments

I would like to thank:
Mr H. L. King; Mr A. L. Kipling; Mr S. L. Nash; Mr E. E. Stott, Royal Aircraft Establishment, Farnborough; Prof. C. Thomas, M.A., F.S.A., Hon. M.R.I.A., and Mr A. E. White.

Squadron Leader A. J. Cockle, H.Q. Rhodesian Air Force, Salisbury; Major L. N. Masencamp of the Office of the Armed Forces Attaché at the South African Embassy, London, and Major C. A. Morrison, Canadian Defence Liaison Staff in London.

Mr A. Kielland Hauge, Curator of the Haermuseet, Oslo.

Captain H. Ringoir, Hon. Gunner of the R.N.A.

Mr L. A. T. Ege, Director of the Royal Danish Air Force's Historical Branch and Mrs Inga Fl. Rasmussen, Curator, Tøjhusmuseet, Copenhagen; and Mr J. P. Champagne.

P. M. Pavasovic, Lieut.-Col. Royal Yugoslav Artillery, President of the Royal Yugoslav ex-Combatants' Association 'Drazha Mihailovich' in Great Britain, and his son Mr Milan P. Pavasovic, who was responsible for translations and the organisation of the material relating to the Royal Yugoslav Air Force.

Mr C. G. Sweeting, Curatorial Assistant, Aeronautics, at the National Air and Space Museum, Smithsonian Institution, Washington D.C. and Mr Pierre C. T. Vereye.

Col. Pilota G. Battazzi, Air Force Attaché at the Italian Embassy in London, and Geom. L. Granata.

Lieut.-General, CA, Chang Ju-ho, Deputy Chief of General Staff for Personnel, Ministry of National Defence, Republic of China.

Mr A. Mollo; Mr F. Ollenschläger and G. I. Paprikoff, M.D.

Mr M. Melkko, Director, Sotamuseo, Helsinki; Commander I. Balaban, Mr I. Ratiu, M.A., LL.B.

Mr K. Barbarski, Vice Curator of the Polish Institute and Sikorski Museum in London; Captain W. Milewski and Lieut.-Colonel B. Mincer. Lastly my thanks to Diana, my wife, for her assistance.

Great Britain

Plate 1. Historical Background

The first aeronautic venture of significance began in the late 1870s with the setting up of a Balloon School at Chatham and soon after interest was captured by airships, the next obvious stage of flight.

Meanwhile a great deal of individual efforts were dedicated to the building of aeroplanes, until finally, in April 1911, the Air Battalion, Royal Engineers, was officially formed at Farnborough. It was divided in two detachments, one specialised in airships, the other in aeroplanes. Other experiments had taken place at Eastchurch where the Naval Flying School was established in 1911.

In order to unify these disjointed efforts a Royal Warrant was issued on 13 April 1912 sanctioning the formation of the Royal Flying Corps, with a Naval and a Military Wing, both served by the same Flying School. However, the Royal Navy kept its own school at Eastchurch and eventually on 1 July 1914 the Naval Wing of the Royal Flying Corps became the Royal Naval Air Service.

At the outbreak of World War 1 there were no armed aircraft in Britain and the first experiments with machine-guns took place in the following year, 1915. Initially, the only flyers were pilots and observers but during the war the observer also became air gunner.

Pilots wings, in gilt metal with brooch pin at the back, and in embroidery, were granted in 1913 for full dress and service dress, respectively. The observers obtained their own badge (Plate 3) in September 1915.

The cap and collar badges of the Royal Flying Corps resemble those of the Royal Engineers, the forerunners of British aviation, while the cap badges of the Royal Naval Air Service maintained their naval flair, with an eagle in flight in place of the anchor. The personnel of the latter wore naval uniforms; the flying officers wore the eagle on the left sleeve above the distinction lace and, from 1916, also on the left shoulder board. The observers were given their own badge in 1917, a winged 'O' which was worn on both sleeves and shoulder straps. Later in the same year a winged 'A' was adopted for officers of the Royal Naval Reserve and Royal Naval Volunteer Reserve attached to the Royal Naval Air Service.

Many other badges were introduced during World War 1: ratings wore a red embroidered eagle on the right sleeve and specialists had propellers and other devices placed under their eagles. Metal and cloth shoulder titles and other badges were also adopted, even cap tallies inscribed 'ROYAL FLYING CORPS' in gold standard lettering on black.

The Royal Flying Corps, Military Wing, had its own uniforms from 1913, with an unusual double breasted service dress tunic which was known as the 'maternity jacket'. During World War I the officers wore their rank badges on the shoulder straps or alternatively on the cuffs.

There were two classes of warrant officer, wearing the Royal Arms and the Royal Crown respectively. The Quartermaster-Sergeant had four inverted chevrons ensigned by the propeller of the Flight Sergeant who had three 'V' chevrons, with a 4-bladed prop- and star-badge as illustrated, and the Royal Crown above. Only the propeller, without its central star, was worn by the Sergeant and two chevrons, without any badge, were worn by the Corporal. In October 1916, a new badge was adopted for Air Mechanic First Class: it depicted a 2-bladed propeller, embroidered in white on khaki, worn on the right upper sleeve above the elbow.

The officers wore metal R.F.C. shoulder titles while other ranks wore cloth titles, embroidered in white on dark blue.

The growth of aviation during World War 1 is remarkable. In August 1914 the personnel of the R.F.C. amounted to 1,244 officers and other ranks while the personnel of the R.N.A.S. comprised a total of about 600 men, flying 272 machines in all. By October 1918 the R.A.F. comprised over 290,000 officers and other ranks manning 198 squadrons and five flights.

At the beginning of that war no one yet knew if the future of aviation lay in the aeroplane or in the airship. Aeroplanes were all-purpose machines, classified by their speed and reliability and by the end of the war there were fighter-interceptors, bombers, observation planes and even aeroplanes for long-range reconnaissance.

New, skilled men were required for this type of warfare: Marconi's 'apparatus' was fitted on the planes so that messages could be transmitted and received and the wireless operators began wearing a brass badge depicting an 'O' for operator, with three lightning flashes on each side. Photographers were trained for aerial observation.

It was the age of the great aces of aviation, who surged to fame by destroying scores of enemy planes; for example, Captain Albert Ball V.C. and Major W. Avery Bishop, V.C., a Canadian who shot down at least fifty enemy planes, out-rivalled by Captain James B. McCudden, who by April 1918 had destroyed fifty-four planes. Twice he destroyed four 4-seater enemy planes in a single day.

In the meantime, it became apparent that a general reorganisation was necessary in order to develop, govern and supply adequately this ever growing new war-machine. The Air Board was expanded to Air Ministry and on 1 April 1918 the R.F.C. and the R.N.A.S. combined to form the

Royal Air Force. In 1924 the Fleet Air Arm was instituted and officers of the Royal Navy were admitted to R.A.F. training schools.

Khaki service dress uniforms, similar to those of the army, were adopted in April 1918 and sky blue uniforms made their appearance as well for a short time after the end of the war, until in September 1919 the familiar grey-blue uniforms were finally introduced. New officers' ranks badges were also introduced in 1918: these were cuff stripes of varying size with a crowned eagle above them. The crown and the eagle were in separate pieces and the latter always faced outwards.

The rank titles were then still the same as those of the Army; the generals wore a large stripe with three, two or one narrow stripes above it. The Brigadier-General had only the large stripe while the Colonel and the Lieutenant-Colonel wore four and three narrow stripes respectively. The Major wore two narrow stripes with a narrower one in between (illustrated); the Captain and Lieutenant had two and one stripe respectively and the 2nd Lieutenant initially wore only the crowned eagle on the cuffs and later one narrower stripe as well.

On 27 August 1919 these titles were changed and the colour of the stripes also changed to match the new grey-blue uniforms. These stripes and rank titles are still in use at the present time.

The officers' grey-blue service dress consisted of the peaked cap, a single breasted jacket with open collar, cloth belt and patch pockets with flaps, breeches with puttees or riding boots, or trousers. The other ranks wore tunics with high neck collar until the late 1930s, although warrant officers and senior N.C.O.s had open collars earlier. A couple of years later, breeches and puttees were replaced by trousers for all ranks.

In 1920 a blue full dress uniform was introduced for the officers, followed the year after by a busby of black leather and short fur, in line with the tradition of the original flying helmets. The tunic of this uniform had a stand-up collar with oak leaves embroidered in gold, depending upon rank: officers of Air Rank had embroidery all round the collar; group captains, wing commanders and squadron leaders only at the front, while all others had only five gold oak leaves at the front. All had the crown and eagle in gold on the shoulder straps and the officers of Air rank had an additional laurel wreath around the buttons (Plate 4). A dress waist belt was worn as well.

The greatcoat and mess dress were adopted in 1920, but the latter was abolished during the war, until 1947 when both greatcoat and mess dress were modified. Grey-blue battledress was adopted and worn by all ranks during World War 2.

In 1921 new badges were issued to airmen serving with the Works and Buildings Services, later discontinued in 1929. Among the many old badges of the Commonwealth air forces I have chosen to illustrate the

1920s' pattern of South African pilots' wings, with the Union's coat of arms in its centre.

Canada, Australia, New Zealand and South Africa had their own independent air forces, although many individuals volunteered to join the R.A.F. as did many others who came from British territories where an organised air force did not yet exist.

The Royal Canadian Air Force traces its origins to the Canadian Aviation Corps founded in 1914, which was reorganised in 1920 and became finally an independent service in 1939. A Canadian naval air branch existed for a short time at the end of World War 1 and was re-formed only in 1946.

The Australian Flying Corps was raised in 1913 and although its personnel manned five squadrons during World War 1, the corps was disbanded in 1919. However it was re-formed the following year and in March 1921 it was renamed Australian Air Force, which became 'Royal' a few months later. The Australians wore dark blue uniforms and the officers had gold stripes on the cuffs, below the crowned eagle.

Earlier, during the war, many New Zealanders served in the A.F.C. or in the R.F.C. as the New Zealand Permanent Air Force was raised as late as 1923. It became Royal New Zealand Air Force in 1934 and an independent service three years later.

The South African Aviation Corps was formed in 1915, disbanded in 1918 and re-formed in 1920 under the designation of South African Air Force.

In Rhodesia an Air Unit was formed in 1935, on a Territorial Force basis, as part of the Rhodesia Regiment and after a period of development in May 1938 the first six Rhodesian pilots received their wings. By the end of August 1939, eight aircraft left Salisbury for Nairobi. During the following months, before Italy's entry into the war, many other pilots were trained in Rhodesia and subsequently by the R.A.F. establishment in Iraq.

In April 1940, the Rhodesia Air Force was absorbed into the R.A.F. and No. 1 Squadron became No. 237 (Rhodesia) Squadron. It was deployed in the war against the Italians in Abyssinia, later in North Africa and the Middle East as an army air support unit, which later became a fighter reconnaissance squadron. In the spring of 1944 the squadron was moved to Corsica and operated in Southern France and Northern Italy until its disbandment in 1945.

Rhodesians fought also in the No. 266 Squadron, a unit raised at Sutton Bridge, England, in 1939. It was designated 'Rhodesian' during the Battle of Britain, later taking part in the invasion of Europe and was disbanded at Hildesheim, Germany in August 1945.

Other Rhodesians were employed in Bomber Command units and in

1941 they were grouped into No. 44 Squadron which became therefore another 'Rhodesian' unit of the R.A.F. No. 44 (Rhodesia) Squadron took part in many bombing raids over Germany, among which the daylight raid of 17 April 1942 should be remembered as, of six Rhodesian Lancasters participating in the operation, only one eventually returned.

Great losses were suffered by Rhodesians during World War 2: out of a total of 2,409 aviators 498 were killed and 228 men received decorations and awards. All wore R.A.F. uniforms and insignia with 'RHODESIA' titles on the upper sleeves.

Men of many nationalities, volunteers from the Commonwealth and British territories and exiles from occupied Europe served in the R.A.F. during the war. The latter used R.A.F. grey-blue uniforms, often with their own badges. These have been dealt with in various chapters of this book.

Women served alongside the men in the air force from the beginning of World War 1. The original Women's Royal Air Force was disbanded in 1920 and later, in 1938 women were once again recruited into the Auxiliary Territorial Service, units of which were attached to the R.A.F.; detachments that became eventually the Women's Auxiliary Air Force, with grey-blue uniforms and badges as men, although their rank titles were different. The W.A.A.F. officers and N.C.O.s wore special peaked caps while the other ranks had dark blue berets, later changed to a head-dress similar to that of the former; cap badges were the same as those of the men. Pay was two-thirds that of the men, depending on the duties performed and the rank held. Teleprinter operators, telephonists, mess staff, cooks and M.T. drivers received 1s. 4d. a day on joining, with prospects of 2s. 4d. a day when mustered as aircraftwomen 1st class and higher rates of pay with further promotions. Those entered for certain special duties, such as equipment assistants and clerks, received 2s. 2d. a day on entering, 2s. 8d. a day when mustered as aircraftwomen 1st Class.*

Plate 2. Cap Badges

The official badge of the Royal Air Force, complete with motto was and is still worn by the officers on the busby of the full dress, adopted in 1921. A gold feather-holder is fitted behind this badge attached at the front of the head-dress, made of leather and fur, the latter resembling the ear flaps of the early flying helmets.

The badge originally devised in 1918 included a garter which in 1922 was modified to a circlet; however, the official description of this badge was promulgated by the Air Ministry only in 1949.

When the R.A.F. was formed in 1918, two new designs of cap badges were adopted for officers and other ranks respectively. The generals,

From Hutchinson's *Pictorial History of the War,* Volume 1.

officers and the Warrant Officers 1st Class wore a badge similar to that illustrated for warrant officers on the peaked cap: it was made of brass and mounted upon a padded backing of black cloth. The other ranks wore cap badges similar to those previously worn by those of the R.N.A.S., in gold embroidery for Warrant Officer 2nd Class and N.C.O.s, in worsted embroidery for the others.

Soon after, new cap badges were adopted following the introduction of the new grey-blue service dress uniforms. The officers of Air Rank were distinguished from the other officers by the use of different cap badges and oak leaves on the visor emphasised rank distinction still further.

The regulations of 1918 prescribed the use of upright metal bars at each side of the badge on the cap band. Lieutenants wore one bar while captains wore two bars; field officers had one row of gold oak leaves on the visor and generals were distinguished by two rows of oak leaves. Later, although the two rows of leaves were maintained for the latter, now known as officers of Air Rank, the one row of oak leaves applied to the rank of Group Captain only. All the other officers had a plain visor, lined with grey-blue cloth.

The chaplains had their own badge, a winged Cross Patee in metal below the Royal Crown. The badge, like those of the other officers, was on a padded dark blue backing.

The warrant officers had the same badge as the officers but made of brass and airmen were given a cap badge that closely resembled that of the R.F.C., with different initials in the centre.

The same type of badges and oak leaves embroideries were worn during the last war by the officers and warrant officers of the Commonwealth air forces whose nationality was usually identified by shoulder titles. However, in the case of airmen, the nationality was disclosed by the cap badge as well, usually by means of initials in the centre of the badge. The South Africans had a different pattern of badge altogether, with the eagle in its centre and the initials of the bi-lingual motto on a separate scroll.

The officers wore the eagle below the crown on the left side of the forage cap; this badge was made in one or two pieces and in the latter case the eagle and the crown were attached by means of a brass backing plate in order to keep the same distance between the two. The generals have worn a small replica of the peaked cap's badge since the beginning of World War 2.

The officers wore the eagle below the crown on the left side of the forage cap; this badge was made in one or two pieces and in the latter case the eagle and the crown were attached by means of a brass backing plate in order to keep the same distance between the two. The generals have worn a small replica of the peaked cap's badge since the beginning of World War 2.

HISTORICAL BACKGROUND

Royal Flying Corps
Cap and Collar Badges

Royal Naval Air Service
Officers' Cap Badge

ROYAL FLYING CORPS

Shoulder Title

Royal Naval Air Service
Chief Petty Officers' Cap Badge

Flight Lieutenant
R.N.A.S.

Flight Sergeant
R.F.C.

Flight Observer
R.N.A.S.

Pilot
R.F.C.

Pilot
South Africa

Shoulder Title

Works and Buildings Services
Cap and Collar Badges

Wireless Operator

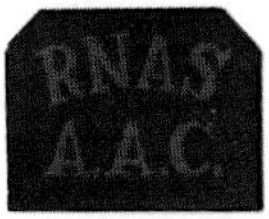

Anti-Aircraft Corps
R.N.A.S.

Major R.A.F.
1918–19

Engineer
R.N.A.S.

PLATE 1

GREAT BRITAIN

CAP BADGES

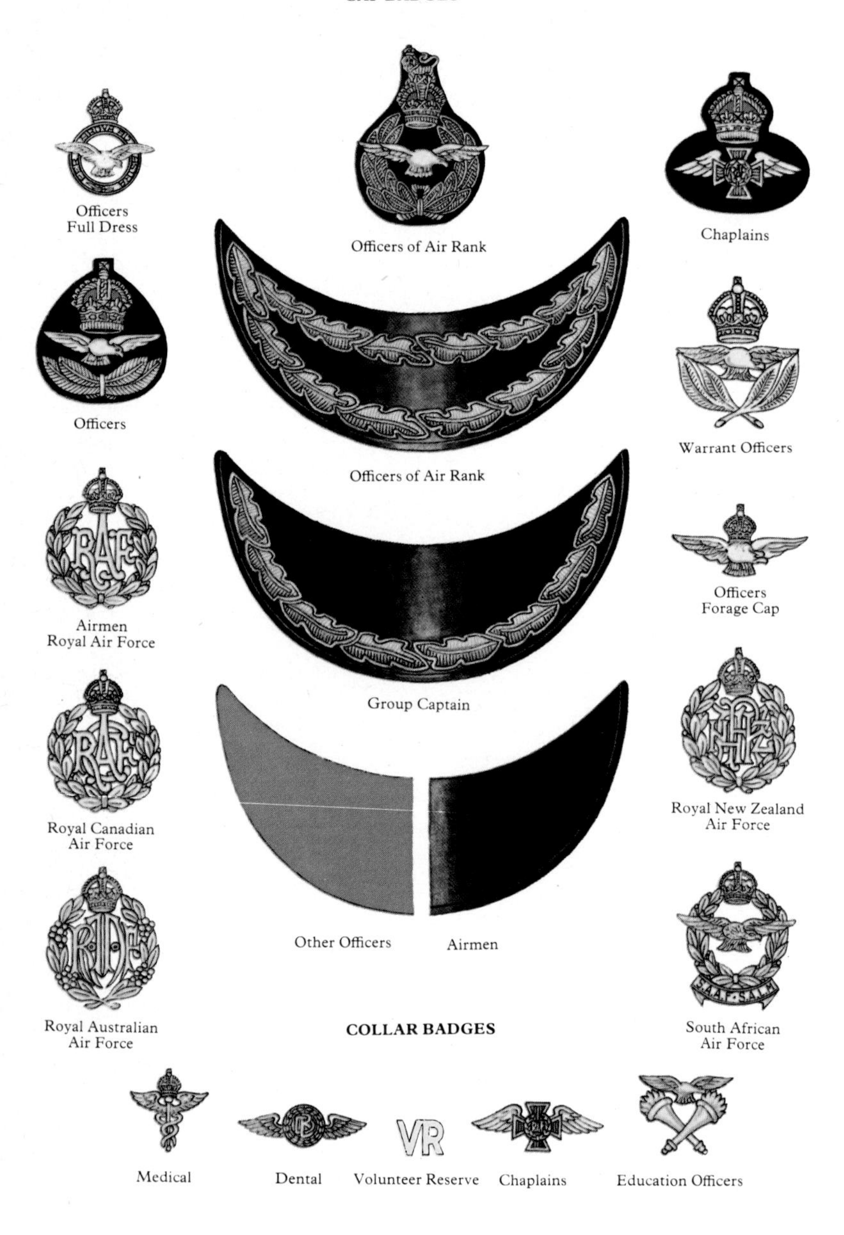

Officers Full Dress

Officers of Air Rank

Chaplains

Officers

Officers of Air Rank

Warrant Officers

Airmen Royal Air Force

Group Captain

Officers Forage Cap

Royal Canadian Air Force

Royal New Zealand Air Force

Other Officers

Airmen

Royal Australian Air Force

South African Air Force

COLLAR BADGES

Medical

Dental

Volunteer Reserve

Chaplains

Education Officers

PLATE 2

PILOTS' WINGS

Pilot R.A.F.
Service Dress

Pilot R.A.F.
Full Dress

Pilot R.C.A.F.

Pilot R.A.A.F.

Pilot S.A.A.F.

Pilot R.N.Z.A.F.

AIRCREW BADGES – R.A.F.

Observer

Navigator

Air Gunner

Wireless Operator
Air Gunner

Flight Engineer

Bomb Aimer

Parachute Training
Instructor

Signaller

Bomb Aimer

AIRCREW BADGES – R.C.A.F.

Navigator

Bomb Aimer

Air Gunner

Wireless Operator
Air Gunner

Flight Engineer

AIRCREW BADGES – R.A.A.F.

Observer

Air Gunner

Bomb Aimer

Signaller

PLATE 3

OFFICERS' RANK BADGES

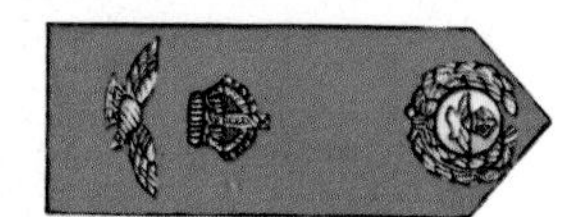

Officers of Air Rank
Full Dress

Marshal of the Royal Air Force

Other Officers
Full Dress

Air Chief Marshal

Air Marshal

Air Vice-Marshal

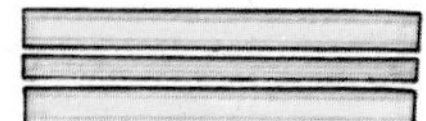

Squadron Leader
Full Dress

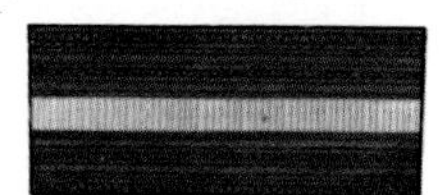

Air Commodore

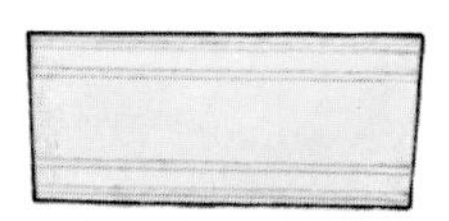

Air Commodore
Full Dress

Group Captain

Wing Commander

Squadron Leader

Flight Lieutenant

Flying Officer

Pilot Officer

Air Marshal
Greatcoat

Flying Officer
Royal Auxiliary Air Force
Battledress

WARRANT OFFICERS' AND N.C.O.s' RANK BADGES

Warrant Officer
(1st Class)

Flight Sergeant

Sergeant

Corporal

Drum-Major

Leading Aircraftman

Good Conduct Stripes

P.T. Instructor

P.T. Instructor

TRADE AND OTHER BADGES

Bandsman

Shoulder Badge

Trumpeter

A
Auxiliary

Parachute Training
Instructor

Ground Gunner

Volunteer Reserve

Ground Gunner

Signaller

GREAT BRITAIN

TRADE AND OTHER BADGES

Combined Operations

R.A.F. Regiment

Air-Sea Rescue Service

Radio Operator/Mechanic

Apprentice

Eagle Squadron

Bomb Disposal

Air Gunner

Wireless Operator

NATIONALITY TITLES

PLATE 6

BADGES OF OTHER FLYING ORGANISATIONS

Air Defence Cadet Corps

Air Transport Auxiliary

Civil Air Guard

Air Training Corps

Air Transport Auxiliary
Flying Wing

Royal Observer Corps

FLEET AIR ARM INSIGNIA

Officers'
Cap Badge

Chief Petty Officers'
Cap Badge

Petty Officers'
Cap Badge

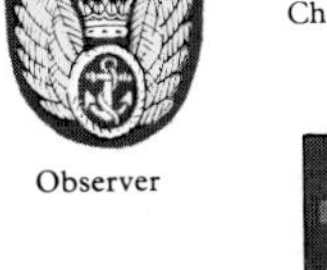
Observer

Aircrewman

Pilot

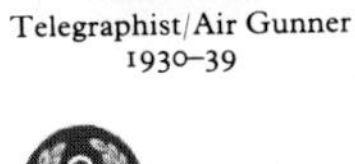
Telegraphist/Air Gunner
1930–39

Aircrewman (U)

R.A.F. Officers
Attached to F.A.A.

Air Branch Lieutenant
1939

Air Branch Officers
1938

GREAT BRITAIN

NON-SUBSTANTIVE BADGES

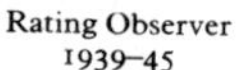

Rating Observer
1939–45

Acting Rating Observer
1939–45

Air Gunner
1st Class
1939–44

Air Gunner
2nd Class
1939–44

Air Gunner
3rd Class
1939–44

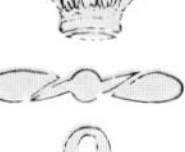

Air Mechanic
Airframes Engines
1939–48

Radio Mechanic
1944–48

Air Mechanic
Electrical Ordnance
1939–48

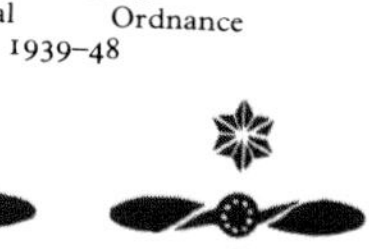
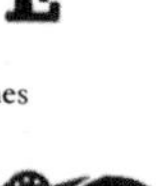

Air Mechanic
Airframes Engines
1939–48

Air Mechanic
Electrical Ordnance
1939–48

Radio Mechanic
1944–48

Air Mechanic
Airframes Engines
1939–48

Air Mechanic
Electrical Ordnance
1939–48

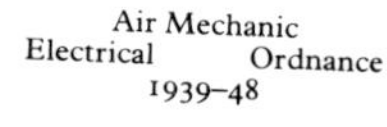

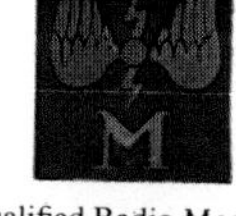

Qualified Radio Mechanic
1944–47

Air Fitter
Airframes Engines
1940–48

Air Mechanic
Unclassified
1943–48

Air Fitter
Electrical Ordnance
1940–48

Airframes Engines Electrical Ordnance

Air Fitter
1940–48

Unclassified
1943–48

PLATE 8

NORWAY

CAP BADGES

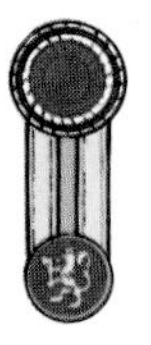
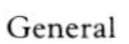
General

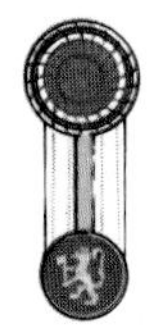
Officer

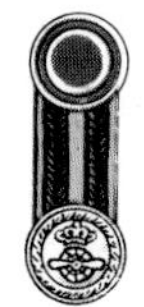
Sergeant

Other Ranks

RANK BADGES

Major-General

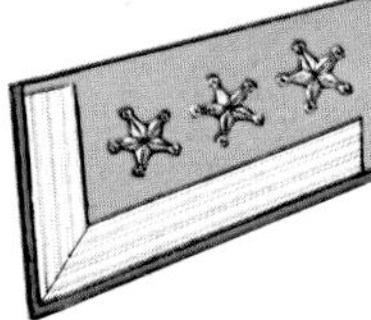
Colonel

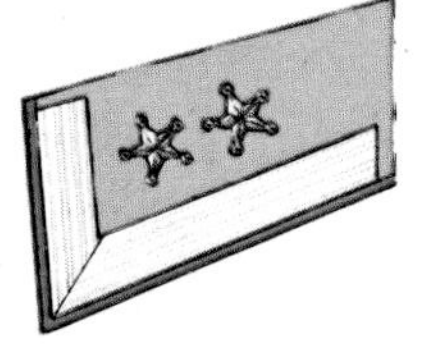
Lieutenant-Colonel

Major

Captain

Lieutenant

2nd Lieutenant

OTHER BADGES

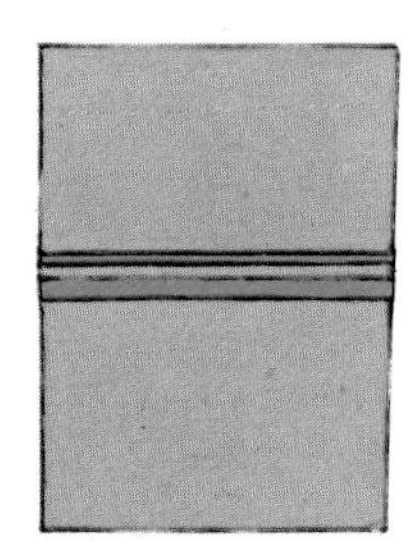
Sergeant

Pilot

Observer

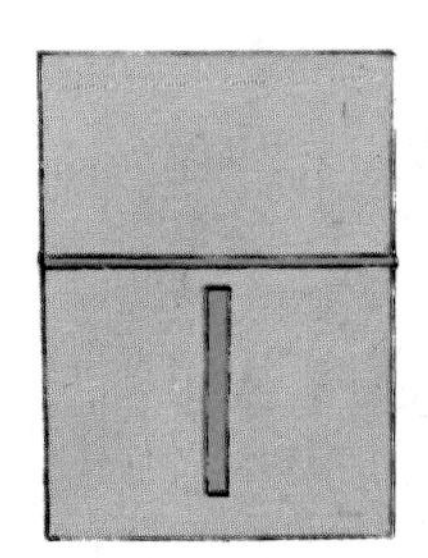
Corporal

Button

PLATE 9

NORWAY

BADGES WORN AFTER 1940

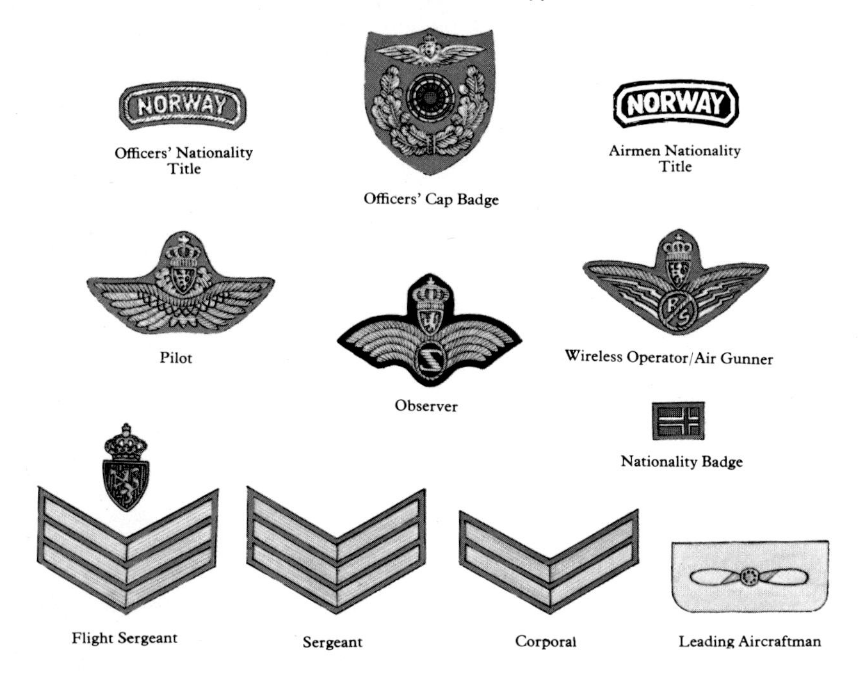

NETHERLANDS

ARMY AIR SERVICE – CAP BADGES

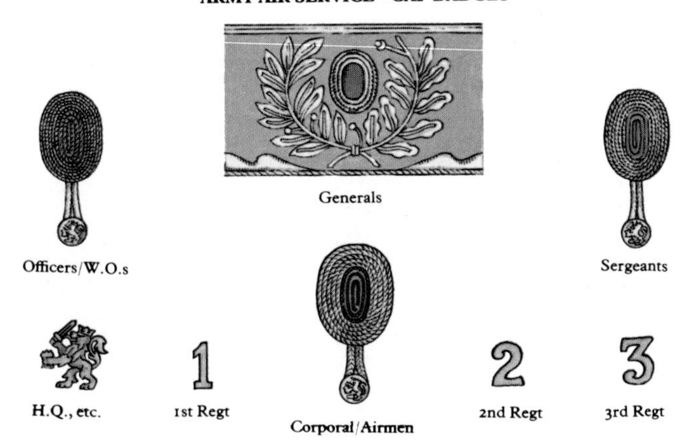

ARMY AIR SERVICE – RANK BADGES

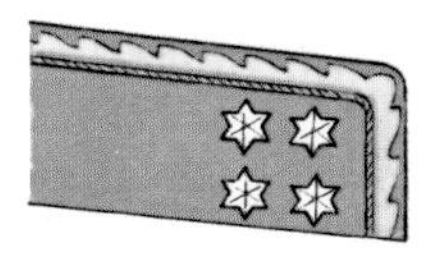
Lieutenant-General

Major-General

Colonel

Lieutenant-Colonel

Major

Captain

1st Lieutenant

2nd Lieutenant

Captain Adjutant

1st Lieutenant Adjutant

Warrant Officer (W.O.1)

Other Ranks

Sergeant-Major

Sergeant 1st Class

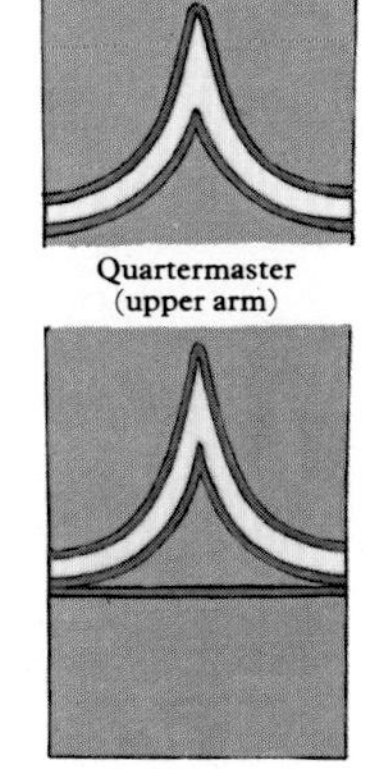
Quartermaster (upper arm)

Sergeant

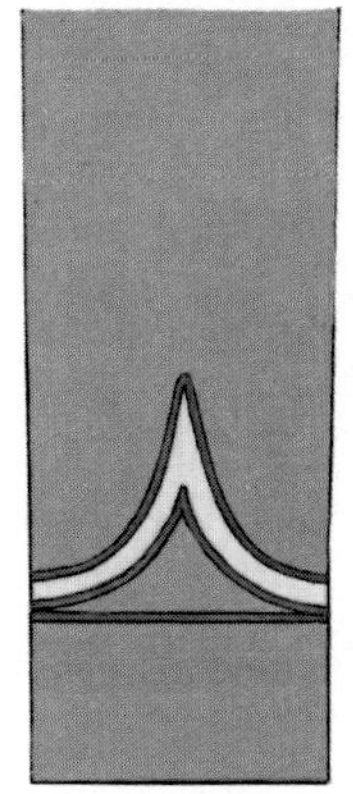
Corporal

NETHERLANDS

QUALIFICATION BADGES
ARMY AIR SERVICE

Pilot

Pilot – Observer

Observer

Pilot
(made in Britain)

Observer
(made in Britain)

ROYAL NETHERLANDS INDIAN ARMY AIR SERVICE

Pilot

Pilot – Observer

Observer

Air Gunner

Bomb Aimer

Flight Surgeon

Photographer

Wireless Operator

Flight Engineer

ROYAL NETHERLANDS NAVAL AIR SERVICE

Air Gunner

Air Telegraphist – Gunner

Telegraphist

TRADE AND OTHER BADGES

R.N.A.A.S.
(nationality title)

Mechanic

Chief Mechanic

Aircraft
Mechanic

NETHERLAND

Airman attached to R.A.F.V.R.

R.N.A.A.S.
(nationality title)

RANK BADGES – ARMY AIR SERVICE AFTER 1940

Lieutenant-General

Major-General

1st Captain Adjutant

Colonel

Lieutenant-Colonel

Major

1st Lieutenant Adjutant

Warrant Officer

Captain

1st Lieutenant

2nd Lieutenant

Airmen

Sergeant-Major

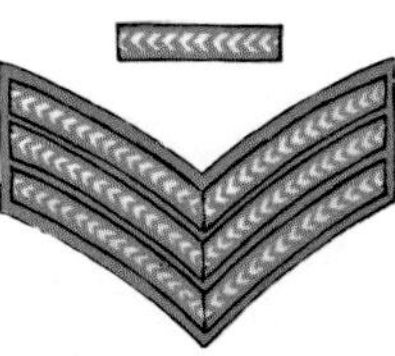
Sergeant 1st Class

Quartermaster

Sergeant

Corporal

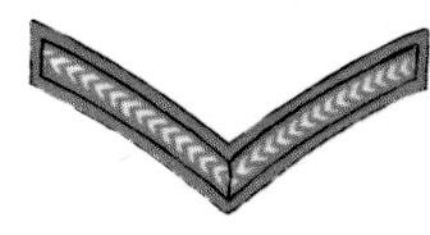
Private 1st Class

NETHERLANDS

ROYAL NETHERLANDS NAVAL AIR SERVICE

Flyer
Warrant and Petty Officers

Officers' Cap Badge

Repairman
Warrant and Petty Officers

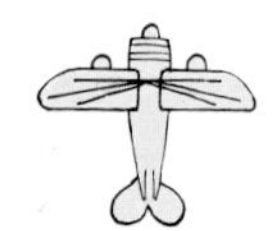

Repairman
Leading Seaman and
Seaman 1st Class

Repairman
Apprentice 3rd year

Flyer
Corporal
Leading Seaman

Repairman
Apprentice 2nd year

Repairman
Apprentice 1st year

ROYAL NETHERLANDS INDIAN ARMY AIR SERVICE

Officers' Cap Badge

Captain
Black Uniform

Colonel
White Uniform

Major-General

Major

Garrison Uniform

Lieutenant-Colonel
Field Uniform

1st Lieutenant
Garrison Uniform

Ensign
Garrison Uniform

Warrant Officer
Field Uniform

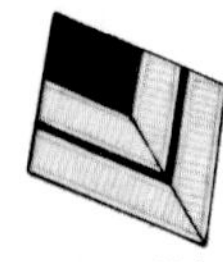

Sergeant-Major
White Uniform

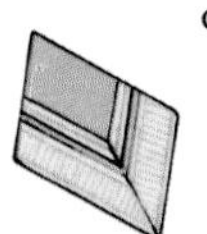

1st Sergeant
Field Uniform

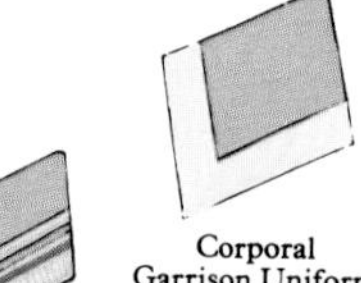

Corporal
Garrison Uniform

QM Sergeant
Field Uniform

ROYAL NETHERLANDS INDIAN ARMY AIR SERVICE – AFTER 1942

Major-General collar badge

Officers' Cap Badge

Major-General shoulder straps' badge

Colonel

Lieutenant-Colonel

Major

Captain

1st Lieutenant

2nd Lieutenant

Ensign

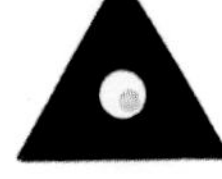
Warrant Officer

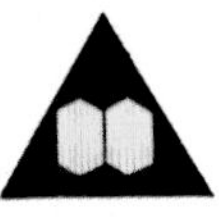
Sergeant-Major

Sergeant

Corporal

Private 1st Class

HISTORICAL BACKGROUND

U.S.S.R.

Aviation and Aeronautics

Pilot
(Imperial Russian)

Observer
(Imperial Russian)

Aviation and Aeronautics – Exemplary Unit

Red Army Aviator

Red Navy Aviator

Aviation Engineer

HEAD-DRESS AND RANK BADGES (1940–43)

Officers' Cap Badge peaked cap

General of the Army

Major-General

Colonel-General

Lieutenant-General

General of the Army sleeves' badge

Other Generals sleeves' badge

Officers' Cap Badge forage cap

Colonel

Lieutenant-Colonel

Major

Captain

RANK BADGES (1940–43)

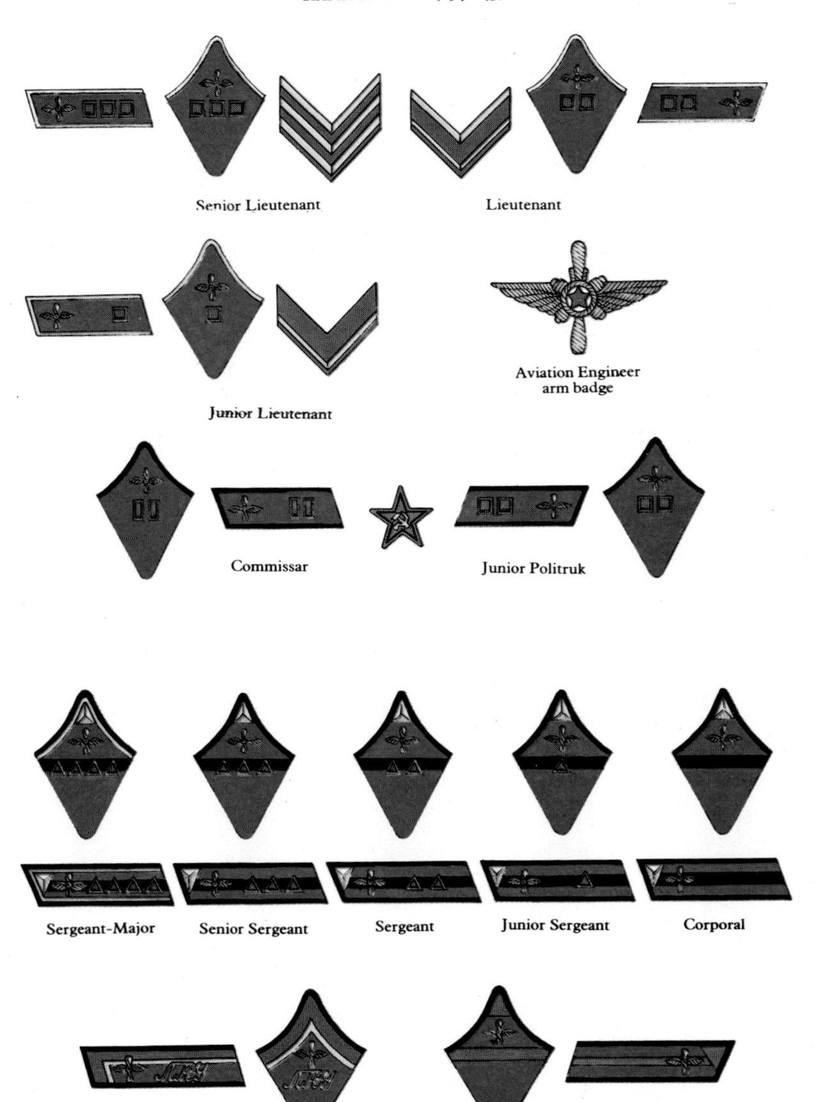

PLATE 17

HEAD-DRESS AND RANK BADGES (1943)

Marshals' and Generals' Cap Insignia
(Parade Uniform)

Collar and Cuffs

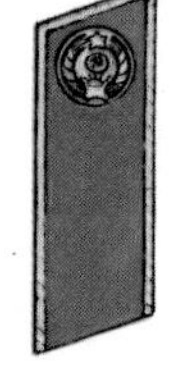

Collar and Cuffs

Marshals

Greatcoat Collar Patches
(Parade) (Ordinary)

Generals

Marshals' and Generals' Shoulder Boards

Marshal
4.2.1943

Supreme Marshal
27.10.1943

Marshal
27.10.1943

General of Army

Colonel-General

Lieutenant-General

Major-General

HEAD-DRESS AND RANK BADGES (1943)

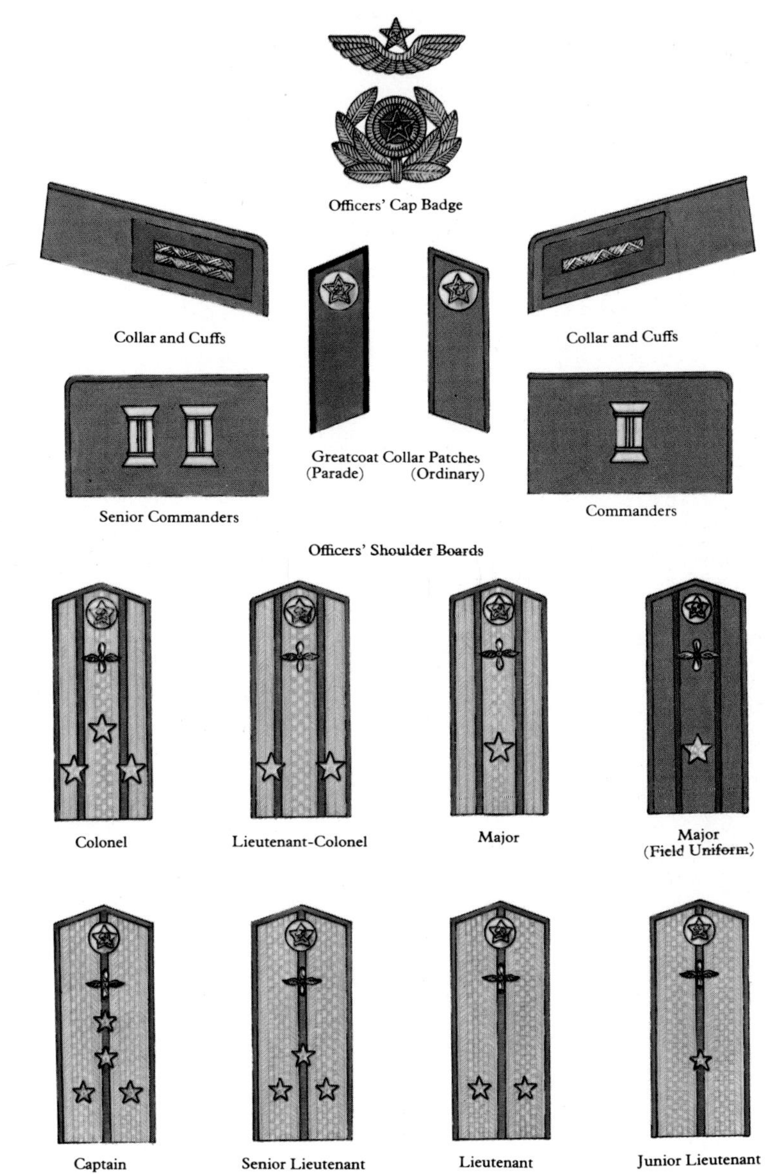

PLATE 19

U.S.S.R.

HEAD-DRESS AND RANK BADGES (1943)

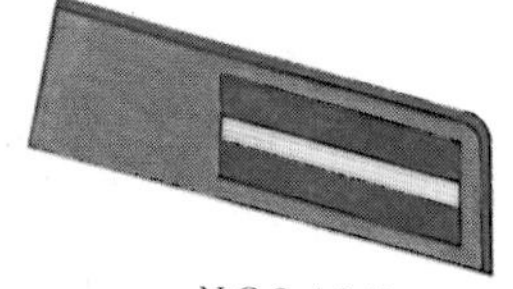

N.C.O.s' Collar

Forage Cap Badge

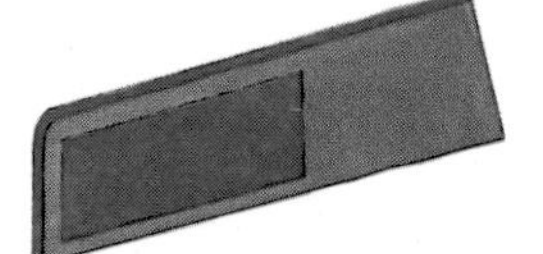

Privates' Collar

N.C.O.s' Shoulder Boards

Sergeant-Major

Senior Sergeant

Sergeant

Junior Sergeant

Corporal

Private

(Parade Uniform)

Sergeant-Major

Corporal

(Field Uniform)

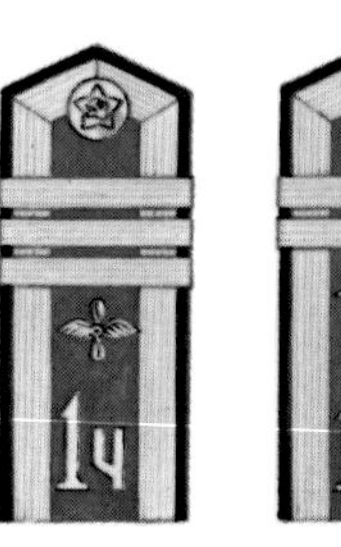

Aviation Specialists' School

DENMARK

MISCELLANEA

Officers attached to R.A.F.V.R.

Pilot

Airmen Attached to R.A.F.V.R.

ARMY OF THE AIR - CAP BADGES

General Member of the Superior War Council or Air Army Commander

General Commander of Region or Air Corps

General of Air Division

General of Air Brigade

Metropolitan

North African

General Staff – Captain

Colonial Aviation – Captain

Rank and File

Mechanic/Specialist Officers

Administrative Officers

Steel Helmet's Badge

QUALIFICATION WINGS

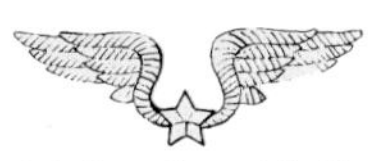

Aviation – General Staff

Aviation Metropolitan and North African

Aerodrome – Metropolitan

Aerodrome – North African

Aviation – Colonial

(Evening Dress)

FRANCE

RANK BADGES

General Member of the Superior War Council or Air Army Commander

General Commander of Region or Air Corps

General of Air Division

General of Air Brigade

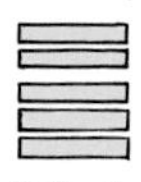
Colonel

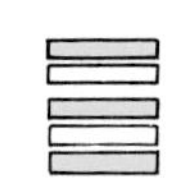
Lieutenant-Colonel

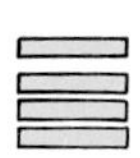
Major

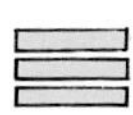
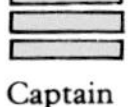
Captain

Lieutenant

2nd Lieutenant

Chief Warrant Officer

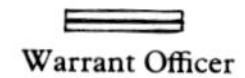
Warrant Officer

Chief-Sergeant

Sergeant (Regular)

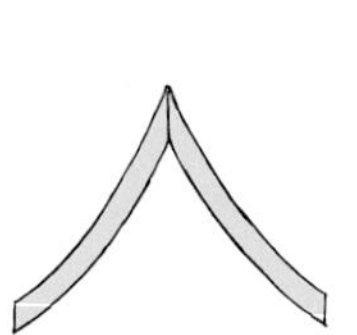
Sergeant

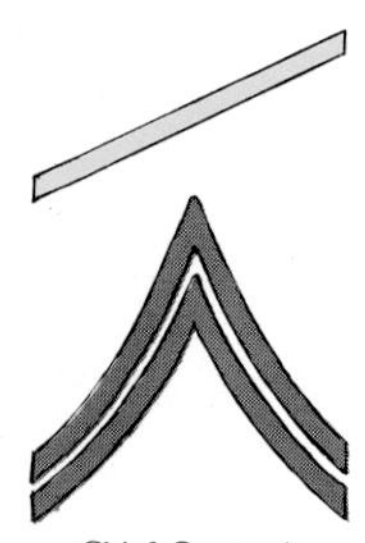
Chief-Corporal

Corporal

Private 1st Class

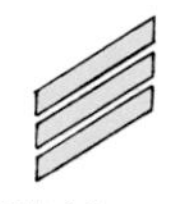
Chief-Sergeant (Field Uniform)

PLATE 22

COLLAR PATCHES – OFFICERS

Mechanic/Specialists

Administration

NON-COMMISSIONED OFFICERS

Fighter Interceptors
Pilot

Mixed Formations
Air Crew

North African A.C.
Ground Specialist

Meteorology

RANK AND FILE

Fighter Interceptors

Mixed Formations

Bombers

Intelligence, Reconnaissance,
Observation

Aerodrome
Base (Aircraft)

Aerostation
Base (Balloons)

Balloon
Battalions

Air Battalions
and Companies

North African
Formations

Colonial
Aviation

Meteorology

Mechanic
Aptitude Certificate

Aerostation Stevedore

FRANCE

QUALIFICATION BADGES – ARMY OF THE AIR

Aircraft Pilot

Airship Pilot

Observer
Cadet Aircraft Pilot

Air Crew

Observer – Mechanic
Cadet Airship Pilot

MARITIME AVIATION

Aircraft Pilot

Arm Badge

Airship Pilot

Aircraft Crew

Captive Balloon
Observer

Pilot Naval Aviation
F.F.N.F.

Aircrew Naval Aviation
F.F.N.F.

FREE FRENCH AIR FORCE

F.F.A.F. Badge

Officers' Cap Badge

F.F.A.F. Badge

Ile-de-France
Group

Alsace
Group

Helmet Badge

Lorraine
Group

Bretagne
Group

FREE FRENCH AIR FORCE

Shoulder Title
Group Normandy in the U.S.S.R.

Military Airline

Shoulder Title
Group Normandy in the U.S.S.R.

Flying Cadre

Shoulder Title
Group Normandy in the U.S.S.R.

Air Mechanics Corps

Air Medical Service

Air Police

Corps of the Administrative Services

Flight Surgeon

Air Commissar

Air Police

Air Musician

Mechanic

Equipment Mechanic

Aircraft Mechanic

N.C.O.s' RANK BADGES

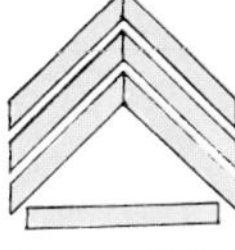

Sergeant-Major

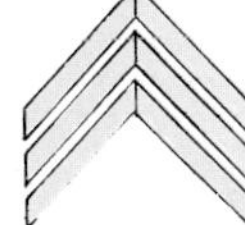

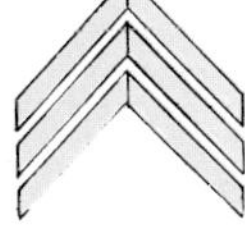

Chief-Sergeant

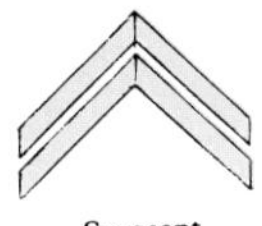

Sergeant
(Regular)

Sergeant

Chief-Corporal

Corporal

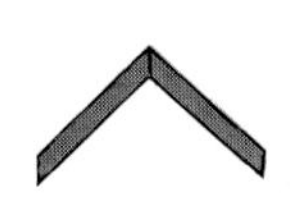

Private 1st Class

BELGIUM

OFFICERS' CAP AND QUALIFICATION BADGES

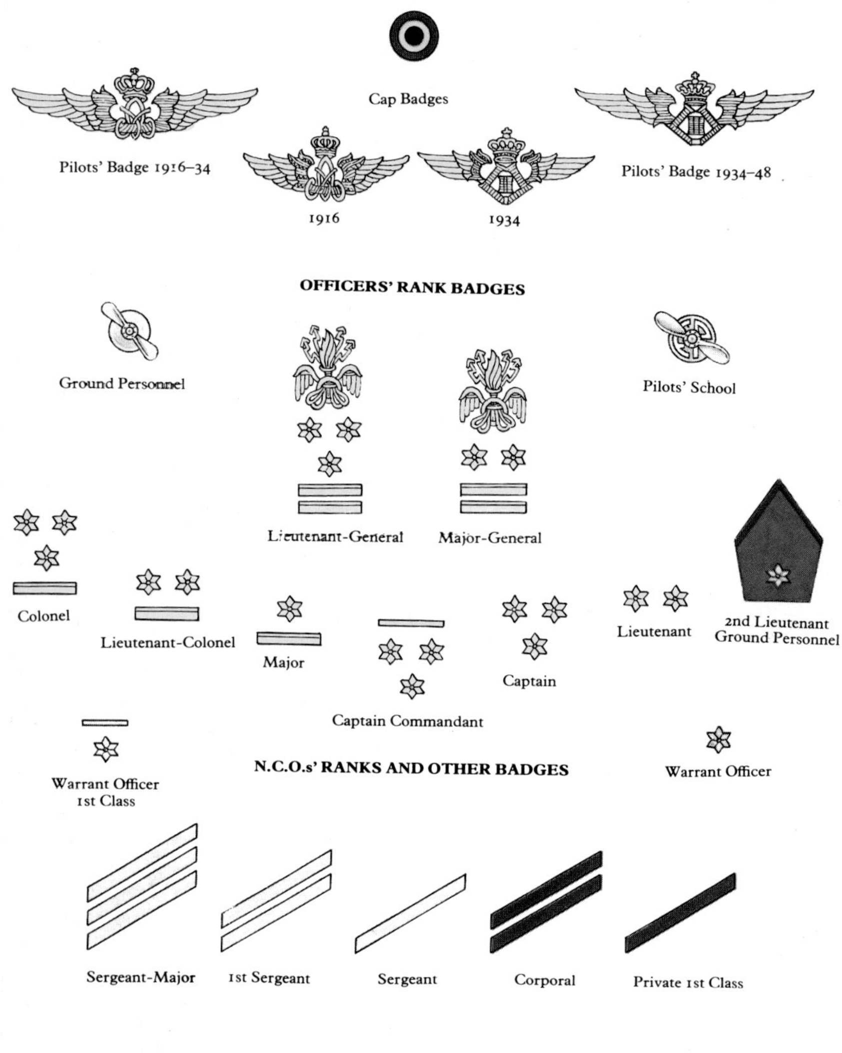

Officers attached to R.A.F.V.R.

Aerostat Officer

Airmen attached to R.A.F.V.R.

BELGIUM

FORMATIONS' BADGES

1/I/1
La Mouette

3/II/1
Feuille de Houx

5/III/1
Hirondelle

Pilots' School

Aviation School

7/IV/1
Diable

9/V/1
Sioux Bleu

11/VI/1
Sioux Rouge

1/I/2
Comète

2/I/2
Chardon

4/II/2
Cocotte Rouge

3/II/2
Cocotte Blanche

5/III/2
Aigle Bleu

6/III/2
Aigle Rouge

1/I/3
Dragon Doré

3/I/3
Dragon Argenté

5/III/2
Aigle Egyptien

7/III/3
Flêche Ailée

YUGOSLAVIA

CAP AND QUALIFICATION BADGES

Officers' Cap Badge

Pilot

Observer

YUGOSLAVIA

RANK BADGES

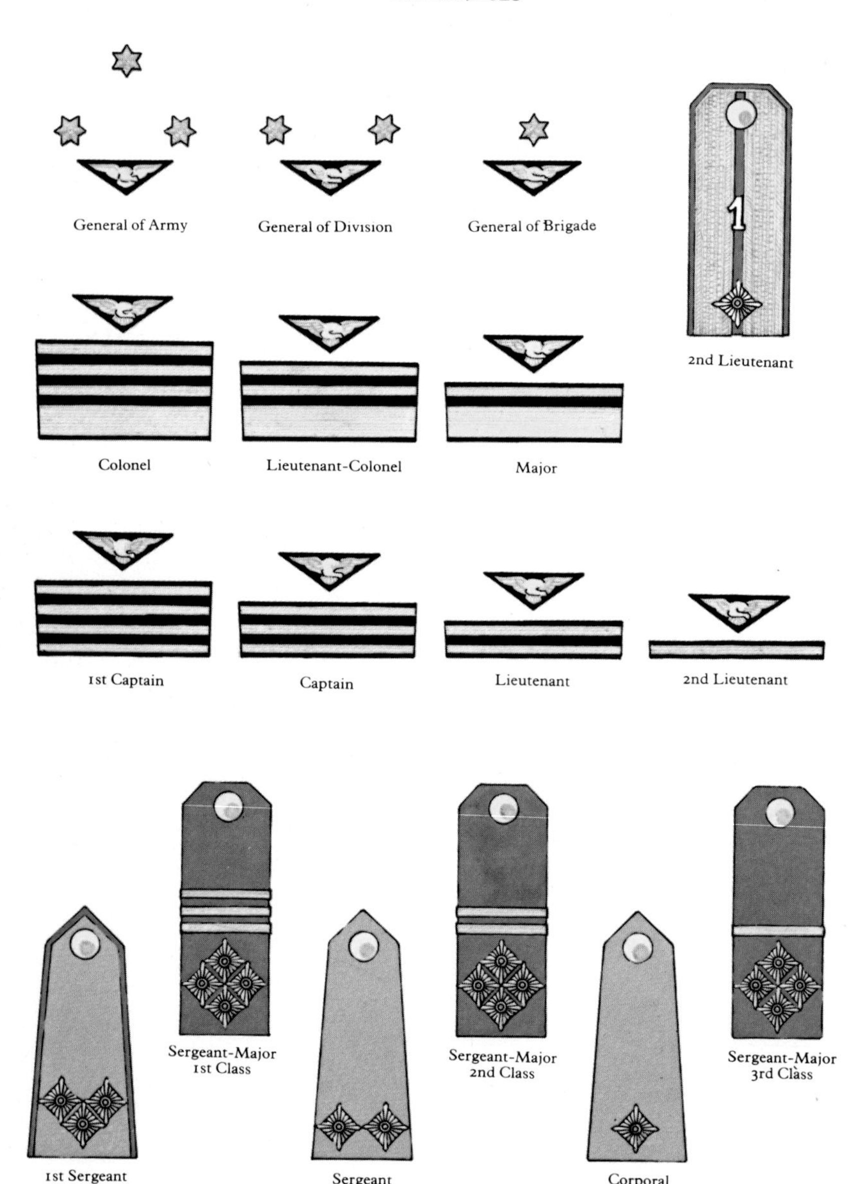

General of Army

General of Division

General of Brigade

2nd Lieutenant

Colonel

Lieutenant-Colonel

Major

1st Captain

Captain

Lieutenant

2nd Lieutenant

Sergeant-Major 1st Class

Sergeant-Major 2nd Class

Sergeant-Major 3rd Class

1st Sergeant

Sergeant

Corporal

HISTORICAL BACKGROUND

Military Aviator 1913

1

2

Military Aviator, Junior and Reserve Military Aviator 1917

A

3

4

B

5

6

7

9

C

D

11

8. Military Aviator – Oct. 1917

Airplane and Balloon Observer

10

12

13

Enlisted Pilot

14

Bombing Military Aviator

Junior and Reserve Military Aeronaut

Military Aeronaut

Junior and Reserve Military Aeronaut

Military Aeronaut
Junior and Reserve Military Aeronaut

Observer – 1919
Qualified as Pilot

Observer – 1918

Enlisted Aviator – Air Service

Airship Pilot

PLATE 29

CAP BADGES AND OTHER INSIGNIA

Cadets
U.S.A.A.F.

Officers
U.S.A.A.F.

Enlisted Men
U.S.A.A.F.

Officers' Collar Badges
U.S.A.A.F.

Warrant/Flight Officer
U.S.A.A.F.

Enlisted Men's Collar Badges
U.S.A.A.F.

Warrant Officer
U.S. Navy Aviation

Officers/Chief W.O.
U.S. Navy Aviation

Petty Officers
U.S. Navy Aviation

U.S. Navy Aviators
(Garrison Cap)

U.S.M.C. Aviation Cadets
Garrison Cap

Officers
U.S.C.G. Aviation

Petty Officers
U.S.C.G. Aviation

Warrant Officers
U.S.C.G. Aviation

Enlisted Men
U.S.C.G. Aviation

Officers (Dress)
U.S.M.C. Aviation

Officers
Collar – right

Enlisted Men
Garrison Cap

Enlisted Men (Dress)
U.S.M.C. Aviation

OFFICERS' AND WARRANT OFFICERS' RANK INSIGNIA

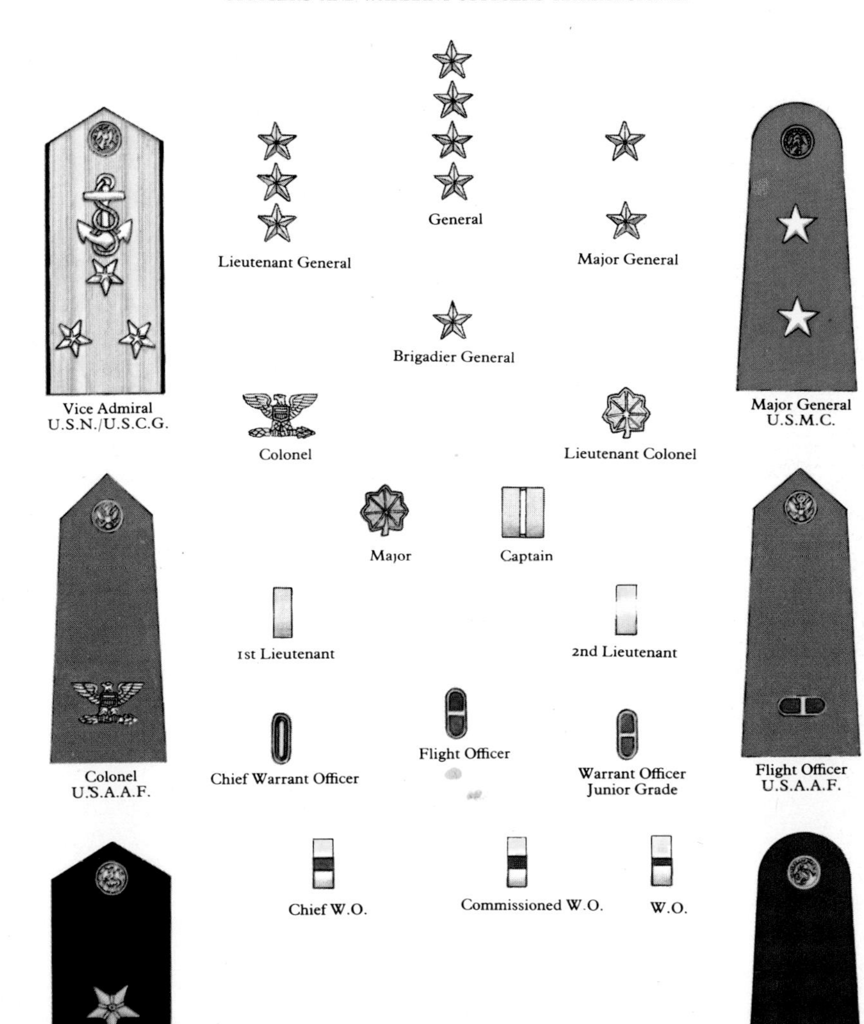

Vice Admiral U.S.N./U.S.C.G.

Lieutenant General

General

Major General

Major General U.S.M.C.

Brigadier General

Colonel

Lieutenant Colonel

Major

Captain

1st Lieutenant

2nd Lieutenant

Colonel U.S.A.A.F.

Chief Warrant Officer

Flight Officer

Warrant Officer Junior Grade

Flight Officer U.S.A.A.F.

Chief W.O.

Commissioned W.O.

W.O.

Chief W.O.s' and W.O.s' Sleeve Stripes

Lieutenant U.S.N./U.S.C.G.

2nd Lieutenant U.S.M.C.

U.S.A.

ARMY AVIATION N.C.O.s' RANK BADGES

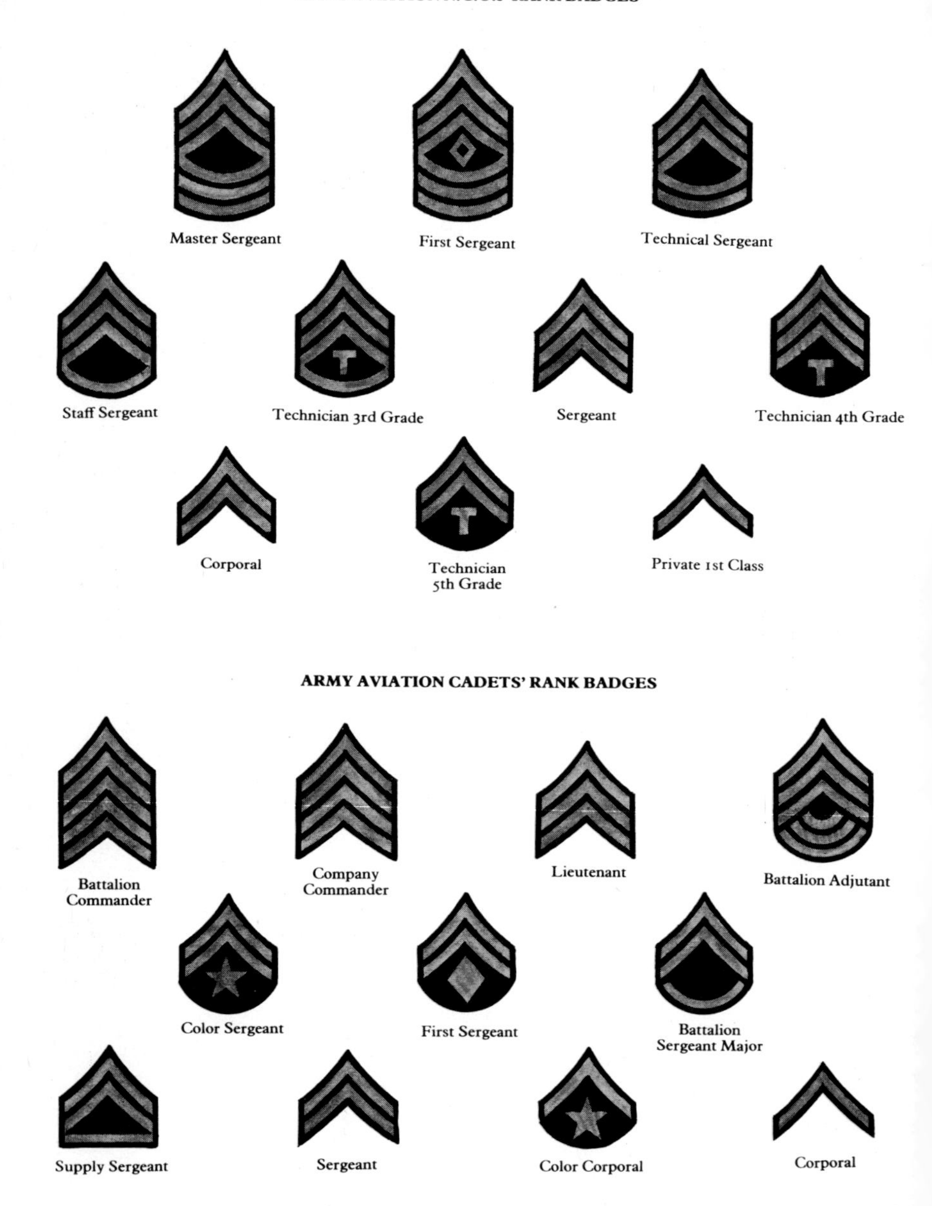

PLATE 32

ARMY AVIATION CADETS' RANK BADGES – OVERCOAT

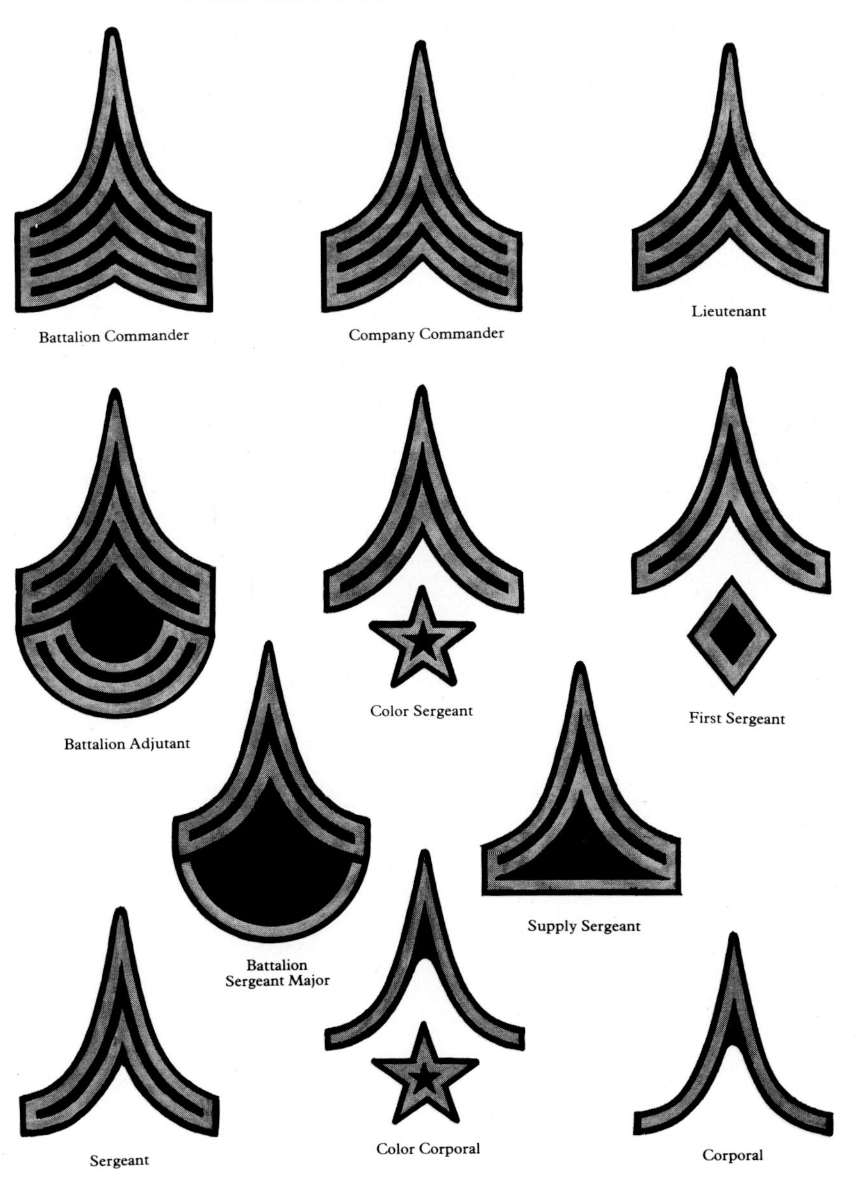

PETTY OFFICERS' RATINGS – U.S. NAVY AND COAST GUARD

Chief Petty Officer
Aviation Metalsmith

Chief Petty Officer
Av. Electrician's Mate
12 years with Good Conduct

Petty Officer 2nd Class
Av. Radioman

Petty Officer 3rd Class
Av. General Utility

Petty Officer 1st Class
Av. Machinist's Mate
8 years Service

Seaman/Fireman
1st Class

Seaman/Fireman
2nd Class

Apprentice Seaman/Fireman
3rd Class

Lieutenant Junior Grade

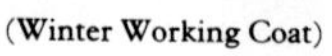

(Winter Working Coat)

(Dress and Blue Service Coat)

Aviation Cadet
U.S. Navy

Aviation Cadet
U.S.M.C.

U.S. Coast Guard shields, for Officers and W.O.s, Chief Petty Officer and Enlisted Men, for winter and summer uniforms

N.C.O.s' RANK BADGES – U.S. MARINE CORPS

First Sergeant

1st Grade Line

Band Leader

1st Grade Staff

2nd Grade Line

2nd Grade Staff

3rd Grade Line

3rd Grade Staff

4th Grade

5th Grade

6th Grade

Enlistment Stripes

1st Class Private Musician

CIVIL AIR PATROL

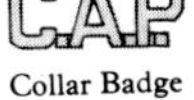
Collar Badge

Cap Badge

Collar Badge

Pilot

Garrison Cap Badge

Duck Club

Observer

QUALIFICATION BADGES

Senior Pilot

Command Pilot

Pilot

Balloon Pilot

Senior Balloon Pilot

Balloon Observer

Aircraft Observer

Technical Observer

Navigator

Bombardier

Aerial Gunner

Air Crew Member

Glider Pilot

Service Pilot

Liaison Pilot

Women's Air Force Service Pilot

Flight Surgeon 1st type

Women's Army Service Pilot

Flight Nurse 1st type

Flight Surgeon 2nd type

Flight Nurse 2nd type

Pilot U.S.N./U.S.M.C./U.S.C.G.

Observer U.S.N./U.S.M.C.

Balloon Pilot U.S.N./U.S.M.C.

Naval Combat Air Crew Member

Flying Instructor

Flight Surgeon U.S.N./U.S.M.C./U.S.C.G.

NAVAL SPECIALITY AND DISTINGUISHING MARKS

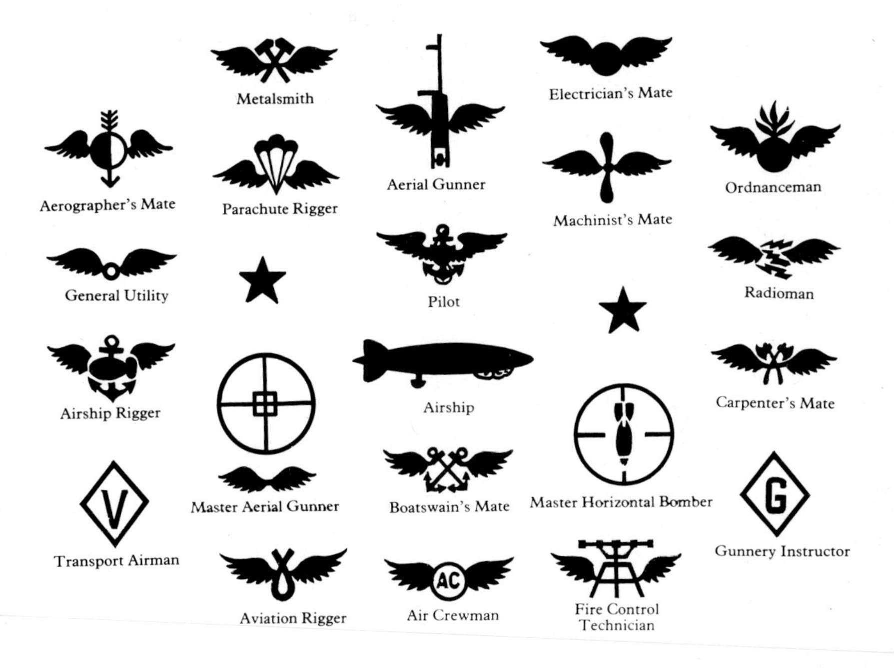

AIR CARRIER CONTRACT PERSONNEL – A.T.C., U.S.A.A.F.

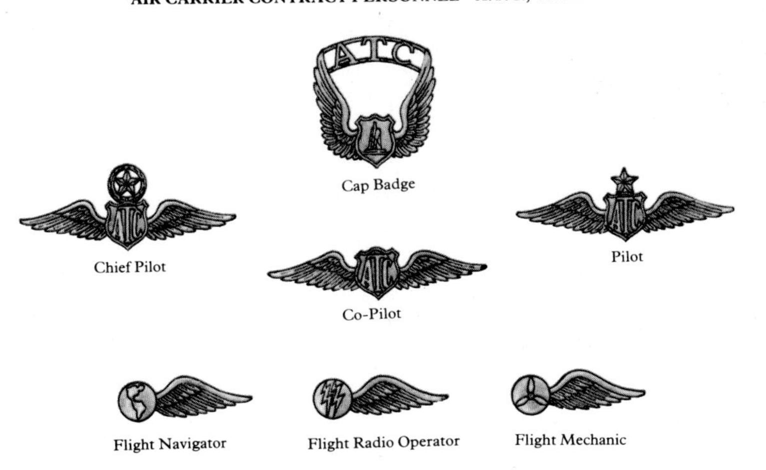

U.S. ARMY AIR FORCES' SHOULDER SLEEVE INSIGNIA

U.S.A.A.F.
Instructor

U.S. Army Air Forces
1st and 2nd type

1st Air Force

2nd Air Force

3rd Air Force

4th Air Force

5th Air Force

6th Air Force

7th Air Force

8th Air Force

9th Air Force

10th Air Force

11th Air Force

12th Air Force

13th Air Force

14th Air Force

15th Air Force

Desert Air Force

20th Air Force

Mediterranean Allied
Air Force

Strategic Air Force

Airborne Troop
Carrier

SPECIALISTS' CUFF INSIGNIA

Engineering
Specialist

Armature
Specialist

Photography
Specialist

Air Force Cadet

Communication
Specialist

Weather
Specialist

Air Force Cadet

U.S. MARINE CORPS, CIVIL AIR PATROL, ETC. SHOULDER SLEEVE AND CUFF INSIGNIA

U.S.M.C. Aircraft 1st Wing

U.S.M.C. Aircraft 2nd Wing

HQ, U.S.M.C. Air Force – Pacific

U.S.M.C. Aircraft 3rd Wing

U.S.M.C. Aircraft 4th Wing

Air Transport Command

HQ Pacific Aircraft Wing

High School Victory Corps – Air

Aircraft F.M.F. 2nd Wing

Aircraft F.M.F. 3rd Wing

Aircraft F.M.F. 1st Wing

1st Marine Amphibious Corps Aviation Engineers

Aircraft F.M.F. 4th Wing

Air Transport Command Ground Personnel

Women's Ferrying Command

Coastal Patrol

Civil Air Patrol

Civil Air Patrol Cadet

Civil Air Patrol Guard

Photography

Liaison Patrol

Forest Patrol

Courier Service

Transportation

Radio

Band

ITALY

HISTORICAL BACKGROUND

Artillery Aviation Shoulder Strap's Title

Aviation – Aircraft 1915–23

87th Squadron Shoulder Strap's Title

Pilot W.W.1

Observer W.W.1

Balloon Observer W.W.1

Aviation-Airship

Machine-Gunner W.W.1

Pilot

Mechanic

Pilot 1923–35

Balloon Engineers 1931

Observer 1931

Ballon Observer 1931

Observer

Airship Commander

Airship 2nd Officer

Airship Crew Officer

Ex-war Pilot Army

Balloon Battalions

1,000,000 Km Award Civil Aviation

PLATE 40

CAP INSIGNIA

Generals
Aviation Engineers

Generals
General of Air Brigade

Officers
Specialists' Role – Fitter

A.E. Technical
Assistants Role

Senior Officers
Lieutenant-Colonel

C.C. Commissariat
Role

Services Role

C.C. Administrative
Role

Junior Officers
Lieutenant

Flying Role

Medical Corps

Forage Cap Badge
Gold Embroidered

Warrant Officers
All W.O.s' ranks

Forage Cap Badge
Yellow machine-embroidered

Forage Cap Badge
Yellow hand-embroidered

Chaplains

Forage Cap Badge
Yellow hand-embroidered

ITALY

OFFICERS' RANK BADGES – SERVICE UNIFORM

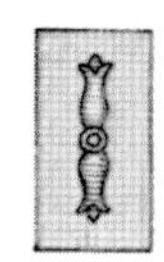
Air Marshal and Generals

Air Marshal

General of Air Army

Generals
Services Role

General of Air Squad
in command of Air Army

General of Air Squad

General of Air Division

General of Air Brigade

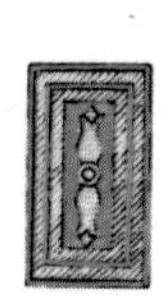
Senior Officer
Flying Role

Colonel

Lieutenant-Colonel

Major

Senior Officer
Medical Corps

Junior Officer
A.E. Engineers Role

Captain

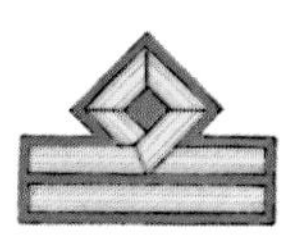
Lieutenant

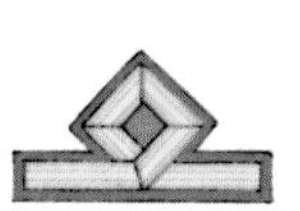
2nd Lieutenant

Junior Officer
C.C. Commissariat Role

Junior Officer
S.R. Photographer

Captain
A.E.Engineers Role

Captain
C.C. Commissariat Role

Junior Officer
Chaplain

OFFICERS' SHOULDER BOARDS FOR FULL DRESS UNIFORM

General
of Air Squad

Lieutenant-General
C.C. Commissariat Role

Major
A.E. Engineers Role

Captain
S.R. Fitter

Captain
Chaplain

OFFICERS' SHOULDER BOARDS FOR COLONIAL AND OTHER UNIFORMS

General of Air Brigade
Medical Corps

Colonel
Flying Role

Lieutenant
C.C. Administrative Role

W.O.s/SERGEANTS FULL DRESS UNIFORM

Chief W.O.
Flying Role

CORPORALS/AIRMEN FULL DRESS UNIFORM

Airman
S.R. Electrician

WARRANT OFFICERS' AND N.C.O.s' RANK BADGES

Aiutante di battaglia
S.R.Radio-Aerologist

W.O. Major
Bandsman

Chief W.O.
Flying Role

W.O.
A.E. Technical Assistant

Sergeant-Major

Sergeant

First Airman

Leading Airman

ITALY

QUALIFICATION BADGES

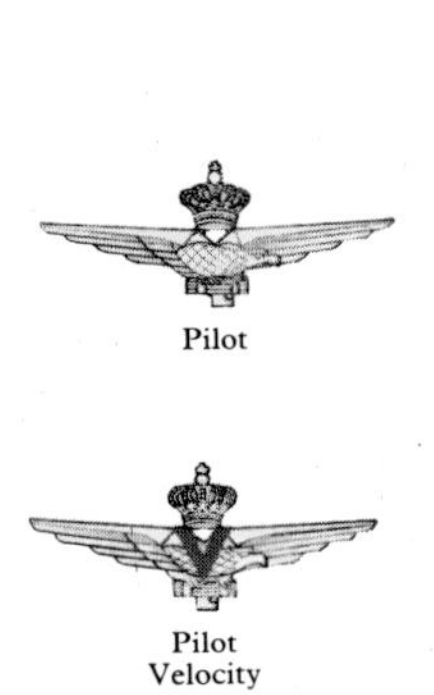

Pilot

Observer

Observer

Pilot
Velocity

Pilot
Stratosphere

Pilot
Atlantic

Air Crew Member

Torpedo Aircraft
Crew Member

Interceptors

Bombers

Torpedo Aircraft

Assault-Combat

Reconnaissance
at Sea

Strategic
Reconnaissance

Diver Aircraft

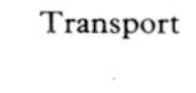

Transport

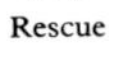

Rescue

Aerial Observation

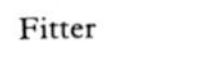

Fitter

A.F. Parachutist
1942–45

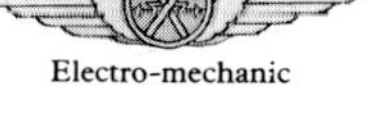

Electro-mechanic

Motorist

Photographer

Armourer

ARM-OF-SERVICE (CATEGORY) BADGES

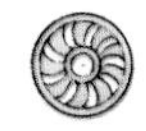
Photographer

Armourer

Electrician

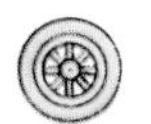
Driver

Mechanic

Fitter

Radio-Aerologist

Fitter Instruments

Technical Assistant

Medical Orderly

Wireless Operator

Troops Admin. Service

ARM BADGES AND MISCELLANEA

Air Force in the Aegean

Assault Pilot

Bandmaster

Fencing Instructor

1st Interceptors Group

★ REGIA AERONAUTICA ★

Tally for Summer Hat

THE AIR FORCE OF THE ITALIAN SOCIAL REPUBLIC

Generals' National Insignia

Officers' and Airmens' Cap Badges

All Other Ranks' National Insignia

Torpedo Aircraft

Interceptors

Torpedo Aircraft

CHINA

CAP AND OTHER BADGES

Officers

Privates

N.C.O.s

OFFICERS' RANK BADGES

Collar Badges

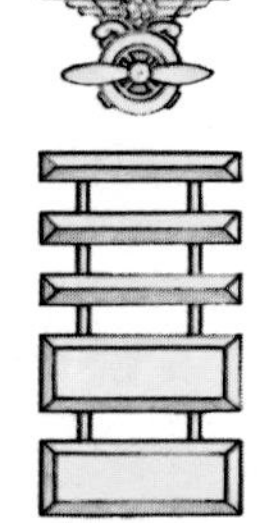

General

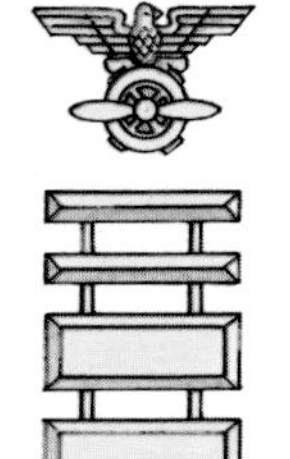

Lieutenant-General

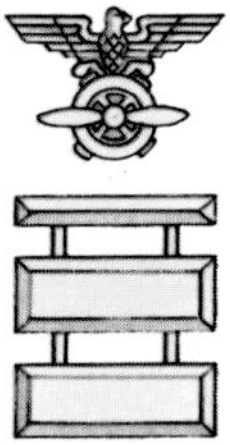

Major-General

General Staff Academy

Colonel

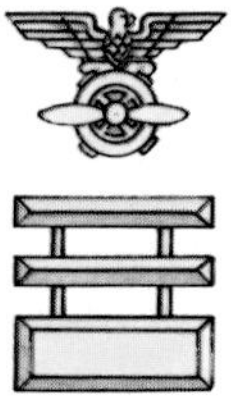

Lieutenant-Colonel

Major

General Staff Academy
Collar Badges

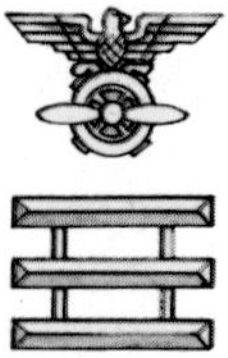

Captain

1st Lieutenant

2nd Lieutenant

Corporal – A.A. School

PLATE 46

CAP, COLLAR AND RANK BADGES

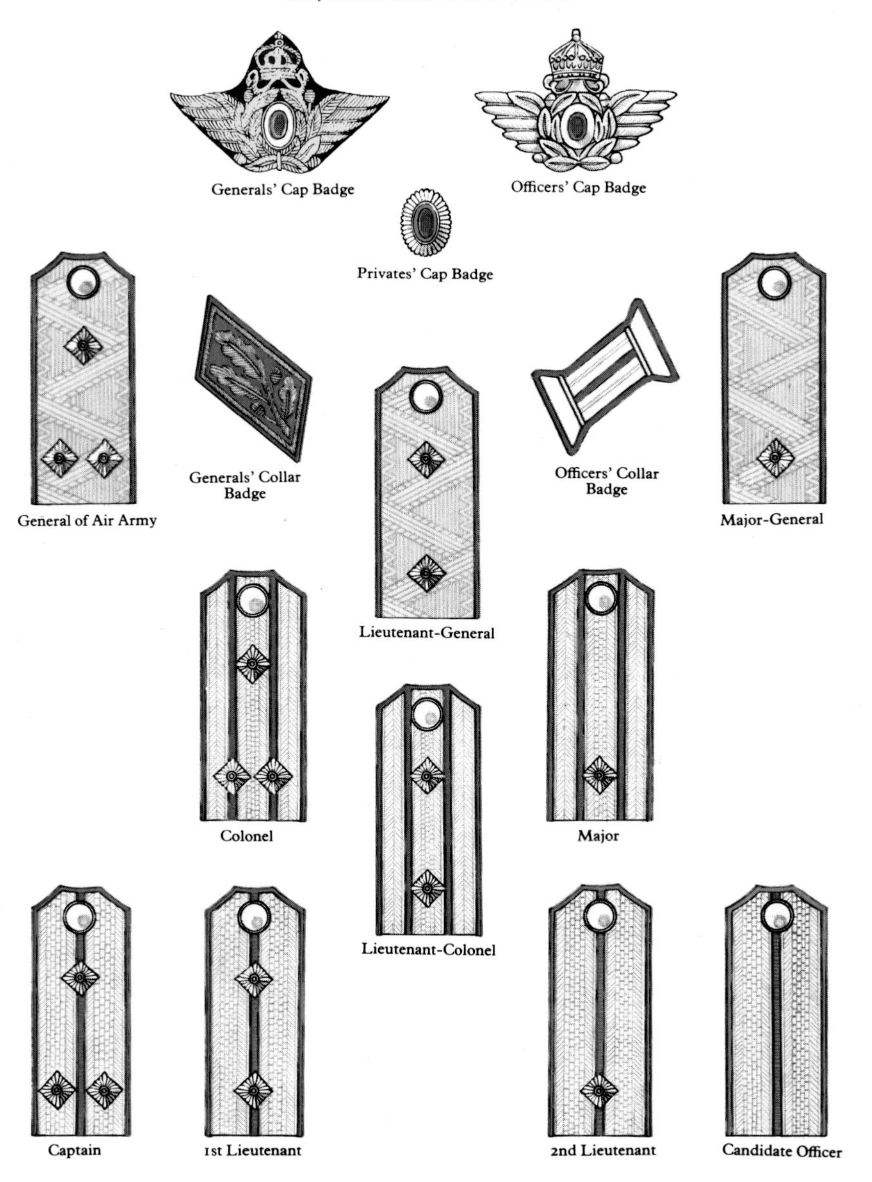
Generals' Cap Badge

Officers' Cap Badge

Privates' Cap Badge

General of Air Army

Generals' Collar Badge

Lieutenant-General

Officers' Collar Badge

Major-General

Colonel

Major

Lieutenant-Colonel

Captain

1st Lieutenant

2nd Lieutenant

Candidate Officer

PLATE 47

BULGARIA

N.C.O.s' RANK BADGES

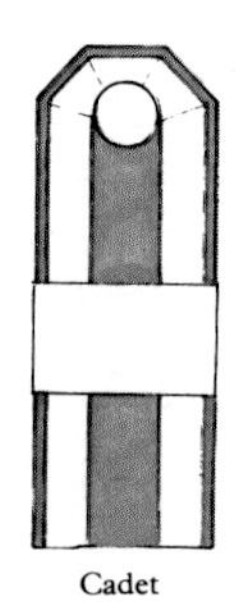
Cadet

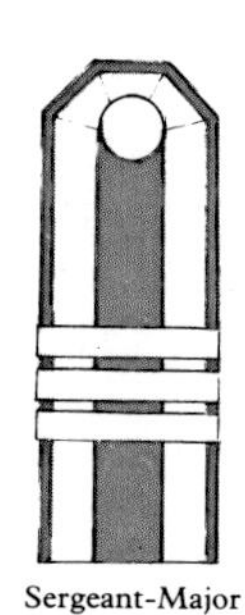
Sergeant-Major

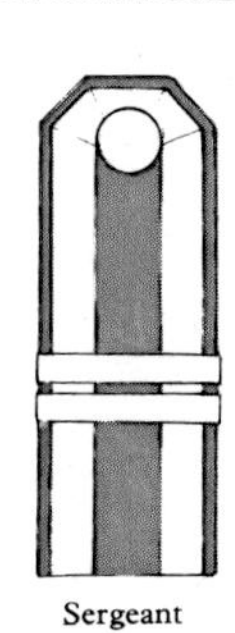
Sergeant

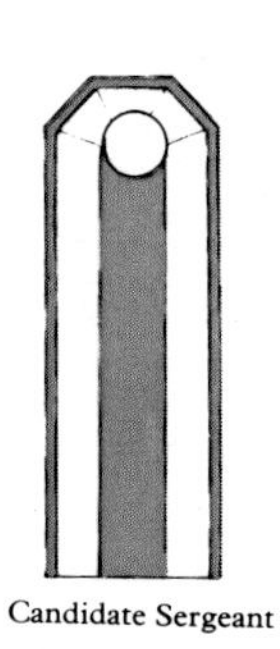
Candidate Sergeant

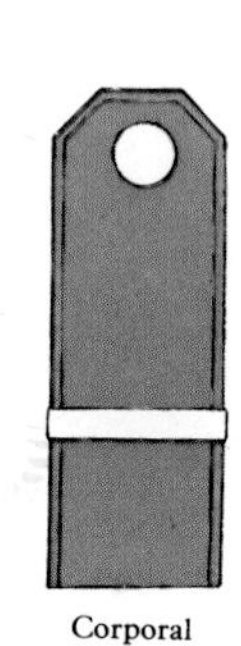
Corporal

GERMANY

HISTORICAL BACKGROUND

Pilot

Observer
(Bavarian)

Observer

Naval Pilot
(Sea)

Aviator
Commemorative Badge

Naval Pilot
(Land)

Airship Crew (Navy)
Commemorative Badge

Naval Observer

Air Gunner

Naval Pilot
Commemorative Badge

Airship Crew (Army)
Commemorative Badge

Naval Observer
Commemorative Badge

CAP INSIGNIA

Reichsmarschall of Great Germany

Generals

Officers

Officers
Side Cap

Other Ranks

Other Ranks
Side Cap

BREAST INSIGNIA

Generals

Other Ranks

Officers

GERMANY

FIELD-MARSHALS' AND GENERALS' RANK INSIGNIA

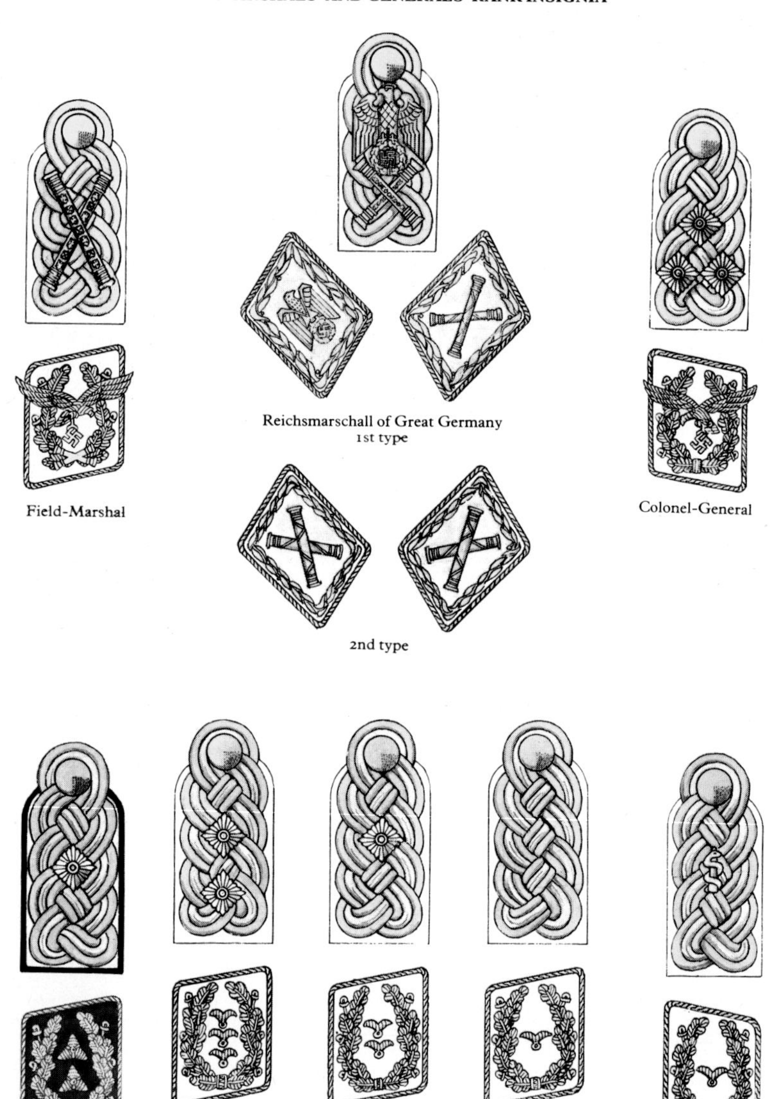

Field-Marshal

Reichsmarschall of Great Germany
1st type

2nd type

Colonel-General

Lieutenant-General (Officials)

General of Aviation

Lieutenant-General

Major-General

Major-General (Medical Corps)

OFFICERS' RANK INSIGNIA

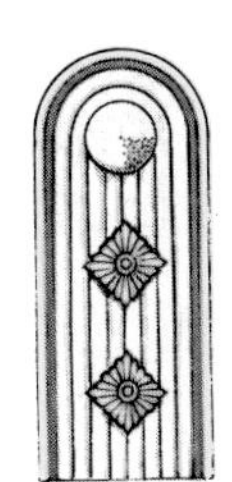

1st Lieutenant
(Flyer Reserve)

Colonel
(General Staff)

Lieutenant-Colonel
(Air Ministry)

Major
(Flyer)
Retired List

Captain Re-enlisted
(Flyer)

Senior Inspector
(Officials)

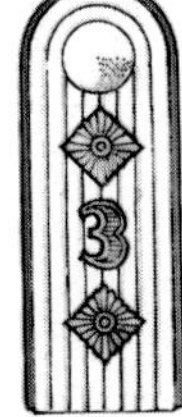

Captain
(Anti-Aircraft)

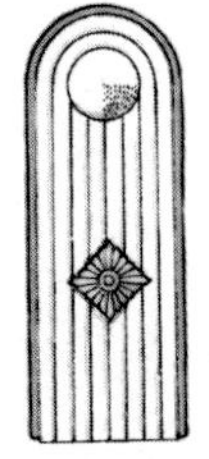

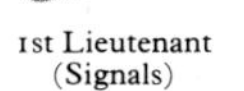

1st Lieutenant
(Signals)

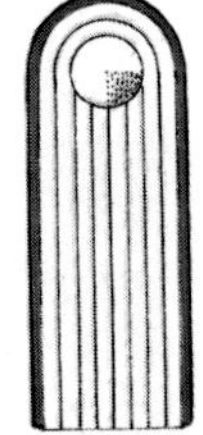

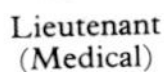

Lieutenant
(Medical)

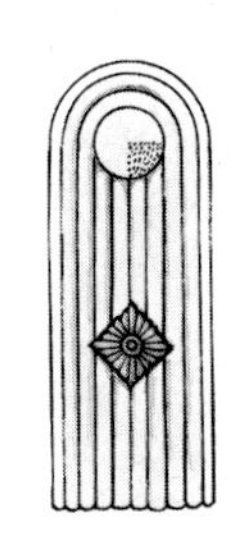

1st Lieutenant
(General Göring)

Officers' Collar Patches of the H. Göring Tank Division
1st and 2nd Pattern

N.C.O.s' RANK BADGES

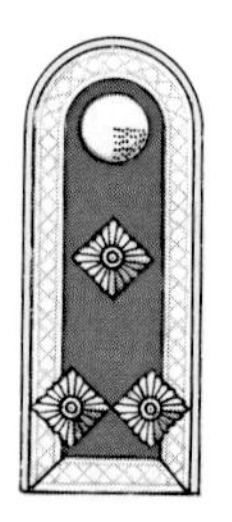
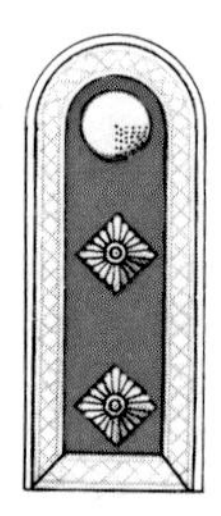
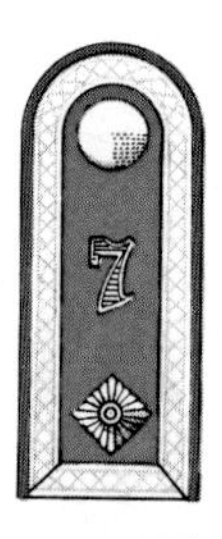
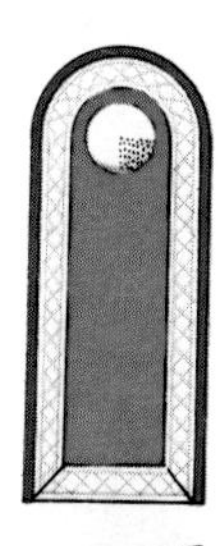
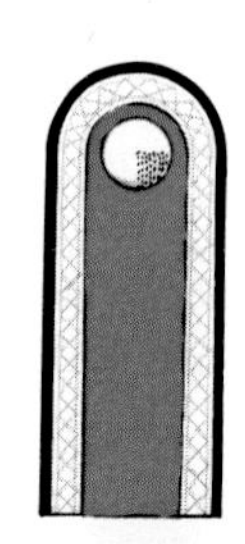

Stabsfeldwebel (Flyer)

Oberfeldwebel (H. Göring Tank Div.)

Wachtmeister (A.A. Artillery)

Unterfeldwebel (Medical Corps)

Unteroffizier (Construction Troops) after 1939

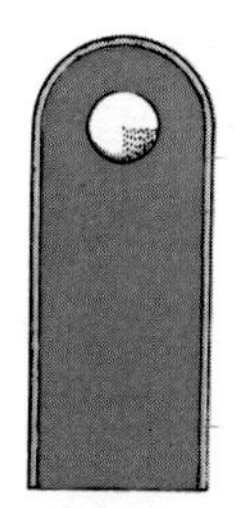
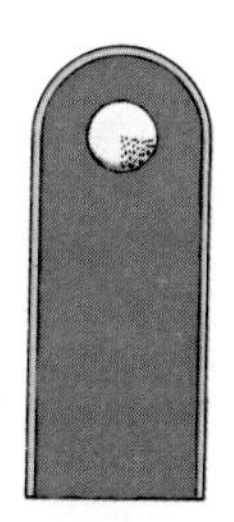
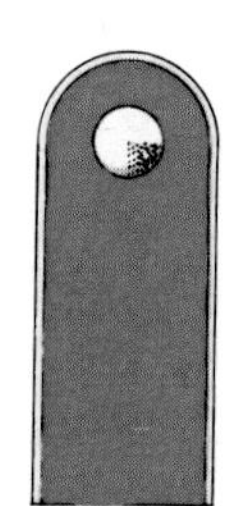

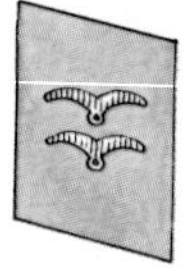
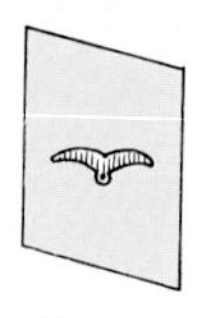

Stabsgefreiter N.C.O. Candidate (Jäger Bn H. Göring)

Obergefreiter (Signals)

Gefreiter (Air Traffic Control)

Flieger (Flying Troops)

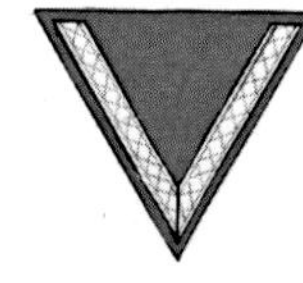

Stabsgefreiter after 1944

Hauptgefreiter until 1944

Obergefreiter

Gefreiter

RANK BADGES FOR FLYING FIELD/UNIFORMS

Field-Marshal

Colonel-General

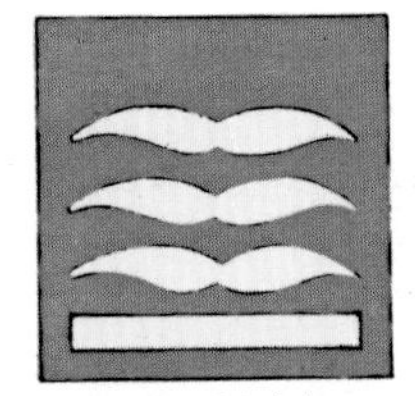
General of Aviation

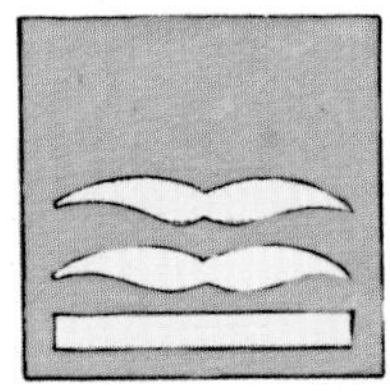
Lieutenant-General

Major-General

1st Lieutenant (Corps of Administrative Officials)

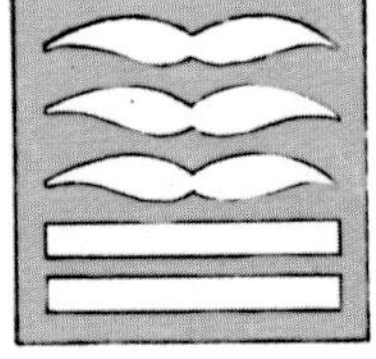
Colonel

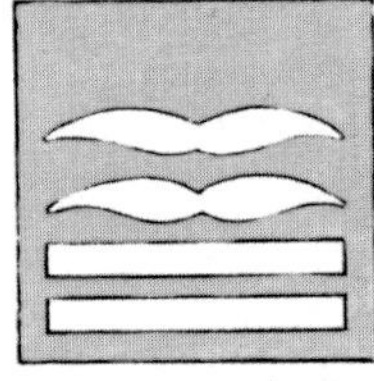
Lieutenant-Colonel

Major

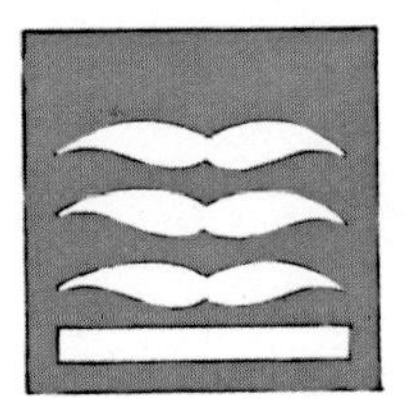
Captain

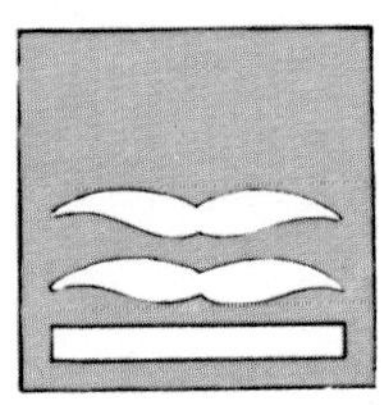
1st Lieutenant

Lieutenant

Stabsfeldwebel

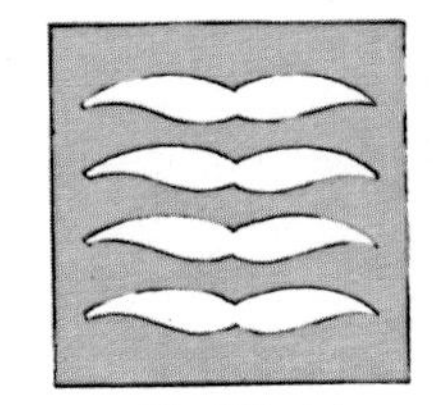
Oberfeldwebel

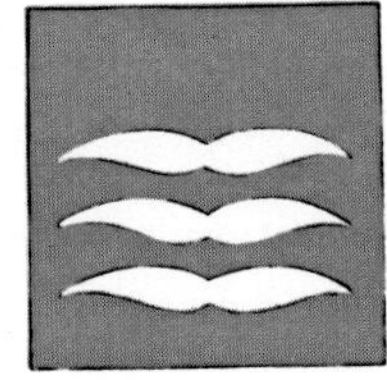
Feldwebel

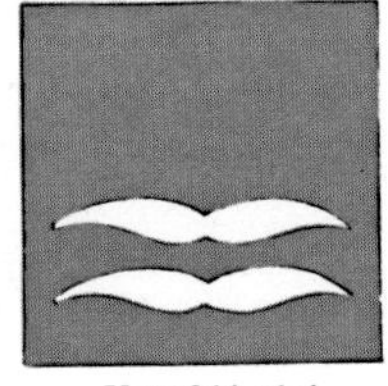
Unterfeldwebel

Unteroffizier

ENGINEERING CORPS' RANK INSIGNIA

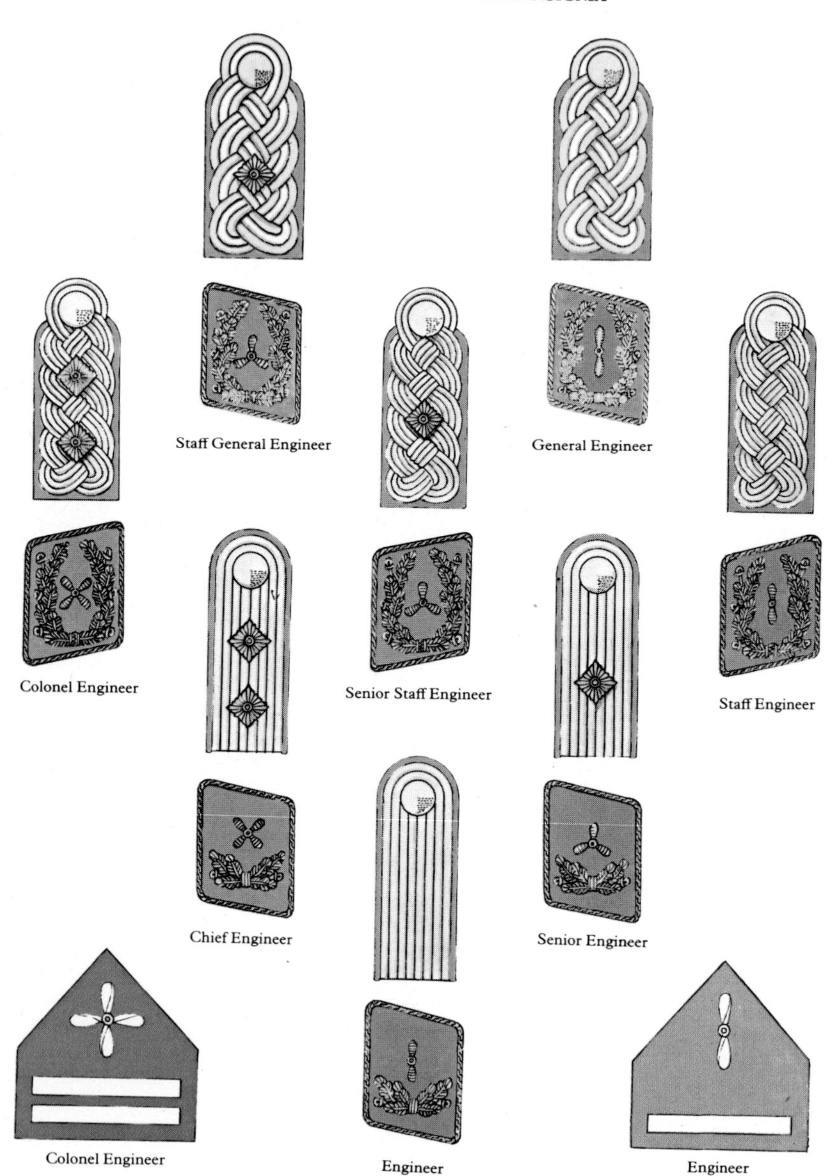

Staff General Engineer

General Engineer

Colonel Engineer

Senior Staff Engineer

Staff Engineer

Chief Engineer

Senior Engineer

Colonel Engineer

Engineer

Engineer

MUSICIANS' RANK INSIGNIA

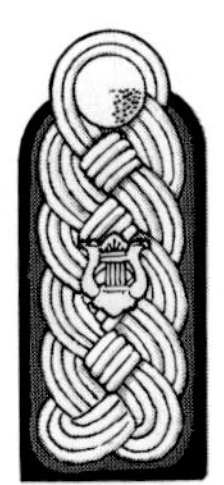

Staff Music-Master
1935–38

Senior Music-Master
1935–38

Music-Master
1935–38

All three ranks
1935–38
(Flying Troops)

Music-Superintendent
1935–38

Note : Arm-of-service colour refers to the branch of service

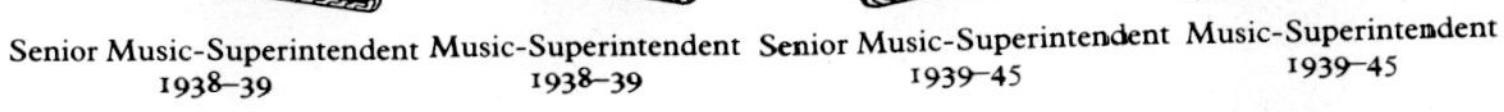

Senior Music-Superintendent
1938–39

Music-Superintendent
1938–39

Senior Music-Superintendent
1939–45

Music-Superintendent
1939–45

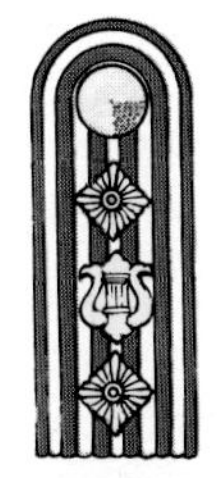

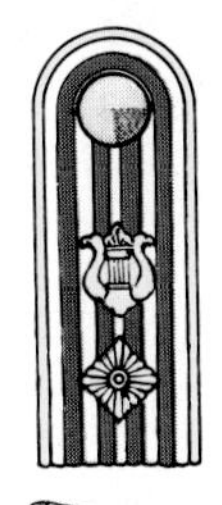

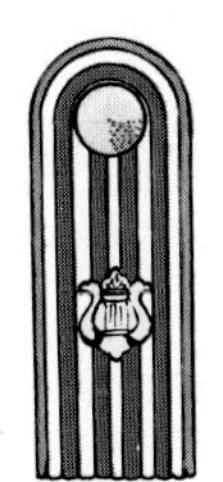

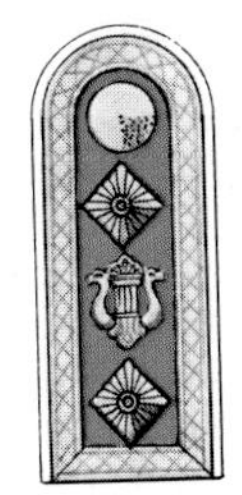

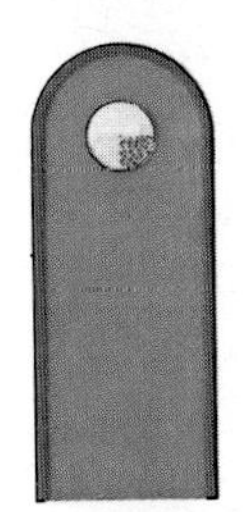

Staff Music-Master
1938–45

Senior Music-Master
1938–45

Music Master
1938–45

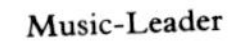

Music-Leader

Musician

CUFF TITLES

Jagdgeschwader Richthofen

Geschwader General Wever

Geschwader Horst Wessel

Geschwader Immelmann

Jagdgeschwader Mölders

Geschwader Hindenburg

Geschwader Boelcke

Jagdgeschwader Udet

Legion Condor

Fallschirm-Division

Fallschirm-Jäger Rgt. 1 .2

Jagdgeschwader Schlageter

General Göring

HERMANN GÖRING

Hermann Göring

AFRIKA

COMMEMORATIVE CUFF TITLES

Jagdgeschwader Frhr. v. Richthofen Nr. 1 1917/18

Jagdstaffel Boelcke Nr. 2 1916/18

QUALIFICATION BADGES AND AWARDS

Pilot
Observer
Air Crew
Pilot-Observer
Air Gunner Flight Engineer
Glider Pilot
Parachutist
Wireless Operator Air Gunner
Ex-Flyer
Un-qualified Air Gunner
A.A. Artillery Award
Ground-Combat Award
100 Ground-Combat Engagements Award
Sea Battle Award
Tank Battle Award
75 Tank Battle Engagements Award

GERMANY

QUALIFICATION CLASPS

Long-Range Fighters and Air-to-Ground Support Aircraft

Day Interceptors

Night Long-Range Fighters and Night Intruder Aircraft

Bombers

Night Interceptors

Reconnaissance

Transport and Gliders

Ground Combat

Air-to-Ground Support

SPECIALITY AND TRADE BADGES AND AWARDS

Technical Aviation Personnel

Flying Personnel

Anti-Aircraft Personnel

Signaller not in Signal Unit

Armourer N.C.O.

Administrative N.C.O.

Ordnance

Armourer N.C.O. Flying and Signal Units

Teletype N.C.O.

Teletype Operator

Qualified Telephonist N.C.O.

Qualified Telephone Operator

Transport N.C.O.

Qualified Radio N.C.O.

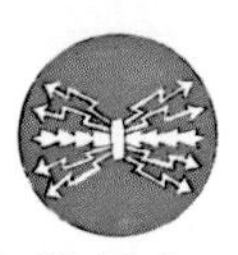

Qualified Radioman

Qualified Sound Location N.C.O.

Qualified Sound Location Operator

SPECIALITY AND TRADE BADGES

Radio Direction N.C.O.

Radio Direction Finder

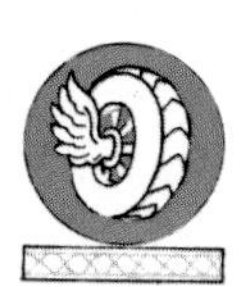
Mechanised Transport Equipment Administrator Candidate

A.A. Artillery

Signal Equipment Administrator

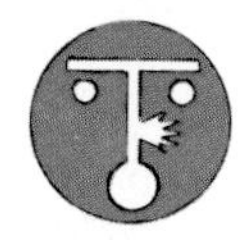
Searchlight Equipment Administrator

Medical Orderly

Military Boats Personnel

'C' Qualified Radioman A.A.

'B' Qualified Radioman A.A.

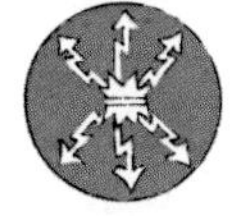
Master Radioman

Air Raid Warning Personnel

Aircraft Equipment Administrator

Driver

Technical Preparatory School Graduate

N.C.O.s' School

Armourer Light Bombs

Technical N.C.O.

Armourer Heavy Bombs

Farrier

Sound Locator Crewman (1 year service)

Range-Finder Crewman (1 year service)

Sound Locator Crewman

Standard Bearer

Range-Finder Crewman

PLATE 59

CZECHOSLOVAKIA

CAP BADGES

Officers
(Non-combatant)

N.C.O.s
(Combatant)

Other Ranks

RANK BADGES

Generals
(Stars on sleeves)

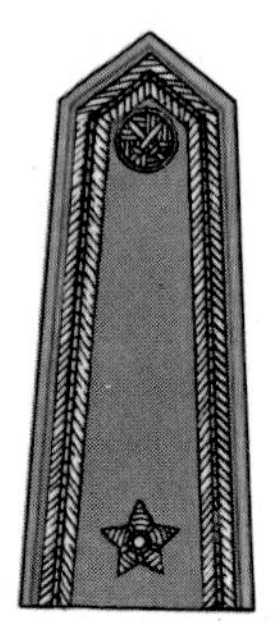
Staff Captain

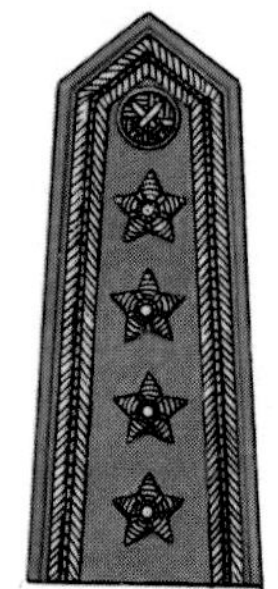
Colonel

Lieutenant-Colonel

Major

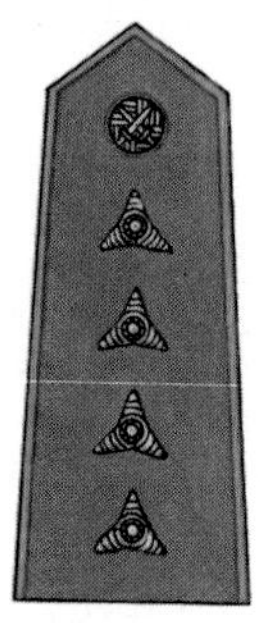
Captain

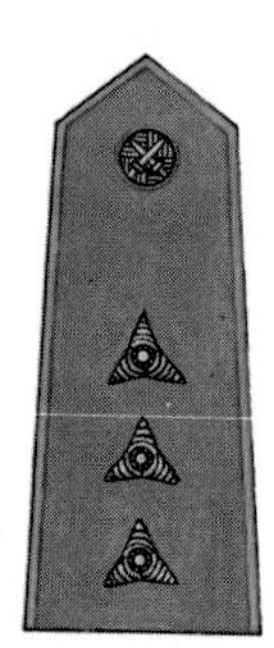
Senior Lieutenant

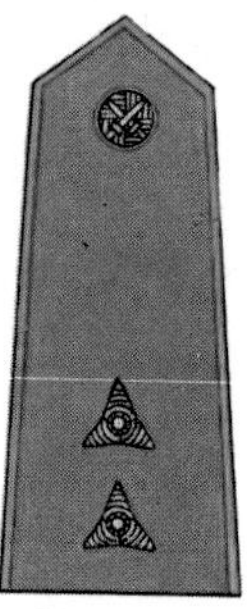
Lieutenant

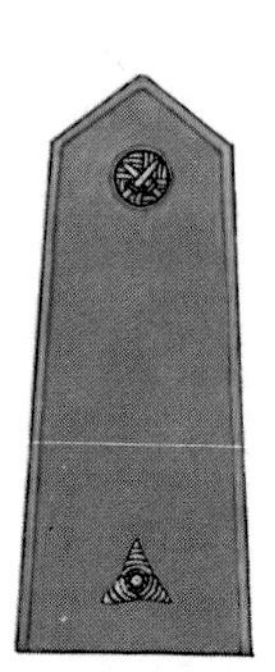
Junior Lieutenant

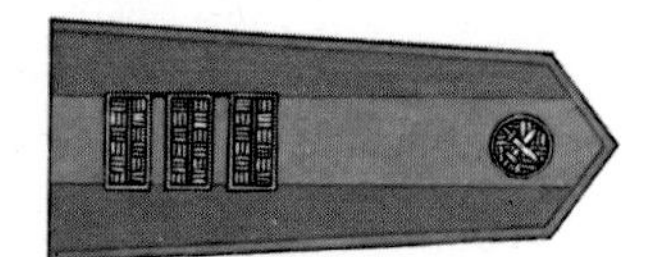
Warrant Officer 1930–38
(3 Ranks)

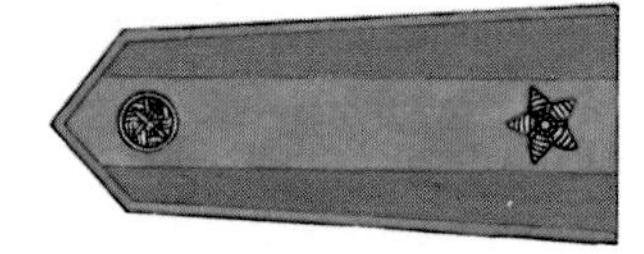
Staff Warrant Officer post–1938

PLATE 60

RANK BADGES

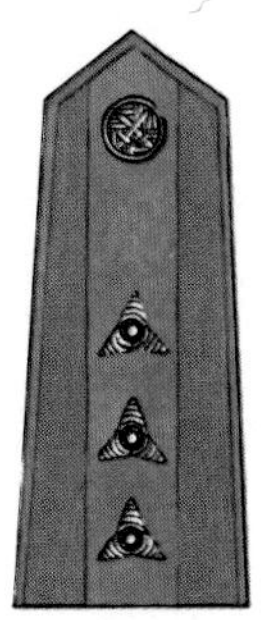
Warrant Officer

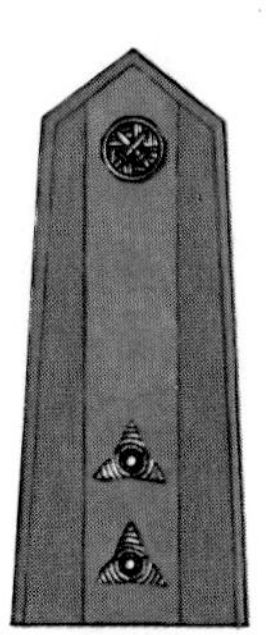
Staff Sergeant

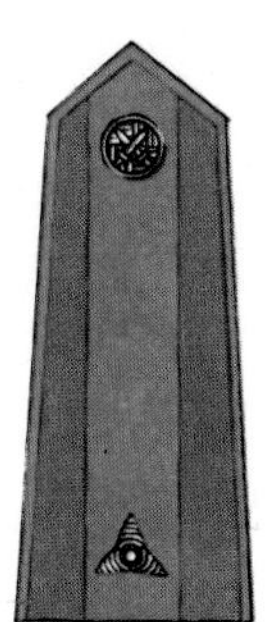
Sergeant

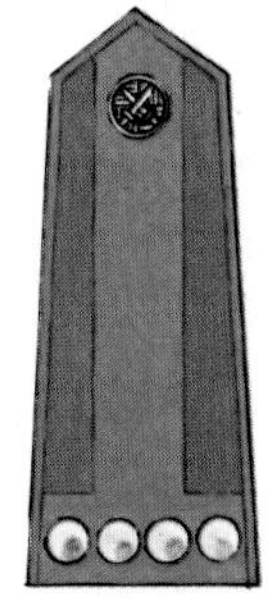
Senior Platoon Sergeant

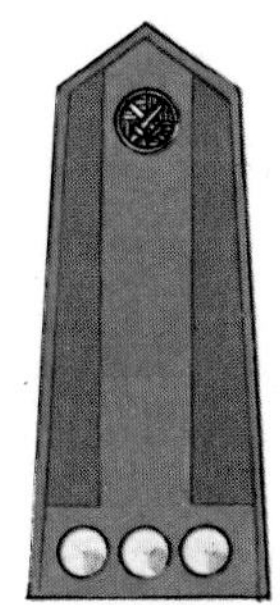
Platoon Sergeant

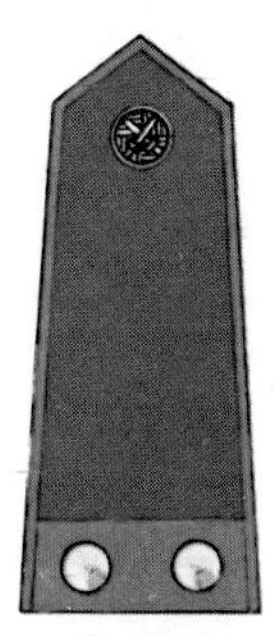
Corporal

Lance Corporal

QUALIFICATION BADGES

Army Observer

Air Gunner

Pilot

Observer

Observer
(Balloon)

Officer attached to R.A.F.V.R.

Pilot
(Balloon)

FINLAND

CAP BADGES

Officers'
Peaked cap

1

2

3

4

OFFICERS' RANK BADGES

Lieutenant-General

Major-General

QUALIFICATION BADGE

Pilot

Colonel

Lieutenant-Colonel

Major

OFFICERS OF THE SERVICES

Lieutenant-Colonel
Doctor

Captain

Lieutenant

2nd Lieutenant

Lieutenant
Technician

N.C.O.s' RANK BADGES

Flight Sergeant

Senior Sergeant

Sergeant

Junior Sergeant

Corporal

Arm-of-service Badge

Airman

POLAND

HISTORICAL BACKGROUND

Aviation in Greater Poland

Aviation in France

Shoulder Straps Badge

1917

1919

Krakow Pilots' School

7th Kościuszko Air Squadron

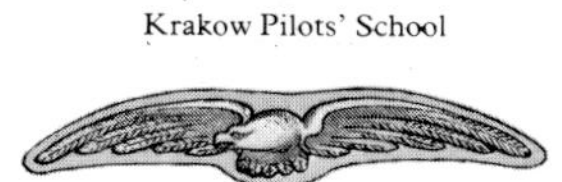

Flyers' Arm Badge Aircraft

Military Aviation Courses

Doctor

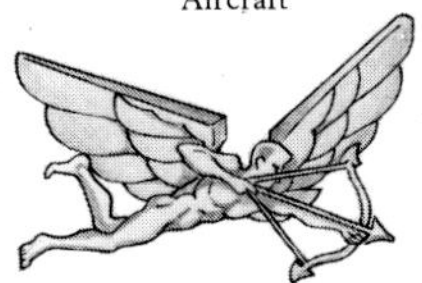

Air Gunner

Photographer/ Surveyor

CAP BADGES (1936)

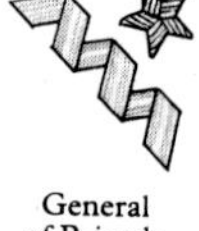

General of Brigade

Officers/W.O.

Lieutenant-Colonel

Captain

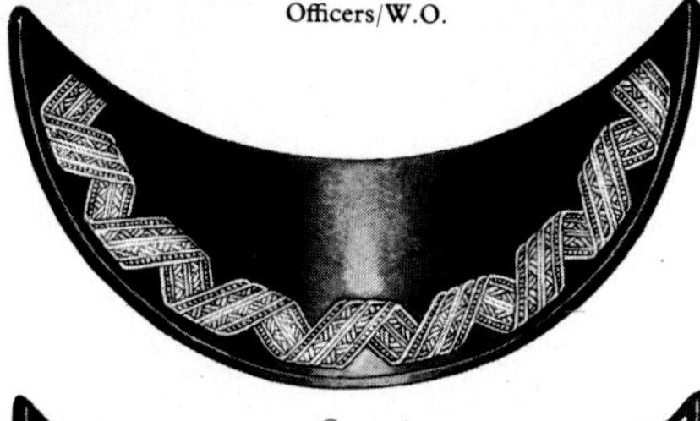

Generals

Warrant Officer

Sergeant

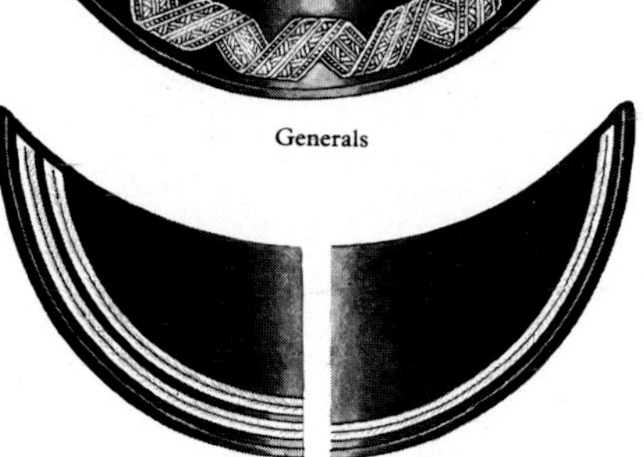

Senior Officers Junior Officers

Lance Sergeant

OTHER RANKS' CAP BADGE AND CAP BAND RANK INSIGNIA

Staff Sergeant

Sergeant

Lance Sergeant

Corporal

Lance Corporal

OFFICERS' RANK BADGES

Generals

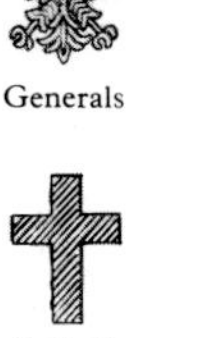

Catholic Chaplain

General

General of Division

General of Brigade

General Staff

Bandmaster

Bandsman

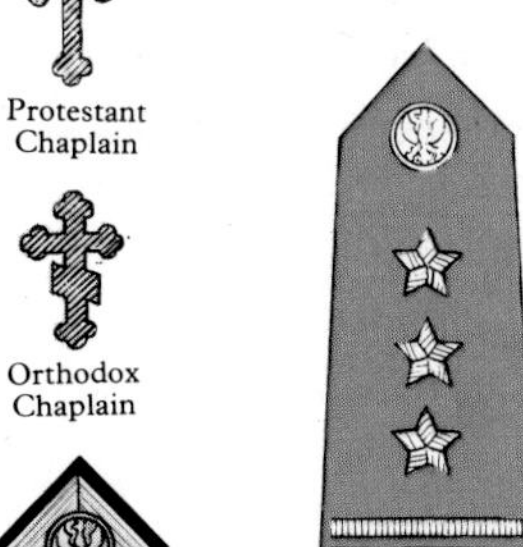

Protestant Chaplain

Orthodox Chaplain

Colonel

Lieutenant-Colonel

Major

N.C.O.s' School

Cadet (Regular)

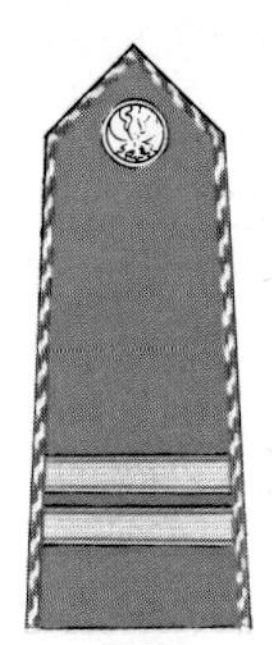

Cadet (Reserve)

Cadet (Regular)

Cadet (Reserve)

Captain

Lieutenant

2nd Lieutenant

WARRANT OFFICERS' AND N.C.O.s' RANK BADGES AND MISCELLANEA

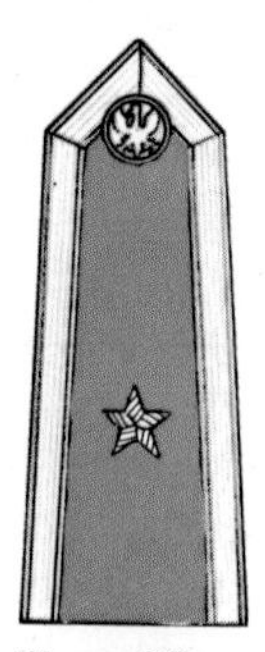
Warrant Officer

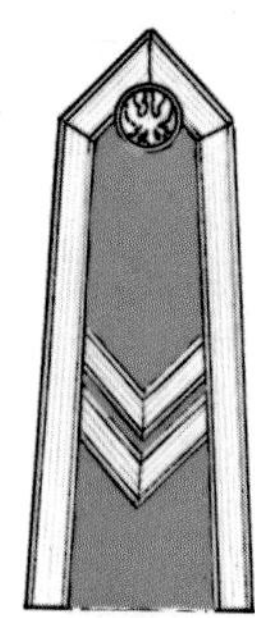
Staff Sergeant

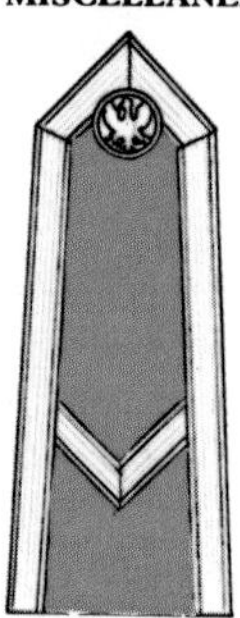
Sergeant

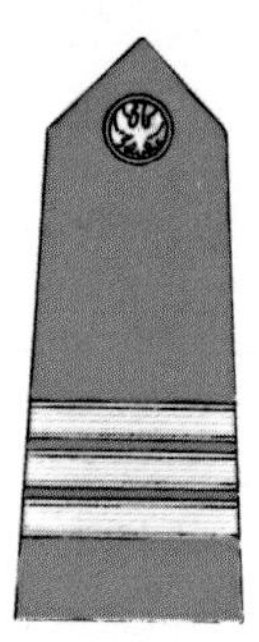
Lance Sergeant

Corporal

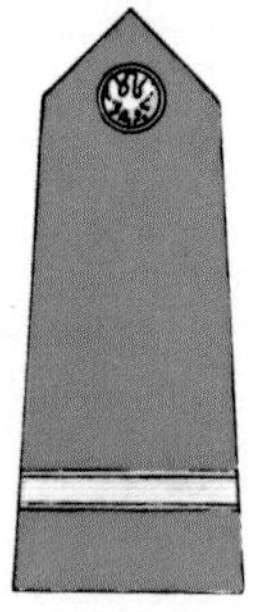
Lance Corporal

Officers' Dress Belt

Examples of Officers' and N.C.O.s' Badges for Flying Uniform

Voluntary Training Flights – Examples of Officers' and N.C.O.s' armlets

CAP BADGES WORN AFTER 1939

Other Ranks

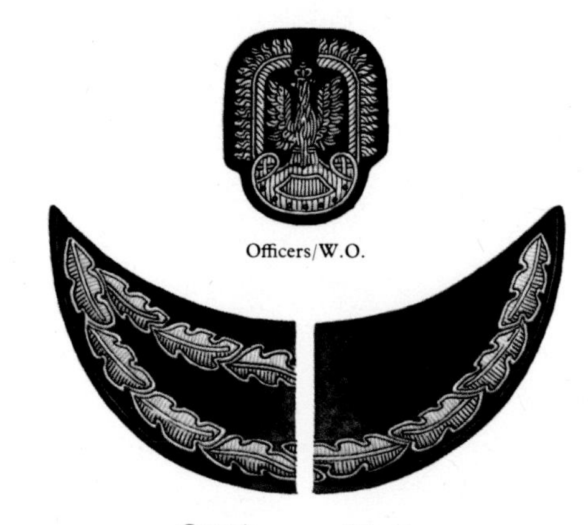

Officers/W.O.

Generals Colonel

All Ranks
Forage cap

SHOULDER FLASHES (AFTER 1939)

Airmen

Airmen

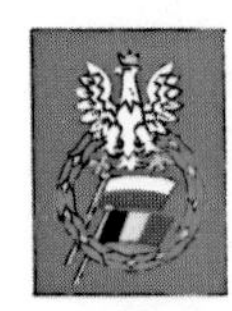

Polish Volunteers from France, Belgium, North and South America

OFFICERS' RANK BADGES (AFTER 1939)

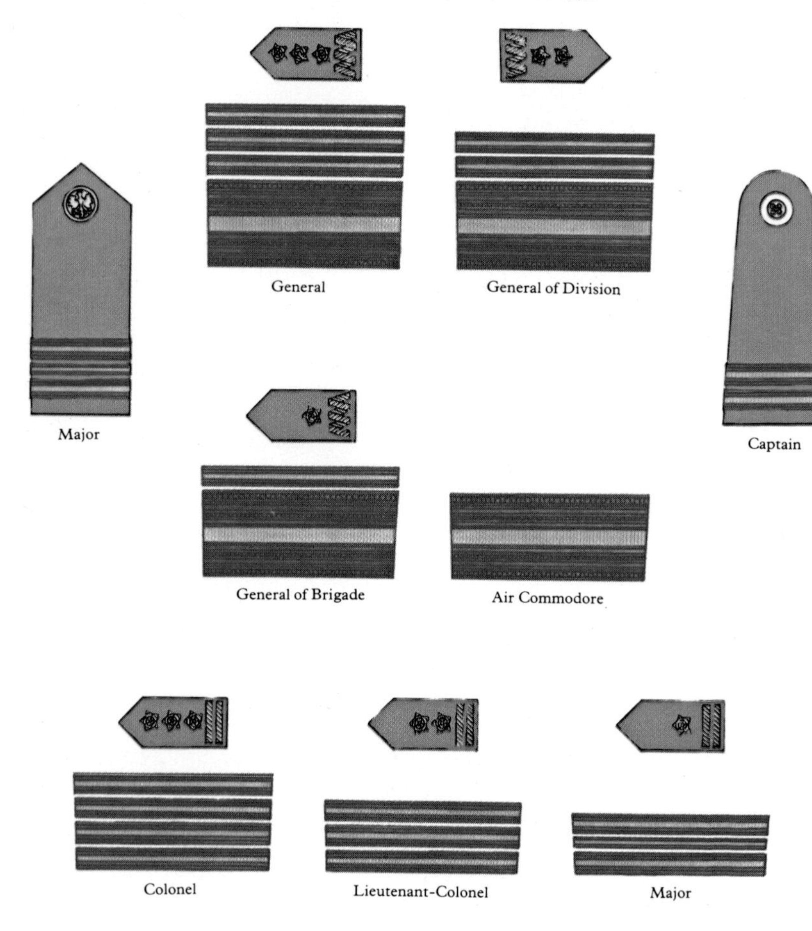

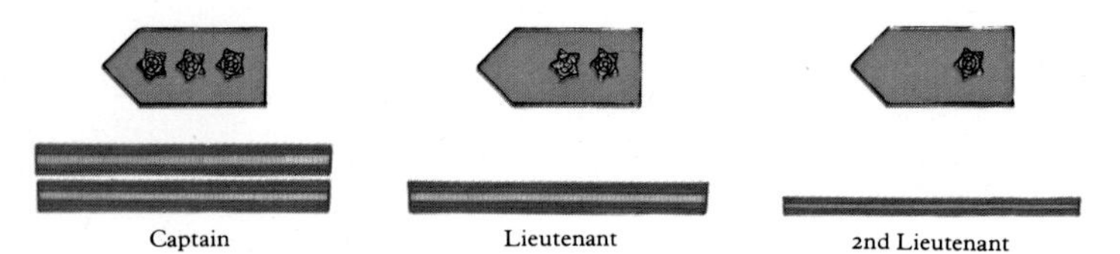

PLATE 68

WARRANT OFFICERS' AND N.C.O.s' RANK BADGES (AFTER 1939)

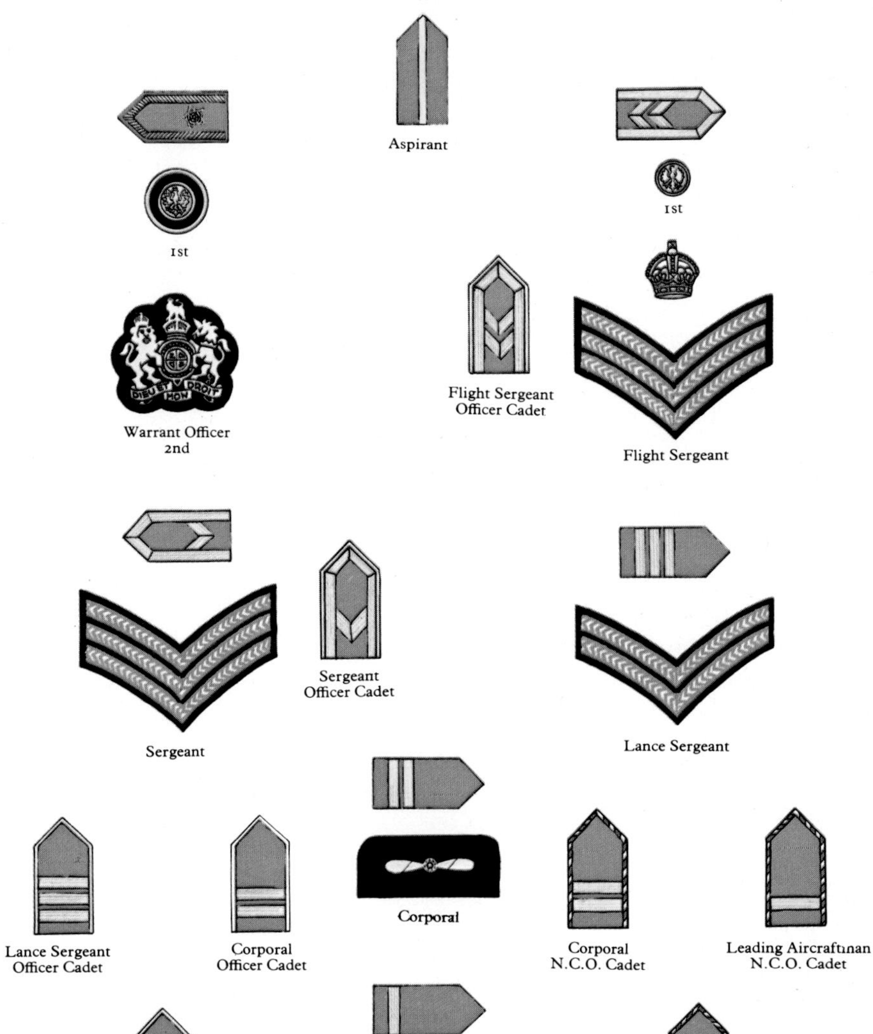

Leading Aircraftman

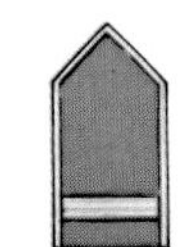

Leading Aircraftman
Officer Cadet

Aircraftman
N.C.O. Cadet

POLAND

QUALIFICATION BADGES

Pilot
1919/42/44

Pilot
1919/33

Pilot 1st Class
1933

Observer (Combat)
1919/33

Pilot 2nd Class
1933

Observer 1919/42/44
Observer 1st Class 1933

Pilot-Observer
(Combat) 1928

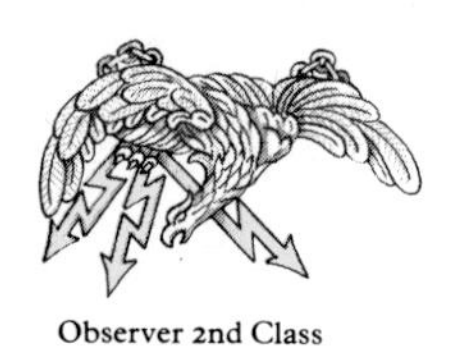

Observer 2nd Class
1933

Pilot-Observer
1928

Air Gunner – Radio Operator
1942

Radio Observer
1942

Air Gunner
1942

Flight Engineer
1942

QUALIFICATION BADGES

Air Gunner – Radio Operator
1944

Air Gunner
1944

Flight Meteorologist
1944

Flight Engineer
1944

Bombardier
1944

Artillery Observer
Aircraft Pilot

Naval Aviation
Pilot 1st Class
1933

Airship Mechanics
1922

Naval Aviation
Pilot 2nd Class
1933

Naval Aviation
Observer 1st Class
1933

Balloon Observer
1st Class
1933

Naval Aviation
Observer 2nd Class
1933

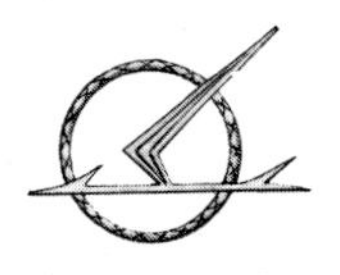

Air Gunner 1st Class
1933

Balloón Observer
2nd Class
1933

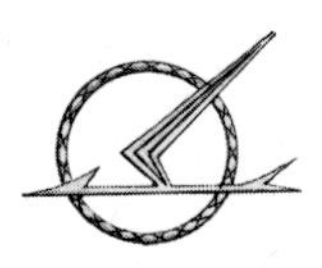

Air Gunner 2nd Class
1933

POLAND

QUALIFICATION BADGES

Specialist N.C.O. 1st Class
1933

Technical Officer 1st Class
1933

Doctor 1st Class
1933

Specialist N.C.O. 2nd Class
1933

Technical Officer 2nd Class
1933

Doctor 2nd Class
1933

OTHER BADGES

Officers' School

Staff College

Balloon Insignia

N.C.O.s' School

No. 55 Squadron

National Aircraft
Factory

1st Aviation Regt

2nd Aviation Regt

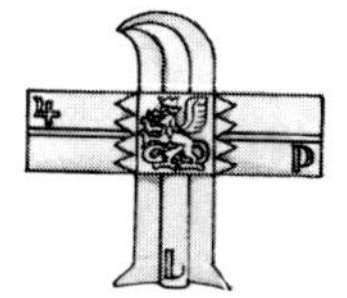
4th Aviation Regt

3rd Aviation Regt

Air Defence League

5th Aviation Regt

6th Aviation Regt

Pilots' School

SQUADRON BADGES

663rd A.O.P. Sq.

No. 300

No. 301

Polish Fighting Team

No. 302

No. 303

No. 304

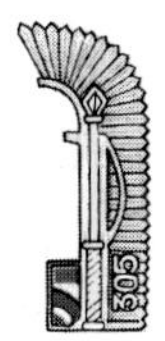

No. 305

No. 306

No. 307

No. 308

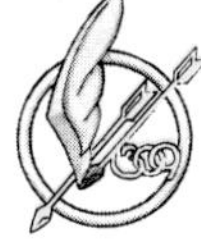

No. 309

No. 315

No. 316

No. 317

No. 318

CAP BADGES OF ARMY AND NAVAL AVIATION

Officers

Officers

Other Ranks

Petty Officers

Ratings

Ratings

Ratings

JAPAN

RANK BADGES

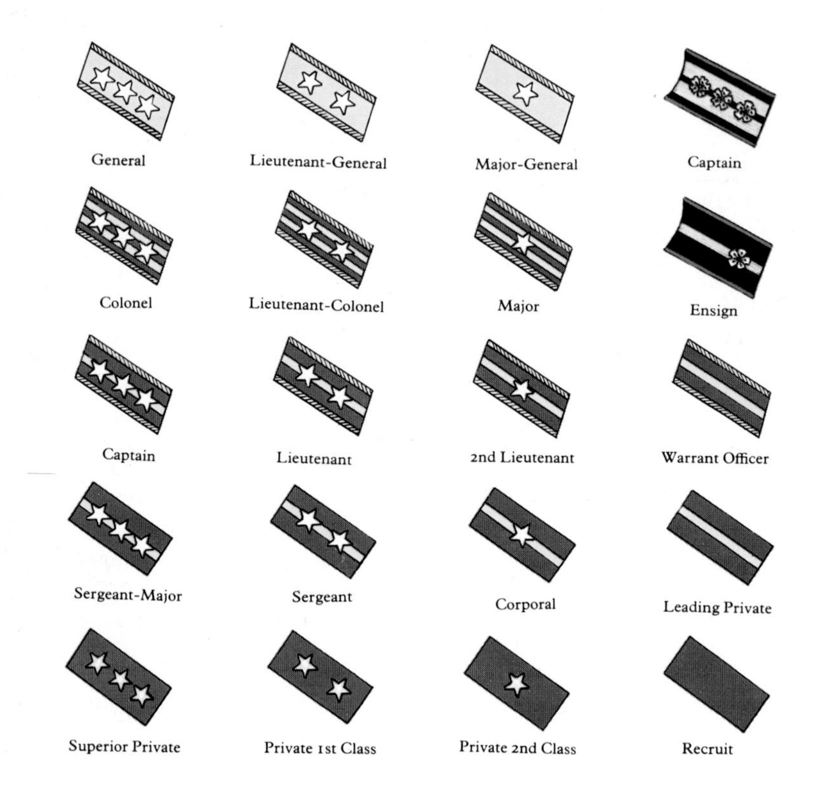

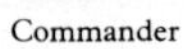
Commander

Vice Admiral

Lieutenant Commander

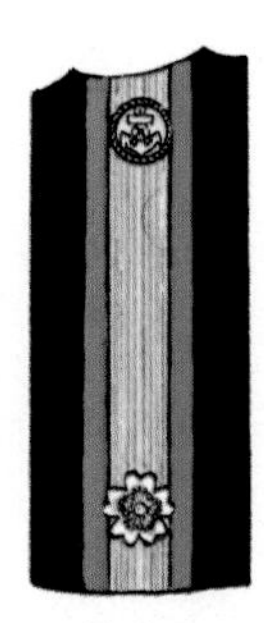
Ensign

PETTY OFFICERS' AND SEAMENS' RANK BADGES

OTHER BADGES

Bomber Pilot

Senior Petty Officer

Petty Officer 1st Class

Petty Officer 2nd Class

Fighter Pilot

Leading Seaman

Senior Seaman

Seaman 1st Class

Aviation Badge

Pilot

Aviation Badge

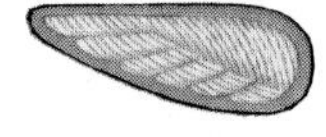
Collar Badge

Collar Badge

Army Aviation School

Officers' Army Aviation School

Kumagai Army Aviation School

22nd Army Air Kikusi Squadron

Army Aviation Maintenance School

3rd Army Aviation Squadron

RUMANIA

RANK BADGES

General Inspector of the Air Force

General of Air Squad

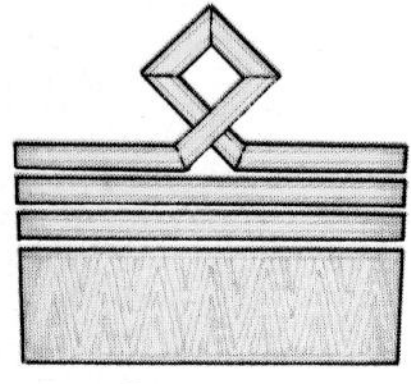
Commander

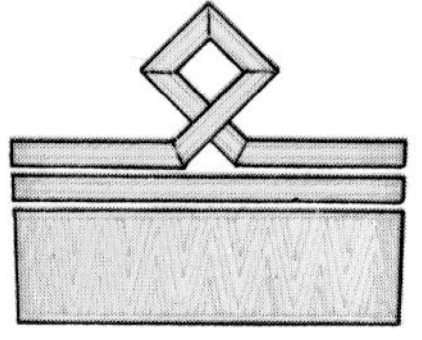
Captain Commander

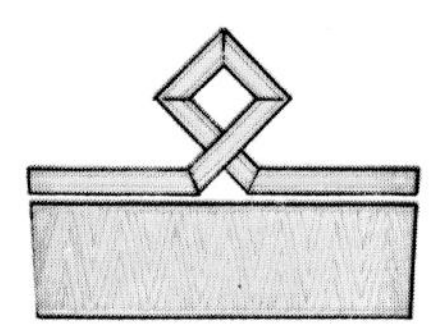
Lieutenant Commander

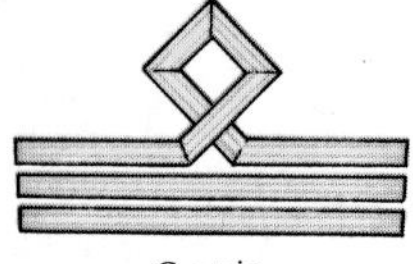
Captain

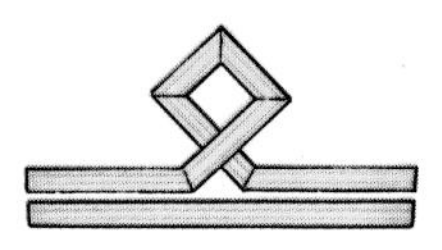
Lieutenant

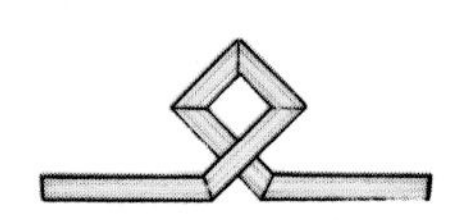
2nd Lieutenant

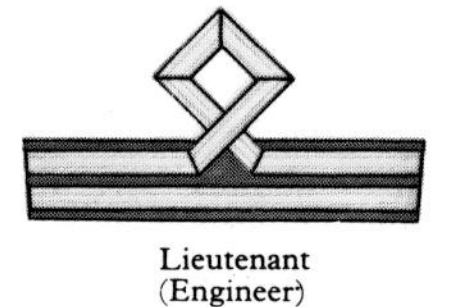
Lieutenant (Engineer)

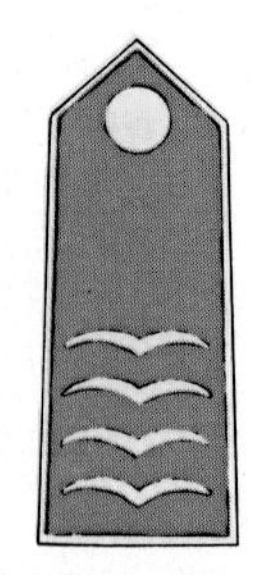
Chief Warrant Officer

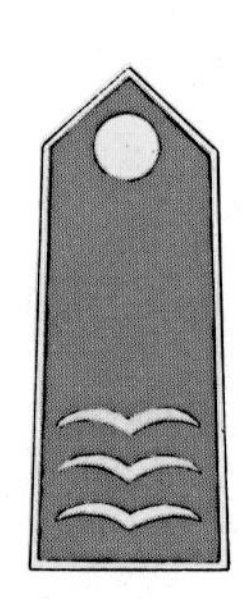
Warrant Officer Major

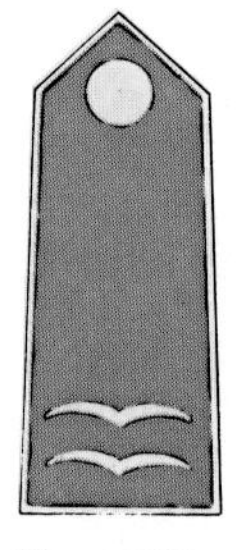
Warrant Officer

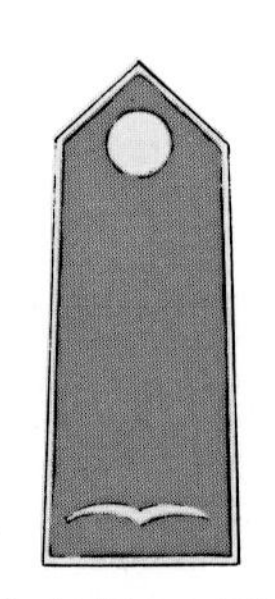
Junior Warrant Officer

RUMANIA

RANK BADGES

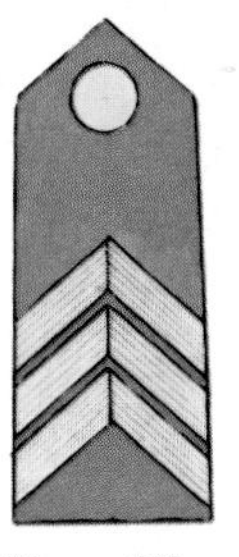

Warrant Officer
(Ground Personnel)

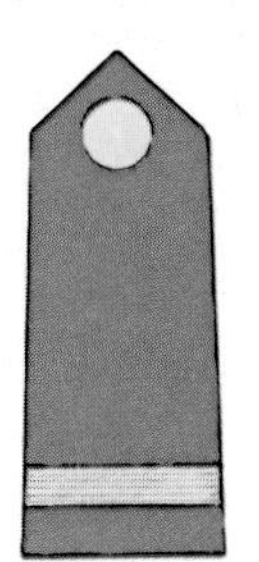

Sergeant

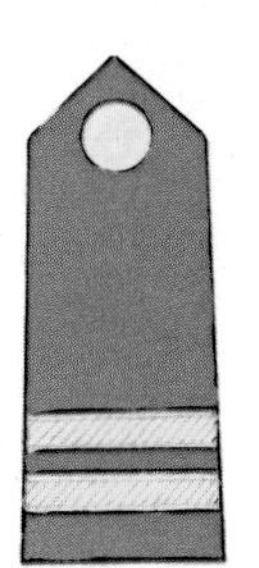

Corporal

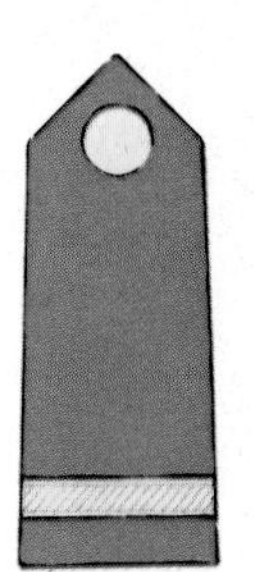

Private 1st Class

ARM-OF-SERVICE BADGES – COLLAR PATCHES

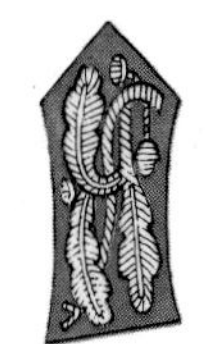

Generals

Physicians

Mechanics

Anti-Aircraft

Reconnaissance

Bombers

Fighters

Engineers

Aerostation

Schools

QUALIFICATION BADGES

Pilot

Pilot-Bomber

Observer

PLATE 77

HUNGARY

CAP INSIGNIA – PEAKED CAP

Officers

Other Ranks' Cap Badge

W.O./Sergeants

FORAGE CAP

Lieutenant-General

Major-General

Colonel

Lieutenant-Colonel

Major

Captain

1st Lieutenant

2nd Lieutenant

Candidate Officer

Warrant Officer

Senior Staff Sergeant

Staff Sergeant

Sergeant

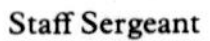

Corporal-Major

Corporal

Senior Airman

OFFICERS' RANK BADGES

Major-General
Flying Suit

Lieutenant-General

Major-General

Lieutenant-Colonel
Flying Suit

Colonel

Lieutenant-Colonel
(General Staff)

Major

Captain

1st Lieutenant

2nd Lieutenant

QUALIFICATION BADGES

Officer Pilot

N.C.O. Pilot

WARRANT OFFICERS' AND N.C.O.s' RANK BADGES

Warrant Officer Flying Suit

Aspirant

Warrant Officer

Senior Staff Sergeant Flying Suit

Senior Staff Sergeant

Staff Sergeant

Sergeant

Corporal Major

Corporal

Senior Airman

Airman

Collar Badge

Collar Badges

The first badge for medical officers was adopted in 1918 and resembles that of the Royal Army Medical Corps, except for the motto which in the case of the R.A.F. badge read 'Nec Aspera Terrent'. A smaller different badge was instituted two years later.

Gilt, silver and brass versions were worn by officers on service dress and mess dress and by orderlies, respectively. Later a different badge was worn by the personnel of the Dental Branch. Chaplains wore their distinctive badge, minus the crown, on the collar of the service and mess dress uniforms; in the case of Jewish chaplains the Cross Patee was replaced by the Star of David.

The Educational Officers of the R.A.F.V.R. obtained their own collar badges in 1940, above which were attached the 'VR' titles. There was also another title in existence: a plain letter 'A' for Auxiliary (Plate 4), and both titles were used in two sizes, for the jacket collar and a larger size for the greatcoat's shoulder straps, plus embroidered variations of both which were worn beneath the shoulder flash by N.C.O.s and airmen. The Auxiliary Air Force was formed in 1924 while the R.A.F. Volunteer Reserve was instituted in 1937.

Plate 3. Pilots' Wings

The first 'wings' were granted to qualified pilots in 1913 and when five years later the Royal Air Force was formed, the initials in the centre of the wings were changed from R.F.C. to R.A.F. It should be noted that the first wings depicted the R.F.C. badge, as worn on the cap and collar, with additional wings on either side. In 1918 the officers' cap badges were changed and collar badges were abolished (for exceptions see previous section), therefore since 1918 the centrepiece of the wings resembles the design of the cap badge of the airmen, who cannot qualify for the badge in any case.

A great number of variations of R.A.F. pilots' wings could be found: there were metal badges with a brooch pin at the back and others embroidered in gold and silver wire on the uniform's cloth, for full dress. Some other wings of the R.F.C. were embroidered in gold and silver on dark blue cloth and were worn on patrol tunics while smaller badges, also embroidered in metal wire were used for the mess dress.

The wings for service dress were embroidered in silk or cotton on a dark blue, or black cloth backing: some of these were flat while others had a padded base. The wings, crown and initials were usually executed with buff coloured cotton while the wreath was brown.

Wings of the same basic design were used in the Commonwealth but the centrepiece of the badge was different. The pilots' wings of the Royal Canadian Air Force had the initials R.C.A.F. in the centre while Australian pilots had the appropriate initials R.A.A.F. in the centre of their badge which was usually white with a light blue wreath.

The South African Air Force wings were made of white silk with a shield in the centre depicting the figure of Hope of the Cape Province, the 'wildebeeste' of Natal, the orange tree of the Orange Free State and the waggon of Transvaal. Early wings, made of brass, depicted the Union coat of arms below the crown, encircled by a wreath with the usual side wings (Plate 1).

The initials 'N.Z.' were present in the centre of the wings of the New Zealand Air Force.

Aircrew Badges—R.A.F.

These qualification badges are commonly known as 'half-wings' and as with the pilot's wings are worn above the left breast pocket, and above any ribbons or decorations.

The Observer's badge was adopted in September 1915 and was replaced in 1942 by the Navigator's badge as by then the functions of the Observer had been taken over by the more complex duties of the latter. The badge of the former depicted a wing with fourteen feathers protruding from an 'O'. The wing of the Navigator and the other aircrew's wings usually have twelve feathers only.

Another early qualification badge which has been illustrated among arm badges (Plate 6) is that of Air Gunner; it depicts a winged bullet, all made of brass. It was adopted in 1923 and in December 1939 was superseded by a half-wing with the letters 'A.G.' in the centre. Other aircrew qualification badges were adopted in 1942 and, in the following years, with their own appropriate initial or initials in the centre.

The Parachute Jumping Instructor badge was adopted shortly after World War 2 and this was the first time that the P.J.I.s were formally awarded aircrew status. It shows an open parachute in the centre instead of the usual initials.

These half-wings were all embroidered on dark blue or black backing cloth and, like the pilot's wings, there are flat and padded variations. A smaller, flat variation of these exists as well: this was usually worn by foreign aviators who had other badges on the breast as well.

Personnel of the Pathfinder squadrons, employed in finding and marking targets for oncoming bombers obtained their own distinctive badge in 1942. It was worn on the flap of the left breast pocket, 4.8 mm. below the seam. This was the eagle as worn on the forage cap, but in this case without the Royal Crown.

Aircrew Badges—R.C.A.F.

The Canadian aircrew members were eligible for the same qualifications as R.A.F. personnel but their badges were different. These half-wings carried the Royal Crown and the initials R.C.A.F. as well. However, the earlier Observer's badge was the usual winged 'O' which was granted during World War 1 to all Observers of the R.F.C. regardless of nationality.

Aircrew Badges—R.A.A.F.

The Australians had dark blue uniforms, therefore their aircrew badges were embroidered on bluish-grey felt, and the wreath was usually light blue, although variations exist which have all been embroidered in white.

Plate 4. Officers' Rank Badges

The R.A.F. officers' ranks that we know today were introduced on 27 August 1919 and new black and blue cuff stripes were adopted to be worn on the new grey-blue service dress. Gold stripes were worn on full dress and mess dress. Previously, khaki stripes were used on the war-time khaki uniform and gold stripes on the short lived sky blue uniforms.

The air force rank titles compare to the equivalent army ranks as follows:

Royal Air Force	Army
Marshal of the R.A.F.	Field-Marshal
Air Chief Marshal	General
Air Marshal	Lieutenant-General
Air Vice-Marshal	Major-General
Air Commodore	Brigadier-General
Group Captain	Colonel
Wing Commander	Lieutenant-Colonel
Squadron Leader	Major
Flight Lieutenant	Captain
Flying Officer	Lieutenant
Pilot Officer	2nd Lieutenant

The rank was shown by a combination of stripes of varying width: officers of Air Rank were distinguished by a wide stripe (2 inches) while the other officers had narrower stripes of two widths (½ inch and ¼ inch) appropriately combined.

On the greatcoat and on the blouse of the war-time grey-blue battle-dress the stripes were worn across the shoulder straps, as illustrated. The service dress jacket had no shoulder straps while the tunic of the full dress had shoulder straps with eagle and crown embroidered at the ends; officers of Air Rank wore an additional wreath embroidered in gold below the shoulder straps' button.

The women serving in the Women's Auxiliary Air Force had the same rank badges as the men but had different titles as shown in the following comparison chart:

W.A.A.F.	**R.A.F.**
Senior Controller	Air Commodore
Controller	Group Captain
Chief Commandant	Wing Commander
Senior Commandant	Squadron Leader
Company Commander	Flight Lieutenant
Deputy Company Commander	Flying Officer
Company Assistant	Pilot Officer

These rank titles were modelled after those of the A.T.S. but were changed in 1942 as follows:

W.A.A.F. 1st pattern	**W.A.A.F. 2nd pattern**
Senior Controller	Air Commandant
Controller	Group Officer
Chief Commandant	Wing Officer
Senior Commandant	Squadron Officer
Company Commander	Flight Officer
Deputy Company Commander	Section Officer
Company Assistant	Assistant Section Officer

Later the ranks of Commandant-in-Chief and Air Chief Commandant were also introduced, and compare with those of Air Marshal and Air Vice-Marshal respectively.

Plate 5. Warrant Officers' and N.C.O.s' Rank Badges

The warrant and non-commissioned ranks of the R.F.C. and later of the R.A.F. derive from those of the army, although some naval flavour is attached to the title of Leading Aircraftman.

The warrant ranks, of 1st and 2nd Class, existed until the beginning of World War 2: the former wore the Royal Arms on the forearm of both sleeves and the other a large Royal Crown, 45 × 45 mm. in size. The pre-war badges were usually embroidered in fine light blue silk, while later versions were embroidered in cotton on dark blue, or black felt. Eventually the two ranks were merged into one, of Warrant Officer, with the Royal Arms as its distinctive badge.

The Flight Sergeant was the top N.C.O.s' rank, with three worsted grey-blue chevrons and a crown above them. The latter was usually made of brass but light blue embroidered variations were used as well. Three- and two-chevron ranks identified the Sergeant and the Corporal while the army's one-chevron rank of Lance-Corporal was substituted by the two-bladed propeller badge of the Leading Aircraftman. The Leading Aircraftman, Aircraftman of 1st and of 2nd Class were graduation titles of airmen and the former became a rank title only in 1950 although the propeller badge existed since World War 1.

Four inverted 'V' chevrons below a drum were worn on the forearm by the Drum Major. Similar individual chevrons were also worn on the forearms and were known as good conduct stripes.

Initially the N.C.O.s' rank titles of the W.A.A.F. were different from those of the R.A.F.: there were Senior Section and Assistant Section Leaders, and Aircraftwomen of 1st and 2nd Class. Later the rank of Under Officer, equivalent to the R.A.F. Warrant Officer, was instituted and the women's rank titles were the same as those of the men.

Trade and Other Badges

Most of the following badges were worn on the sleeve and therefore have been illustrated together in this and in the following plates.

The eagle of the R.A.F. was worn on both upper sleeves, below the shoulder seam, by all those below the rank of Warrant Officer 1st Class; only the nationality title could be worn above the R.A.F. eagle. This badge was adopted in 1918 and was originally red for the khaki uniform of that period but subsequently its colour was changed to light blue when the grey-blue uniform was introduced. However, red eagles as well as other badges were worn on the khaki tropical uniforms of World War 2.

Airmen of the Royal Auxiliary Air Force and those of the Royal Air Force Volunteer Reserve wore the initials 'A' and 'VR' respectively, embroidered in light blue on dark blue background, immediately below the eagle badge.

The Warrant Officer wore the same badge below the rank badge. The same initials but made of brass were worn by the officers on the lapels of the service dress jacket and on the shoulder straps of the battledress and of the greatcoat (Plate 4). The letter 'A' was used also by personnel of the Women's Auxiliary Air Force. Later, during World War 2 the use of these initials was abandoned.

Bandsmen of the R.A.F. wore a brass badge depicting a lyre and wreath with the crown above, while musicians of voluntary bands had the same badge but without the crown. Trumpeters, pipers and drummers wore their own appropriate arm badges: crossed trumpets, a Scottish bagpipes and a drum, respectively.

The badge of Physical Training Instructor was already in use in the early 1920s and its original brass pattern was reproduced in cloth versions during World War 2 for reasons of economy. The remaining four badges illustrated in this plate were adopted during the last war: The Gunners were later taken over by the R.A.F. Regiment: the badge with two 'G's stands for Ground Gunner. The Parachute Instructor badge appeared in 1943 and was worn on the right upper sleeve as with that of Gunner, while the Signallers' badge was worn on both sleeves and was introduced in 1944 for qualified personnel of the R.A.F. Regiment.

Plate 6. Trade and Other Badges

The Combined Operations badge illustrated was worn by a member of the 3207 R.A.F. Servicing Command, one of several units with the new task of activating airstrips constructed by the Royal Engineers. These provisional airstrips, usually made of metal sheeting, were sited near the front line and were used as re-fuelling bases by fighter squadrons stationed in Britain. The Servicing Commando kept an airstrip going until the front line moved on and eventually passed its duty to normal R.A.F. units, before advancing to prepare another airstrip closer to the front line.

The Royal Air Force Regiment was raised in 1942 and was formed by ground personnel employed primarily in the defence of R.A.F. installations. All ranks wore a distinctive shoulder title on both upper arms.

Personnel engaged in Air-Sea Rescue wore a special badge on the right upper sleeve from 1943 to 1948.

Already, during World War 1, a special brass badge was created to distinguish Wireless Operators (Plate 1); the 'sparks' badge remained in use after the war and later the 'O' was replaced by a clenched fist, worn by Radio Operators and Mechanics, while Radio Operators had the initials 'RO' instead of the fist; other badges with different initials between the forks of lightning existed as well.

A brass badge, depicting a four-bladed propeller in a ring, was adopted in 1919 for boy apprentices and was worn on the left upper sleeve. The Air Gunner's badge was also made of brass: it has been mentioned already in the chapter on Aircrew badges.

The Bomb Disposal badge was adopted in 1941 for wearing on the right upper sleeve. The badge of the Eagle Squadron is a very exclusive item as it was worn from 1940 onward by Americans only, serving in that squadron. It was worn on both upper sleeves.

After dealing with each of these badges it becomes apparent that most pre-war badges were made of brass while war-time versions were later made in cloth purely for reasons of economy as thousands of men were by then wearing them. The cloth badges exist in embroidered and printed patterns, in light blue on dark blue background for grey-blue uniforms and red on khaki for khaki tropical uniforms.

The vast majority of the above-mentioned badges were used by N.C.O.s and airmen, therefore these had a dark blue or black background, while officers' badges were embroidered on a grey-blue background, to match the colour of the uniform.

Nationality Titles

During World War 2 the R.A.F. absorbed a number of servicemen from the Commonwealth and exiles from countries over-run by the enemy. The latter group is dealt with in their own national chapters in the book.

The colour of these nationality titles follows the general rule: the officers wore curved titles embroidered in light blue on grey-blue background, while the others had titles in light blue on dark blue or black background which was usually rectangular. All ranks wore red and khaki shoulder titles on the tropical uniform.

However, many badges that did not follow the rule were also made because many manufacturers were engaged in making these titles and they tried to improve on the average standard. In many instances the R.A.F. eagle and the nationality title were combined in the same badge, and different styles of lettering were applied. For instance, there are titles depicting the eagle above the initials U.S.A., others with 'CANADA' above the eagle and others with both national titles and the eagle in between. On the other hand, British airmen serving in Canada started wearing the 'GT. BRITAIN' title, and others appeared—i.e. the title 'SCOTLAND'.

All commonwealth nations, colonies and British territories were represented in this form and only a very few examples can be illustrated. Some other odd shoulder titles can be found as well, for instance that of 'MEXICO', probably worn by ex-residents in other nations.

Plate 7. Badges of Other Flying Organisations

Some extra-ordinary organisations were created during the years of national danger, giving a chance to many thousands to contribute in the cause of common defence. Only some representative badges of these organisations have been illustrated.

The Air Defence Cadet Corps was raised in 1938 to provide preliminary aviation training. The usual grey-blue R.A.F. uniforms were worn, with silver lace rank stripes. The officers' cap badge has been illustrated, the badge of cadets did not carry the wreath.

The Air Transport Auxiliary was an organisation employed in ferrying aircraft and general transportation. Many of the pilots were women. Dark blue uniforms were worn by its personnel with gold stripes on the cuffs, in a background in branch colour. The cap badge is illustrated but another variation existed, made of metal, with a scroll inscribed 'Aetheris Avidi'. Wings, half-wings and arm badges were worn as well by qualified personnel.

The personnel of the Civil Air Guard also had special badges; the pilots' wings depicted the initials as in the cap badge sided by straight wings. The Air Training Corps was created with the cadre of the Air Defence Cadet Corps in 1941. R.A.F. uniforms were used with R.A.F. stripes and chevrons and additional A.D.C. badges. The officers wore the 'VR' initials of the R.A.F. Volunteer Reserve in which they were commissioned.

Soon after it was raised, the Observer Corps was granted the prefix 'Royal' for its magnificent performance. The badge depicts an Elizabethan Coast Watcher, holding a torch above the motto 'Forewarned is Forearmed', surrounded by a wreath and ensigned by the Royal crown. The officers wore the initials 'ROC' on the lapels of the collar. The other ranks had an embroidered breast badge which, in a ring surmounted by the crown, shows the R.A.F. eagle surrounded by the title 'Royal Observer Corps'.

Fleet Air Arm Insignia

The Fleet Air Arm was formed in 1924 as a subordinate organisation to the R.A.F. and the seaborne contingent of the Fleet Air Arm came under the command of the Royal Navy in 1937 only.

Naval uniforms were worn by its personnel, with naval cap badges and rank insignia. In 1925 qualified pilots were granted a gold and silver embroidered badge which was worn on the left forearm above the rank stripes. The badge depicted an anchor surrounded by a wreath, below the Royal Crown, with an albatross wing on each side. A metal variation of this badge has been worn since 1933 on the breast on the white uniform only. R.A.F. officers attached to the Fleet Air Arm wore a similar badge but with out crown and wings.

Pilots who were recruited before the beginning of the war and did not belong to the naval establishment, therefore could not command H.M. vessels and were given a special badge — a silver 'A' surrounded by a gold wreath, which they wore above the rank insignia on the left sleeve. In 1939 a small letter 'A' was adopted in its place, worn inside the curl of the top stripe of both sleeves. The latter badge, however, was also worn by other officers of the Air Branch with qualifications other than that of pilot.

In 1942 a special arm badge was introduced for the Observers of the Fleet Air Arm: Air Gunners wore a similar badge and so, later, did other Aircrewmen ratings. These were embroidered in red for blue uniforms and in blue for white uniform, with or without crown.

Plate 8. Non-substantive Badges

These badges indentified the qualification, or specialisation of petty officers and seamen of the Royal Navy. The chief petty officers wore them in pairs, embroidered in gold on the lapels of the collar while larger badges, red for blue uniform and blue for white uniform were worn on the right arm by the other ratings. Gold badges were worn on full dress.

In 1930 the Telegraphist-Air Gunners of the Fleet Air Arm were granted a special badge which depicts an aeroplane with straight wings (Plate 7). Later, in 1935, a similar badge but with a 6-pointed star above the aeroplane was given to Air Gunners; a similar badge but with a crown instead of the star to Acting Observer's Mates, while the Observer's Mates had the aeroplane with the crown above and the star below.

These qualifications were reorganised in 1939 and the design of the aeroplane was also modified, as illustrated. The Air Mechanic qualification was instituted in the same year and that of Air Fitter in 1940. The badge of the former was a 2-bladed propeller while fitters wore a 4-bladed propeller. There were four sections of each of these qualifications: Airframe, Engine, Electrical and Ordnance.

The Chief Petty Officer Air Mechanic wore a crown above the propeller and a letter below referred to the section of specialisation. The leading ratings wore a star above the propeller and the letter, while the other ratings had the propeller and the letter only.

The crown was not worn with any of the fitters' badges. Unclassified badges, i.e. without the section's letter, were worn after 1943 by Air Mechanics and Fitters not yet qualified.

The Radio Mechanics of the Fleet Air Arm used the badge of the Royal Navy.

Norway

Plate 9. Cap Badges, Rank and Other Badges
At the outbreak of World War 2 Norway had a small Army Air Force and a Naval Air Service, both in existence since 1915. The aviators wore army or navy uniforms respectively, with additional qualification wings.

The army uniforms were modified in 1934 and the colour of piping and chevrons was changed from red to green. The officers' service dress consisted of a kepi or forage cap, a tunic with high folded collar and four patch pockets of usual pattern, Sam Browne belt, breeches and riding boots or long trousers and shoes. Double-breasted greatcoats and fur hats were used in winter. The other ranks wore the forage cap, a field-grey tunic with four patch pockets, a leather waist belt with a plain rectangular buckle, long trousers and boots. The buttons were shown on the greatcoat only.

A dual-badge was worn on the head-dress by officers and N.C.O.s, with stripes of gold, silver or black lace to identify class of rank. The officers had a silk cockade in the national colours at the top while that of the other ranks was made of metal and painted blue, white and red. The national emblem, the Norwegian Lion, was carried on the badge placed below by the officers, and on an arm-of-service button by the N.C.O.s. The officers' badge was made of gilt and enamel and was semi-spherical in shape. The privates wore the cockade only at the front of the forage cap.

Rank distinction was shown on the kepi, on the collar of the tunic and on the shoulder straps of the greatcoat or, in the case of N.C.O.s, on the cuffs.

Rank stripes were worn all around the kepi, above the chin strap. They were made of gold for generals and silver lace for the other officers; the former had also a special chin strap made of gold cords. The senior officers were identified by a large silver stripe with narrower rank stripes below while the lower three ranks had only the narrow stripes. The sergeants had narrow double green stripes placed vertically on the sides and on the back of the kepi, above the cap band. The Corporal wore single stripes in the same position.

There were two generals' ranks in 1940: the rank of General with three silver stars and of Major-General with one star only. A Colonel commanded the Army Air Force until 1924, later a Major-General.

Green piping was worn on the kepi, on the collar of the tunic, as illustrated, on the cuffs and on the shoulder straps of the greatcoat.

The generals had a large gold lace stripe at the front of the collar of the tunic, with large stars embroidered in silver thread. The senior officers had a silver stripe, 15 mm. wide, at the front of the collar and white metal 5-pointed stars identified the actual rank. Only the stars were worn by the junior officers, as illustrated.

These Norwegian officers' stars could be readily identified as at the end of each arm they have a small round loop which is used for stitching on to the uniform.

The stars and the senior officers' stripe were applied on the greatcoat's shoulder straps as well. The latter was stitched next to the outer green piping, all around the strap, except for the outer end that was attached to the shoulder seam.

The Sergeant wore one green stripe below the cuff piping of the tunic and the Corporal had a vertical green stripe on the cuff of both sleeves.

Wings were worn by qualified Pilots and Observers above the right breast pocket of the tunic. Both were embroidered in silver on a background of arm-of-service colour: red before 1934 and green from 1934 to 1940. Double wings, surmounted by the national coat of arms, were worn by Pilots while a half-wing, the Norwegian Lion in a shield below the crown was the badge of the Observers; both badges were instituted in February 1926. Naval aviators wore uniforms and badges of the Navy with the above-mentioned wings, embroidered in gold on dark blue background.

Plate 10. Badges worn after 1940

After the German invasion of Norway, in the spring of 1940, King Haakon VII and his government left for Britain where subsequently the Norwegian armed forces and the merchant marine were reorganised. At that time the Norwegian merchant marine was then the fourth largest in the world and as the majority of it joined the Allied cause, eventually it provided a considerable revenue which was used for continuing the war from bases abroad.

After the subjugation of Norway, 120 officers and airmen and a few battered old aircraft were all that remained of the Norwegian Air Force, by then in England. In 1940 a training centre was set up in Canada at Toronto which became the birthplace of the new modern air force. It was named 'Little Norway' and trained thousands of Norwegians who came from all over the world. This number included many escapees who came across the North Sea to Britain in small boats and others who escaped to Sweden in order to eventually join in the fight.

The Norwegian Naval Air Service operated as part of R.A.F. Coastal Command from British bases while the Army Air Force provided two fighter squadrons. Incidentally, a Norwegian squadron became famous among the Allied air forces' units for its performance and score of victories. In 1944 the two services were amalgamated to form the Royal Norwegian Air Force which was at last an independent arm.

The Norwegians with the R.A.F. wore grey-blue uniforms of British pattern, while those in the Naval Air Service had dark blue naval uniforms. The officers of the former wore a new badge on the peaked cap: this badge was in three separate pieces attached to a shield-shaped grey-blue background. Generals had gold twisted cords as a chin strap, senior officers had two thinner twisted silver cords while the others wore the usual leather chin strap. The old round cap badges, illustrated in the previous plate, continued to be worn on the front of the forage cap while the winged badge, which was at the top of the peaked cap badge, was worn on its own on the left side of the forage cap.

Airmen, as well as officers and N.C.O.s, wore two badges at the front of their forage caps, but without any lace in between. The cockade in national colours was attached at the top and a plain button with the Norwegian Lion below.

The same type of officers' rank insignia was used, but now the stars and the lace were placed at the front of the lapels of the collar of the grey-blue service dress jacket, or on the collar of the grey-blue battledress. The N.C.O.s' ranks were modified to conventional chevrons of silver lace and followed the R.A.F. pattern. The ranks of a Flight Sergeant, wearing three chevrons below the crowned shield of Norway and a Leading Aircraftman at the lower end, wearing a 2-bladed propeller badge, were added.

All wore the 'NORWAY' nationality title on the left upper sleeve and a small Norwegian flag on the right upper sleeve. The nationality title was placed in a frame with trimmed corners; the officers' title was usually embroidered in silver or white thread on grey-blue background while the other ranks' title was in white on dark blue, or black background.

The Pilot's wings remained basically the same although the new wings for Pilots, Observers and Wireless Operators/Air Gunners were now embroidered in silver on grey-blue for those serving in ground based units, and in gold on dark blue for personnel of naval units. Two examples of the former pattern and one of the naval pattern have been illustrated. The Observer's and Wireless Operator/Air Gunner wings were adopted during the course of the war in response to the need for creating new aircrew qualifications.

Netherlands

The interest in aeronautics captured the imagination of many people in Holland as it did in the rest of the world. Early experiments in flight took place some time before the establishment of the Aviation Arm of the Royal Netherlands Army on 1 July 1913. A great deal of enthusiasm, in conjunction with the need to modernise the country's defences before the outbreak of World War 1, lead to a steady development in the field of aviation. The Royal Netherlands Indian Army, in the Far East, raised its own independent Air Service on 20 October 1915 and eventually the Navy also raised its own aviation.

In the period between the wars lack of funds prevented any further expansion and even modernisation of the existing establishment. Therefore the Netherlands possessed only a few, rather obsolete aircraft at the beginning of World War 2. In 1938 the Aviation Arm was renamed Military (i.e. Army) Air Service and hurried preparations for defence were initiated.

The badges of these three different pre-war air branches, and those of new organisations which were raised during the war, have been grouped separately and will be dealt with in different chapters of the text.

Plate 10. Army Air Service–Cap Badges

This establishment was part of the army and therefore field-grey army service uniforms were worn by all ranks; in fact many officers who qualified as pilots or observers were eventually employed as army officers due to the lack of aircraft. Only just before the war, when the Army Air Service was somewhat expanded, were all the aviators employed in their true role, although even in 1940 only about 124 aeroplanes could be mustered.

The service dress and the field uniform were field-grey and the common head-dress for all ranks, with the exception of the generals, was the kepi. The generals wore a peaked cap and a section of the front of the cap band has been illustrated. It shows the cap badge, which was an oval orange cockade in a gold frame, surrounded by a branch of laurel and one of oak leaves with a gold soutache around the top of the cap band and a wavy gold embroidery at the bottom.

The kepi was of Austrian pattern, with a visor covered in field-grey cloth and brown leather chin strap with buckle at the front. The cap band was visible above the chin strap to show the piping on either side and another stripe of piping ran along the top of the kepi. The arm-of-service colour of the Army Air Service was blue.

The national cockade was applied on the upper front of the kepi: the officers' cockade was made of orange silk and gold wire; the N.C.O.s' cockade was all made of silk, while that of the corporals and privates was made of brass with its centre painted orange. A thin cord was attached to the bottom of the cockade and in the loop of this cord there was a button depicting the Lion of Nassau. The cap badge of the lowest ranks had the cord and loop made of metal. Regimental numbers or the Lion of Nassau, made of bronze, were worn on the cap band below the button.

Plate 11. Army Air Service—Rank Badges

Rank distinction was shown in the form of piping on the head-dress while insignia of rank were worn on the collar of the tunic and greatcoat.

The senior officers had three stripes of gold piping on the kepi, one at the top and above and below the cap band; junior officers had gold piping only on either side of the cap band and blue piping at the top of the kepi; warrant officers (W.O.1) had only one gold stripe on the top side of the cap band and N.C.O.s wore only blue piping. The officers and warrant officers had gold piping also on the forage cap while the others had blue piping; the badges or numbers on the forage cap were always painted orange.

All ranks wore field-grey tunics with high collar and blue piping all around it. The generals wore four 6-pointed stars all made of silver, or in gold and silver, and gold embroidery instead of coloured piping. Silver stars and gold bars identified the senior officer while only the former were worn by junior officers. Captains and 1st Lieutenant Adjutants had their first star made of gold and warrant officers (W.O.1) wore a round white metal stud on each side of the collar.

A gold or bronze aircraft engine with propeller, the badge of the air service, was worn on both sides, of the collar.

Stars and bars were worn by officers on either side of the greatcoat's collar while warrant officers in this case wore a special badge: the usual stud but mounted on to brass double bars.

The non-commissioned officers wore inverted-V chevrons, 1·5 cm. in width, on both sleeves just above the cuffs. The sergeants had gold chevrons, the corporals yellow chevrons, mounted on a cloth backing of arm-of-service colour, blue for air force and other corps. The Sergeant 1st Class had a gold soutache above his chevron while the Quartermaster-Sergeant had an extra chevron on the left upper sleeve. The Sergeant-Major Administrator had a gold crown above his chevrons while an Instructor wore a silver crown.

Plate 12. Qualification Badges—Army Air Service
Badges for qualified Pilots and Observers were instituted on 14 October 1919, to be worn on the left breast, above the pocket and eventual service ribbons. The former depicts an eagle in flight above an orange circle, the other shows a winged blue circle and the initial 'W', which stands for 'Waarnemer', i.e. Observer. Up to 1940 these badges were made of gold embroidery but later during the war some metal versions were made in London.

A combined badge for Pilot-Observer was created on 30 December 1930.

R.A.F. wings and half-wings were granted to Dutch aviators who qualified in Britain during the war and which—now known as 'memorial badges'—are still worn by those entitled.

Royal Netherlands Indian Army Air Service
Entirely different qualification badges, made of bronze, were adopted in the colonies for Pilots and Observers on 25 November 1921 and later, on 9 September 1932, a composite badge was made for the Pilot-Observer. The Flight Surgeon's wings appeared in 1940 and all the others, for Air Gunner, Bomb Aimer, Photographer, Wireless Operator and Flight Engineer, were adopted in 1941.

Royal Netherlands Naval Air Service
Qualified flyers of the Naval Air Service wore the badges of Pilot, Observer and Pilot-Observer of the Army Air Service, plus the three special half-wings illustrated. Further details of the insignia of this separate organisation can be found in the chapter relating to Plate 14, where some other naval badges are illustrated.

Trade and Other Badges
Three trade badges were worn until 1940 on the left upper sleeve by mechanics of the Army Air Service. All depict the aircraft engine and with crown and without in gold were worn by Chief Mechanics and Mechanics respectively, while gold or red badges depicting the engine and a 2-bladed propeller were used by Aircraft Mechanics.

The remaining illustrations show nationality titles worn during World War 2 by Dutch airmen in the United Kingdom.

Plate 13. Rank Badges—Army Air Service after 1940
About 250 men, including eight instructors and eighty trainees from the training schools of Flushing and Haamstede arrived in Britain at the end

of May 1940, via France. At about the same time, eight aeroplanes of the Naval Air Service crossed the Channel with their crews. They went to form No. 320 (Dutch) Squadron of Coastal Command and were later joined by other Dutch personnel from the East Indies.

Initially Dutch exiles joined the R.A.F.V.R. and from April 1942 volunteers were trained as pilots, and eventually joined No. 320 and other squadrons, mainly Nos. 118 and 167. In June 1943 the latter was re-designated No. 322 (Dutch) Squadron, R.A.F. Men attached to the R.A.F.V.R. wore British grey-blue uniforms and badges with 'NETHERLAND' shoulder titles embroidered in light blue on grey-blue or dark blue for officers and airmen respectively.

As the Netherlands' armed forces were slowly rebuilt in Britain, during the course of the war a new Dutch air force was organised with its own identity. The Nassau Lion was the main emblem of the new Royal Army of which the Air Service was still part. Only one small section of the army dress regulations published in 1944 was dedicated to the uniforms and badges of the air force, which of course were different to those of the army.

However, the air force badges followed the pattern of those of the parent service, with the exception of the cap badges which were those of the R.A.F.

New 'NEDERLAND' shoulder titles were adopted, in this case with the Dutch spelling, as were badges with the Nassau Lion above the nationality title. The latter were inspired by the army titles which depicted an orange lion and title embroidered on khaki. Some officers of the air force wore for a time the same badge in golden orange embroidery on grey-blue but later the embroidery was changed to light blue, or silver.

Eventually, during the last year of the war, men were recruited in Holland and truly independent national armed forces were established. The Army Air Service and the Netherlands Indian Army Air Service were amalgamated to form the Royal Netherlands Air Force, an independent service. The cap badges were changed to a new Dutch pattern and eventually the nationality title of the arm badge was changed to the motto 'JE MAINTIENDRAI'.

All Dutch aviators in the United Kingdom wore British uniforms and badges with their own nationality shoulder titles. As the war progressed it became apparent that as the former Dutch rank insignia of the officers could not be applied to the new uniforms, new badges had to be devised. Additionally, as the British uniforms had no piping, coloured collar patches were adopted in order to show rank and branch of service at the same time. These appeared in the 1944 dress regulations which became mandatory in February 1945.

Air Force personnel wore Cambridge blue patches, pointed at the top, with rank distinction identified by stars and bars, as worn before the war;

generals' patches had a narrow embroidery at the top which resembled that previously worn by generals on the tunic's collar. Doctors and chaplains wore special breast pocket badges.

The non-commissioned officers wore R.A.F. chevrons and the Leading Aircraftman the propeller badge, but later the original ranks were developed into four sergeants' grades, one Corporal and a Private 1st Class, the latter with one chevron. The 1944 regulations prescribed two Sergeant-Major's badges: the first was a British badge for the service and field uniforms while the second, the Netherlands Royal Crown was worn with dress uniform only. Both badges were worn on the forearm.

Plate 14. Royal Netherlands Naval Air Service

The Royal Netherlands Navy was a very powerful organisation and, as it was partially based in the Dutch East Indies it was not shattered by the surprise attack that hit the Army in Holland.

The Naval Air Service was raised in 1917, with establishments in Holland and in the colonies. In May 1940 all that could be saved of the former was moved to France and later to Britain. In 1942, units of the Naval Air Service in the East moved to Australia and Ceylon following the Japanese invasion of their colonies.

Naval uniforms and insignia were worn by the personnel of this service: it should be noted however that there was not a unique cap badge for all naval officers but corps emblems were placed in its centre, below the crown. The officers of the Air Service had the familiar aircraft engine and 2-bladed propeller, as illustrated.

The personnel of the Naval Air Service was made up of flyers and repairmen, the former with the above-mentioned badge, while the repairmen's badge depicted the silhouette of an aeroplane. These badges were worn on the left upper sleeve by those eligible and were of the same colour as the chevrons, i.e. gold, yellow or red, depending upon rank.

Royal Netherlands Indian Army Air Service

Following the formation of the Army Air Service in Holland, two years later, on 20 October 1915, an aviation branch was also raised in the Dutch Indies, as part of the army.

The uniforms and badges of the new corps were basically the same as those of the army, already described in another volume of this series, and aviators could only be recognised by their arm-of-service colours and by the engine and propeller badge worn on the shoulder straps or on the collar.

A round cockade with orange centre was the head-dress badge in the

East Indies: it was made in gold, yellow silk or cotton, depending upon the rank of its wearer.

Four types of uniforms, the same as in the army, were used before the Japanese invasion. The dark blue, virtually black, ceremonial dress uniform was worn with kepi and an Attila tunic and the former could also be worn with the white uniform in some special circumstances. Below the cockade of the kepi there was the loop and button, as also were shown below the cockades used in Holland, while the round cockade on its own was worn on the cap band of the peaked cap. The Attila had a black collar with blue piping and additional gold lace for generals and senior officers. The arm-of-service badge was worn on the collar.

The badge was worn on the shoulder straps of the white uniform and only the rank was shown on the collar: generals and field officers had the stars on gold lace patches; junior officers, the ensign and warrant officers had their stars or studs attached directly on to the collar. Sergeants had stripes on black patches. The shoulder straps were the same as those of the army, made of gold interlaced cords for generals, woven in gold with a zig-zag pattern for senior officers, plain gold for junior officers and black for N.C.O.s, all with a silver propeller-badge attached.

The two remaining uniforms, the garrison and the field uniform, were both field-grey, with collar patches of different shape on the collar, because their collars were different. Bronze arm-of-service badges were worn on the shoulder straps.

The gold lace patches of the generals and senior officers had coloured piping all around the edges, and in this case junior officers, the ensign and warrant officers, wore black collar patches, the former with a gold stripe inside the edges.

Plate 15. Royal Netherlands Indian Army Air Service—After 1942

The Japanese attack compelled the Dutch units to retreat in 1942 and the Air Service moved to Australia and Ceylon continuing the fight against the invaders. Some pilots were already in Australia before the fall of Java, and due to take over American aircraft. On 1 May 1942 they formed No. 18 (Netherlands East Indies) Squadron, R.A.A.F. This unit was composed of 242 Dutchmen and Indonesians and 206 Australians.

In the same month the Royal Netherlands Military Flying School was created in America, at Jackson, Mississippi, under the command of Major-General L. H. van Oyen. The Royal Netherlands Indian Army and Naval personnel trained there wore American khaki uniforms with Dutch badges; General van Oyen wore his rank insignia on the lapels of the collar of his khaki jacket in the form of four stars above a V-shaped gold stripe, as illustrated.

Trained aviators were sent back to Australia, where in December 1943 they formed No. 120 (Netherland East Indies) Squadron, R.A.A.F., a fighter unit, in Canberra. Later, after the surrender of Japan, No. 121, another fighter squadron and No. 20, a transport squadron, were raised and fought in the Dutch-Indonesian conflict of 1945–50.

The Union of Socialist Soviet Republics

Plate 15. Historical background

Balloons were used in Russia for tactical observation many years before the invention of the aeroplane and an aerostation already existed in the 1890s. Its personnel wore a special breast pocket badge which depicted a winged anchor surmounted by the Czarist double-headed eagle clutching two crossed axes, the whole set on a wreath.

In 1910 six officers were sent to France to be trained to fly aircraft and an Aviation School was formed with branches at Sevastopol and Gatchina (Petersburg).

Some aircraft were bought abroad; later new prototypes were built in Russia and eventually the Imperial Russian Aviation Corps was formed, keeping pace with similar military establishments that were raised all over Europe.

The qualified aviators, i.e. Pilots, were granted a special badge and a similar one, but with an additional telescope was instituted in 1916 for the Observers.

After the Revolution aviation was reorganised under the name of Red Air Fleet of Workers and Peasants which in 1924 was redesignated Soviet Military Aviation Forces.

The personnel of the former wore army uniforms which displayed a light blue arm-of-service colour in various manners according to type of uniform. Uniforms and insignia were standardised in 1919 and in 1922: the latter regulations officially confirmed the use of a metal winged propeller badge for army aviators and a winged anchor for the naval branch.

A special arm badge 100 mm. in width and 63 mm. in height was adopted on 3 April 1920 and a similar one, but with an additional 15 mm. red edge all around, with the inscription 'Exemplary' appeared in September 1922. Some different arm badges were introduced in August 1924 to identify army and naval aviators; their design followed the pattern of the arm-of-service badges of the two branches. A third badge of this type for wearing on the left upper sleeve was issued in 1925 to Aviation Engineers.

In 1924 blue uniforms were adopted; rank insignia previously worn on the forearms was moved on to the collar and collar patches were changed from plain light blue to blue with additional red piping. The arm-of-service badge, to be worn on the collar patch after rank insignia, was also modified; the new one had shorter wings and a rather squarish looking propeller.

The Aviation Engineers, however, kept to army uniforms and had blue collar patches with black piping, ensigned by the winged propeller badge.

New blue uniforms with open collar were adopted in 1935 and saw the Soviet aviators into World War 2.

Plate 16. Head-dress and Rank Badges (1940–43)

The blue uniform was used as parade, service and walking-out dress while for everyday wear khaki uniforms were used, with aviation blue cap bands, piping and patches. In July 1940 an additional grey dress uniform was prescribed for the Marshal of the Soviet Union and for the generals.

A composite badge was worn on the peaked cap while only the red star on blue backing was used on the forage cap.

New collar patches, as well as new uniforms were adopted in 1935: these were light sky blue, with gold piping for officers and black piping for political personnel and other ranks. Oblong patches, 100 mm. × 32.5 mm. in size were worn on the collar of jackets and tunics and larger ones, 110 mm. in height and 90 mm. in width, cut to the shape of the collar were worn on the greatcoat. The winged propeller and rank insignia were placed on the patches as illustrated.

Rank badges in the form of red enamelled diamonds, rectangles, squares and triangles, each corresponding to a class of rank, were introduced in 1924, as a development of pre-existing badges adopted in 1919 and modified in 1922. The structure of ranks was also modified several times during this period as already detailed in another volume of this series.

The senior officers at that time were called senior commanders, the junior officers commanders, and the N.C.O.s were known as junior commanders.

In July 1940 the generals' diamonds were replaced by gold embroidered stars; the illustrations show their patches as worn on the special generals' tunics with stand-and-fall collar. The rank of Marshal of the Soviet Union was above the corps and service cadres and therefore is beyond the scope of this book. The ranks from Colonel to Captain were identified by red rectangles, from four to one.

Gold and red chevrons for wearing by officers on the forearms were adopted in 1935 and modified in 1940. Initially gold chevrons were used by generals and red chevrons by the other officers, but later, in 1940, a single large gold chevron with a narrow red stripe at the bottom, and a gold star above it was prescribed for all the generals except that of the top rank, who had a larger gold star and a red stripe also above the gold chevron. The other officers' chevrons showed a combination of gold and red stripes.

Plate 17. Rank Badges (1940–43)

The lieutenants were identified by square-shaped red enamelled badges, which from three to one were worn on the collar patches; they also wore chevrons on the forearms.

The political personnel were an integral part of the armed forces and were divided into Commissars, i.e. senior ranks, and Politruks, the junior ranks. They wore black instead of gold piping on the collar patches and a red star with hammer and sickle on the sleeves.

A new arm badge for Technical Engineers was introduced in April 1942; a small replica of the same was worn on the collar patches in place of the winged propeller. This one and the arm badges previously mentioned (Plate 15) cannot be classified as 'wings' and flyers on the whole were identified only by the gold wings and star on the peaked cap.

The N.C.O.s wore collar patches with black piping and black central stripe on which the sergeants attached their triangular rank badges. The Sergeant-Major had an additional 3 mm. stripe of gold braid parallel to the piping. Both tunic and greatcoat patches carried a triangular device designed to mark the angle on which the patch was to be set. The tunic's patches had a 5 mm. black stripe in the centre while the stripe of the greatcoat's patches was twice as wide.

Cadets of special schools wore the usual patches with additional embellishments, as illustrated.

Plate 18. Head-dress and Rank Badges (1943)

Uniforms and badges were modified by new regulations which appeared in 1943. New uniforms were adopted with gold shoulder boards 140–160 mm. in length, 65 mm. wide for marshals and generals and 60 mm. for the other officers, with piping and rank insignia.

This plate illustrates the badges of the generals and marshals, the latter's ranks having been created in February of that year. The collar and cuffs of their grey dress tunic were modified in accordance with the regulations issued on 15 January, which prescribed gold oak leaves on the cap band, collar and cuffs of the Marshal of the Soviet Union and gold laurel leaves on the cap band and collar of the generals, and three gold embroidered double bars on each cuff.

On 4 February 1943 a new rank was created, that of Marshal of Aviation, with a silver star 50 mm. in diameter, the same as that of the Marshal of the Soviet Union, on the shoulder boards but with the winged propeller in place of the emblem of the Soviet Union. Later, in October, the marshal's rank was divided into two classes: that of Supreme Marshal and of Marshal and the size of their shoulder boards' star was reduced to 40 mm. to make room for a silver laurel wreath which was added around the star of the former.

The new marshals were authorised collar and cuffs facings in arm-of-service colour, blue in the case of aviation.

New collar patches were applied to the collar of the greatcoat. The buttons of the marshals and generals depicted the emblem of the Soviet Union while those of all the other ranks had the star with crossed hammer and sickle in its centre.

Plate 19. Head-dress and Rank Badges (1943)

The regulations of 15 January 1943 brought many changes to the officers' uniforms also. New tunics had to be adopted on which the new insignia could be applied: all officers had shoulder boards of gold lace for parade and service uniform or made of plain cloth for use on the field uniform. The latter type had blue piping and longitudinal dark red stripes, while the gold shoulder boards had piping and stripes in arm-of-service colour. Senior officers, then still known as commanders, had two stripes and silver stars 20 mm. in diameter while the lieutenants' shoulder boards had one stripe only, and stars 13 mm. in diameter.

The parade dress tunic had collar patches and double bars on the cuffs. The former were blue patches with two or one embroidered stripes according to class of rank which was also shown by the double bars on the cuffs: senior commanders, i.e. senior officers, wore two on each cuff while commanders, i.e. junior officers, had only one.

Aviation personnel had embroidered collar stripes of gold with a narrow silver zig-zag design while Engineering/Technical Staff wore silver stripes with gold zig-zag.

Plate 20. Head-dress and Rank Badges (1943)

The same regulations also dealt with the uniforms and badges of the other ranks: shoulder boards with stripes replaced the collar patches with red triangles and new patches were devised for the collar of the parade/walking-out tunic. The latter were blue, with an additional stripe of gold lace 6 mm. wide, for N.C.O.s, the rank class then known as junior commanders. Engineering/Technical Staff had silver stripes.

Blue shoulder boards with black piping were used on the parade/walking-out tunic: they had additional gold stripes according to rank, metal arm-of-service badge, number and initial of the formation or unit.

The shoulder boards of the field uniform were khaki, edged with blue piping; dark red stripes identified rank.

Cadets had a stripe of gold lace around the edges of their shoulder boards and as they graduated in the same way as the N.C.O.s, they could wear additional stripes as did the latter. Narrower shoulder boards with narrow lace were worn by the cadets of the Aviation Specialists' School. Numbers and Cyrillic letters were worn below the winged propeller as further means of identification.

The 1943 regulations made the blue uniforms obsolete as the Soviet Military Aviation was technically a branch of the Army; aviators wore khaki uniforms with their own arm-of-service colour and badges.

The Naval Aviation existed also as an integral part of the Navy, and its personnel wore naval uniforms but their insignia differed from that of the personnel of the Line. They had army rank titles, wore only shoulder boards and army cuff ornaments instead of naval stripes. The officers of the Aviation Engineering had silver shoulder boards.

Denmark

Plate 20. Miscellanea

Danish military aviation begins in 1911 when the Army Air Service and Navy Air Service were formed, although only one locally built aircraft was available. Two years later four French aircraft were acquired and as a result two Danish officers were sent for training in France.

Denmark remained neutral during World War I and as aircraft were unobtainable from other countries a few seaplanes were built locally; other aircraft were built under licence after the war.

The air services were redesignated Army Flying Corps and Naval Flying Corps in 1922 and four years later a Danish Fokker CV flew from Copenhagen to Tokyo, returning via Siberia and Russia. A reorganisation took place in 1932, planes were bought and built in an effort to reach the planned strength of five Army Flying Corps squadrons, two of fighters and three for reconnaissance, and two naval squadrons.

The German invasion of 1940 cut short this programme: on 9 April German troops crossed the frontiers and aircraft attacked Vaerloese Air Station, north of Copenhagen, destroying a large number of aircraft on the field.

A number of Danish aviators escaped to Britain and to Sweden. Subsequently many served in the R.A.F. and in the Norwegian Air Force raised in Britain, and a Danish dive-bomber squadron was formed in Sweden.

The old flying corps were part of the Army or Navy and their personnel wore the uniforms and badges of the parent service. Only the Pilots were distinguished by the wearing of breast wings.

Danes in Britain wore R.A.F. uniforms with their own nationality titles, embroidered in light blue on grey-blue for officers and light blue on dark blue, or black, for airmen. Twenty-six Danish flyers were killed in action.

France

Flying experiments with balloons and aircraft began in France many years before the official institution of the Military Aviation, in 1910. A Naval branch, called Aviation Service, was formed in the same year.

Great progress was made in a short time and by the outbreak of World War 1 the Military Aviation had twenty-five squadrons, four of which were stationed in the colonies. France was by then the leading nation in the field of aeronautics, a standard achieved by the cooperation of extremely skilled, enthusiastic engineers and aviators of world-wide reputation.

Further, during World War 1, French machines, pilots and specialists were sent all over the world to improve or even to build up from scratch the aviation of various nations. Innumerable problems had to be dealt with to keep up the production of aircraft. Firstly, there was a constant lack of manpower as both the armed forces and industry progressively needed more and more men. New, improved aircraft had to be conceived and built continuously to keep up with the adversaries' technical advance.

The Naval Aviation Service also made its own valiant effort during World War 1 and towards the end of it attempts were made to operate aeroplanes directly from ships, a phase culminating with the launching of the first French aircraft carrier in 1925.

In the years between the wars, French air power declined due to low expenditure programmes and other problems common to many other nations at that time. However, the Military Aviation and the Aviation Service of the Navy were renamed the Army of the Air and Maritime Aviation, respectively, and a programme of reorganisation and modernisation began in the middle 1930s.

By 1935, the metropolitan territories of France were divided into four Air Regions each under the command of a General of Air Division; the 5th Air Region supervised the air force in Algeria. Each region, with the exception of the latter, was formed of two brigades, each in turn composed of demi-brigades, which, commanded by a Colonel, consisted in peacetime of one base and one or two escadres. There were escadres of fighters, of day and night bombers and of reconnaissance aircraft, each divided into two or three groups. These groups, in turn, were formed of two or three escadrilles.

The personnel of the Air Battalions and some independent companies were in charge of administrative tasks.

The Maritime Aviation operated from shore bases along the coastline, which was divided into Maritime Districts as, although another two aircraft carriers went into production they were not finished in time to become operational.

The uniforms of the Army of the Air in use at the beginning of World War 2 were adopted in the years 1934–35. The officers were entitled to wear an evening dress, a full dress and a walking-out uniform, service and field uniform.

French aviators wore dark blue uniforms, the shade of which was known as 'Bleu Louise', although white and khaki uniforms were worn in hot climates.

The evening dress followed the conventional fashion of that time and was worn with peaked cap and cape; it was blue in France and white in the colonies, although a white spencer could be worn in France during summer. Minor variation of detail transformed it into the evening dress for grand, i.e. official and small, i.e. private ceremonies.

The main components of the other uniforms, (the peaked cap, the jacket and the trousers) were basically the same, all made of blue cloth. The blue, white and khaki jackets were single-breasted with open collar and four pockets of the inset or patch type, depending on the type of uniform. Long trousers were usually worn although breeches could be used with the field uniform. The Sam Browne belt, shoes and leather flying jackets were made of black leather, while flying overalls were usually brown.

The warrant officers had uniforms similar to those of the officers with the exception of the evening dress; the sergeants had a walking out uniform, the same as that of the officers and a service dress similar to that of the rank and file. The rank and file wore a blue uniform composed of a peaked cap, jacket with closed, folded collar and trousers, which was used for parades and when walking out; they wore a dark grey uniform when on ordinary duties, composed of a beret, jacket and trousers with puttees.

All personnel of the Maritime Aviation wore naval uniforms and badges and were distinguished by some special aviation badges, which will be mentioned further on in this text.

Plate 21. Army of the Air—Cap Badges

The peaked cap was the common head-dress of French aviators of any rank and was worn with almost every uniform. It was Louise blue with black cap band and black visor and during summer it could be worn with a white cover.

Basically, there were two peaked caps for officers, one for dress uniform and the other for service use. Both displayed insignia of rank and of branch of service. All officers, including the generals, wore gold embroidered wings at the front above the cap band: the wings were the emblem of aviation and above these the generals wore their individual stars of rank, while the other officers wore branch insignia which were usually the formation numbers on their own in the case of metropolitan formations, or above a crescent if the formation was a North African one. A gold anchor was the emblem of the colonial aviation and a star that worn by staff officers. The same badge was worn on dress and service caps. The mechanic and specialist officers had cap badges embroidered on violet velvet and the administrative officers on brown velvet. They also wore coloured collar patches and coloured backing under their rank stripes. These badges, but made of metal, were worn on the tropical helmet.

Gold cords, in lieu of the chin strap, were worn by all officers and warrant officers on the dress cap and by all, with the exception of generals, on the service cap. The service peaked cap of the latter had a conventional chin strap with small gold oak leaves embroidered along its centre. The officers' dress cap carried gold stripes of rank around the cap band, while on the service cap these stripes were embroidered on a padded cloth background, oval in shape, which was fixed on the cap band at the front.

The dress cap band of the generals was ornamented with silver soutache, and two or one rows of gold embroidered oak leaves, depending on rank.

The non-commissioned officer, i.e. from Chief Sergeant to Chief-Corporal, wore a gold chin strap 12 mm. in width and at the top of the cap band a 2 mm. soutache in the same colour, gold or orange, of the chevrons. The blue peaked cap of the rank and file had a blue cap band with orange stripes at the top and bottom. The sergeants wore cap badges as did the officers, while the Chief-Corporal and the rank and file wore the wings on the top and the formation number below, on the cap band, in gold for the former and in orange for the others.

The officers also wore a blue beret with winged star in gold embroidery and small rank insignia. The other ranks had a dark grey beret with rank insignia and metal badges, in gilded brass for N.C.O.s and bronze for the rank and file. A 4-bladed propeller on a wreath was the common emblem, but mechanics wore a winged 2-bladed propeller and other specialists wore different badges.

Qualification Wings

Flying personnel wore wings above the right breast pocket of the jacket; in France these were called speciality insignia and existed in embroidered and metal versions for blue uniforms and linen uniforms respectively. On the evening dress, the wings were replaced by an eagle embroidered in gold.

Aviation personnel had a 5-pointed star between the wings while aerodrome personnel had a cog-wheel instead; formation numbers and badges the same as those on the cap badge were placed in between the wings.

Plate 22. Rank Badges

The officers' rank insignia were worn on the forearms of the blue jacket and greatcoat and on the shoulder straps of the evening dress and summer linen uniforms. As we have already seen, the generals wore their stars on the cap badge as well as on the sleeves.

All other officers wore gold lace stripes, except the Lieutenant-Colonel who had three gold and two silver stripes alternated. Circular stripes were worn above the cuffs of the full dress and walking-out uniform while only short stripes, 35 mm. in length, were used on the other uniforms, stitched on a backing patch, usually blue but in the case of mechanic/specialist or administrative officers violet or brown, respectively.

The evening dress shoulder straps were made of gold lace and bore the rank stripes at the outer ends and the eagle in flight in Louise blue. The Lieutenant-Colonel had three Louise blue and two lighter blue stripes.

The full dress blue jacket had gold shoulder cords while the ordinary jackets had only narrow gold embroidered tabs across the shoulders, near the seam.

Warrant officers and sergeants had shoulder tabs as well, which were a short length of their chevron's lace on blue background. The former wore stripes on the sleeves similar to the officers: the Chief Warrant Officer had a gold strip with a narrow red central line, the Warrant Officer had a silver stripe with red line instead.

All the non-commissioned officers wore 12 mm. chevrons above the cuffs of the blue jacket and stripes of reduced size on the field jacket and on the beret.

The Chief-Sergeant wore three gold chevrons or stripes, the regular, career Sergeant had two chevrons while the Sergeant not in the N.C.O.s' cadre, i.e. conscripted, wore only one gold chevron. The Chief-Corporal and the Corporal wore two orange woollen chevrons, the former with a gold oblique stripe on the left upper sleeve. The Private 1st Class wore only one woollen chevron. Non-flying personnel of aerodrome units wore chevrons instead of short stripes on the field uniform.

Plate 23. Collar Patches

The flying officers did not use collar patches while non-flying officers wore collar patches instead of the qualification wings of the former. The mechanics and specialists wore violet patches and the administrators wore brown velvet patches with their formation number in gold in the centre.

These patches were sewn on the corners of the lapels of the collar and therefore have been illustrated in different shapes. The ground officers' patches were smaller as they carried the formation number only, while the other ranks' patches had piping, numbers and often badges as well and were necessarily larger. In addition, the rank and file wore a tunic with closed, folded collar, which was wider than the lapel of the N.C.O.s.

All the other ranks of the flying and ground cadre wore collar patches made of Louise blue felt, with coloured piping consisting of stripes of Russia braid, numbers and badges, that identified the branch of service and unit of the wearer. Flying personnel wore also metal qualification badges on the breast.

The branch colours of the piping were as follows:

Colours	**Branch of Service**
Green	Fighter Interceptors
Yellow	Mixed Formations (escadre)
Scarlet	Bombers
Sky blue	Intelligence, Reconnaissance and Observation
Violet	Aerodrome Personnel
Ash grey	Air Battalions and Companies
White	Metereology
Orange	Balloon Battalions

Personnel of units grouped into a corps wore three stripes of piping instead of two.

The numbers and badges on N.C.O.s' collar patches were embroidered in gold, while the rank and file had orange formation numbers and badges. Some specialisations were identified by means of badges shown on the collar patches: a winged 5-pointed star was worn by qualified pilots and observers; a winged wheel was the badge of qualified aerostate personnel, observers of captive balloons, pilots and mechanics of airships. A winged grenade was worn by air gunners, wireless operators and flight engineers and a cog-wheel by ground specialists.

Personnel of North African formations wore a crescent and those of the colonial aviation had an anchor, without formation number.

Personnel in possession of a certificate of aptitude to be engaged as aircraft mechanics wore a half cog-wheel above a thin chevron on the left upper sleeve, in gold or orange depending on rank. Stevedores wore an interlaced stripe of braid.

Plate 24. Qualification Badges—Army of the Air

These badges were made of metal and were worn on the right breast of the tunic by other ranks with flying qualifications.

The badges, which included a 5-pointed star, were intended for aircraft personnel while those with the steering wheel were worn by airship and balloon personnel. The winged 2-bladed propeller was worn by aircrews, i.e. flight engineer, bomb aimer, wireless operator, air gunner, etc., serving with aircraft and airships alike. Cadet pilots wore all-silver badges.

Maritime Aviation

The Maritime Aviation was a branch of the French Navy and therefore naval uniforms and basic badges were worn by all ranks.

A special arm badge distinguished the aviators: it was worn on the left sleeve and depicted, regardless of rank, a gold embroidered winged anchor with a star in the centre. Some pilots, but not officers, eligible for the special title of Superior Pilot or Chief of section had a golden 5-pointed star and a wing on each side of the collar.

Metal badges were worn on the right breast, regardless of rank, by qualified personnel. They were rather similar to those of the Army of the Air, although a cable substituted the wreath and an anchor was appropriately added on the background. Wings, as usual, stood for aviation, the 5-pointed star represented aircraft flying qualifications while the steering wheel identified airship or balloon qualifications.

Free French Air Force

After the German invasion of France many French aviators joined the R.A.F., but the majority of them were eventually drawn into French units. The status of the Free French in Britain was somehow different from that of other exiles as they could exert more pressure on the British Government because they already had fighting formations in Africa and the Middle East.

Although the Free French Armed Forces depended on the Allies for equipment, they never entirely adopted foreign uniforms and kept to their own badges.

The Cross of Lorraine, the French emblem dating back to the time of the Crusades, became the symbol of the Free French in 1940, and some new badges were made showing this cross. It appeared on the new air force officers' cap badge and in the centre of the new helmet badge. A breast badge of the Free French Air Force was also introduced and two different variations were used: one made in London had the French tricolour starting with the red at the top while the colours of a badge made in Syria started with the blue, on the left.

The Free French Naval Force was also organised with British and American help and, with it, a small Naval Aviation unit which took part in the landing in Sicily and later in the South of France. These aviators wore qualification badges, made in London, which were the same as the previous ones except for an additional Cross of Lorraine.

The first formation of the Free French Air Force raised in Britain was the No. 2 Fighter Group 'Île-de-France' or No. 340 (French) Squadron, R.A.F., formed at the end of 1941 by personnel of the ex-Army of the Air and Maritime Aviation.

The No. 1 Fighter Group was raised at Rayak, in Syria, in September 1941; this was the 'Alsace' unit formed by the Strasbourg and Mulhouse escadrilles, i.e. flights. Later this group was transferred to Britain where it was number No. 341 Squadron.

It should be noted that at this time the French used to name their air groups after French Regions and the two flights of the group after towns of that region. Previously the air formations were identified by numbers only.

Another group which eventually, in 1943, became No. 342 (French) Squadron, R.A.F., a bomber formation, originating from units in the French African colonies, fought in Abyssinia and North Africa where it was known as the Free French Squadron. Later it was named Lorraine Group, formed by the Metz and Nancy Flights.

Another bomber formation that fought in North Africa was the Bretagne Group, with the Rennes and Nantes Flights. It originated from units in the Tchad and, after the North African campaign the Bretagne Group was based in Sardinia and later in France.

Breast pocket badges were worn by the personnel of groups and of some escadrilles and specimens of these have been illustrated. These badges were made of metal and enamel and depicted the coat of arms of the French regions and towns the formations were named after. Often several variations of the same badge can be encountered as they were made at different times, by different manufacturers, in different countries.

Plate 25. Free French Air Force

The Military Air Lines were organised in 1941 as a necessary means of communication and way of supplying the Free French units dotted around all over the world. Its badge symbolised this deployment exactly.

The No. 3 Fighter Group Normandy was formed in Syria in 1942 and initially was formed by three flights, Le Hâvre, Rouen and Cherbourg.

Later, for a period, a fourth unit named Caen was part of the group. The Normandy was sent to the Soviet Union in November 1942 where it remained until the end of the war. During this time it was awarded the battle honour Niémen and therefore it became known as the Normandy-Niémen Group. Nationality shoulder titles were worn on the blue walking-out uniform: the French version was worn on the left and the Russian version on the right upper sleeve. A shoulder title 'Normandy', written in cyrillic characters, was used as well. Various enamel badges were adopted each showing the common motif of the two leopards of Normandy.

Another two groups, the Artois and the Picardie, were formed in Africa and in the Middle East for coastal defence duties. Later the Nos. 329 and 345 (French) Squadrons, R.A.F., were based in Britain and eventually were transferred to the Continent where they took part in the final stages of the war.

By 1944, the Free French were back at home where they were able to reorganise their forces and to strengthen them with new manpower. The Free French Air Force was renamed once again the Army of the Air and some badges were modified appropriately as the new recruits were not, obviously, Free French.

French, American and British uniforms were used, depending on the source of supply. The former was worn as a walking-out uniform and on formal military occasions when available, but the other two types of uniform were more common at that time.

Rank badges were also worn in different positions and a new rank, that of Sergeant-Major, was introduced also. Long stripes and chevrons were still worn on the forearms of the Louise blue French uniforms or short ones, 5 cm. in length, on a blue background, were worn on the forearms of the khaki American jacket, or on the shoulder straps of the American blouse. Rank insignia were on the shoulder straps of the British uniform and all summer shirts.

The Cross of Lorraine was eliminated from the officers' cap badges which were embroidered on branch of service colour as in the following list:

Colours	**Branch of Service**
Black	Flying Cadre
Violet (velvet)	Mechanics' Cadre
Brown (velvet)	Administrative Cadre
Bordeaux red (velvet)	Medical Personnel
Blue	Air Police

The Army of the Air was formed by the following corps, the personnel of which wore one or the other colour of the above list:

Officers	Other Ranks
Flying Cadre	
Air Officers Corps	Flying Personnel Corps
Sedentary Cadre	
Air Mechanic Officer Corps	Mechanical Personnel Corps
Corps of the Officers of Air Administrative Services	General Service Personnel Corps
Air Commissariat Officers Corps	
Air Police Officers Corps	Air Police Personnel Corps
Military Air Engineers Officers Corps	

These were followed by the officers and other ranks of the Air Medical Service, Chaplains, Musicians and female personnel.

In order to further define the individual's duties, the pre-war qualification badges were reinstated, with the exception of the airship qualifications that had become obsolete. Also breast wings, embroidered on Louise blue backing, were reintroduced officially and others, for Equipment and Aircraft Mechanics, were worn on the sleeve.

Belgium

Plate 26. Officers' Cap and Qualification Badges
The Belgian Military Aviation was created in 1910 to test and fly balloons and aircraft. At that time the Aviators' Company was in charge of aircraft, becoming the Aviation Militaire in 1915. It expanded considerably during World War 1, in line with the air forces of the Entente and later, in the early 1930s, the Belgians adopted the training methods of the R.A.F. as by then many British machines were in use.

By 1940 the Military Aviation's primary role was that of army support although aviation and anti-aircraft were technically part of the Territorial Air Defence.

Flying personnel wore grey-blue uniforms while ground personnel wore khaki uniforms, the same as the army's. The latter wore distinctive collar patches, sky blue with scarlet piping. The grey-blue uniform was similar to that of the R.A.F., with long trousers or breeches and riding boots. All officers had a black cap band with the Aviation's badge at the front, sided in the case of generals by a vertical gold bar on each side. The senior officers had gold piping at the top of the cap band. All wore the tricoloured Belgian cockade just above, in the centre, at the front of the peaked cap.

A similar but larger winged badge was worn on the left sleeve and later during the war on the left breast above the ribbons. This badge, embroidered in gold for officers and in silver for other ranks on dark blue or black background, depicted the crowned Royal Cypher of the reigning monarch, sided by wings. Flying personnel other than pilots wore the same cypher but with one wing only. Aerostate officers who were qualified balloon observers wore a gold embroidered balloon on the sleeve of the jacket.

The non-commissioned and other ranks of the ground personnel wore a special badge, a propeller on a disc, on the left side of the forage cap and on both shoulder straps, in the latter's case above the regimental number (1, 2 or 3). A similar badge with additional initials 'EP' standing for École de Pilotage, i.e. Pilots' School, existed.

The rank titles and corresponding badges were the same as those of the Army; as the officers and warrant officers of the flying cadre wore no collar patches their stars and bars were embroidered directly on the collar. The 3-star badge was often worn with the single star above as well as below the two stars.

As a result of the German Blitzkrieg in 1940 the majority of Belgian aircraft were destroyed on the ground and eventually many aviators joined the R.A.F. and were grouped to fight in Nos. 349 and 350 (Belgian) Squadrons, R.A.F., both fighter units, which eventually combined a score of 161 victories. During this period they wore British uniforms, R.A.F. rank insignia and were distinguished by nationality titles only.

Plate 27. Formations' Badges

Initially these badges were painted on the aircraft but later metal and enamel versions were adopted for wearing on the left pocket of the jacket. The three aviation regiments of 1940 were divided into groups which in turn were divided into escadrilles, squadrons. The abbreviated numbers that identify the badges start with the squadron number and end with the regimental number. The Roman numbers identify the group.

The 1st Aviation Regiment had the role of Army Corps observation, the 2nd was a fighter regiment while the 3rd Regiment's role was reconnaissance and bombing in support of the ground armies.

The Pilots' School badge depicted a penguin because of the hesitant behaviour of this non-flying bird—an association with the school's young cadets.

Yugoslavia

Plate 27. Cap and Qualification Badges

The Royal Yugoslav Air Force traced its origins to the Military Aviation of the Kingdom of Serbia. On 24 April 1912 six Serbian officers were sent to France to train as pilots and the nucleus of an air force was formed during the same year with its first headquarters near the town of Nish. During the ensuing Serbo-Bulgarian War, on 8 March 1913, the pilot Miodrag Tomich dropped four ordinary cannon grenades on a bridge on the River Bojana; this action is recorded as the first bombing mission ever made.

After World War I Yugoslavia became an independent nation and Serbs, Croats and men from other ethnic groups joined the armed forces. Some had served already as aviators in the Austro-Hungarian Air Force during the war and therefore were recruited in the newly formed Military Aviation, which was initially a branch of the Army. Designers and technicians, many of whom had had practical experience abroad set up an aeronautic industry that as well as producing aircraft on licence, built and tested its own.

The German-Italian attack on 6 April 1941 caught the Air Force with an array of different aircraft and the disproportion of the forces in the field left no doubt of the final outcome.

At that time only the officers and sergeants wore grey-blue air force uniforms while the other ranks still wore the field grey uniforms of the Royal Yugoslav Army.

The officers had a special badge embroidered in gold and silver on the peaked cap; the generals had two rows of gold laurel leaves on the visor and the senior officers one row only. A similar but smaller badge was worn by officers and was attached at the front of the forage cap. The N.C.O.s, corporals and privates wore the oval cockade of army pattern.

Pilots and observers wore special metal badges above the right breast pocket of the jacket.

Plate 28. Rank Badges

The officers wore rank badges on the sleeves and shoulder boards similar to those of army officers, but on sky blue backing. The generals had gold twisted shoulder cords; the officers wore gold shoulder boards which in the case of junior officers had a central blue stripe. Silver pips identified rank in the usual manner.

On the sleeves the generals wore gold 6-pointed stars above an eagle in flight while the other officers had stripes below the eagle. The eagle was worn by flying personnel only. The four junior officers wore gold stripes 5 mm. in width while the senior officers had the same stripes but worn above a larger one, 15 mm. in width. Stripes and eagles were placed above a black background.

The Sergeant-Majors wore shoulder boards similar in shape to those of the officers but made of sky blue cloth; all had four gold pips, and three, two or one stripe, depending on the class of rank. The 1st Sergeant, Sergeant and Corporal wore shoulder straps, the former with blue piping.

Many Yugoslav airmen managed to escape to the Middle East and to Britain where eventually they manned two R.A.F. squadrons. At that time the Yugoslav government was reorganised in Britain and eventually new regulations were published in order to standardise the Yugoslav badges, by then worn on British uniforms.

The air force officers obtained new shoulder straps, made of grey-blue cloth on which the junior officers wore from one to four gold 6-pointed stars, the senior officers wore the stars, from one to three, below a crown and the generals had crossed swords between the crown and the stars. The Field-Marshal (Voivoda) wore the crowned White Eagle of Yugoslavia on the shoulder straps and a gold crown above the cuffs. Stripes, as before, were worn on the cuffs, but the generals wore from one to three large gold stripes below a 6-pointed gold crown. The officers of the Anti-Aircraft wore grey-blue uniforms with the usual pre-war air force cap badge on the peaked cap but also wore black facing on the collar, gold stripes on the shoulder straps and crossed cannons ensigned by the eagle in flight above the cuffs. Rows of gold leaves were embroidered on the peaked cap's visor as before the war.

Later, when Communist orientated Yugoslav forces were organised under the name of National Liberation Army, new rank badges were adopted for wearing on the sleeves. They consisted of a combination of 6-pointed stars and stripes, made of silver for N.C.O.s and gold for officers.

The United States of America

Plate 29. Historical Background

As early as the American Civil War balloons were used for tactical observation by the Union and Confederate armies and in 1892 a Balloon Section was attached to the telegraph branch of the Signal Corps. Balloons fitted with telegraph apparatus were used again during the Spanish-American War and in 1902 a balloon unit was formed at Fort Myer, Va.

On 1 August 1907 an Aeronautical Division was created in the Office of the Chief Signal Officer 'to study the flying machine and the possibility of adapting it to military purposes'. The new organisation was composed of one officer and two enlisted men.

The first successful flight took place at Fort Myer in 1909 in a Wright brothers' biplane piloted by Orville Wright, with Lieutenant (later Major General) Frank P. Lahm as a passenger; it lasted 1 hour, 20 minutes and 40 seconds. Lieutenants Lahm and F. E. Humphreys subsequently became the first qualified pilots.

On 18 July 1914 an Act of Congress created the Aviation Section of the Signal Corps and in the following September the 1st Aero Squadron was formed at San Diego, California, with a strength of sixteen officers and seventy-seven enlisted men.

The first badge of Military Aviator, which was instituted on 27 May 1913 depicts the American Eagle clutching the crossed flags of the Signal Corps, the whole suspended from a tablet; it is a reminder of the early association of the aviation with the corps. The badge was made of 14 kt. gold and was intended as an award compared to the marksmanship and gunnery badges, not as a qualification badge.

The aviators wore, of course, the collar badges of the Signal Corps, but by 1917 manufacturers added small wings to the original badges of the Signal Corps. These unofficial officers' badges became very popular with the result that many variations appeared on the market. In most cases the wings were made of silver and were attached to the centre of the bronze badges (A, B); small and larger variations of this pattern were in existence. Another variation of the aviators' collar badge shows the wings in bronze at the top of the badge, which has no torch (C). Officialdom had eventually to recognise the need for a special badge for aviators and on 27 April, 1918 a new collar badge was authorised showing the usual signal device with a winged hemisphere superimposed on its centre (D). A variation of this badge shows a smaller hemisphere and somewhat straighter wings. The enlisted men wore the same device but on a bronze disc.

When World War 1 broke out in 1914 the American military aviation had five aircraft while by the end of that war it had received no less than 2,500: these figures reflect the expansion of the Aviation Section, which in May 1918 was renamed the Air Service Branch of the Signal Corps. Later in 1926 it became the Air Corps and in 1941 Air Forces. Aviation broke its links with the Signal Corps in August 1915 and was under the General Staff until March 1942, when it became autonomous (U.S. Army Air Forces) as was the case with the Army Ground Forces and Army Service Forces.

The United States of America entered the first conflict on 6 April 1917 and sent an Army Expeditionary Force to Europe. Earlier many American volunteers had joined the Allied cause, for instance Major Raoul Lufbery, French by birth, who at the age of six in 1891 emigrated with his parents to the United States. Later he became the mechanic of a famous French stunt flyer. During the war he joined the Escadrille Lafayette, composed of American volunteers and in April 1918 became the commander of the U.S. 94th Aero Squadron. He was killed on 19 May 1918. Captain Eddie Rickenbacker, the American ace with 25 victories, became the squadron commander the following September. The 94th Aero Squadron's badge, painted on its planes, depicted a top hat, painted with stars and stripes, which flies through a ring.

The first qualification badges were authorised on 15 August 1917. The American Shield sided by wings was granted to the Military Aviator (1) and the shield with one wing only to the Junior Military Aviator (9). However, this ruling was changed on 27 October when a star was added to the wings of the Military Aviator (8) and the original badge, without star, was given to the Junior and Reserve Military Aviator.

The original badges were embroidered in silver wire, with gold initials 'US' on the shield, on dark blue cloth background. As each badge was individually hand embroidered many varied in style and shape (1, 3); by the summer of 1918 manufacturers had introduced metal badges, in three separate pieces mounted on a dark blue felt background (2, 4). Subsequently the three parts were attached together (6, 10) and finally the blue background was discarded and a pin was fixed at the back of the badge (7).

In the meantime, as has been already mentioned, in October 1917 the Junior and Reserve Military Aviator changed from the half-wing to the full-wing without star, and the half-wing became the badge of the Observer until 29 December 1918, when the letter 'O' with one wing was adopted as his badge (11) and the previous one was definitively discarded. Eventually metal 'O' badges appeared (12), then badges with the rounded 'O' were introduced (13) until finally, on 21 December 1918 a solid metal pattern was adopted (14).

On 29 December 1917 wings embroidered in white silk were authorised for Military Aeronaut and Junior and Reserve Military Aeronaut, with and without star respectively. Such badges were also made in silver embroidery and later in metal also.

The Enlisted Pilot's wing and the large square sleeve patch illustrated at the bottom of this plate were also made of white silk and, as usual, variations exist of both: the latter is a 1918 specimen; early badges had numbers at the top to identify the squadron; enlisted airmen wore only the propeller below the number, mechanics wore a ring around the propeller and balloon mechanics had a balloon in place of the propeller.

An official badge depicting a bomb sided by wings was worn during the first war by Bombing Military Aviators.

A process of standardisation started after the end of World War 1: on 25 January 1919 the definitive qualification wings made of oxidised silver were introduced for Military Aviator and Junior and Reserve Military Aviator (see Plate 36, Pilot); for Military Aeronaut and Junior and Reserve Military Aeronaut (see Plate 36, Balloon Pilot); for Observer Qualified as Pilot and a half-wing was awarded for Observer.

On 12 November 1920 more changes took place: the winged American Shield became the badge of the Airplane Pilot and another badge, an airship superimposed on wings was created for the Airship Pilot, the Observer's half-wing was abolished and a round winged 'O' with blank centre was adopted for the Airplane Observer and the winged balloon (see Plate 36, Balloon Pilot) became the badge of the Balloon Observer. More changes took place later, as will be explained in connection with the wings illustrated on plate 36.

In 1926 embroidered badges were re-introduced for wearing on the wool service coat.

Plate 30. Cap Badges and Other Insignia

Various cap and collar devices worn by American aviators during World War 2 are illustrated in this plate. Although the U.S. Army Air Forces was the organisation that eventually became the modern U.S.A.F., the U.S. Navy, Marine Corps and Coast Guard had their own aviations also. The personnel of these organisations wore the normal cap badges of their parent services, i.e. the U.S. Army, Navy, etc. but in the context of this book these technically become air force insignia.

All ranks of the U.S.A.A.F. wore appropriate cap badges as their counterparts of the U.S. Army. Aviation cadets wore the winged propeller instead. Towards the end of World War 1 the N.C.O.s of the Air Service used a bronze unofficial cap badge which depicted the winged propeller surrounded by a wreath similar to that of Warrant/Flight Officer illustrated.

The winged propeller was the branch of service badge of aviation and as such was worn by all ranks on the collar. The first development of this badge has been seen already in the historical background of this chapter. The actual winged propeller device was adopted on 17 July 1918, on its own for officers and on a disc for enlisted men. These badges were made of blackened bronze although the propeller was usually silvered. Many slightly different variations exist because these badges were manufactured in America, Britain and France. A smaller badge was worn by officers on the shirt's collar.

After that war gilded badges were introduced for officers and brass ones for enlisted men; the officers' propeller was still made of silver. Olive-drab plastic badges were used by enlisted men during World War 2. The branch of service badge was worn together with the 'U.S.' national insignia and during the last war the officers wore these badges in pairs on the service jacket, the 'U.S.' on the collar, the winged propeller on the lapels. The latter and the rank badge were worn on the shirt's collar. Enlisted men wore the 'U.S.' disc on the right and the branch badge on a disc on the left side of the collar. The arm-of-service colours of the Air Corps were ultramarine and orange.

The aviation personnel of the U.S. Navy, Marine Corps and Coast Guard wore the cap badges of their parent services although naval aviation officers and aviation cadets of the U.S.M.C. had different badges attached on the left side of the garrison cap. The Naval Aviator and Naval Aviation Observer wore a miniature gold metal aviation insignia on the left side of the green winter working garrison cap until the spring of 1943 when they were obliged to follow naval regulations, and replaced it with a small replica of the usual cap device. Aviation Cadets of the U.S.M.C. wore a bronze winged propeller on the garrison cap and shoulder straps during the same period and a gold and silver device with the dress uniform. Eventually they became part of the U.S. Navy until commissioned and the above-mentioned badges were abolished.

All the officers and the Chief Warrant Officer of the U.S. Navy Aviation wore the normal naval cap badge made of metal or embroidery, the eagle of which faced left until May 1941, and right as its correct placing should be, from then on. The American Shield, below the eagle reappears on the cap badges of the U.S. Coast Guard of which it is the major insignia, and on its own is worn on the shoulder boards, above the cuff stripes. It is worn in white or blue version according to uniform, on the cuffs of enlisted men.

All ranks of the U.S. Marine Corps wore the Marine Corps emblem on the head-dress and collar. The larger badges were worn on the peaked cap in gilt and silver for officers' dress uniform, brass for enlisted men's dress uniform and bronze for all ranks' service uniform. The rope of the officers' badges was free of the anchor while in the case of enlisted men the rope and the anchor were in one piece. There was no rope in the smaller badges worn on the garrison cap, and on the collar. In the latter case badges were worn in pairs.

Plate 31. Officers' and Warrant Officers' Rank Insignia

The aviation personnel used the rank insignia of their parent service, i.e. the U.S.A.A.F. had those of the U.S. Army, the U.S. Navy Aviation those of the U.S. Navy and so on, in accordance with dress regulations.

The metal badges illustrated in the centre of this plate were common to all. These rank badges were primarily used by the U.S. Army and U.S. Marine Corps while the main rank insignia of the U.S. Navy and Coast Guard were worn in the form of stripes on the sleeves and on the shoulder boards. Their rank titles also differed from those of the first two services.

The rank of Flight Officer was instituted in the summer of 1942 as an opportunity for cadets who did not qualify for a commission in the U.S.A.A.F. The rank was equivalent to that of Warrant Officer, Junior Grade.

The marines' warrant titles and badges differed from those of their army counterparts: initially, during World War 2, the Chief (commissioned) Warrant Officer wore a gold and blue bar and had the title of Chief Marine Gunner, Chief Pay Clerk, Chief Quartermaster Clerk or Chief Quartermaster Clerk (A. and I.). The latter initials were added to distinguish this title of the Adjutant and Inspector's Department from that of the Quartermaster's Department. The Warrant Officers (not 'chief') wore their departmental insignia in lieu of a rank badge.

Later the titles were changed to Commissioned Warrant Officer and Warrant Officer, and different rank badges were adopted also.

The main uniforms of the U.S.M.C. were the blue dress, the green service uniform and light khaki shirt and trousers for summer wear; on the latter smaller rank badges were used, about five-eighths of the normal size for shoulder straps. Gold/Silver or bronze departmental badges were used according to uniform.

There were blue, green, grey, white and light khaki naval uniforms, with rank insignia on the sleeves, on the shoulder boards or on the collar accordingly. Both the sleeve stripes and shoulder boards were worn on the overcoat only, otherwise only one or the other type of insignia was used.

The flag officers wore stars and the fouled anchor on their shoulder boards or stripes on the cuffs, contrary to the other officers who had stripes only, on both.

There were stripes of 2 in. in width for the flag officers, ½ in. and ¼ in.

for the other officers in gold and black variations, the latter for naval grey working uniform and the green working uniform of aviation officers.

The Chief (commissioned) Warrant Officer and the Warrant Officer were identified by broken stripes of different width as illustrated: gold and blue or black and grey, according to uniform. (See also Plate 34.) Small metal rank badges were worn by the officers on the light khaki summer shirt.

Plate 32. Army Aviation N.C.O.s' Rank Badges

The Non-commissioned Officers of the U.S.A.A.F. wore army pattern chevrons, consisting of actual chevrons and arcs, on both upper sleeves. Technicians' grades were introduced in January 1942 and they wore the initial 'T' below their chevrons. Some unauthorised versions were manufactured and worn by Line N.C.O.s before and during World War 2, with a small winged propeller in place of the Technicians' 'T'.

All chevrons were 80 mm. in width and were machine embroidered in khaki (O.D.) silk or woven in sandy grey silk (for summer shirt) on a dark blue background.

Oblique single khaki (O.D.) stripes on the left forearm identified each three years of honourable Federal service. Small yellow inverted chevrons on the left forearm each identified six months of World War 1 overseas service while yellow stripes were granted for World War 2 service. One yellow inverted chevron was worn on the right forearm for each wound received in combat before the introduction of the Purple Heart.

Plate 32/33. Army Aviation Cadets' Rank Badges

The Flying Cadets originally wore slate blue uniforms with black chevrons similar to those worn by the cadets of the U.S. Military Academy. Later they were re-designated Aviation Cadets and were given khaki uniforms with khaki chevrons on dark blue background. The chevrons worn on coats are 80 mm. in width while those worn on overcoats are 190 mm. wide and, as shown on Plate 33, they differed considerably from the former.

Plate 34. Petty Officers' Ratings—U.S. Navy and Coast Guard

Besides the more obvious similarity in dress between the U.S. Navy and the Coast Guard, the latter in peace-time depends from the Secretary of Treasury while in war-time it comes under the control of the Secretary of the Navy.

Both had the same rating badges, which consisted of the eagle, the arc and chevrons and speciality mark that in the case of ordinary petty officers were blue on white background for white uniform, while for the blue uniform the eagle and speciality mark were white and the chevrons red, all on blue background.

The Chief Petty Officer wore officers' type uniforms, the arc above the chevrons and, on the blue coat, had the option of wearing silver or white eagle and speciality mark. The Chief Petty Officer of outstanding record, i.e. with not less than 12 years of service, three consecutive good conduct awards, or equivalent qualifications, wore gold chevrons with silver embroidered eagle and speciality mark.

Personnel of the Seaman Branch (Boatswain's Mate, Quartermaster, Fire Controlman, etc.) wore the rating badge on the right upper sleeve while the personnel of Aviation and other branches had the badge on the left sleeve. Initially the eagle always faced left as did the eagle of the officers' cap badge but during World War 2 some new regulations ordered that the eagle of the rating badges should always face towards the front of the wearer, regardless if placed on one or the other sleeve.

Only speciality marks were shown on rating badges, never distinguishing marks (Plate 37) which were proficiency badges.

Enlistment stripes of the same colour as the chevrons were worn one for every four years of service on the forearm, below the rating badge. White cuff markings were worn on blue and white dress jumpers and identify Fireman or Seaman class. They were 120 mm. long, made of a narrow white ribbon, 5 mm. in width, sewn on both cuffs.

The aviation cadets did not wear the line star on the cuffs and shoulder boards until 1943 and the winged propeller worn by U.S.M.C. cadets was abolished at about the same time.

The personnel of all branches of the U.S. Coast Guard wore their distinctive shield above the stripes both on the cuffs and shoulder boards or in the case of ratings and seamen on the right forearm. The shield was about 25 mm. in height and was embroidered in gold for officers and warrant officers; in silver for chief petty officers and white or blue for enlisted men, according to uniform. The shield was black on green winter aviation uniform.

Plate 35. N.C.O.s Rank Badges—U.S. Marine Corps

The U.S. marines used three types of chevrons: gold on red background for the dress blue uniform, green on red for green winter uniform and on light khaki for summer shirt.

The N.C.O.s of the Line have chevrons joined by arcs while those of the Staff had theirs joined by ties, i.e. straight bars. The marine advanced into the Line or Staff careers by becoming a Private 1st Class (6th Grade) but only when he reached the 3rd Grade rank did the arc or the tie identify the branch to which he belonged. Aviation N.C.O.s wore ties under their chevrons as aviation was one of the seven specialisations of Staff.

The lozenge within the First Sergeant badge was adopted during World War 2 while the badge with three chevrons and three arcs was worn by the Sergeant Major and Master Gunnery Sergeant (1st Grade Line). The Master Technical, Paymaster and Quartermaster Sergeant wore the 1st Grade Staff badge. Two arcs were used by the Gunnery Sergeant and two ties by the Technical and Supply Sergeants and Drum Major, one arc by the Platoon Sergeant and one tie by the Staff Sergeant. The remaining ranks were those of Sergeant, Corporal and P.F.C.

Before September 1942 the rank badges were worn on both upper sleeves but new orders were issued on the 9th of that month, which prescribed the use of chevrons only on the left sleeve.

Enlistment, or service stripes, were worn one for each four years of service.

Civil Air Patrol

The Civil Air Patrol was a civilian volunteer organisation which became an auxiliary body of the U.S.A.A.F. by Executive Order of 29 April 1943.

The C.A.P.'s activities included patrolling the coastal water in an anti-submarine defence role, air courier and transport services, etc., as well as its pre-military training programme for youths between 15 and 18 years of age.

The organisation derived from the Office of Civilian Defence from which it adopted the basic blue disc and white triangle badge. A C.A.P. aviation wing existed in every State and its members wore military uniforms and ranks with the badges illustrated on this plate. All except cadets had red shoulder straps as further means of identification.

The officers wore army type rank badges and the N.C.O.s had chevrons but on red background. Qualification badges were worn by those entitled above the left breast pocket and one short gold stripe was worn on the left forearm for each period of six months service. Small blue, red and white triangles of cloth were worn above the left pocket in lieu of merit awards.

The Duck Club badge was worn by personnel who had made a forced landing at sea. Some shoulder sleeve insignia of C.A.P. have been illustrated in Plate 39.

Plate 36. Qualification Badges

The wings worn during World War 2 were made of sterling silver, as embroidered badges were finally abolished by the regulations issued on 16

March 1938. The appearance of the actual wings was standardised to a design by Herbert Adams, adopted in 1919.

On 10 November 1941, three classes of Pilot's wings were authorised thus distinguishing pilots with longer service and a higher average of flying hours.

The winged balloon was reinstated to the Balloon Pilot and a new badge was authorised for Balloon Observer, with an additional 'O' on the balloon. Balloon pilots with 10 years of service, who had piloted military airships or motorised balloons for 100 hours were granted a new badge with star and the qualification of Senior Balloon Pilot. A new badge was adopted on the same date for the Technical Observer.

More badges appeared in the following year: that of Navigator has an armillary in its centre and that of Bombardier depicts an aerial bomb on a target. The qualified Service, Liaison and Glider Pilot were granted new badges with the initials 'S', 'L' and 'G' in the central shield. The Liaison Pilot wings were worn regardless of rank by men assigned to organic air observation of the field artillery. Later the granting of this badge to enlisted men was discontinued.

The Aircrew Member wings were worn by men regularly assigned aircraft personnel who had shown proficiency in performing their duties. The centrepiece of the Aerial Gunner wings shows appropriately a flying bullet; was adopted on 29 April 1943 for qualified gunners if regular members of a combat aircrew.

The Flight Surgeon wings originally adopted were gold-plated and were changed to silver in September 1944. Smaller gold wings, 5 cm. in span, were adopted in 1943 for the Flight Nurse and subsequently were changed to silver.

The Flying Instructor badge was authorised in metal, in January 1919 and re-issued in March 1943 to be worn, now embroidered in gold colour, on the right sleeve at 10 cm. from the end.

The wings of the Women's Air Force Service Pilots (WASPS) illustrated belonged to the 319th Training Detachment and the 'W1' identified first class graduation. WASPS were engaged in non-combat flying missions and training duties under U.S.A.A.F. control. Earlier during the war women were engaged in ferrying aircraft under the organisation known as Women's Auxiliary Ferrying Squadron (WAFS), but later women were deployed in other fields of duty as well. Another pattern of women's badge depicts a plain diamond between the wings.

Wings were adopted by the U.S. Navy only at the beginning of 1919 although official approval to the project was stated in Change 12 to Uniform Regulations, issued on September 1917. A gold metal badge with a pin at the back was finally chosen as the Naval Aviator's device. The badge did not change a great deal although the original pattern was solid, and later versions varied in style more than in design.

A Naval Observer's badge appeared in 1922: it consisted of a gold embroidered fouled anchor with the rope forming the shape of an 'O' in the centre, sided by one single wing. Five years later a similar badge, but made of gold metal and with the American Shield in place of the 'O' was authorised to identify the Balloon Observer. The aircraft Observer's badge used during World War 2 depicted an anchor within an 'O' in silver finish, sided by gold metal wings. The badges of Flight Surgeon and Combat Aircrewman were adopted during the course of the war.

The U.S. Marine Corps and Coast Guard used the same qualification badges as the U.S. Navy. Some smaller wings, approximately half size of the normal ones were worn by officers on the evening dress and the white mess jacket.

Plate 37. Naval Speciality and Distinguishing Marks

The speciality marks identified the specialisation or trade of a seaman and the badge eventually became part of his rating insignia, and was worn above the chevrons. The distinguishing marks were only proficiency badges and were worn usually on the sleeve if regulations did not prescribe otherwise. Dark blue badges were worn on white uniform and vice versa.

Air Carrier Contract Personnel—A.T.C., U.S.A.A.F.

The personnel of this organisation wore army uniforms with special bronze badges and one, two or three stripes on the sleeves of the service jacket, or short bars on the shoulder straps of the trench coat.

The National Memorial at Kitty Hawk, N.C., in remembrance of the first flight performed there by the Wright brothers in 1903 is the badge of the Air Transport Command (Plate 39) and is in the shape of a small round disc worn on the shoulder straps and by non-supervisory ground personnel on the service and garrison cap as well. A large version of the same badge was worn as a shoulder patch on the left sleeve with a number in a circle embroidered below.

Personnel sent on overseas duties wore the non-combatant patch on the right sleeve: it depicts the letters 'US' in black on a white equilateral triangle (side 9 cm.) on a black square background.

Plate 38. U.S. Army Air Forces Shoulder Sleeve Insignia

From 1921 to 1942 the fuselage marking of American aircraft depicted a white 5-pointed star with a round red centre set on a round blue background; the red disc was abolished in August 1942 and two white bars, one on each side of the emblem, were added in June 1943. Until the following September the emblem was outlined in orange, and later in blue. The star with red centre remained however the main emblem in all war-time insignia, except for the earlier patch of the U.S.A.A.F. authorised on 20 July 1937 for wear by personnel of GHQ Air Force. The badge symbolised a spinning propeller and was executed in the colours of the Air Corps, ultramarine blue and orange.

The U.S. Army Air Forces was created on 20 June 1941, following a decision to convert the existing Air Districts (Northeast, Northwest, Southeast and Southwest) into Air Forces, numbered from 1st to 4th respectively. The first two districts became Air Forces on 9 April, the SE Air District on 24 May and the SW Air District became the 4th Air Force on 31 March 1941.

A new shoulder patch was approved for personnel of the U.S.A.A.F. on 21 March 1942, and later for the continental Air Forces as well.

On 5 February 1942 the Far East Air Force was redesignated the 5th Air Force, the Caribbean Air Force the 6th, the Hawaiian Air Force the 7th and the Alaskan Air Force became the 11th Air Force. The reorganisation of the former, heavily engaged against the Japanese, was completed by the following September in Australia; its patch was authorised on 25 March 1943. The 6th Air Force was formed to protect the Canal Zone and the Caribbean area while the 7th and the 11th became engaged in active operations in the Pacific. The latter with headquarters in the Aleutians covered the northern Pacific theatre of operations. The badge of the 7th was approved on 21 May and that of the 11th on 13th August 1943.

The 8th Air Force was activated at Savannah, GA., on 28 January 1942 and by the following May some of its units were transferred to Britain from where, on 27 January 1943, it carried out its first bombing raid over Germany. The 8th's patch was officially approved on 20 May.

In the meantime, on 12 February 1942, the 10th Air Force was activated at Patterson Field, Ohio, and became operational in the India-Burma area, where soon afterwards it began ferrying supplies to China, across the Himalayas. This task developed into the setting up of the China Air Task Force which on 10 March 1943 gave birth to the 14th Air Force at Kunming, China. The latter's badge, approved on 6 August 1943, depicted a flying tiger in memory of the American Volunteer Group (The Flying Tigers) in China which had been taken over by the 23rd Fighter Group, 10th Air Force, in July 1942.

The U.S. Army Middle East Air Force was formed in the summer of 1942 in Egypt and on 12 November it was redesignated the 9th Air

Force, a tactical formation which was transferred to Britain in 1944. Its badge was approved on 16 September 1943. The 12th Air Force was raised at Bolling Field, D.C. in August 1942; during the following November it supported the invasion of North Africa and as a tactical formation it took part in the invasion of Italy. Another formation, the 15th Air Force, was activated on 1 November 1943 in the Mediterranean area for strategic operations. The 13th Air Force was raised already in January in the Southwest Pacific area.

After the raising of the 15th Air Force and the transfer of the 9th to Britain, the U.S.A.A.F. and R.A.F. achieved a perfect balance of strategic and tactical power and were able to co-ordinate strategic raids on central Europe from the west with the 8th and from the south with the 15th Air Force, thus the U.S. Strategic Air Force was formed as a supervisory headquarters. The 20th Air Force, with headquarters in Washington, D.C., directed the strategic air offensive against Japan. The Mediterranean Allied Air Force was a combined U.S. and British organisation.

Specialists' Cuff Insignia

The five triangular badges illustrated were authorised on 25 January 1943 to be worn by specialists of the U.S.A.A.F. on the right forearm 10 cm. above the end of the sleeve of all uniforms, except fatigue, on which the badge is worn on the left breast pocket.

The last two badges with the winged propeller were worn on the sleeve by cadets.

Plate 39. U.S. Marine Corps, Civil Air Patrol, etc. Shoulder Sleeve and Cuff Insignia

Cloth badges were very seldom granted to the marines and in March 1943 only, the commandant of the Corps authorised the wearing of a limited number of shoulder sleeve insignia by personnel of the first three marine divisions and of some other formations. The shield-shaped Aircraft Wing patches were adopted at that time but were later replaced by the kite-shaped patches with a winged Corps' emblem in the centre.

Personnel of the 1st Amphibious Corps were granted large blue patches with white stars symbolising the Southern Cross and different badges in the centre, on a red background. The Aviation Engineer's badge depicted a winged castle.

The Air Transport Command was formed from the conversion of the Ferrying Command on 20 June 1942 and was composed of a Ferrying and an Air Transportation Division. The original Air Transport Command was redesignated Troop Carrier Command. There were two patches of

Air Transport Command, one on light blue and the other on yellow background, the latter for ferrying formations.

The High School Victory Corps, as well as the C.A.P., ran programmes of training for youths and 'Air' was only one of the H.S.V.C.'s specialisations. Others were entitled Land, Sea, Community and Production, each represented by a badge. The basic badge of this organisation was a thick red 'V', for Victory, on which round specialisation badges were superimposed at the top.

During World War 2, the personnel of the Civil Air Patrol (see Plate 35) wore three main shoulder patches and rectangular patches on the left sleeve above the cuff. The latter identified personnel of Active Duty units or one's speciality. The Active Duty Units performed various tasks: the Forest Patrol, for instance, was basically concerned with fire prevention while the Coastal Patrol was engaged in coastal security duties and the Southern Liaison Patrol kept watch on the Rio Grande.

Most of these badges were worn until 1947 when a reorganisation took place; later blue patches with white emblem were worn on the forearm.

Italy

Plate 40. Historical Background

Captain of Artillery Carlo Piazza made the first operational flight in Libya on 25 October 1911, during the Italo-Turkish War. He flew on another thirty operations during that campaign and a colleague of his recorded a total of fifty-four operational flights.

A new era had begun, with its accompanying new weapons of destruction. On 24 May 1915, when Italy entered World War 1, only a few dozen planes were available whereas at the end of that war (4 November 1918) 1,758 Italian aircraft dominated the sky, and 1,784 aviators had fallen in the meantime. Among the many that should be remembered, I mention only Major Francesco Baracca, who scored thirty-four victories until finally, in June 1918, he was shot down by rifle fire.

The aviators wore the grey-green field uniforms of the Army and the badges of the branch of service to which they belonged originally, usually the Artillery and Engineers. Aircraft personnel had a small propeller added to the centre of their cap badges, while personnel manning airships and balloons wore their own special devices on the cap badges. Qualification badges were worn on both sleeves, halfway between the shoulder and the elbow: the qualified pilots had an eagle surmounted by the Royal Crown and observers wore a winged sceptre and an 'O'. When the observer took on the additional task of a machine-gunner the 'O' was replaced by an 'M'. The balloon observers had a small dragon instead of the sceptre.

Cloth titles were also worn at the outer ends of the shoulder straps by the men of some units. Antonio Segni, a future president of the Republic of Italy, served as an aviator of the artillery and wore a self-explanatory shoulder title.

The 87th Squadron was named 'La Serenissima' after the city of Venice and bore the large, handsome Lion of St. Mark painted on its planes. Supreme Headquarters employed this squadron on many missions of long range reconnaissance, including the flight on Vienna, inspired by the poet Gabriele D'Annunzio, himself an observer. This expedition was mounted on 9 August 1918 with the purpose of dropping leaflets on the Austrian capital and was accomplished by seven planes which flew a distance of over 1,000 kilometres in one hour and fifty minutes.

After the flight, the squadron's command was taken over by Captain Natale Palli, one of its participants, whose brother, a pilot in another squadron, was shot down on 3 November, a day before the end of the war.

Later, on 20 March 1919, Natale's plane crashed on the Alps while attempting the Padua-Paris raid.

The first shoulder title of the squadron read 'SQ' above 'SERENISSIMA' in white on black, but in 1919 its late commander's name was added on to the shoulder titles.

A new pilot's badge was adopted at about that time: it depicted a winged propeller. For Mechanics the propeller was replaced with an aircraft engine. Army uniforms were still in use but with an additional cobalt blue collar; qualification wings were moved on to the breast in the early 1920s.

In 1923 the 'Regia Aeronautica' became a service in its own right and new blue-grey uniforms were adopted for its personnel. Peaked caps and forage caps appeared when army personnel were to continue to wear the old soft kepi for another ten years. The new officers' jacket had an open collar, patch pockets with flaps and a cloth belt. Trousers or breeches were worn in different circumstances. Warrant officers, sergeants, and officer cadets had similar uniforms, with single-breasted jackets and gilded buttons while the rank and file wore tunics with high closed collar until 1934 when new jackets were introduced. Both patterns were single-breasted, initially with wooden buttons covered by a fly patch and later, from 1932, with five exposed brass buttons. Both had four patch pockets with flaps and shoulder straps. Grey-blue breeches and puttees and black boots completed the uniform.

The officers' grey-blue uniform is still more or less the same in the 1970s. White and khaki uniforms were used during summer and in hot climates, and greatcoats of usual style were used in winter. The rank and file's clothes were greyer, lighter in colour than those of the higher ranks, because they were made of a rather coarse melton cloth, while the latter had their peaked caps, jackets and trousers of gaberdine cloth of a considerably darker shade.

The newly formed Royal Aviation instituted qualification badges made of metal, to be worn by all entitled on the left breast, above the ribbons. The pilots wore a crowned eagle in flight, while the other aviators had wings, with a central device. The Commander, 2nd Officer and Crew of airships, still popular at that time, had crowned crossed anchors as the wings' central device, with red enamel in the crown of the former, a plain gilt badge for the 2nd Officer and the same but with silver crown for the Crew Officer. Balloon observers and aircraft observers of the army had their own wings which appear in the 1931 dress regulations, although probably they were adopted much earlier.

The same regulations show that the engineers in charge of balloons still had their own cap badge in 1931, with a small balloon embroidered in the centre of the engineers' badge. A larger balloon, embroidered on grey-green, was worn on the upper left sleeve.

Army personnel who, as aviation pilots, had taken part in the Italo-Turkish War 1911–12, or World War 1, or subsequent operations in Albania from November 1918 to August 1920, or any military operation in Libya or Somaliland from October 1912 to 1923, could apply to the War Ministry for the concession of a special silver badge: a winged sword with crown superimposed. Civil airline pilots who had flown over 1,000,000 km. were granted a special badge in the late 1930s.

From 1923 to the early 1930s all flying ranks had double wings and the Royal Crown on the shoulder straps, while specialists wore brass winged badges instead.

Plate 41. Cap Insignia

The spread eagle surrounded by a laurel wreath and surmounted by the Royal Crown was adopted in 1923 as the badge of the Air Force. Large gold embroidered badges were worn on the peaked cap by officers, warrant officers, and sergeants, and smaller gold badges on the forage cap; the airmen usually wore the forage cap and therefore had only small cap badges, machine- or hand-embroidered in yellow thread.

The generals, from the rank of General of Air Squad and above, and Inspector General of the Aviation Engineers, wore cap badges with purple-red backing under the crown, while all the other officers, except Chaplains, had blue backing. The Chaplains had violet backing under the cap badge's crown, and a red cross on the chest of the eagle.

The laurel branches of the flying personnel's badges were plainly joined at the bottom while specialists had an additional roundel, with a badge or device, in its centre. These latter cap badges were abolished during the course of World War 2. Another distinguishing feature was the coloured piping and backing to rank insignia.

By the 1930s the Royal Aviation was a very complex but functional organisation, and besides the Flying Role, the following specialisations existed also:

Specialisation		**Badge**
Services Role		Savoy Knot
Aviation Engineers	Engineers' Role	Roman helmet
	Technical Assistants' Role	Roman helmet above crossed hammer and axe
Commissariat Corps	Commissariat Role	Oak wreath
	Administrative Role	Laurel wreath
Medical Corps		Aesculapius staff

Specialists' Role—divided into categories, each with its appropriate badge. (See Plate 45.)

Some officers of Flying Role had also badges with the roundel with the number of the Stormo, or higher formation they belonged to.

The whole of Italy was divided into Territorial Air Zones (4) plus the air forces in the colonies: nine planes formed a Squadriglia, two or more Squadriglie formed a Gruppo, two or more Gruppi a Stormo. During the war two Stormi were joined under the Air Brigade and Air Divisions and Air Squads were organised as well, as part of an Air Army. The general organisation of the Royal Aviation however was modified from time to time to take losses and dispersion of strength into consideration, as expeditionary forces were deployed on all battle fronts, including the North of France, for the Battle of Britain (Italian Air Corps).

Officers' and warrant officers' rank was shown by stripes on the cap band, with an additional gold embroidered greca in the case of the generals. These insignia corresponded with the rank badges worn on the sleeves of the service uniform, except for warrant officers who all wore only one single stripe on the cap band, regardless of class of rank. Contrary to the stripes on the sleeves, which were individually stitched on a cloth backing, the cap band stripes were woven in one piece with 2 mm. grey-blue or coloured space between one stripe and the other. They were slightly narrower than those of the sleeves. The sergeants wore a plain cap band, without any rank distinction on the head-dress.

Plate 42. Officers' Rank Badges—Service Uniform

The conventional shoulder straps of the officers' service uniform were replaced in the early 1930s by small shoulder tabs, which identified the class of rank and the branch of service of the wearer. The tabs for the jacket were 55 × 28 mm. while those for the greatcoat were 65 × 30 mm. in size, and were applied on the shoulder at 4 cm. from the sleeve's joint.

The generals had gold lace tabs, the senior officer had two gold embroidered edges of 1.5 mm. each on uniform's cloth, and the junior officer had one gold edge only. Branch of service badges were embroidered in the centre of the shoulder tabs. Black tabs with violet piping, gold edgings denoting class of rank and a gold embroidered square cross were worn by Chaplains. They also had a large red cross stitched above the left breast pocket of the service uniform.

All the officers of the Flying Role, including the generals, wore a sceptre on their shoulder tabs while the others wore their appropriate badges, already described, and coloured piping around the tabs, as below:

Specialisation		Colour
Services' Role		Emerald green
Aviation Engineers	Engineers' Role	Crimson
	Technical Assistants	Black
Commissariat Corps	Commissariat Role	Red
	Administrative Role	Black
Medical Corps		Methilene blue
Specialists' Role		Black

The same colours, in the form of a cloth backing, were shown under the rank stripes, on the sleeves. Initially, in the 1920s, the officers of the services had sleeves' stripes without the square loop. Branch of service colours were abolished in the first years of the war.

As the officers' service jacket had no cuffs the rank stripes were applied at 90 mm. from the lowest edge of the sleeve and were 80 mm. long; smaller, gold embroidered stripes were worn on the sleeves of the ceremonial uniform. The generals' greca, stripes and loop were always embroidered in gold wire, on felt matching the uniform's colour or coloured background for the commanders of branches other than the Flying Role. They were known by different rank titles, such as Major- or Lieutenant-General, or Inspector General in the case of the Aviation Engineers, due to the fact that they did not command an operational formation.

The General of Air Squad had two stripes as did the general of Division but with a crown below the greca and usually commanded a Territorial Air Zone, in army terms corresponding to an Army Corps. The General of Air Squad 'in Command' of an Air Army wore the crown and an additional sceptre below the greca.

The crown superimposed on crossed swords identified a Promotion for War Merit and, as in the Army and the Navy, were as follows:

In silver on uniform's colour backing for holders of junior officers' rank at the moment of promotion.

In gold on uniform's colour backing for holders of senior officers' rank at the moment of promotion.

In gold on red backing for holders of general's rank at the moment of promotion.

The officers' rank stripes were made of gold lace: the narrow ones were 12 mm. in width and the larger base stripes for senior officers were 22 m. in width.

The same type of badges, but without the loop, were worn by all officers including generals, on the front, left side, of the forage cap.

Plate 43. Officers' Shoulder Boards for Full Dress Uniform
The full dress uniform for officers of the Royal Aviation was abolished during the first years of the war: it consisted of the usual grey-blue peaked cap, jacket and trousers, but with a white shirt and black tie, with additional shoulder boards, dress waist belt, blue sash, sword, metal decorations and medals. Aiguillettes were worn by eligible personnel. The wearing of the blue sash, sword, decorations and medals only was permitted after 1941. The sword, steel helmet and a brown leather Sam Browne belt with pistol and breeches were worn on parades and similar military events.

The generals' shoulder boards were made of grey-blue gaberdine material or coloured velvet or cloth depending on the branch of service, covered with gold lace at the top, with grey silk at the bottom, leaving the arm-of-service colour to protrude all around the sides. The other officers' shoulder boards, except those of the Chaplains, were made of uniform's cloth, like the generals', with, in some cases, an additional underlay of coloured velvet or cloth forming a piping all around. Chaplains had black shoulder boards with violet, often purple, piping.

Twisted gold cords were added on those of the generals and senior officers, while junior officers had twisted gold cords with blue specks woven into it. The Royal Crown, the branch of service badge and the rank badge were embroidered in the centre, between the cords.

The shoulder boards of the Evening Dress Uniforms for winter were similar but their background was black instead of grey-blue.

The warrant officers' and sergeants' full dress uniforms were similar to that of the officers, although the latter were not entitled to wear a sword, and their waist belt was made of brown leather; neither wore the blue sash. Their full dress shoulder boards were also different from the officers' ones: they were made of blue woven silk, with gold stripes for warrant officers, without rank identification for sergeants. All bore the branch of service badge, in gold embroidery or metal at the outer ends. It should be noted that warrant officers and sergeants of Flying Role had a wing as their badge, and not the sceptre of the officers.

The airmen's full dress uniform had brass buttons and the Air Force badge, in brass, on the shoulder straps.

Officers' Shoulder Boards for Colonial and Other Uniforms
Another type of shoulder boards was worn on khaki and white colonial uniforms and on the summer ceremonial uniform: they were similar to the previous pattern but, in the case of generals and senior officers, with a gold embroidered stripe instead of the gold twisted cords. Junior officers had plain boards, with the Royal Crown, branch and rank insignia.

The background to the cap badge and shoulder boards of the colonial uniforms was grey-blue; no rank insignia were worn on the sleeves.

Warrant Officers' and N.C.O.s' Rank Badges

The service uniform of warrant officers and sergeants had grey-blue shoulder tabs 55 × 28 mm. in size, with branch of service badge and, those of the warrant officers, with rank stripes at the front. The sergeants wore gold chevrons and the airmen red chevrons on both upper sleeves.

Plate 44. Qualification Badges

During the last war qualification badges were worn by pilots, observers and air crew members. The first two were modified in the early 1930s to suit the fashion of that time. The realistic design of the previous badges were replaced by a stylish, contemporary conception and the fascio was added at the bottom.

Earlier, some pilots were granted special badges with coloured letters enamelled in the centre. Pilots who had flown high velocity planes had a red 'V' on the badge, others had an 'S' for flying at high altitude and those who crossed the Atlantic were granted the badge with a blue 'A'. These daring exploits of early aviation were recaptured in the new 'Fascist' badges. Some unofficial wings existed as well: the pilots of the 'Green Mice' Squadron had three small green enamelled mice on their wings.

However, although pilots took to wearing their new badge with the fascio, the vast majority of observers wore the new pattern badge without the fascio.

All air crew members, regardless of specialisation wore a circular badge, 18 mm. in diameter, ensigned by the Royal Crown. At least three versions of this badge existed: one was made all in white metal, another had red enamel inside the crown and another had also blue enamel in its centre. Later the crew members bought privately and wore on uniform some unofficial wings which were their arm-of-service badges, illustrated in the next plate, with added wings. Two types of these wings were made, in white metal with realistically drawn wings and in grey metal with streamlined wings.

Aviators were granted metal breast badges for good performance in their deployment: there were three grades of badges, in gold, silver and bronze, although in the case of the former only the central device was gilded. During the war the badges of the first two grades appear to have been made in aluminium, and the central device of those of the first grade were painted yellow.

A special badge for the Parachute Battalion of the Air Force was adopted in 1942, and was worn until the end of the war.

The Parachute Battalion of the Air Force was raised in the spring of 1942 as a special task force to be deployed in the projected assault on Malta; i.e. its companies should have occupied and restored the island's airfields so that they could be used immediately by the Axis air forces. Later this project was abandoned and on the 16 November the Battalion arrived at Bizerta by sea and was subsequently employed as an infantry unit, which was swallowed up in the North African battlefield.

All ranks wore Army-type parachute uniforms, berets, collarless Saharian jacket and baggy trousers, all made in grey-blue cloth. Air Force cap badges and shoulder tabs were worn together with parachutist's collar patches and arm badge. Air Force rank stripes were worn on the cuffs and stars, as with the Army, on the left side of the beret.

A special badge, the pilot's eagle with parachute, was adopted in 1942 as the qualification insignia of the Parachute Battalion of the Air Force. The same badge was re-introduced after 1943 for the newly formed parachute units of the Republican Air Force.

Plate 45. Arm-of-Service (Category) Badges

While the Air Force officers were divided into Corps and Roles the airmen were divided into categories, depending on the specialisation, identified by small round badges on the shoulder straps. Technical Assistants of any rank wore the same badge and others of these badges were also worn by the officers of the Specialists' Role, while in the case of Administrative personnel, the officers' badge was a laurel wreath, the airmens' a capital 'G', which stands for Governo.

All these badges are self-explanatory; for instance the badge of Photographers depicts the camera's shutters, the Armourers had a grenade above crossed rifles, etc. The 'M' in the Fitter's badge stands for Montatore and the additional 'S' stands for Strumentista.

Arm Badges and Miscellanea

Assault Pilots, Bandmasters and Fencing Instructors wore special badges, embroidered in metal wire, on the upper left sleeve halfway between the shoulder and the elbow.

A peculiar wide brimmed straw hat used to be worn by airmen when in fatigue uniform in hot climates, and the tally illustrated was worn on this hat. The only other badges on this uniform were the national five-pointed stars, woven in white on a circular grey-blue background.

Other badges also existed: the Air Force in the Aegean had a beautiful enamelled breast badge 38 × 30 mm. in size, surmounted by the crown, and groups and squadrons had also their own badges. The badge of the 1st

Squadron depicted Disney's Donald Duck, rolling up his sleeves and the badge of the 4th Bomber Squadron depicted Pluto and a bee. The badge of the 1st Interceptors Group, illustrated, shows the Rampant Horse which, during World War I used to be the emblem of Captain Baracca's squadron.

These badges were the small replicas of the formation emblems worn on flying overalls, one of which, of the Red Devils, is illustrated on the cover of this book. After September 1943 this became the badge of the 5th Squadron of the 2nd Interceptors Group and from 1957 to 1959 it became the National Acrobatic Patrol, of the 6th Air Brigade.

The Air Force of the Italian Social Republic

After the Armistice of 8 September 1943 with the Allies, by then well on their way to occupy all the south of Italy, the new Republican Air Force was formed in the north, while the Regia Aeronautica continued its existence in the south. The latter did not change badges and therefore this text will now only deal with the Air Force in the north.

During this period the Aeronautica Repubblicana raised three groups of fighter-interceptors, each with three squadrons, which were numbered from 1st to 9th, and minor units most of which were eventually absorbed in the groups; the Autonomous Group of Torpedo Aircraft, with three squadrons, plus a complementary, HQ Training Squadron. There were also two transport groups, each with three squadrons, and a liaison unit. At this time the anti-aircraft artillery was placed under the command of the Air Force. All the necessary support units, training schools and administrative echelons existed as well making this small Air Force into a fully independent and very effective service.

Towards the end of 1944 Germany retrieved its operational formation from its Southern flank, the defence of which was then left to the Republican Aviation, already mauled by the Allies' air superiority and frustrated by constant lack of fuel.

Although new regulations were published which introduced new uniforms and new badges the vast majority of aviators continued to wear the old uniforms and the old badges, from which the Royal Crown was simply cut off. A new cap badge was machine-woven for the airmen as the crown could not be eliminated from the old badge without defacing it altogether.

A new national insignia replaced the stars on the collar: it was known as the 'gladio' and depicted a Roman sword with 'Italia' inscribed on the hilt, superimposed on a wreath of oak. As with the previous stars, the generals wore gold badges while the other ranks had white metal ones.

Two special badges were worn by personnel of the Torpedo Aircraft Group: the first illustrated on the left was made of metal and was worn on the right breast pocket while the larger badge on the right was embroidered in gold and was worn on flying jackets. In June 1944 ten aircraft of this group attacked the harbour of Gibraltar and later operated in the Adriatic and Aegean seas. In less than one year 223 men of the group, including thirty pilots, lost their lives. Statistics based on the production and losses of aircraft during the course of World War 2 indicate that an Italian pilot had only an average 4 hours of operational flight before being shot down.

China

Plate 46. Cap and Other Badges

Experiments in the field of aviation started before the foundation of the Republic of China in 1911, as in the second year of the reign of Emperor Hsuan Tsuan in the Ching Dynasty the General Staff established an airplane experimental factory at Wu-li-tien, east of Nanyuan.

Later some regional air forces were formed and finally in 1920 Generalissimo Chiang Kai-shek activated the Aviation Bureau at Ta-sha-tou, Canton. This organisation was composed of a headquarters with the Adjutant and General Affairs Divisions, and the 1st and 2nd Airplane Groups.

General unrest prevented the Central Government from asserting its control over the whole of China and other regional air forces remained active at the time. In 1934 an American Mission provided some more aircraft and later, after the Japanese attack of 1937, the Soviet Union also aided the Chinese government. The first confrontation recorded between Chinese and Japanese aircraft took place over the Chien bridge, Hangchou, on 14 August 1937, in which six Japanese planes were downed. During the long struggle that followed the Chinese Air Force lost air supremacy and eventually an American Volunteer Corps, known as the Flying Tigers, was raised in the spring of 1941, with a strength of about ninety Curtiss P-40B fighters.

These planes were made famous by the genial shark's face painted at the front. Initially the A.V.C. defended the Burma road to China, was later moved to China and eventually was absorbed into the 10th U.S. Air Force.

During World War 2 Chinese aviators wore khaki uniforms, the same as those of the Army, but with different badges. The Officers' and N.C.O.s' badge for peaked cap consisted of the national emblem above gold or silver wings respectively, while the other ranks wore the national emblem only, at the front of their soft cap.

Rank insignia were initially worn on the forearms and were embroidered in gold wire, as separate stripes but in 1940 they were moved on to the shoulder straps. Metal bars had appeared by then and eventually new badges were introduced with the bars joined together by two strips of metal.

The winged propeller was worn on both sides of the tunic's collar: several variations of this badge existed during the war.

The Chinese armed forces made use of a great number of fully written identification badges; one of triangular shape has been illustrated. Below the national emblem the wording means 'Aeronautic Committee', the second row of characters means 'AAA School', the third reads 'Corporal (Rank) Chang Te-kung (Name) and the last reads' Issued in 1942'.

Some other badges with Chinese lettering, and a set of collar badges of the General Staff Academy, have been illustrated.

Bulgaria

Plate 47. Cap, Collar and Rank Badges

The Bulgarian armed forces were comprised of an aviation branch during the Balkan War of 1912–13 and subsequently during World War 1. However, in both instances the branch was disbanded after the wars, as foreign machines flown by foreign pilots were used; further, as Bulgaria took the side of the Central Powers, it was forbidden to possess an air force after World War 1.

The Bulgarian Air Force was raised in 1937, once again as a branch of the Army, and although grey-blue uniforms were adopted for the new service they were worn mainly by officers and senior N.C.O.s. The grey-blue and the army khaki uniform had the same pattern, only the colour of the material changed.

The peaked cap had a short leather visor, with cords for officers and senior N.C.O.s and leather chin strap for the other ranks. Tunics with stand-and-fall collar were later replaced by jackets with open collar, although the former was always worn by the lower ranks, to the end of the war. The officers and N.C.O.s had breeches, or occasionally long trousers, while the other ranks had trousers tucked in high boots.

There were embroidered and metal versions of the winged cap badge of the aviators; the generals wore gold badges, the others silver badges, as silver and sky blue were the distinctive colours of the Air Force. Gold, as a rank distinction, was worn by the generals on the shoulder boards and collar patches also.

The tunic's collar patches of generals and officers have been illustrated, the other ranks had plain oblong sky blue or sky blue patches with silver stripes according to rank. Corporals and privates had a button at the rear end of their tunic's patches, but no button on the greatcoat's collar patches. The officers wore oblong patches with button on the collar of the greatcoat.

The officers wore silver shoulder boards on tunics and greatcoats: these had sky blue piping and central stripes, two for the senior officers and one for the junior officers with silver stars for all ranks. The King's monogram or other badges often appeared on shoulder boards and on other ranks' shoulder straps.

Plate 48. N.C.O.s' Rank Badges

Senior N.C.O.s had a stripe of silver lace around the loose sides of the shoulder straps, and narrower stripes to denote rank. The Corporal wore only one narrow stripe.

The rank of Potential Officer, practically a warrant officer's, was instituted during the war as the highest N.C.O.s' rank.

Germany

Historical Background

At the beginning of the century the Germans saw the potential of flight only as a means of aerial reconnaissance and employed airships for this purpose. The first aircraft were constructed in 1910 and soon after the Military Aviation Service and the Naval Air Service became operational, and were equipped with both airships and aircraft.

During World War 1, although the interest of most nations converged on to aircraft, Germany continued developing the airship which had a wider operational range than the former. Aerial freedom was Germany's only counterpart to the sea blockade that surrounded her, and long range bombing raids were the direct result. Airships and large bombers were deployed on these raids and the former became obsolete only after the invention of the incendiary bullet, which the Germans could not match by the invention of a non-combustible gas to fill their airships.

The organised fighter-interceptor warfare developed only after the invention of a synchronised gear which enabled a machine-gun to fire through the propeller. The inventor was A. Fokker, a Dutchman working in Germany. The purpose of aviation, which started as aerial reconnaissance had developed into a new kind of warfare, aimed at obliterating the enemy's machines from the air.

Aviators like Oswald Boelcke, Baron Manfred von Richthofen and many others accumulated scores of victories until eventually most of them were in turn shot down.

The Military Aviation Service was organised by the Corps of Engineers in 1913 and thus engineer uniforms were worn by all ranks, although the officers seconded to the Air Corps during World War 1 continued wearing the uniform of the corps they belonged to originally. On the pre-war uniform all wore a winged propeller badge on the shoulder straps, the other ranks with the unit's number below, but the use of the latter was discontinued early in the war.

The first qualification badges, worn on the breast, were adopted in January 1913 for Army and Navy Pilots and one year later a badge was granted to the Observers. The Aviator Commemorative Badge was adopted at the same time. The Naval Pilots operating on land and Naval Observers received badges in May 1915 and smaller, commemorative badges for Naval Pilots and Observers were granted in October 1916. The Air Gunner badge was adopted in January 1918. Bavarians wore similar badges but with the Bavarian crown instead of the Imperial crown at the top. There were Bavarian badges for Pilots', Observers, Air Gunners' and Aviators' Commemorative Badges. The bronze badges for Airship Crews were adopted in August 1920.

After World War 1, the clauses of the Treaty of Versailles prevented the raising of a conventional air force and flying was an activity confined to the sports clubs formed by a few enthusiasts. In March 1933 these clubs were amalgamated in a single institution, the Deutscher Luftsport-Verband which had branches specialising in aeroplane, glider and balloon flying. The members of this association wore uniform and insignia, which disguised also the officers of the air corps, the organisation of which was secretly set up at about the same time.

The German Air-sport Association was embodied in the National Socialist Flying Corps in March 1935: the latter was a politically orientated para-military organisation that technically prepared its members for active service in the Luftwaffe. The corps' rank insignia and titles were modelled on those of the S.S.

The Luftwaffe, the German Air Force, came into existence on 1 March 1935 and expanded rapidly in the following years: the anti-aircraft was part of it thus unifying the air defence branch. Parachutists, tank and other ground formations were also part of the Air Force: some came into existence almost incidentally, others were raised for a specific purpose.

The General Göring Regiment developed from the Landespolizeigruppe General Göring which in the early 1930s was a para-military bodyguard unit. A number of volunteers were drawn from the regiment in November 1935, received parachute training at Stendal in 1936 and eventually constituted the parachute unit of the General Göring Regiment. In 1938 it became the 1st Battalion of the 1st Parachute Regiment (FJR 1), which later became part of the 7th Air Division of the Air Force (Fliegerdivision 7), which in turn was re-numbered the 1st in early spring 1943. Ten airborne divisions were subsequently formed during the war. 1st Parachute Army, which included two Parachute Assault Gun Brigades, was organised by Generaloberst Student in France in March 1944.

The remaining units of the original Hermann Göring Regiment developed into the Hermann Göring Tank Division another formation of the Air Force, which later during the war was expanded into a tank corps (Fallschirm Panzer Korps).

The Luftflotte was the main tactical organisation of the air force divided into Fliegerkorps and Fliegerdivisionen. The Geschwader was usually commanded by a colonel or lieutenant-colonel and, depending on its assignment could be classified in:

Kampfgeschwader	Bombers
Jagdgeschwader	Single-engine fighters
Zerstorergeschwader	Twin-engine fighters
Nachtjagdgeschwader	Night fighters
Schlachtgeschwader	Air-to-ground attack aircraft
Lehrgeschwader	Tactical, training and experimental aircraft

The Geschwader usually consisted of three Gruppen, each with an average of twenty-seven aircraft and the Gruppe was in turn divided into three Staffeln.

Plate 49. Cap Insignia

All ranks of the German Air Force wore peaked caps, forage caps and from 1943, also another head-dress, with cloth peak, modelled after the Army's mountain cap.

The peaked cap was of conventional German type, with chin strap cords in gold for generals and silver for other officers, and leather chin strap for other ranks.

After Hermann Göring's promotion to Reichsmarschall, in 1940, he started wearing a new pigeon-grey uniform with gold embroidered laurel wreath around the cockade and, often, an additional row of laurel leaves all around the cap band. His new rank badges are shown in the next plate. The generals' cap badges, cords and piping were all made of gold, while the other officers' were made of matt silver. The cockade, oak wreath and side wings, all in one piece were embroidered on black cloth backing, matching the colour of the cap band, while the eagle was embroidered on cloth of uniform's colour.

The same badges but made in aluminium were fitted on the other ranks' cap. A summer service cap with white removable cover and white metal eagle was also used, together with the old style soft, officers' peaked cap without cords above the visor and a tropical cap, all made of brown khaki cloth including the visor, with woven cap badges.

Smaller badges without oak leaves wreath were worn on the other two head-dresses, in gold, silver and grey for generals, officers and other ranks respectively. The latter also wore a composite badge, with the eagle and cockade machine-embroidered on a one-piece of grey-blue cloth. Alternatively, some badges were embroidered on khaki for use on the tropical uniform.

On steel helmets the national colours were placed on the right side and the eagle on the left.

Breast Insignia

The Luftwaffe emblem, the eagle in flight holding a swastika, was worn above the right breast pocket, with its base stitched above the pocket's flap. Several variations of this badge are in existence, embroidered on grey-blue, white, khaki, or in white metal with brooch pin for the white summer uniform.

The rule of gold badges for generals, silver badges for officers and grey woven badges for other ranks, was applied as usual.

Plate 50. Field-Marshals' and Generals' Rank Insignia

On 19 July 1940 Field-Marshal Göring was appointed to the new rank of Reichsmarschall of Great Germany thus becoming entitled to wear a special pigeon-grey uniform with new badges. This uniform consisted basically of peaked cap, tunic with folded collar and buttons covered under a flap, breeches and riding boots. Interlaced gold cords with gold badge were worn on the shoulders and special patches, with gold embroidery on a silver base, appeared on his collar. The gold eagle embroidered on the right patch was replaced in March 1944 by crossed batons, already present on the other collar patch.

The rank of Generalfeldmarschall, or Field-Marshal, was instituted in February 1938 while that of Colonel-General dates back to 1936. The former had gold cords and silver crossed batons on the shoulders while the latter had two gold and one silver cords interlaced on the shoulder and three silver pips. The collar patches of both were similar, depicting the eagle above a wreath in gold, with additional silver crossed batons for the Field-Marshal.

Bar exceptions, the backing to all marshals' and generals' shoulder cords was white and the backing to the Field-Marshals' and other generals' collar patches was also white. The pips were 18 mm. in size, in silver since 1935. The Major-General of the Medical Corps wore the arm-of-service badge instead of the conventional pip, with white backing and since 1944 with dark blue backing under the rank badges. Other colours were granted in 1944 to identify the generals of some other branches of service.

Administrative officials with the rank of general had white and dark green backing under their shoulder cords and dark green collar patches with gold embroidery. The white colour identified their rank and the dark green the branch of service. Also other colours were used instead of white during different periods, as specified below:

Red	15.4.1935–23.10.1935
Black	23.10.1935–1.4.1937
Red	1.4.1937–16.2.1940
White	16.2.1940–1.5.1944
Red	1.5.1944 to the end of the war

The arm-of-service colour of the Court Martial Generals and Judicial Generals Officials were Bordeaux red and wine red respectively.

All collar patches were edged by three narrow gold cords, twisted into one and those of the last three ranks had a gold oak leaves wreath, with from three to one wings embroidered in the centre. Following the German tradition the last rank of the class had no pip on the shoulders.

Plate 51. Officers' Rank Insignia

The shoulder straps and the collar patches had the dual purpose of identifying the rank and the branch of service of the wearer; rank was shown by pips on the former and wings on the latter while the background colour of both identified branch of service as follows:

White	Generals (see below for H. Göring units)
Crimson	General Staff
Golden yellow	Flying personnel and Parachutists
Golden brown	Signals
Scarlet	A.A. Artillery and Ordnance
Dark blue	Medical Corps
Black	Air Ministry (until 1939)
	Construction Troops (from 1939)
Dark green	Administrative officials
Light green	Air Traffic Control
Pink	Engineers Corps (Plate 54)

Officers of the Reserve had additional light blue inner piping on the shoulder straps and collar patches; officers who had served during World War I and were subsequently re-enlisted wore an additional light grey inner piping on the shoulder straps only. Retired officers were identified by a stripe of silver lace protruding from under their shoulder straps.

On 23.3.36 all personnel of the General Göring Regiment were issued with standard Air Force uniforms but with white arm-of-service colour. The regiment was formed by two rifle battalions, one of which was a parachute-rifle battalion, and by an anti-aircraft battalion. The N.C.O.s and men of the two rifle battalions wore rifle green piping around their white collar patches, while the gunners had red piping instead.

After the redeployment of the regimental parachute battalion the two remaining battalions were brigaded and in June 1942 the Hermann Göring Tank Division came into existence, with its personnel wearing black tank uniforms and tank patches with skull and crossbones, with white piping. The identification of the various divisional branches of service made necessary the adoption of further colours that from 4 January 1943 were applied as piping to the collar patches, as follows:

White	Grenadier Regiment/Guards Regiment
Pink	Tank and Reconnaissance Troops
Red	Artillery and A.A. Artillery Regiments
Golden brown	Signals Battalion
Light blue	Supply Troops/Administrative Troops/Military Police

All had white piping on the shoulder straps.

In April 1943 white collar patches were adopted for all and the coloured piping was moved on to the shoulder straps, with the following additions:

Rifle green	Rifle Regiment
Golden yellow	Flügbereitschaft
	Reconnaissance
Black	Pioneer Battalion

The following June the military policemen changed their piping from light blue to orange.

From the end of 1942 the Air Force started to organise Field Divisions, twenty-two of which eventually came into operation, until they were disbanded or transferred to the Army by the end of the next year. The officers wore rifle green collar patches with metal twisted cords and shoulder straps piping in arm-of-service colours while other ranks had a narrow piping also around their rifle green collar patches. The arm-of-service colours were the same as those described above.

The Corps of Administrative Officials included many branches, depending on specialisation, which was identified by the colour of the inner piping of their shoulder straps. During World War 2 all except Court Martial and Judicial Officials had dark green collar patches, all with 3-pointed pips instead of wings; the Court Martial Officials wore Bordeaux red patches and Judicial Officials wine-red patches and inner piping on the shoulder straps. The usual square metal pips were worn on the shoulder straps.

The officers' collar patches were 40–48 mm. wide, 60 mm. in height with a full oak leaves wreath in silver embroidery for senior officers and six leaves and two acorns for junior officers; all had silver cords piping. Rank was identified by small silver wings, one for each successive rank. The shoulder straps consisted of silver double cords, plain for junior officers and interlaced for senior officers. Yellow metal pips, and sometimes numbers and badges were worn on these shoulder straps.

Plate 52. N.C.O.s' Rank Insignia

The titles of these ranks have been transcribed in the original German version due to difficulty and confusion that could be caused by translating these rank titles into English.

The N.C.O.s wore rank badges on the collar and the senior N.C.O.s also on the shoulder straps. On the collar, rank was shown by wings attached to patches of the same colours as those of the officers. The collar patches illustrated were used on the greatcoat as they have the stripe of lace attached on the patch itself, while on the jacket the silver lace was stitched all around the collar instead. White metal pips were worn on the shoulder straps.

Following tradition the personnel of the Artillery used the title of Wachtmeister instead of Feldwebel in their terminology of rank. An additional rank, that of Hauptfeldwebel was used after March 1938: its badges were the same as those of the Oberfeldwebel, plus a stripe of silver lace on the lower sleeves, above the cuffs.

The junior ranks wore additional chevrons on the upper left sleeve instead of the silver stripe of the senior N.C.O.s: the ranks of Hauptgefreiter, Obergefreiter and Gefreiter were used until May 1944, when the title of Stabsgefreiter replaced that of Hauptgefreiter. The latter was never used in the Anti-Aircraft Artillery and in the General Göring Regiment. The title Flieger means flyer, a private of the Anti-Aircraft Artillery was called Gunner and a parachutist Jäger, i.e. Rifleman.

Plate 53. Rank Badges for Flying Field Uniforms

Special rank badges were worn on the upper sleeves of the flying uniforms and overalls: the background of these badges matched the colour of the material of the uniform on which they were worn and therefore grey-blue, sandy brown and others were used by officers and N.C.O.s.

The Field-Marshal and Colonel-General had oval badges with a yellow embroidered eagle on an oak wreath, the former with additional white crossed batons at the base of the wreath. The rank badge of all the others was shown by a combination of wings and bars, in yellow for generals and white for officers and N.C.O.s. The Stabsfeldwebel wore a pip under four wings. Corporals wore their usual chevrons on the upper sleeves.

The personnel of the Corps of Administrative Officials, who were not combat flyers, wore 3-pointed pips instead of the wings and their patches were of a different shape.

Plate 54. Engineering Corps' Rank Insignia

The engineer officers of this corps wore special rank badges on the collar patches and their arm-of-service colour was pink; these badges were introduced on 20 April 1935 but in May 1940 the propellers on the collar patches were replaced by the usual wings, as worn by the flying officers.

A 4-, 3- and 2-bladed propeller identified the actual rank on the collar patches, while large or small wreaths and the metal of embroidery, gold or silver, identified the class of rank as usual. The engineer officers wore normal shoulder straps with pips but of course on pink underlay.

Propellers instead of wings, combined with bars, were worn on flying uniforms: generals had yellow insignia, while officers wore two or one bar with propellers according to rank.

Plate 55. Musicians' Rank Insignia

The Bandmasters had special rank titles and were identified by distinctive rank badges; the former have been translated into English according to their meaning and the title 'Inspizient' has been translated as Superintendent.

Rank titles and badges were changed a few times from 1935 onwards. Initially the following ranks existed:

Music-Superintendent (Musikinspizient)
Staff Music-Master (Stabsmusikmeister)
Senior Music-Master (Obermusikmeister)
Music-Master (Musikmeister)

and Bandsmen. The rank of Music-Leader (Musikleiter) was instituted then, because there was a shortage of music-masters.

The Music-Superintendent belonged to the category of officials and therefore he had double underlay under the shoulder cords. The inner underlay was red from April to October 1935; it was then changed to black and back to red again in April 1937. The other ranks wore underlay in arm-of-service colour. The Music-Superintendent supervised all matters connected with music at the Air Ministry. The music-masters were classed as 'Portepee Uffz' before 1938.

A general reorganisation took place in 1938 and the top rank was divided into two grades:

Senior Music-Superintendent (Obermusikinspizient)
Music-Superintendent (Musikinspizient)

both classed in between the officers and the N.C.O.s. They were followed by the same ranks as before, but with different rank insignia.

The alternate silver and red cords were adopted at this time in twisted form for the superintendents and straight for the music-masters. The former wore them with black underlay and black collar patches until 30 June 1939, when ordinary arm-of-service colours were adopted instead.

The lyre on the Music-Leader's shoulder straps was added in 1936 and the year after it replaced the usual four wings on the collar patches. Bandsmen could attain any rank up to Stabsfeldwebel or Stabswachtmeister while fifers and drummers could reach ranks up to Hauptgefreiter only.

Bandsmen on duty wore the uniform of their unit with 'swallownest' type epaulettes in arm-of-service colour and additional lace and fringes according to rank and unit.

Plate 56. Cuff Titles

The personnel of some special formations wore an embroidered armlet above the cuff of the right sleeve. The officers' version was embroidered in silver and the other ranks' in grey thread; the officers and N.C.O.s of the Rgt/Div. Gen. Göring, H. Göring and Fallschirm-Jäger Rgts 1–2 had additional edging stripes of silver and grey thread respectively.

The general idea was to name an air formation after a World War 1 ace, a party hero or otherwise to identify a special unit. As all are self explanatory no captions have been added and the illustrations have been arranged in order to take advantage of the space available as much as possible.

The lettering was usually on dark blue, except for the titles of the Parachute Division (Fallschirm-Division) and Parachute Rifle Regiments (Fallschirm-Jäger Rgt 1–2) the backgrounds of which were dark and light green respectively.

One cuff title commemorated the German Condor Legion that participated in the Spanish Civil War and another was worn by those who served in North Africa. Two versions of the Hermann Göring title existed, one in Gothic and the other, a later type in Latin capitals. Göring's regiment was granted the General Göring cuff title which was changed later to the Hermann Göring pattern for brigade, divisional and later, army corps personnel.

Other cuff titles were worn as well, one with the inscription 'Kriegsberichter der Luftwaffe' was worn by officers only, another one with the inscription 'Tannenberg' was used by all ranks of the Aufkl. Gruppe 10. The cuff title 'Führer-hauptquartier' or 'Führerhauptquartier' was made initially with gold and later with silver lettering; it was worn on the left sleeve.

Plate 57. Commemorative Cuff Titles

The two armlets illustrated were worn by ex-members of famous World War 1 formations commanded by Oswald Boelcke and Freiherr Manfred von Richthofen.

Boelcke after shooting down forty enemy aircraft died in an air collision in October 1916 while von Richthofen at that time was a member of the former's squadron 'Jasta II', before assuming his own command in the following February. Later he took command of a group of squadrons and on 21 April 1918 was shot down and fell behind the British lines. He had been credited with eighty victories, of which seventy-nine were over British planes.

Qualification Badges and Awards

The first badge in the centre of this plate was adopted officially in January 1935, for Pilots and Observers of the newly formed Luftwaffe. It used to be worn, as were most of these badges on the left breast pocket or just below by holders of the Iron Cross 1st Class. Some new badges were introduced in March 1936 for Pilots, Observers, Pilot/Observers and for Wireless Operator/Air Gunners.

However, some of these were used before their official sanction, by qualified members of the German Air-sport Association.

The Air Gunner/Flight Engineer's badge was instituted in June 1942, while unqualified Air Gunners who had participated in at least ten operations in that role were granted a similar badge, but made of reversed metals, in April 1944.

Parachutists were issued with badges in November 1936 and Glider Pilots in December 1940. The former wore theirs on the left pocket. On 26 March 1936 a special badge was granted to aviators who had been honourably discharged from flying duties: appropriately it depicts an eagle standing on a rock, the whole surrounded by the usual wreath.

All the other badges illustrated in this plate were given as an award to non-flying personnel of the Luftwaffe and were worn on the left breast pocket, or below the Iron Cross 1st Class. All were adopted during the course of the war. The Ground-Combat and Tank Battle badges were adopted in 1942 and 1944 respectively for personnel of the ground divisions formed and manned by the Air Force. Higher grade awards of both badges were instituted in November 1944, with numbers (25, 50, 75, 100) at the bottom of the wreath to identify the number of combat engagements in which an individual had taken part. A black tank badge with matt silver eagle was worn by crews of armoured vehicles other than tanks (reconnaissance units) and personnel of 'Panzergrenadier' formations.

The Anti-Aircraft badge was an award primarily given for shooting down enemy aircraft or cooperating in this purpose. It was instituted in January 1941 while the last badge illustrated, which was also the last to be instituted on 27 November 1944, the Sea Battle badge, was created for the benefit of the Air Force's sea branch.

Plate 58. Qualification Clasps

These clasps were instituted on 30 January 1941 for wearing on the left breast, above service ribbons; they were in fact awards given for a number of specific operational flights. The issue of clasps was modified during the course of the war and therefore only the final, definitive set of clasps have been illustrated.

The badge consisted of a central device surrounded by a wreath, with a spray of oak leaves on either side. Cloth versions could be worn as well as metal ones. Bronze, silver and gold identified the class of the clasp, parts of which were made of bronze or were black according to qualification.

In June 1942 a gold pendant was added to the gold clasp as a reward for further operational flights, up to 500 in the case of Fighter and Transport formations. Later, in 1944 the pendant was replaced by a tablet with the appropriate number of operations inscribed in its centre. The lowest number was 200, and increased by 100 at a time: only one tablet could be worn below the clasp.

The Ground Combat clasp was instituted on 3 November 1944 for ground personnel who had taken part in close combat: the central device was made of silver while the rest of the badge was in bronze, silver or gold for 15, 30 or 50 days respectively of close engagement with the enemy. Those wounded in action received the badge for shorter periods.

Speciality and Trade Badges and Awards

These badges were worn by N.C.O.s and men on the left forearm and as a rule they identified a specialisation or trade; the Anti-Aircraft personnel badge, however, was worn as a meritorious award only by those eligible for it.

The device was embroidered in matt silver or grey thread on a grey-blue backing and some N.C.O.s' badges had an additional edging of silver twisted cords.

Plate 59. Speciality and Trade Badges

Other badges have been illustrated in this plate as well as the above mentioned: crew men specialised in Sound Location or Range Finding were entitled to gold edging around their badges after one year of meritorious service and standard bearers wore a special badge on the right upper arm. The crossed flags were embroidered in colour according to the branch of service of the wearer.

N.C.O.s' School graduates wore the 'US' initials on the right forearm. The A.A. Artillery badge was worn on the left sleeve in the period between October 1936 and July 1937 only; the badge illustrated in the previous plate was used later.

Czechoslovakia

Plate 60. Cap Badges

Czechoslovakia became an independent republic after World War 1 and subsequently managed to build up a considerably strong air force which technically was a corps of the Army.

All ranks' uniforms were khaki, with army type badges but with distinguishing light blue arm-of-service colours shown by means of piping and stripes.

The officers wore gold metal cap badges, the N.C.O.s silver ones and the rank and file wore bronze badges. The latter's badge depicted the Czech Lion on a shield, while the higher ranks had the shield superimposed on a square diamond-shaped base (sides 31 mm.), with or without crossed swords for combatant and non-combatant personnel respectively.

All officers' peaked caps had gold twisted chin strap cords and the generals wore an additional gold embroidery on the visor while the others had a plain visor covered by khaki material. The rank and file wore a forage cap with the badge on the top, left side.

Rank Badges

The badges of rank were placed on the shoulder straps of all officers and other ranks, with the exception of generals who had special embroidered straps and who wore their rank stars on the sleeves, above the cuffs. The generals' embroidered ornaments on the peaked cap's visor, on the collar patches and shoulder straps repeated a lime leaves motif, the emblem of Czechoslovakia.

There were four senior and four junior officers: the former were identified by a gold embroidered stripe all around the loose sides of their shoulder straps and wore from one to four gold embroidered 5-pointed stars. The junior officers had plain straps with piping and from one to four 3-pointed stars.

The N.C.O.s were divided into senior and junior ranks; the former included the Warrant Officer, the Staff Sergeant and Sergeant whose rank was identified by rectangular silver badges until 1938 and later by 3-pointed silver stars.

The rank of Staff Warrant Officer was instituted in March 1939. Buttons with or without crossed swords were used by the personnel of combatant and non-combatant units respectively and gold, silver and bronze buttons were worn according to the type of metal of the cap badge.

Plate 61. Rank Badges

The N.C.O.s' rank badges were placed on the shoulder straps, on an additional light blue stripe which in the case of the senior ranks was sewn along the centre and for the junior ranks across the outer ends of the straps. Career junior N.C.O.s, on long term enlistment, wore both stripes.

In 1938 the rectangular badges of the higher ranks were replaced by silver 3-pointed stars, and later the rank of Staff Warrant Officer was also introduced, identified by a single silver 5-pointed star.

The junior N.C.O.s wore from one to four plain round silver studs on the outer ends of their shoulder straps.

The cadets of the Reserve Officers' School had other ranks' shoulder straps with light blue piping, junior N.C.O.s' studs on the light blue stripe and additional silver lace stripe at the bottom or on both sides of the latter according to graduation. The officer candidates of the Military Academy wore on the outer end of the shoulder straps a gold stripe, 10 mm. wide, for each year of attendance, while flight cadets had blue stripes instead. The same light blue stripe but arranged in a loop was worn at the Flight Specialists' School.

There is a great amount of confusion about the rank insignia of the senior N.C.O.s, due to contradictory information relating to this complex period of Czech history. Germany annexed the Sudetenland in autumn 1938, and the rest of Czechoslovakia in the following March. Armed forces personnel fled to neighbouring countries and eventually to France and to Britain. Others found their way to the Middle East. Rank insignia were often modified for wearing on new uniforms and the 3-pointed star, which could not be found abroad, was replaced by a 5-pointed star. Czech cap badges were eventually made in Britain.

Qualification badges

Qualified Pilots and Observers wore special metal badges on the right breast of the jacket. Crossed cannons appear on the badges of balloon personnel because balloons were deployed as a means of artillery observation.

The R.A.F. organised four Czech squadrons, the personnel of which wore national titles in the usual manner: embroidered in light blue on grey-blue uniform's colour for officers and light blue on dark blue for airmen.

Finland

Plate 62. Cap Badges

Finland declared its independence in December 1917 and its newly raised armed forces became engaged against the Russians in the ensuing campaign for independence. The Air Corps which was formed in this period later expanded and became eventually an autonomous service.

During World War 2 field grey uniforms of army pattern were widely used although officers and regular senior N.C.O.s wore also a blue service dress which had been adopted before the war. This dress consisted of a peaked cap with gold chin strap cords and embroidered cap badge, single breasted jacket with open collar and four patch pockets with flaps, breeches with riding boots or long trousers and shoes.

The regular officers' cap badge depicted a gold Finnish Lion on a round, protruding red enamel background, on a gold base. On the peaked cap this badge was centred between two sprays of laurel leaves, below an eagle in flight; on other head-dresses the round badge was worn on its own or below a round cockade in the national colours, white, blue and white.

The cockade of N.C.O.s, also used by officers, was made of coloured enamels while that of the other ranks was made of tin metal and painted in the national colours. Another cap badge similar to that of the officers but for lower ranks depicted the Lion and was all made of metal like a button, for wearing on a head-dress which required two badges.

Officers' Rank Badges

The officers of the Air Force wore two different types of rank insignia according to uniform: rank badges of army pattern, on branch of service collar patches were used on the tunic of the field grey uniform while gold stripes were worn on the front of the forearms, above the cuffs of the blue jacket. Stripes were also used on the greatcoat and, sewn on a removable patch, they were attached by means of two buttons on the forearms of the leather coat. These stripes have already been dealt with in another volume of this series on Army badges. The generals wore narrow stripes above a large one, the senior officers wore narrow stripes below a medium one and the junior officers had only narrow ones; the captain wore two narrow stripes with a still narrower one in between.

The collar patches of the field grey uniform were blue with black embroidered frames differing according to class of rank, and with black fir twigs at the front. The frame of the generals comprised one large and one narrow stripe, the senior officers had two narrow stripes and the junior officers one narrow stripe only.

The generals' individual rank was identified by small gold Finnish Lions and that of the officers by gold roses, larger for senior ranks and smaller, 13 mm. in diameter, for the others. The officers of the services had branch of specialisation badges on the collar instead of the fir twigs.

Qualification Badge

Pilots wore a special badge on the left breast pocket. It depicted a swastika surrounded by six rotating wings, the whole ensigned by a stylised crown. It is noteworthy that the swastika was an old, traditional Finnish-Estonian emblem, unrelated to the then contemporary German swastika.

Plate 63. N.C.O.s' Rank Badges

The N.C.O.s had collar patches in arm-of-service colours but without the fir twigs: rank chevrons were sewn in the centre, a large chevron for the Flight Sergeant and from one to four narrower ones for the other ranks. On field and fatigue tunics without collar patches, chevrons or plain stripes were worn on the shoulder straps.

A winged propeller was the arm-of-service badge of the Air Force and was worn on the shoulder straps, in the case of officers above a gold metal lion.

Poland

Historical Background

Poland regained its national independence in 1918 after World War 1 and due to the precarious circumstances of that time it started immediately to organise armed forces to defend its new status.

However, Polish aviation history dates back to the years before 1918: Adolf Warchalowski, for instance, held the Austrian Pilot Brevet No. 1; two Poles were among the first six Russian officers to train as pilots in France in 1910, and Wlodzimierz Mazurkiewicz, also a Pole, was in fact Bulgaria's first pilot; he flew during the Balkan War 1912–13 and later became a flying instructor in the Chinese Army.

Before World War 1 Poland was partitioned between Russia, Austria and Germany but enthusiasm for flying knew no boundaries and later, during the war, it became the common denominator among Poles fighting under different flags.

The Russian Revolution gave an opportunity to the Poles in the East to organise their own units which often became entangled in local events and also found their way home barred by the Austrian and German armies. The 1st and later the 2nd Polish Combat Aviation Unit were raised at that time in Russia, but both were eventually captured and disarmed by the Germans. In the meantime Polish aviators were trained in France where eventually they formed seven squadrons comprising about 100 aircraft, which in 1919 were sent to Poland.

By the end of October 1918 the Poles started to take over control of their own country from the Central Powers which were collapsing. Military installations and airfields were occupied by local Polish soldiers and volunteers which together with others who arrived from Russia, France and other countries, eventually constituted the Polish armed forces that in the next few years secured Poland's independence.

One of the first aviation units to be raised at that time which became internationally famous, was the 3rd Aviation Squadron, formed at Rakowice Aerodrome, near Krakow, in November 1918. It was redesignated the 7th Aviation Squadron on 21 December and the 7th Kościuszko Air Squadron in the following year, after some American volunteers had joined the unit.

Initially the squadron was commanded by Captain C. Perini and participated in the defence of Lwów and subsequent liberation of the Malopolska.

A group of American aviators, some of whom had been members of

Hoover's Relief Mission at Lwów, while watching the military parade of 14 July 1919 in Paris conceived the idea of offering their services to Poland as Kościuszko had done for the cause of American Independence. In October 1919 the first seven American pilots joined the Squadron which was engaged in war operations from the following April to the end of that war. Later the squadron was transferred to Warsaw, where it was renumbered the 111th and became part of the 1st Regiment.

Initially Polish airmen wore a variety of uniforms, mainly Austrian, Russian or French, but all had the Polish Eagle as their head-dress badge, some examples of which have been illustrated. Those who came from Russia had dark blue uniforms and wore a winged propeller badge on the left upper sleeve while those from France had horizon blue uniforms of French pattern but with the square-shaped czapka instead of the kepi. On this head-dress they wore the Polish Eagle and below, on the cap band, they wore the rank stripes set on a padded oval 3 × 4 cm. in size. The officers wore an eagle, embroidered on a red circular background on the shoulder straps; this badge was also used as a beret badge. They had French aviation collar patches with the 5-pointed star followed by a wing, in the shape of a falling star.

The Polish aviators' uniforms of units formed in the former Russian and Austro-Hungarian territories developed separately from those of units in the former German territory (Greater Poland). The former units adopted field grey army uniforms but as their arm-of-service colour was dark yellow and that of the military police was light yellow, dark blue uniforms were adopted in January 1919 for the personnel of the Military Aviation. However, by then the other ranks had already been issued with field grey uniforms and the officers continued wearing the uniforms they possessed. Many changes and modifications took place in a relatively short time: the dark blue round peaked cap initially had piping around the top of the crown and along the centre of the cap band; then the second piping was moved to the top of the cap band and later the leather visor was covered dark blue cloth, edged with dark brown leather. The rank badges were also changed and ultimately they were adopted in the form of stars on trefoil-shaped shoulder cords.

Field grey uniforms were worn in the former German territory, with the Polish czapka instead of the round peaked cap. The eagle, but with shield, was worn at the front and a trefoil-shaped silver ornament on the left side of it. On the round peaked cap of the uniforms previously described the usual eagle above the shield was worn and a white and red metal cockade was attached to the cap band.

Other significant insignia introduced during this period are the arm badges for flying personnel: i.e. an eagle in flight embroidered in silver or made of white metal, on dark yellow background, was worn by aircraft personnel and a winged anchor by balloon personnel of the former Russian and Austrian territories. In the ex-German territory some dark blue velvet collar patches with yellow piping were used instead. A silver wing and an anchor with wing were shown on these patches by aircraft and balloon personnel respectively. A silver embroidered winged propeller on yellow background was also worn on the left upper sleeve.

New regulations appeared on 27 December 1919 and during the following year all army uniforms were standardised to a new khaki pattern; the Military Aviation was part of the Army and therefore conformed to the rule.

Square peaked caps with brown leather visor and chin strap were introduced; the visor was edged by a white metal rim and the new cap badge was slightly larger than the previous pattern. Dark yellow collar patches with 'zigzag' ornament, differing from the later pattern, were worn on the stand-and-fall collar of the tunic and silver or white metal badges were worn on the left arm.

Rank insignia were initially worn on the cuffs and on the shoulder straps but later the former were abolished. These regulations were strictly applied in order to standardise the Polish uniforms once and for all: by 1 February 1920 all the officers had to wear the new rank insignia and the new caps and by July all had to wear the complete new uniform.

Additions and modifications were prescribed in due course; a dark yellow cap band was adopted in 1930 and the tunic's buttons, for instance, originally five were increased to six and then to seven. Officers and warrant officers and N.C.O.s wore blue trousers with yellow stripes for evening occasions. The former had two large stripes with piping in between while the N.C.O.s had only one stripe on the trousers' sides. A ceremonial dagger replaced the sword in 1924.

Although the Military Aviation remained part of the army, new steel grey uniforms were issued to its personnel in May 1936. The major change was that the new uniform's jacket had an open collar, showing grey shirt and black tie. There was one pattern for officers, warrant officers and sergeants and another one for the other ranks.

Plate 64. Cap Badges (1936)

The steel grey uniforms were adopted on 30 May 1936. The peaked cap was round in shape, with black cap band and black leather visor and chin strap.

The officers' class of rank was shown on the visor by a silver zigzag ornament for generals, double silver stripes for senior officers and one stripe only for the junior officers. Individual rank was identified by silver embroidered stars at the front of the cap band below the cap badge, which was embroidered in silver wire.

The other ranks had an oxidised white metal cap badge and wore small replicas of their shoulder straps' rank insignia on the cap band: these insignia were in this case embroidered in silver on black felt. The Warrant Officer wore one silver star, like the 2nd Lieutenant but had no stripe on the visor. Later, by 1939 the N.C.O.s' badges were changed to the army's pattern, slightly smaller, and embroidered on red felt, as already illustrated in another volume of this series.

Rank badges were also worn on the left side of the black beret, but it had no cap badge. The officers' badges were similar to those they wore on the shoulder straps; the Warrant Officer had a silver star above a 30 mm. long red stripe and the others wore the same insignia, chevrons or stripes, as on the peaked cap's band.

Plate 65. Officers' Rank Badges

The officers' steel grey jacket was single-breasted with four patch pockets with flaps and oxidised white metal buttons. A grey shirt was usually worn but white shirt was worn on evening dress; the neck tie was always black. Steel grey trousers or breeches were used in different circumstances, the latter with black riding boots.

The generals had a silver zigzag on black background on the cuffs of the jacket and black 15 mm. double stripes with black inner piping on the trousers while the other officers wore a 15 mm. stripe on the cuffs and trousers. The arm-of-service colour of Doctors and officers of the Commissariat was cherry red and royal blue respectively and was worn in the form of piping on the cuffs and trousers.

The basic rank badge of all officers was the silver embroidered 5-pointed star and stars were worn on the shoulder straps above the generals' zigzag, above the senior officers' double bars or on their own by junior officers. The zigzag and the double bars were embroidered in silver at about 15 mm. from the outer seam; the latter were 15 mm. in width.

Regular and Reserve officer cadets wore different shoulder straps and as they could attain N.C.O.s ranks, chevrons and stripes were worn accordingly, in silver lace by the former, and silver with red edging by the latter. The shoulder straps of the regulars had silver piping while the piping of the reserve cadets consisted of white and red twisted cords. They wore cuff stripes the same as the army cadets; the stripe of the Reserve officer cadets after training was made of silver but had a narrow red strip along its centre.

The Regular officer cadets had black stripes on the trousers; up to the 3rd year's course they wore narrow stripes, 2 mm. wide, exactly the same as those of the N.C.O.s and subsequently the officers' stripes. All had special badges on the collar and the regulars wore badges on the shoulder straps as well; the initials 'SP' mean 'Szkola Podchrazych', i.e. Officers' School.

Plate 66. Warrant Officers' and N.C.O.s' Rank Badges and Miscellanea

The Warrant Officer and regular N.C.O.s wore officers' type uniforms, the former with officers' stripes on the cuffs and trousers, the regular N.C.O.s with a 2 mm. wide black stripe on the trousers only. The others had steel grey uniforms of 1936 army pattern.

The Warrant Officer and senior N.C.O.s (Staff-Sergeant and Sergeant) were identified by a silver lace stripe edged in red on the loose sides of the shoulder straps; the former wore an additional star, while the sergeants had chevrons. The junior N.C.O.s wore from one to three stripes on the shoulder straps. As already mentioned, all wore rank insignia on the head-dress also.

On flying suits different rank badges were worn on the forearms. They consisted of the usual stars combined with zigzag or double bars, or chevrons, according to rank applied in the centre of a cloth roundel with silver edging.

The officers' dress belt was made of black silk and had an oxidised silver buckle, with fittings at the front. The actual belt was 45 mm. in width and the buckle measure 52.5 mm. in diameter.

The pilots of the Reserve who volunteered for additional flights, in excess of the normal compulsory period of flying when on duty wore an armlet on the left upper sleeve of their civilian clothes. The armlet was made of steel grey cloth, 80 mm. in width, with an eagle and the initials 'OR' on the left and the rank insignia on the other side as illustrated. Double bars, stars, chevrons and stripes identified rank as usual; the Warrant Officer had one silver star and a red stripe.

Plate 67. Cap Badges Worn After 1939

On 1 September 1939, the day of the German attack, the Polish Air Force had 397 first line combat aircraft which fought gallantly during the following weeks until the 17th when all hope was lost after the Soviet invasion from the East. Following General Headquarters' instructions, personnel and aircraft commenced evacuation to neighbouring countries, mainly to Rumania.

The vast majority of Polish airmen eventually made their way to France, where General Sikorski had formed the Polish Government in exile. In

December, the first Polish contingents were transferred to Britain in accordance with previous agreements.

On 22 February 1940 the Polish Air Force became an independent service, its personnel in France was re-organised and eventually, by the following May they manned four fighter groups, two reconnaissance groups and one bomber group. The German offensive of May 1940 caught these units still in the process of training and only some fighter formations were able to take part in the subsequent campaign.

During the months of June and July, about 5,500 Polish airmen arrived in Britain from France, adding to the 2,300 who had been admitted earlier.

The Air Ministry had initially decided to recruit Poles in Bomber Command only, but eventually some better terms of collaboration were secured by the Polish Government, then in Britain. Initially an autonomous Polish air organisation was set up within the R.A.F. and all airmen became part of the R.A.F.V.R.; officers were all commissioned to the rank of Pilot Officer, regardless of their previous position.

However, on the strength of a new agreement signed on 5 August 1940 the Polish Air Force became a nationally independent organisation and by the end of that month Nos. 302 and 303 fighter squadrons were operational. Other squadrons were raised during the course of the war as described in the following pages (Plate 73).

Polish aviators wore basically French uniforms during the first phase of their exile: officers had uniforms of Polish pattern made with French 'Louise bleu' cloth while the other ranks wore the available French uniforms. All wore Polish insignia.

Grey-blue R.A.F. uniforms were issued to the Poles in Britain and were worn with the usual Polish cap badges, in silver embroidery for officers and Warrant Officers and oxidised white metal for other ranks. Badges were eventually made in Britain and some variations to the original pattern also appeared; gold and silver embroidered badges were worn by the officers and W.O.s. The peaked cap's visor ornaments were changed to rows of gold embroidered oak leaves for generals and colonels only, following R.A.F. custom.

Polish Eagles of Air Force or Army patterns were used on the forage cap while the other ranks in the R.A.F. usually wore the brass cap badge of the R.A.F.

Shoulder Flashes (After 1939)

The first Polish contingent to train in Britain was issued with R.A.F. uniforms and the Polish Eagle was worn on the left breast pocket. Nationality titles soon appeared in the usual pattern, with light blue lettering on grey-blue background for officers and light blue on dark blue or black for airmen. There were straight and curved titles for the latter, for wearing above the R.A.F. Eagle on the upper sleeves, and a third variation existed with the title and the Eagle on the same background.

In order to encourage the influx of Polish volunteers, Poles residing in other countries, some special arm badges were adopted: they depict the Polish Eagle above a wreath containing the flag of the country of the volunteer's former residence. Four different badges were adopted for volunteers who had been living in France, Belgium, and North and South America.

Plate 68. Officers' Rank Badges (After 1939)

Officers wore standard R.A.F. grey-blue service dress or battledress with additional Polish rank patches on the collar. Gilt buttons with the Polish Eagle were used on the service jacket and British stripes on the forearms, while the stripes were worn on the shoulder straps of the battledress and of the greatcoat, according to R.A.F. regulations.

The rank patches worn on the collar measured about 60 × 25 mm. in size and were made in the shape of a shoulder strap, with gold embroidered small zigzag, double bars and stars, according to rank.

Army rank titles were used by the Polish Air Force contrary to R.A.F. custom but ranks were equivalent, except for that of Air Commodore which did not exist in the Polish Air Force. However, as the ranks on the collar and those on the sleeves showed Polish and British commissions, unrelated to each other, often the two ranks of an officer differed one from the other. As initially all Polish officers were granted the rank of Pilot Officer, many showed a higher rank on the collar patches or, vice versa, many officers rose in rank faster in the R.A.F. than in their own organisation.

The following was the rank comparison between the Polish Air Force and the R.A.F. in October 1941:

P.A.F.	R.A.F.
General	Air Chief Marshal
General of Division	Air Marshal
General of Brigade	Air Vice Marshal
—	Air Commodore
Colonel	Group Captain
Lieutenant-Colonel	Wing Commander
Major	Squadron Leader
Captain	Flight Lieutenant
Lieutenant	Flying Officer
2nd Lieutenant	Pilot Officer

As, however, there was no Polish General/Air Chief Marshal and as on the other hand the need existed to standardise British and Polish ranks, in May 1944 the generals' ranks were all lowered by one; i.e. the General comparing to the Air Marshal, the General of Division to the Air Vice Marshal and the General of Brigade to the Air Commodore.

Chaplains and Bandmasters wore their old badges (Plate 65) on the lapels of the jacket, while Doctors and Dentists wore R.A.F. badges (Plate 2). Regulations prescribed the wearing of the Medical badge without the crown but usually the crown was used as well. Generals and staff officers wore a small Polish Eagle on the cuffs above the stripes.

Plate 69. Warrant Officers' and N.C.O.s' Rank Badges (After 1939)
Also the Warrant Officer and N.C.O.s wore bi-national rank insignia as did the officers. On the collar they all had rank patches which in the case of the Warrant Officer and senior N.C.O.s had additional gold edging at the top and on the sides. The edging, chevrons and stripes were made of gold lace or were embroidered in yellow thread. The Warrant Officers' star was embroidered in gold wire or yellow thread matching the type of edging. A patch with edging and star of gold embroidery has been illustrated.

Aspirant Officers wore special patches with a stripe along the centre, while officer cadets, who graduated, wore N.C.O.s' collar patches with an additional silver edging. Officer cadets in training were identified by white and red twisted cord around their collar patches, as illustrated.

British type of rank badges were worn as well on the forearms by Warrant Officers and on the upper arms by the N.C.O.s. The former used three badges. In 1941 regulations prescribed the wearing of a large button on a black round patch of material superimposed on a larger light blue one, changed in 1944 to an embroidered cap badge but usually the normal R.A.F. insignia was worn instead.

Accordingly, the Polish regulations prescribed the wearing of a small button and later a metal eagle instead of the crown above the Flight Sergeant's chevrons, but the crown was worn as well. Three or two chevrons or the usual 2-bladed propeller were worn by the other ranks.

Plate 70. Qualification Badges
All the Polish qualification badges worn from 1919 to 1945 have been illustrated together for the purpose of clarity and because even very early patterns were worn during World War 2 by those who still possessed them.

All depicted an eagle in flight, about 65 mm. wide from wing tip to wing tip; most eagles held a wreath in the beak and some clutched symbolic lightnings in their claws according to qualification. The metal with which they were made also identified different qualifications. The wreaths of combat badges were usually made of green enamel, although this ruling was not always observed.

They were worn high on the left breast near the lapel under which a small chain was suspended by means of a hook and, although the eagle itself seemed to be suspended by this chain, in reality it was fixed by means of a screw with nut, at the back of the badge.

The first two badges, of Pilot and Observer, were instituted in 1919 and a third badge was adopted in 1928 for aviators with the dual qualification of Pilot-Observer. Five years later the Pilots and Observers were divided into two classes and new badges were issued subsequently.

More badges were instituted during World War 2 by the Polish Air Force in Britain, to match the half-wings which were issued to R.A.F. personnel.

Plates 71/72. Qualification Badges

Four badges were created in 1942 but due to the advent of other aircrew assignments as the war progressed, a new set of qualifications with relative badges was devised in 1944. These badges carried initials on the wreath to identify each individual specialisation.

Artillery Observers qualified as aircraft Pilots were granted a special badge in 1945; this was the last badge issued during the war.

Qualification badges of different design existed as well, for Air Gunner, Balloon Observer and Naval aviators; all were divided into two classes in 1933.

The Naval Aviation manned seaplanes and its personnel wore navy blue uniforms without any distinctive insignia, except for the Pilots' and Observers' wings. The branch was re-formed in October 1944 and an 'L' was then adopted for wearing in the loop of the cuffs' stripes as a special insignia. Technical officers wore red backing showing between the stripes.

Other Badges

A miscellany of badges, usually worn on the breast pocket of the tunic have been illustrated in this plate. Most were worn in Poland before the German invasion, others later in the 1940s.

The basic air formation was the 'eskadra' which, before the war consisted of nine aircraft; two, three or more eskadras formed a 'dywizjon', a division, which grouped eskadras of the same deployment, i.e. fighters, bombers, observation and army support aircraft. Eskadras of different deployment formed the regiments, which were the tactical units defending the territory of Poland.

The 1st, 2nd and 3rd Air Regiments were formed during the summer of 1921, and were based in Warsaw, Kraków and Poznán, respectively. The 4th Air Regiment was raised at Toruń in 1925, the 5th was formed from units of the former 11th Air Regiment at Lida Air Base which was raised in 1925 and disbanded in 1928. The 6th Air Regiment was raised at Lwów in May 1925.

The badges of the Officers' and N.C.O.s' Schools and of the Staff College were worn in Poland and later, during the war, in Britain as well, while the Balloon and Pilots' School badges were used only in Britain.

The badge of the 55th Eskadra has been illustrated as an example of an unofficial badge, the design of which was based on the emblem painted on aircraft. This formation was the former 24th Eskadra of the 2nd Air Regiment, transferred to the 5th, as part of the 2nd Army Support Division, in 1928.

Plate 73. Squadron Badges

Squadron badges were later authorised in Britain for the following formations which were raised from July 1940 onwards and disbanded as No. 300 Źiemia Mazowiecka Bomber Squadron. This unit, named after the Land of Mazovia, was formed in July 1940 at Bramcote. Aircrew who had flown at least one combat mission could wear a crowned figure 300, in gold for officers and silver for N.C.O.s, pinned on the tie knot.

No. 301 Żiemia Pomorska 'Obrôńków Warszawy' Bomber Squadron. It was a unit of the Land of Pomerania, known as the 'Defenders of Warsaw' which was raised at Bramcote in July as was the former; it ended the war as a transport formation.

No. 302 Poznański Fighter Squadron—formed in July 1940 at Leconfield and was named after the city of Poznań. Its personnel wore a light chocolate brown scarf.

No. 303 T. Kosciuszko's Fighter Squadron—was formed in August 1940 at Northolt. Its personnel wore a scarlet scarf.

No. 304 Prince J. Poniatowşki Żiemia Sląska Bomber Squadron—was formed in August 1940 at Bramcote; was part of Coastal Command and later Transport Command.

No. 305 J. Piłsudski's Żiemia Wielkopolska Bomber Squadron—formed in August 1940 at Bramcote, was named after the territory of Greater Poland.

No. 306 Toruńki Fighter Squadron—was formed in August 1940 at

Church Fenton and was named after the city of Toruń. Its personnel wore a green scarf.

No. 307 Lwówski Night Fighter Squadron—formed in September 1940 at Kirton-in-Lindsey, named after the town of Lwów. Its personnel wore a turquoise blue scarf.

No. 308 Krakówski Fighter Squadron—formed in September 1940 at Squires Gate, named after the town of Kraków. Its personnel wore a white scarf.

No. 309 Żiemia Czerwieńska Army Support and Fighter Squadron—formed in October 1940 and its personnel wore a dark blue scarf with white dots.

No. 315 Deblinski Fighter Squadron—formed at Acklington in January 1941. Its personnel wore a blue scarf.

No. 316 Warszawski Fighter Squadron—formed in February 1941 at Pembrey. Its personnel wore a claret red scarf.

No. 317 Wileński Fighter Squadron—formed in February 1941 at Acklington and named after the town of Wilno. Its personnel wore a blue scarf.

No. 318 Gdnański Fighter-Reconnaissance Squadron—formed in March 1943 at Detling and operated in the Mediterranean theatre with 2nd Polish Corps as an army support unit. It disbanded in Austria after the end of the war.

No. 663 Air Observation Point Squadron. It was formed at Eboli, Italy, in September 1943 as part of the 2nd Polish Corps. As it was an army unit its personnel wore khaki uniforms and special collar badges which depicted the red and white Polish aircraft insignia on crossed cannons with a wing at one side.

The Polish Fight Team 'Skalski's Circus' was a very small unit formed in the Middle East, as part of the Desert Air Force.

Japan

Plate 73. Cap Badges of Army and Naval Aviation

The Imperial Japanese Army and Navy each had an aviation branch, the personnel of which wore the uniforms of the parent service with very few additional badges, therefore most of the badges illustrated technically belong to one or the other service and have been illustrated only because they were worn by aviators as well.

Both the Army and Naval Aviation were instituted in 1911 and due to the technological achievements of the 1920s Japan built up a strong air force, including air carriers, during the next decade.

Army aviators wore khaki uniforms and peaked caps with red band or the soft cap with cloth visor, both with the 5-pointed star at the front. Metal, cloth or leather versions of the star were usually worn on the flying helmet as well. Naval cap badges of various pattern, according to rank or type of uniform were used by the personnel of the Naval Aviation.

Plate 74. Rank Badges

Army and naval officers had the same rank titles and were identified by the prefix Army, or Navy, before their rank title. The personnel of naval corps had the corps name before the rank title.

During World War 2 the personnel of the Army Aviation wore the M 98 khaki uniforms adopted in 1938, with rank insignia on the collar. Individual rank was identified by stars on collar patches about 40 × 18 mm. in size. Rank class was shown by gold stripes, commencing with the generals who wore all-gold patches and ending with the N.C.O.s who had only a narrow gold stripe along the centre of their red patches. Privates wore red patches with small metal or embroidered stars to identify graduation. One patch on its own could be worn on the left breast or left upper sleeve or field uniform or flying suits.

The naval aviators wore Navy uniforms and rank badges. They had gold stripes on the cuffs of the blue dress uniform and on the shoulder boards which were worn on the white uniform and overcoat only. Collar patches were worn on blue and on khaki service uniforms. On the former black lace stripes were worn on the cuffs as well. Sky blue was the arm-of-service colour of the Naval Aviation.

Collar patches were worn only by the officers and by the Warrant Officers and were different from those of the Army. They were intended to repeat the pattern of gold stripes shown on the shoulder boards: small silver cherry blossoms identified rank, down to the rank of Ensign. The Midshipman had an anchor on both sides of the collar and a gold stripe, without any cherry blossom on the shoulder boards; the Cadet wore an anchor on both and the Warrant Officers wore a stripe instead.

Plate 75. Petty Officers' and Seamens' Rank Badges

The lower ranks of the Navy wore red inverted 'V' chevrons which during World War 2 were changed to special badges, composed of yellow stripes, a cherry blossom and an anchor, and an additional wreath for the petty officers. The cherry blossom was yellow for personnel of the line, coloured for personnel of the Corps, light blue in the case of the Naval Aviation.

The badge was worn on the upper left sleeve and was usually embroidered on dark blue, although some were embroidered on material corresponding to the colour of the uniform.

Other Badges

The other ranks as well as officers could train to become pilots, and the Bomber Fighter Pilot wore speciality badges, similar in shape to the usual naval speciality badges. These badges were embroidered in red thread on dark blue for blue uniforms and dark blue on white for use on white uniforms.

The aviation badge used by the Army Aviation was worn on both sides of the collar, behind the collar patches, but only in peace-time or in the rear areas. Later their use was discontinued and coloured arm-of-service chevrons, sky blue in the case of aviation, were adopted instead, for wearing above the right breast pocket.

A selection of various badges has been illustrated also, including the Pilot's wings, which were worn above the right breast pocket, and others, mainly patches of aviation schools.

Rumania

Plate 76. Rank Badges

An Army Flying Corps was formed in Rumania in 1910 and again after World War 1, in which the Rumanians were defeated by the Central Powers.

The Royal Air Force, as it was designated during World War 2, adopted the grey-blue uniforms in 1931: the officers wore jackets with open collar, while the other ranks wore tunics with stand-and-fall collar. The cap badge depicted an eagle with spread wings above a wreath, the whole ensigned by a crown.

The officers had gold stripes at the front of both forearms: large stripes of varying width identified generals' and senior officers' class of rank and individual rank was shown by narrow stripes, the uppermost of which was folded to form a square loop. The junior officers had narrow stripes only.

The warrant officers of the flying cadre, known as Adjutants, had their rank badges on the shoulder straps, in the form of stylised wings.

Plate 77. Rank Badges

The Warrant Officer of the ground personnel wore inverted 'V' chevrons on the shoulder straps.

The Sergeant wore one gold lace stripe on both shoulder straps while the Corporal and the Private 1st Class had two and one yellow woollen stripes respectively.

At the beginning of the war these badges were worn in the form of 'V' shaped chevrons on both upper sleeves, those of warrant officers were applied on to a backing in arm-of-service colour.

Arm-of-Service Badges—Collar Patches

All ranks of the Air Force wore collar patches in arm-of-service colour. The generals had special patches, with gold embroidered oak leaves on their own colours, which were dark red for generals of the Army and light blue for those of the Air Force, approximately 75 × 35 mm. in size. The others, officers and other ranks, had plain coloured patches with pointed ends.

The following were the basic colours of the various branches of service, although some changes took place during the course of the war:

Fighter units	Deep green
Bomber units	Deep red
Reconnaissance units	Light blue
Physicians	Cherry red
Engineers	Royal blue
Mechanics	Violet
Aerostation/Signals	Brown
Anti-Aircraft	Black
Schools	Orange

A German wall chart of Rumanian insignia, published in 1939, reports that yellow patches were used by the Reconnaissance units, light blue patches with black piping by the Anti-Aircraft and light blue patches with brown piping were used by signallers.

The personnel of the Seaplane Flotilla wore a gold metal anchor on patches as above.

Qualification Badges

Rumanian aviators wore metal qualification badges on the left breast: the badge of the Pilot depicted the crowned Shield of Rumania between wings, while the Pilots of bomber aircraft had a different badge, initially with the cypher of the reigning monarch, and later with the Shield of Rumania on the breast of the eagle. The Observer had a badge similar to that of the Pilot, but with the King's cypher in its centre.

The same crowned cypher on a sword, sided by wings or an embroidered winged propeller was the badge of the members of the civilian Aero Club.

Hungary

Plate 78. Cap Insignia—Peaked Cap/Forage Cap

The personnel of the Hungarian Army Air Force wore khaki uniforms, many details, of which resembled the old uniforms of the Austro-Hungarian Empire.

The uniforms of the Air Force officers, warrant officer and sergeants differed from those of their Army counterparts in many details: first of all the Aviators' jacket had an open collar, rank insignia on the shoulder straps instead of on the collar, and the flaps of the formers' jackets were rectangular while those of Army personnel had three points, of Austrian pattern.

The other ranks had army uniforms with khaki forage cap or beret.

The officers, warrant officers and sergeants wore khaki peaked caps or forage caps: the former carried at the front an eagle in flight surmounted by the Hungarian Crown, in gold or silver according to rank, embroidered on black background. The national cockade and rank stripes were worn at the front of the forage cap, as in the Army.

The other ranks wore a khaki beret with a black tally, with a bronze badge at the front, on a triangular black backing.

The forage cap's cockade showed the red, white and green national colours, which were surrounded by a gold, silver or bronze frame, according to rank. The frame was made of wire embroidery or plain metal. The rank stripes were placed underneath and were shaped like an inverted 'V' chevron with the above-mentioned cockade at the apex. Their setting following the same rules as for the stripes on the shoulder straps, except for those of the lowest ranks, who had white stripes on the shoulder straps, and black stripes on the forage cap.

Plate 79. Officers' Rank Badges

The shoulder straps illustrated were 40 mm. in width and various lengths, according to the size of the jacket's shoulders. The edging consisted of two twisted gold cords, and rank stripes on arm-of-service colours were shown inside.

There were three widths of gold lace stripes, the large to identify the generals' rank class; the medium for senior officers, while the narrow stripes identified individual ranks. The generals had a gold embroidered wreath above the stripes; combat personnel had a 'V' chevron above the stripes, while services personnel wore the stripes only.

The generals had red shoulder straps while those of the other officers, barring exceptions, were black. The officers of the General Staff wore shoulder straps with a red inner stripe, while the Engineer Officers had shoulder straps made of cherry red velvet; the other officers of Aviation Engineering wore cherry red straps made of felt.

Rectangular Insignia, similar to the shoulder straps but without the rounded ends, were used on flying overalls, for wearing on both forearms.

Qualification Badges

In Hungary there was a qualification badge only for Pilots. It was worn above the right breast pocket of the jacket, and was similar to the cap badge, embroidered in gold or silver for officers and warrant officers, and for N.C.O.s respectively.

Plate 80. Warrant Officers' and N.C.O.s' Rank Badges

The other ranks wore their rank insignia on the shoulder straps, or on the forearms of the flying overalls, in the same manner as the officers. The Aspirant and the Warrant Officer wore the same basic badge as illustrated but with gold or silver edging to the shoulder straps respectively.

The Sergeants wore silver stripes, silver edging and white metal buttons, while the rank and file wore a narrow white chevron and stripes without edging to the shoulder straps. Their buttons were made of bronze.

The winged propeller was worn by the latter on the collar of tunics and greatcoats.

Index

This is not a complete index but it is intended only as a cross reference between illustrations and description.

Book II
Naval and Marine Badges and Insignia

BOOK II
CONTENTS

Acknowledgments

I would like to thank:

Miss Ursula Stuart Mason, Head of Public Relations and Mr J. Mundy, Keeper of the Department of Weapons and Antiquities, of the National Maritime Museum; Mr Stan A. Statham, Lieutenant Hugh F. Wolfensohn, R.N. and Major A. G. Brown, M.B.E., R.M.

Captain 3rd Rank A. Goroziy, Assistant Naval Attaché at the Soviet Embassy in London and Mr M. Fateev, Head Keeper of the Naval War Museum at Leningrad.

Mrs Inga Fl. Rasmussen, Curator of the Tøjhusmuseet, Copenhagen.

Dr Freidrich Herrmann.

Mr Bernard Jamin.

Geom. Licio Granata.

Commander James H. Cromwell, J.A.G.C., U.S.N. and Y.N.I. W. J. Tilton, U.S.N., Public Affairs Officer of U.S.S., Holland.

Mr K. Barbarski and the Polish Institute and Sikorski Museum.

Captain H. Ringoir, Hon. Gunner of the R.N.A., Commander F.C. van Oosten, R.N.N.(Rtd), director of Naval History at the Historical Department of the Naval Staff.

Mr Markku Melkko, Director of the Sotamuseo, at Helsinki.

The Prince Consort Library, Aldershot.

My most sincere thanks to my wife Diana for her assistance.

Great Britain

The Royal Navy

The Royal Navy traces the origins of its power to Elizabethan times, when the period of great expansion started, as Britain could expand only across the seas. In later years, the Royal Navy, its organisation and uniforms set a pattern that was followed by other nations all over the world.

The first uniform regulations were issued by Lord Anson's Board of Admiralty in 1748 in order to set a distinction between naval and other officers, as well as from the need to lay down more precise rules of rank and predence among naval officers themselves.

The seamen were issued with simple garments, the cost of which was deducted from their wages; the navy bought these clothes from a slop seller and ship's commanders occasionally tried to improve the appearance of their own men. In 1757, the Navy Board set up its own Slop Office, which, in 1827, became a responsibility of the Victualling Board and, 5 years later, of the Controller of Victualling under the Admiralty.

Meanwhile, new orders and regulations continued to modify the officers' dress. Regulations published in 1825 sanctioned the use of a blue cloth cap and of a round jacket and, when coats were ordered to be worn buttoned up, the elaborate lapels were discarded. Pantaloons or trousers replaced the white breeches and, finally, blue trousers were adopted in 1856.

Distinction lace on the sleeves of flag officers was introduced in 1783 and was extended to the other officers in 1856, with the addition of the curl in the uppermost row of lace for officers of the executive branch only. Non-executive officers, i.e. of the 'civil' branches, wore different uniforms until 1890: rank stripes without curl but with the addition of coloured velvet, later cloth, in between the stripes from 1864. In January 1915, the use of the curl was extended to engineer officers and, in 1918, to the other branches.

In 1919, the flag officers' narrow stripe was reduced from $\frac{5}{8}$ in (15.9 mm) to $\frac{1}{2}$ in (12.7 mm) in width and the order stated that the modification had obtained the King's approval, but in fact His Majesty had not been consulted at all. He, therefore, ignored the new rule and members of the Royal Family have continued to wear the old stripes on naval uniform to the present day. The $\frac{1}{2}$ in (12.7 mm) gold lace stripe was replaced by a larger stripe, $\frac{9}{16}$ in (14 mm) in width, in 1931.

The officers' uniform regulations were first published in book form, with plates of illustrations, on 1 January 1825 and later editions were issued in 1879, 1891, 1924 and 1937.

Plate 1. Cap and Other Insignia

The officers' cap was made of navy blue cloth, fitted with peak, chin strap and a black mohair band $1\frac{3}{4}$ in (44.5 mm) in width.

The cap badge consisted of a wreath of gold laurel leaves surrounding a silver foul anchor with the Royal Crown above embroidered in gold and silver; the whole anchor could be either embroidered in silver or partly made of silver metal.

This badge was adopted in 1856 in two versions: as above, embroidered in gold and silver for executive officers or in gold for officers of the civil branches. From about 1870 to 1891 the cap badge was usually embellished by a gold ring around the anchor; earlier badges were considerably smaller than those prescribed in the 1937 Uniform Regulations, which were $2\frac{9}{16}$ in (65 mm) high by $3\frac{5}{16}$ in (85 mm) broad.

By the end of World War 1 all naval officers wore the same type of cap badge but later, in 1940, the chaplains obtained a new badge with the crown and anchor in gold and silver as usual and the laurel wreath embroidered in black silk, veined with gold wire. A khaki cap with a bronze badge could be worn with khaki uniform when exposed to enemy fire.

The chin strap was made of black patent calf leather, the peak of the cap of senior ranks entitled to embroidery was covered with blue cloth and bound with leather and that of all the other officers was made of plain black leather.

The embroidery for flag officers and the Commodore 1st Class depicted gold oak leaves in two rows, each $\frac{3}{4}$ in (19 mm) wide, while the Commodore 2nd Class, Captain and Commander had only one row of gold oak leaves embroidered along the front edge of the peak.

The embroidery was introduced in the mid-nineteenth century, originally in the form of a gold stripe, which became oak leaves, for executive officers only, in 1860. The use of oak leaves was extended to engineer officers in 1915 and to all branches in 1918.

The Admiral of the Fleet, Vice-Admiral and Rear-Admiral of the United Kingdom, Aide-de-Camp to the King, Honorary Physician and Surgeon to the King and Naval Equerries to the King or to members of the Royal Family wore the Royal Cypher in dull silver on the plaited shoulder cords of the aiguillette, on the epaulettes, or on the shoulder straps. The officers of flag rank had the cypher below the crown, the others had it superimposed upon the lowest row of gold lace, the bottom of the cypher being even with the lower edge of the stripe.

The Personal Aide-de-Camp to the King wore a special cypher with block letters, each $\frac{11}{16}$ in (17.5 mm) in height. In the case of both devices, when more than one Royal Cypher was worn, the actual cyphers were smaller as, in specific cases, an officer who had held an appointment under more than

CAP AND OTHER INSIGNIA

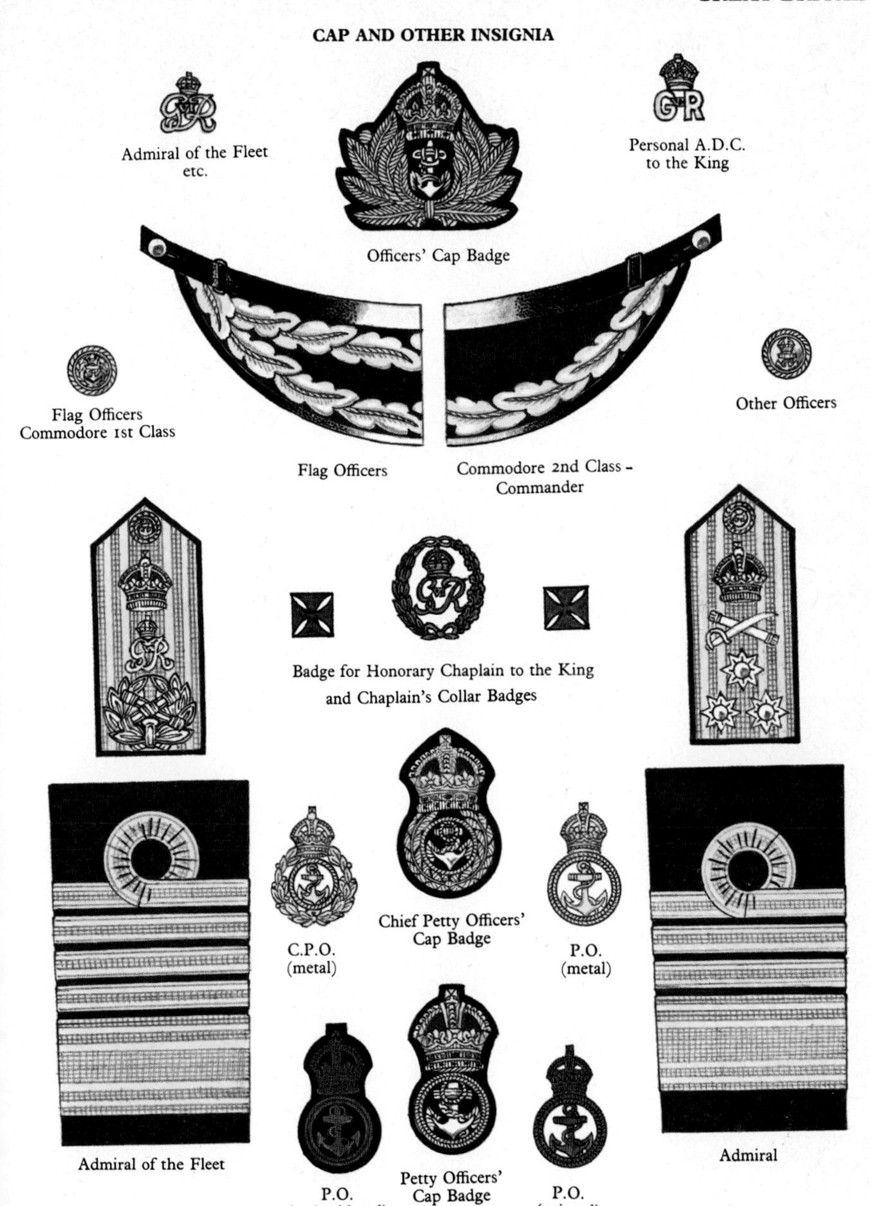

Admiral of the Fleet etc.

Officers' Cap Badge

Personal A.D.C. to the King

Flag Officers Commodore 1st Class

Other Officers

Flag Officers

Commodore 2nd Class - Commander

Badge for Honorary Chaplain to the King and Chaplain's Collar Badges

C.P.O. (metal)

Chief Petty Officers' Cap Badge

P.O. (metal)

Admiral of the Fleet

Admiral

P.O. (embroidered)

Petty Officers' Cap Badge

P.O. (painted)

GREAT BRITAIN

R.N. OFFICERS' RANK INSIGNIA

Vice-Admiral

Rear-Admiral

Commodore
1st Class

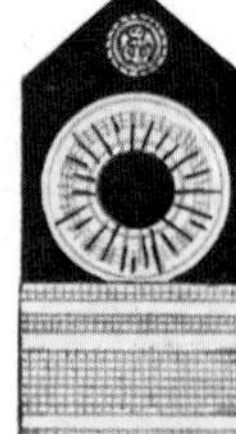
Commodore
2nd Class

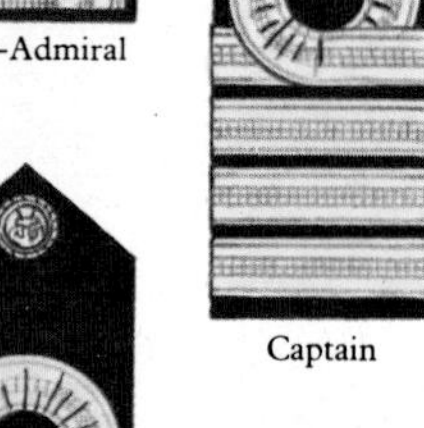
Captain

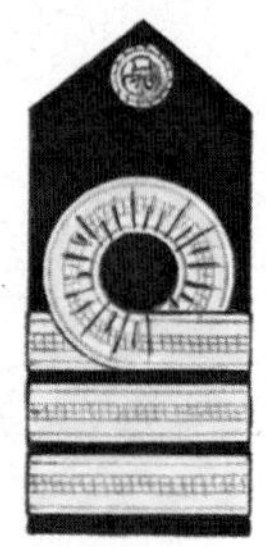
Commander

Lieutenant-Commander

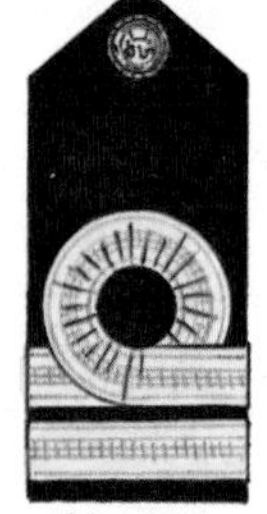
Lieutenant

Naval Cadet

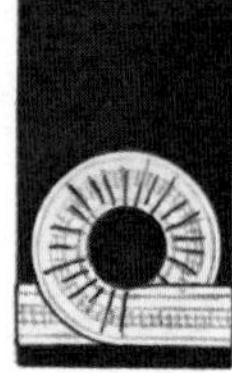
Sub-Lieutenant

Warrant Officer

Midshipman

Paymaster
Commander

Engineer
Vice-Admiral

Doctor
Commodore 1st Class

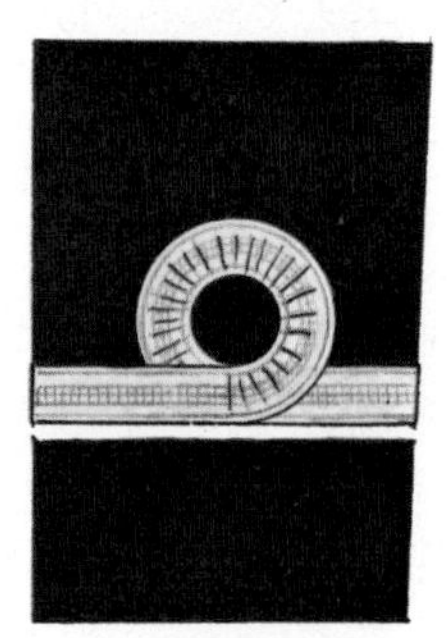
Paymaster
Sub-Lieutenant

R.N.R. OFFICERS' RANK INSIGNIA

Lieutenant-Commander

Commodore
2nd Class

Captain

Sub-Lieutenant

Commander

Lieutenant-Commander

Lieutenant

Sub-Lieutenant

Skipper

Paymaster
Lieutenant-Commander

Paymaster
Lieutenant-Commander

Paymaster
Lieutenant

Paymaster
Lieutenant

Midshipman

R.N.R. Cadet

PLATE 3

R.N.V.R. OFFICERS' RANK INSIGNIA

Lieutenant-Commander

Commodore 2nd Class

Captain

Sub-Lieutenant

Commander

Lieutenant-Commander

Lieutenant

Sub-Lieutenant

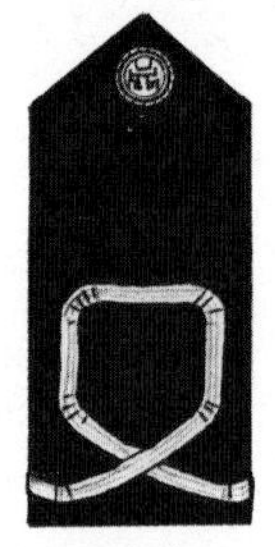
Skipper

Paymaster Lieutenant-Commander

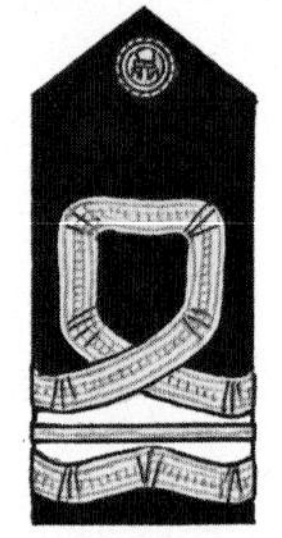
Paymaster Lieutenant-Commander

Paymaster Lieutenant

Paymaster Lieutenant

Midshipman

R.N.V.R. Cadet

R.N. BRANCH OFFICERS' RANK INSIGNIA

Air Branch Pilot

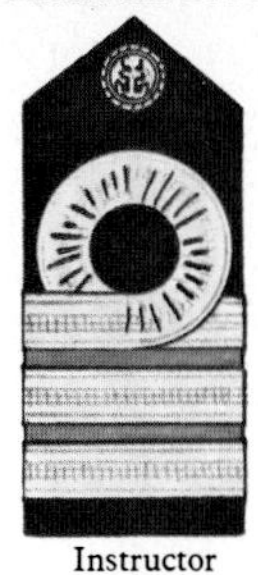
Instructor Commander

Commissioned Electrician

Air Branch Lieutenant

Observer

Air Branch Officers 1938

WOMEN'S ROYAL NAVAL SERVICE

Officers' Cap Badge

Director

Chief Officer

1st Officer

Medical Superintendent

Deputy Director

2nd Officer

Superintendent

Chief Petty Officer

Petty Officer

3rd Officer

PLATE 5

GREAT BRITAIN

PETTY OFFICERS' AND NON-SUBSTANTIVE BADGES

Visual Signalman
1st Class

Stoker P.O.

Chief Petty Officer

Air Mechanic
Ordnance

Leading Torpedoman
(Low Power)

Regulating P.O.

Petty Officer

Leading Seaman

Wireman

Seaman Gunner
Defensively Equipped Merchant
Ships

Armourer's Mate

Chief Shipwright

Torpedo Coxwain
Coastal Force Coxwain

Torpedo Gunner's
Mate

Rangetaker 1st Class

Director Layer 1st Class
Gunlayer 1st Class

Stoker
Fire Fighter

NON-SUBSTANTIVE BADGES

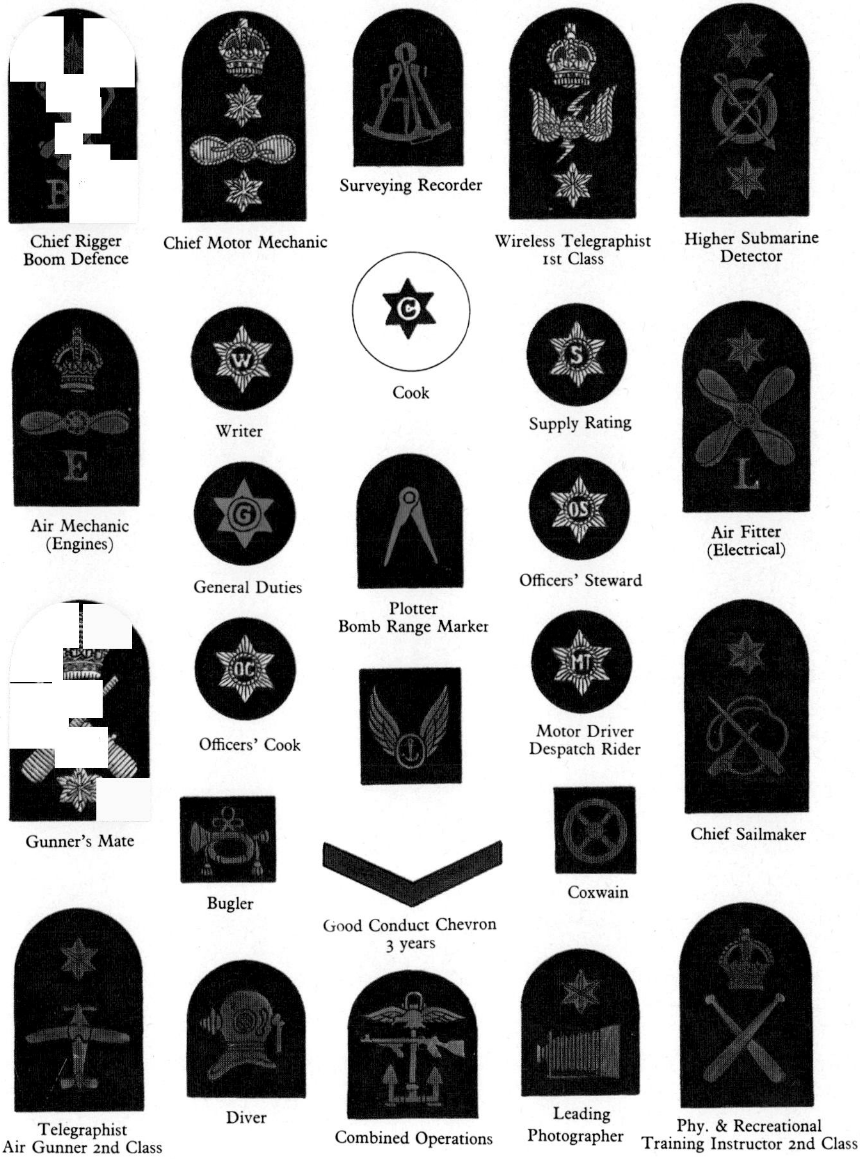

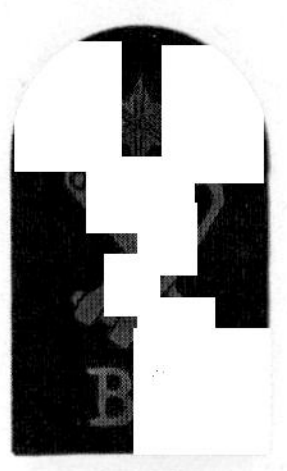

Chief Rigger
Boom Defence

Chief Motor Mechanic

Surveying Recorder

Wireless Telegraphist
1st Class

Higher Submarine
Detector

Cook

Air Mechanic
(Engines)

Writer

Supply Rating

Air Fitter
(Electrical)

General Duties

Plotter
Bomb Range Marker

Officers' Steward

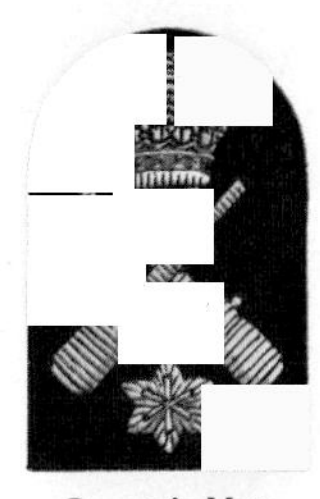

Gunner's Mate

Officers' Cook

Motor Driver
Despatch Rider

Chief Sailmaker

Bugler

Good Conduct Chevron
3 years

Coxwain

Telegraphist
Air Gunner 2nd Class

Diver

Combined Operations

Leading
Photographer

Phy. & Recreational
Training Instructor 2nd Class

PLATE 7

GREAT BRITAIN

NON-SUBSTANTIVE BADGES

Sick Berth Rating

Signalman

Bomb Disposal

Sharpshooter

Master-at-Arms

CAP TALLIES

H.M.S. GLORIOUS.

H.M.S. COSSACK.

H.M.S. EFFINGHAM.

H.M.S. NEPTUNE.

H.M.S. VICTORY.

H.M.S.

Royal Navy

Royal Navy
Youth Entries

S.A

South African Naval Forces

H.M.C.S.

Royal Canadian Navy

H.M.A.S.

Royal Australian Navy

H.M.N.Z.S.

Royal New Zealand Navy

H.M.I.S.

Royal Indian Navy

MERCHANT NAVY – ROYAL NATIONAL LIFEBOAT INSTITUTION

Chief Officer
(Certified)

Merchant Navy

Officers'
Cap Badge

Royal Naval
Patrol Service

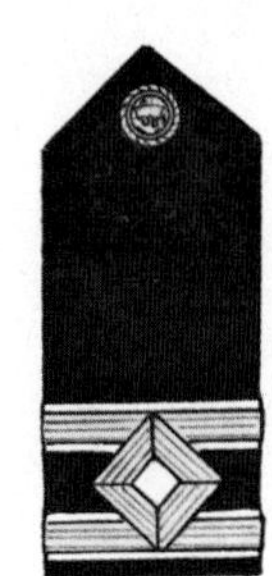

2nd Officer
(Certified)
Purser

Coxwain
Royal National
Lifeboat Institution

Captain
(Certified Master)

Senior Surgeon

Other Ratings
Royal National
Lifeboat Institution

H.M. COASTGUARD

Chief Inspector

Inspectors', Higher Grades'
and District Officers'
Cap Badge

Station Officers

District Officers and Higher Grades

H.M.C.G. Other Ratings

Station Officers and Coastguardsmen

BADGES OF THE ROYAL MARINES

PLATE 10

BADGES OF THE ROYAL MARINES

R.M. Division
116th R.M. Bde

34th Amphibian
Support Regt

117th R.M. Bde

R.M. Engineers

104th R.M. Trng Bde
R.M. Trng Group

R.M. Shoulder Title

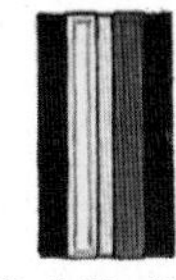
Bush Hat Flash
Far East 1944-45

R.M. Beach Commando

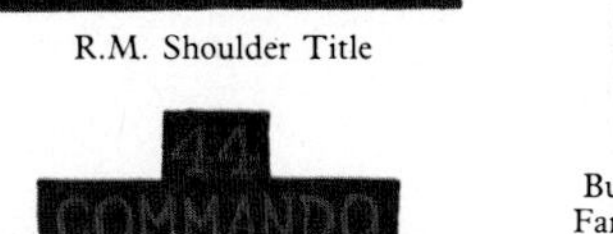

44 R.M. Commando – embroidered

R.N. Personnel Attached
to R.M. Commandos

41 42

R.M. Siege Regiment

7th R.M. Bn
Shoulder Title
1943

44

40
ROYAL MARINES
COMMANDO

40–48 R.M. Commando – woven

30th Assault Unit

CAP AND RANK INSIGNIA

U.S.S.R.

Flag Officers

Officers' Cap Badges
Line Services

Other Officers

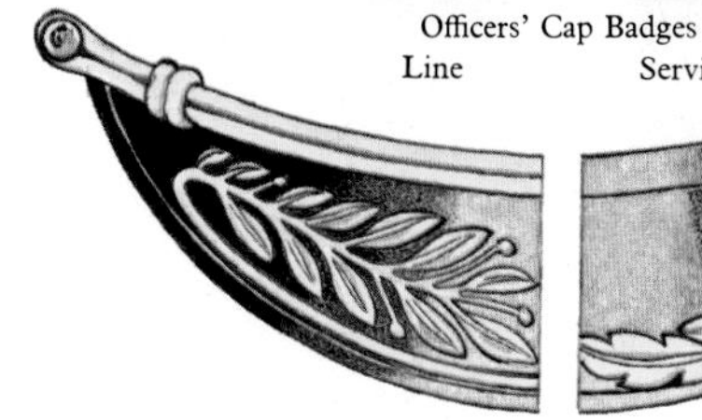

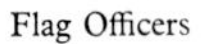

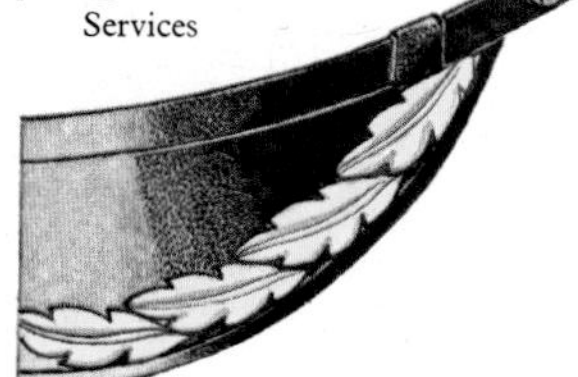
Flag Officers Captains

OFFICERS' RANK INSIGNIA

Admiral

Marshal of the Fleet of the Soviet Union (1955)

Captain 2nd Rank

Admiral of the Fleet

Admiral

Captain-Lieutenant

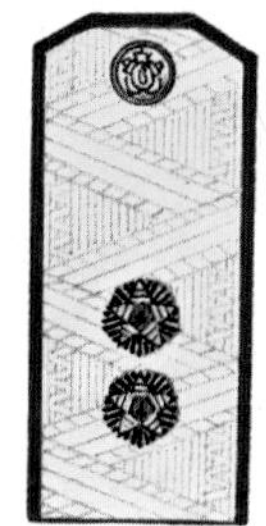
Vice-Admiral

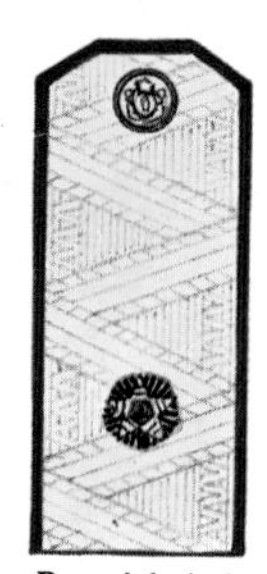
Rear-Admiral

Junior Lieutenant

Captain 1st Rank

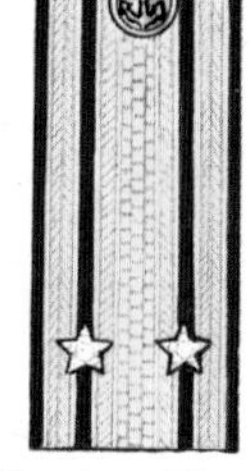
Captain 2nd Rank

Captain 3rd Rank

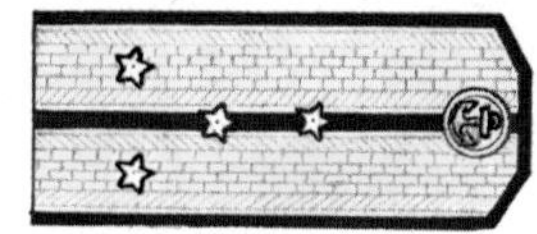
Captain-Lieutenant

Senior Lieutenant

OFFICERS' RANK INSIGNIA

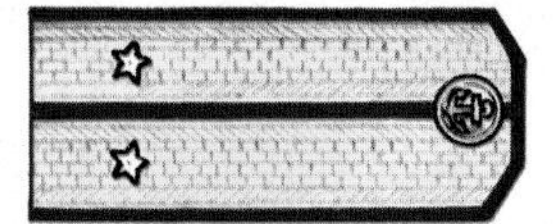
Lieutenant

Guards' Badge

Junior Lieutenant

Flag Officers
Naval Aviation

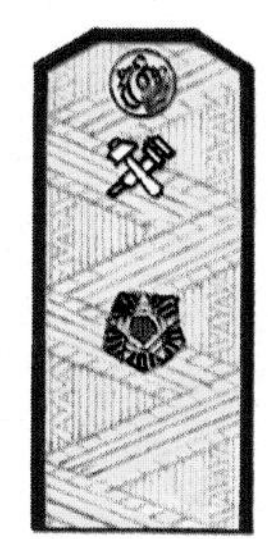
Rear-Admiral
Line Engineering

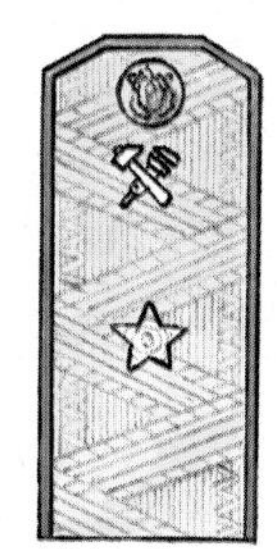
Major-General
Aviation Engineering

Senior Officers
Supply

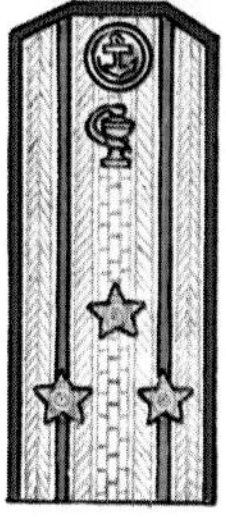
Colonel
Medical

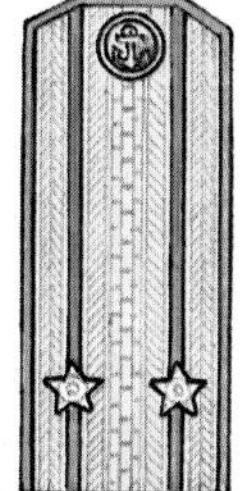
Lieutenant-Colonel
Naval Aviation

Major-General
Coast Defence

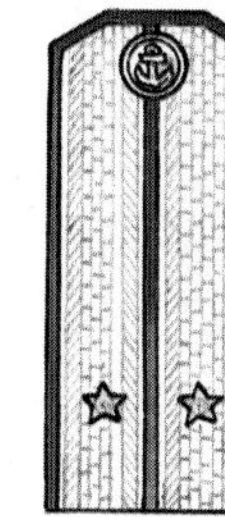
Lieutenant
Supply

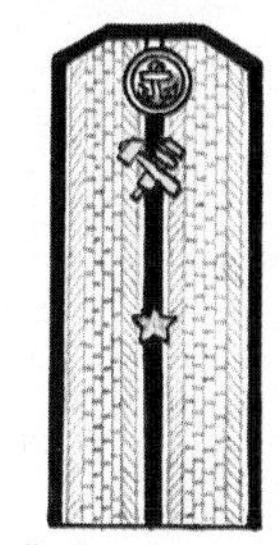
Junior Lieutenant
Naval Constructions

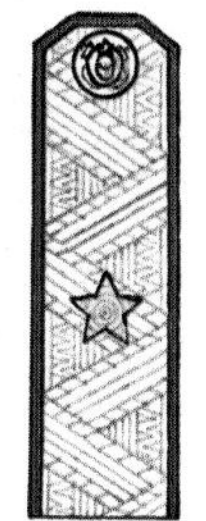
Major-General
Administration

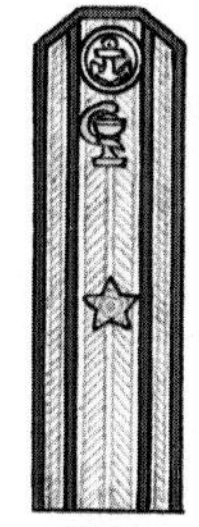
Major
Medical
(non-mil.trained)

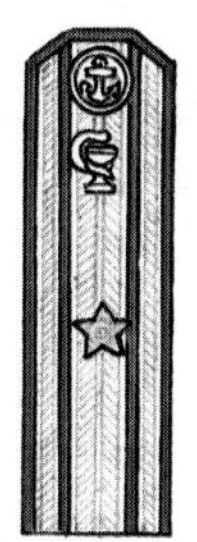
Major
Veterinary

Captain
Legal

CAP AND RATE INSIGNIA

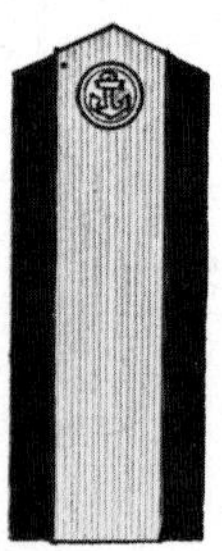

Midshipman

Chief Petty Officer

C.P.O.s'
Cap Badge

Petty Officer 1st Class
Baltic Fleet

Petty Officer 2nd Class
Black Sea Fleet

Leading Seaman
Caspian Sea Flotilla

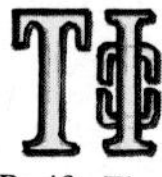

Pacific Fleet

Arctic Fleet

Amur River Flotilla

Volga River Flotilla

Lake Onega Flotilla

Advanced Engineering
School

Anti-Aircraft School

Coast Artillery
School

ИУ

Naval Political
Institute

Л

Lavanevski Naval
Aviation School

Junior Apprentice

Molotov Aviation
Engineering School

С

Stalin Naval
Aviation School

КРАСНЫИ КАВКАЗ

Cap Tally

Marines

Belt Buckle

O.R.s' Cap Badge

OFFICERS' CAP AND RANK INSIGNIA

Flag Officers

Senior Officers

Junior Officers

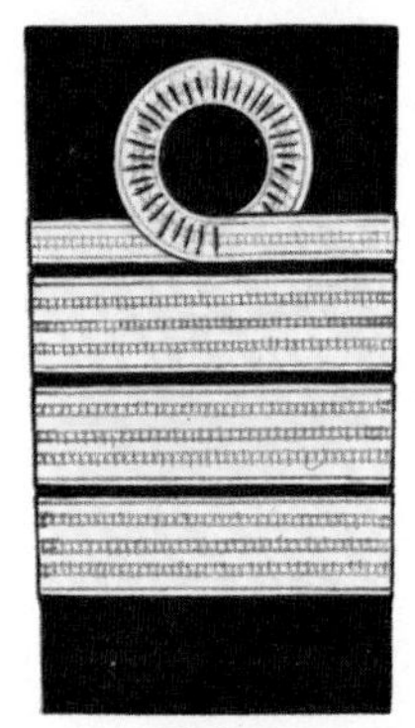
Admiral

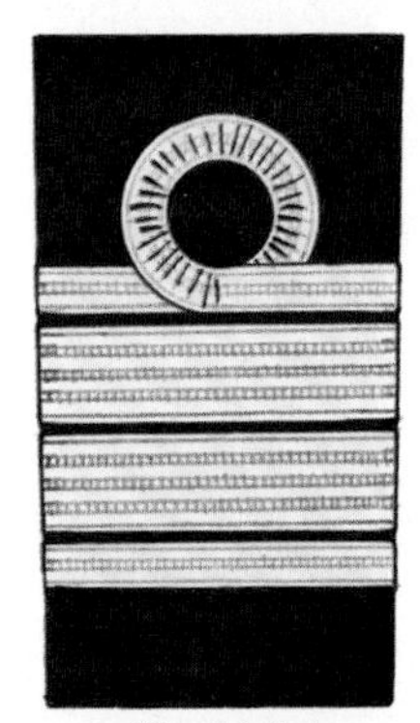
Vice-Admiral

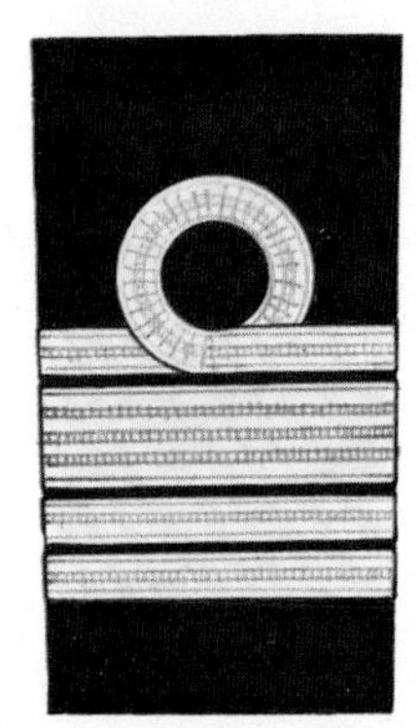
Rear-Admiral

Kommandør

Kommandørkaptajn

Orlogskaptajn

Reserve

Aviation

Coast Artillery

DENMARK

OFFICERS' RANK INSIGNIA

Kaptajnløjtnant

Soløjtnant af 1' Gr.

Soløjtnant af 2' Gr.

Naval Engineer
3rd Grade

Supply Intendant
2nd Grade

Reserve Doctor
Over 3 years Service

MIDSHIPMEN'S, CADETS' AND CHIEF PETTY OFFICERS' INSIGNIA

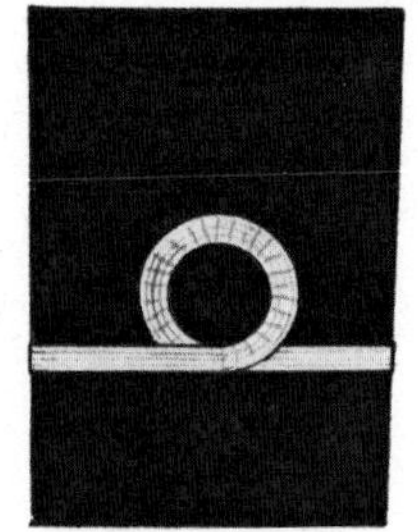
Midshipmen – Cadets
'A' Class

Reserve

Cap Badge

Coast Artillery

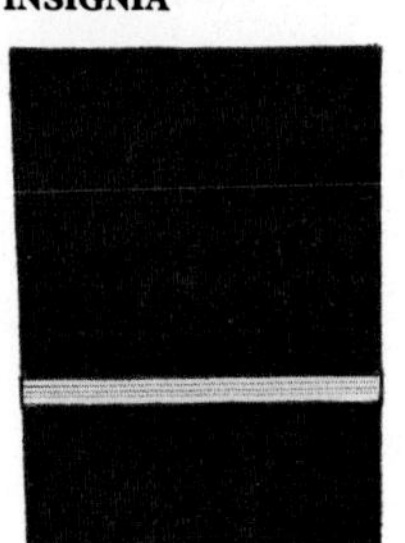
Midshipmen – Cadets
Ordinary

Medical

Engineers

Supply

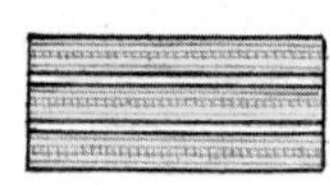
C.P.O. 1st Grade

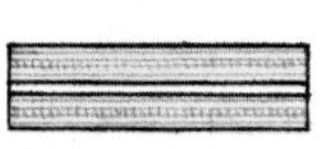
C.P.O. 2nd Grade

C.P.O. 3rd Grade

PETTY OFFICERS' AND SEAMEN'S INSIGNIA

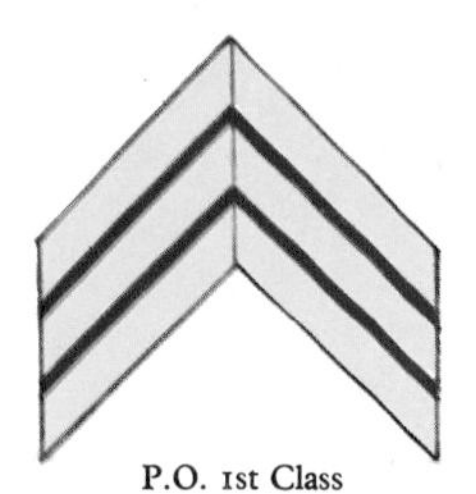
P.O. 1st Class

Petty Officers' Cap Badge

P.O. 2nd Class

TRADE BADGES

Apprentice Seaman

Cook – Storekeeper

Carpenter

Torpedo Mechanic

Signaller

Machinist – Stoker

Supplyman

Telegraphist

Sick Berth Orderly

Mechanic

Gunner

Mineman

Gunner Mechanic

Mine Mechanic

Torpedoman

Expert Rifleman

Expert Signaller

Seaman

Expert Gunner

Expert with Pistol

KGL. MARINE

Cap Tally

GERMANY

CAP AND RANK INSIGNIA

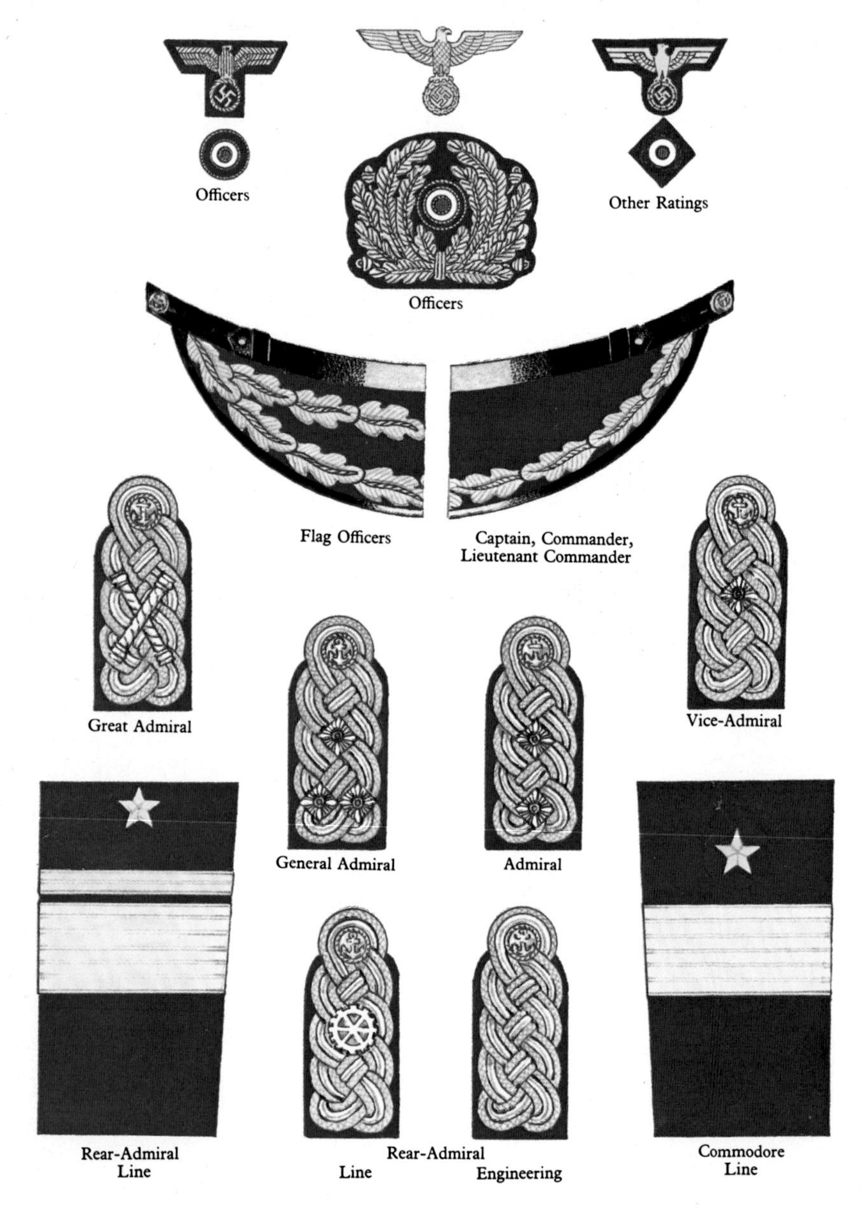

PLATE 18

OFFICERS' RANK INSIGNIA

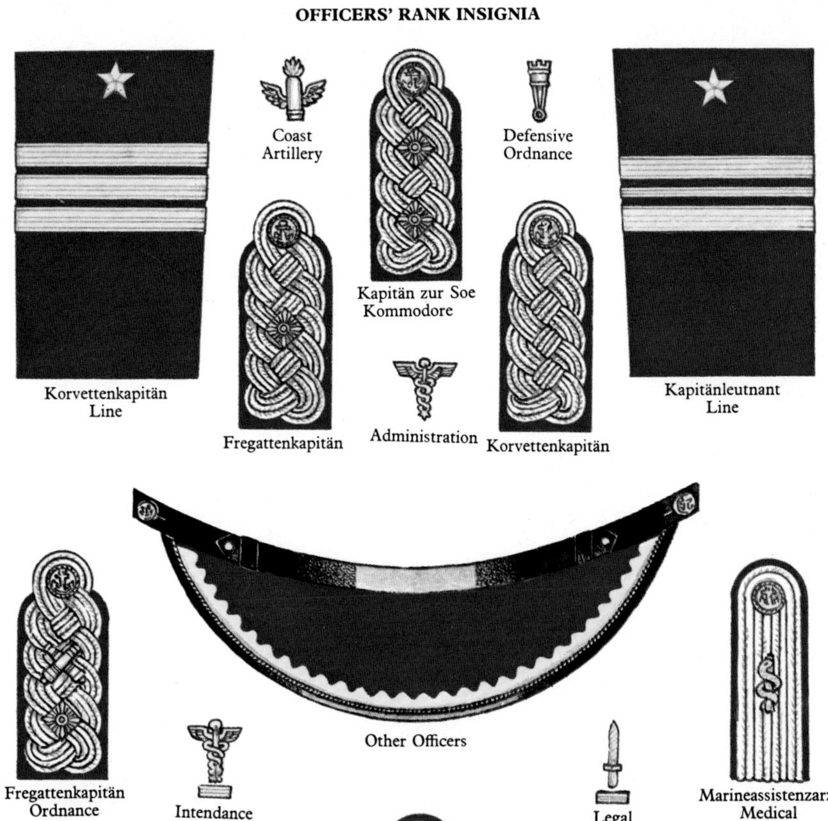

Korvettenkapitän Line

Coast Artillery

Kapitän zur Soe Kommodore

Defensive Ordnance

Kapitänleutnant Line

Fregattenkapitän

Administration

Korvettenkapitän

Other Officers

Fregattenkapitän Ordnance

Intendance

Legal

Marineassistenzarzt Medical

Leutnant Technical Communications

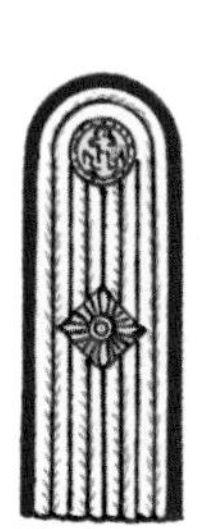

Oberleutnant zur See

Kapitänleutnant

Torpedo Technician

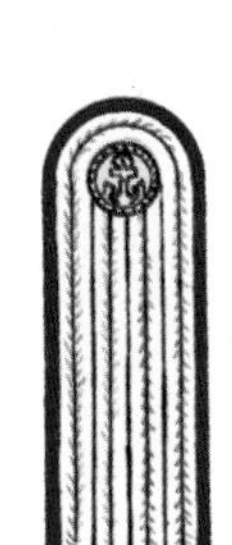

Leutnant zur See

Leutnant Communications Reserve

GERMANY

BREAST INSIGNIA

Embroidered in gold

Woven in gold silk

Embroidered in yellow cotton

Metal

CHAPLAINS' BADGES

Cap and Collar Badges

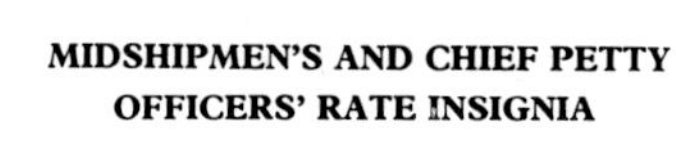

MIDSHIPMEN'S AND CHIEF PETTY OFFICERS' RATE INSIGNIA

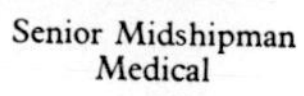

Senior Midshipman
Medical

Gunnery
Artificer

Defence
Ordnance

Gunnery

Midshipman
Line

Stabsoberbootsmann
Line

Stabsmaschinist
Engine Room

Stabssteuermann
Boatswain Branch

Schreiberfeldwebel
Clerical Dept

PETTY OFFICERS' BADGES

Senior P.O. Line

P.O. Line

Signalman

Teleprinter

Radio Telegraphist

Writer

Carpenter

Aircraft Spotter

Driver

Gunner

Sick Berth Orderly

Torpedo Artificer

Boatswain

Gunnery Engineer

Defensive Ordnance Artificer

Gunnery Artificer

Engine Room Specialist

Hydrographer

Administrative Clerk

Bandsman

Candidate Officer Line

COLLAR PATCHES

Petty Officers

Seaman

Kriegsmarine

Cap Tally

GERMANY

DEPARTMENTAL BADGES

Line

Signals

Teleprinter

Radio Telegraph

Clerical

Carpentry

Aircraft Spotting

Motor Transport

Gunnery

Sick Berth

Torpedo Artificer

Gunnery Engineers

Defensive Ordnance

Gunnery Artificers

Engine Room Specialists

Administration

Band

Admirals' Staff

Hydrographer

Seaman 1st Class
8 years' Service

Seaman 1st Class
6 years' Service

Seaman 1st Class
$4\frac{1}{2}$ years' Service

SEAMEN'S RATE BADGES

Seaman 1st Class

Seaman 2nd Class
Awaiting promotion to P.O.

Seaman 2nd Class
Taking P.O. Training

Seaman 2nd Class

WAR AWARDS AND CLASPS

Destroyers

Minesweepers, Anti-Sub. and Escort Vessels

Submarines

Coast Artillery

Auxiliary Cruisers

High-Sea Fleet

Submarine Combat Clasp Bronze

Blockade Runners

Submarine Combat Clasp Silver

Speed Boats

Naval Combat Clasp

Small Fighting Means 7th Class

Small Fighting Means 4th Class

Small Fighting Means 6th Class

Small Fighting Means 5th Class

Small Fighting Means 3rd Class

Small Fighting Means 1st Class

Small Fighting Means 2nd Class

CADETS' BADGES

Line

Engineers

Ordnance

Officials

Medical

Defensive Ordnance

Administration

TRADE BADGES

A.A. Gun Leader (Automatic)

Gun Leader 'E' (Single Gun)

Gun Leader 'T' (Turret) 3 years' Seniority

Gun Leader 'E' 6 years' Seniority

A.A. Gunner (Automatic)

A.A. Gun Leader

Artillery Specialist

Anti-Aircraft Specialist

Coast Artillery Specialist

Coast Artillery Gun Leader

Torpedo Master

1st Class

Torpedo Specialist 2nd Class

3rd Class

Torpedo Assistant Leader

Range Taker

A.A. Range Taker

Mines Specialist

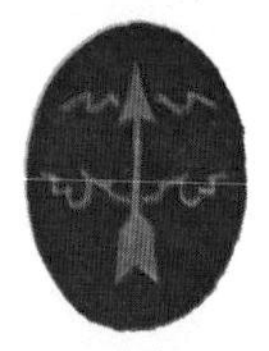
A.A. Listener

Searchlights Specialist Leader

Ship Diver

Torpedo Diver

Surveyor

Motor Engineer 3rd Course

Motor Engineer 2nd Course

TRADE BADGES

Underwater Detector Specialist

Electrician 3rd Course

Electrician 2nd Course

Electrician 1st Course

Drummer – Piper

Underwater Detector Course

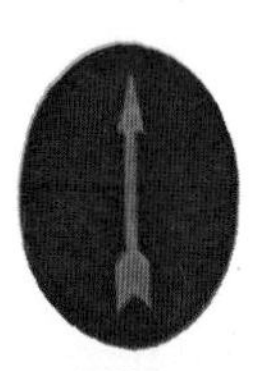
A.A. Detector Listener

P.T. Instructor

Gunnery Leader Coast Artillery

Drummer – Piper

BANDMASTERS

Music Master 1st type

Senior Music Superintendent

Music Superintendent

Music Master 2nd type

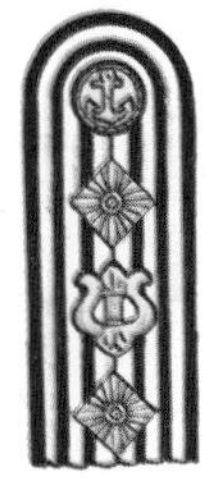
Staff Music Master

Senior Music Master

Music Master

BADGES FOR FIELD GREY UNIFORM

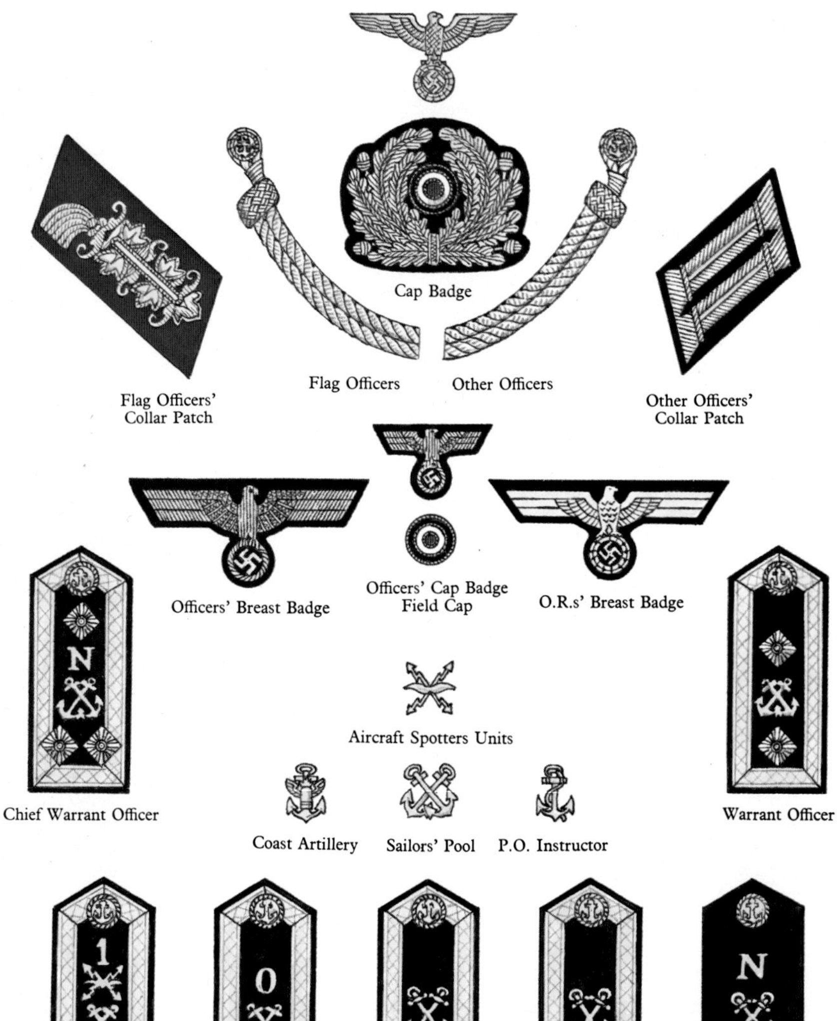

Cap Badge

Flag Officers — Other Officers

Flag Officers' Collar Patch — Other Officers' Collar Patch

Officers' Breast Badge — Officers' Cap Badge Field Cap — O.R.s' Breast Badge

Aircraft Spotters Units

Chief Warrant Officer — Coast Artillery — Sailors' Pool — P.O. Instructor — Warrant Officer

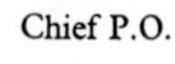

Chief P.O. — P.O. 1st Class — P.O. 2nd Class — P.O. 3rd Class — P.O. Aspirant

PLATE 26

OFFICIALS' INSIGNIA

Cap and Breast Insignia

Administrative Branch

Technical Branch

Sea Service Branch

Administrative Branch

Legal Branch

Technical Branch

Engine Room Technicians

Laboratory Branch

Pharmacy Branch

Dentistry Branch

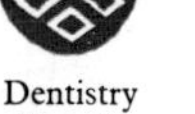

Instructors Branch

Warrant Officer Technician

Legal Branch

C.P.O. Administration

FRANCE

FLAG OFFICERS' CAP AND RANK INSIGNIA

Flag Officers

Other Officers

Admiral of the Fleet, Admiral and Vice-Admiral of Squadron

Rear-Admiral

Shoulder Tabs

Flag Officers

Admiral of the Fleet

Admiral
Vice-Admiral of Squadron

Shoulder Tabs

Senior Officers

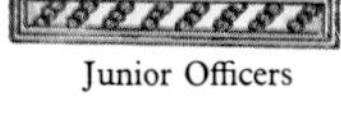

Junior Officers

Midshipman

Vice-Admiral

Rear-Admiral

Admiral
Vice-Admiral of Squadron

Flag Officers of Corps
Cap Badge

Rear-Admiral

OFFICERS' CAP AND RANK INSIGNIA

Capitaine de Vaisseau

Capitaine de Vaisseau

Capitaine de Frégate

Capitaine de Corvette

Capitaine de Corvette

Lieutenant de Vaisseau

Enseigne de Vaisseau
de 1ère Classe

Officers' Cap Badge

Enseigne de Vaisseau
de 2ème Classe

Commissaire de 1ère Classe

Officier de 2ème Classe – Équipage de la Flotte

FRANCE

CAP AND RATE INSIGNIA

PLATE 30

CAP, RATE AND SPECIALITY (ON COLLAR) INSIGNIA

Second Petty Officer Bugler

Fleet Pilot

Ratings' Cap Badge

Inspector and Auxiliary Guard

Bugler

Coast Signalman

Seaman Cap and Collar Badge

Fireman

Coast Signalman

Harbour Services

Pilot Chief of Section

Harbour Services

Fireman

Policeman

Policeman

Driver

Bandsman

SPECIALITY AND OTHER BADGES

P.T. Instructor

Aircraft Pilot

Airship Pilot

P.T. Instructor

Free French Navy

Ship's Badge

Aircraft Crew

Captive Balloon Observer

Free French Navy Seaman

SPECIALITY INSIGNIA (ON SLEEVES)

Ratings

Submarines

Submarines

Fusilier

Superior Certificate

Fusilier

Radio Telegraphist
General Service

A.A. Fusilier
Machine-Gunner
1st Class

A.A. Fusilier
Machine-Gunner

Fusilier Machine-Gunner
Quartermaster
Qualified Master Fusilier

Radio Telegraphist
Coastal

Facing Master

Facing Instructor

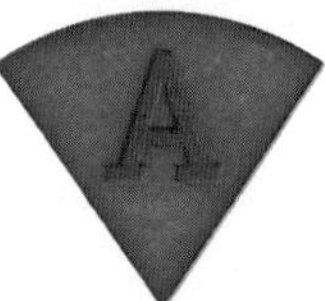

Driver

Recruited Bandsman

Auxiliary Fireman

Radio Signalman
Shore Service

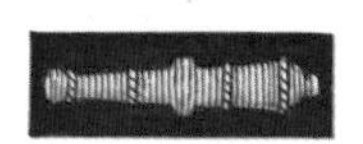

Gunlayer

Range Finder Operator

Aviation Personnel

Master Gunlayer

Gun Aimer

Aviation Radioman

Proficiency Stars for Layer and Aimer

F.N.F.L.

Free French Navy Cap Tally

HEAD-DRESS INSIGNIA

Port Captaincy

Great Admiral

Naval Ordnance

Admiral of Army (Fleet)

Rear-Admiral

Major
Medical

Capitano di Corvetta
Pharmacy

Major
Naval Engineers

Captain
Mechanical Engineers

Tenente di Vascello
Line

Captain
Naval Ordnance

Lieutenant
Commissariat

1st, 2nd and 3rd Chief
Line

Lieutenant
Chaplains

PLATE 33

FLAG OFFICERS' RANK INSIGNIA

Great Admiral

Great Admiral

Admiral of Army
(Fleet)

Admiral of Army
(Fleet)

Admiral of Squad
in Command of Army

Rear-Admiral

Admiral of Squad

Admiral of Division

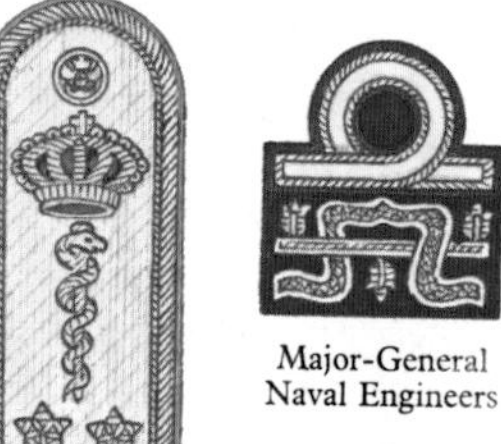

Major-General
Naval Engineers

Lieutenant-General
Naval Engineers Medical

Lieutenant-General
Port Captaincy Commissariat

Submarine Officer

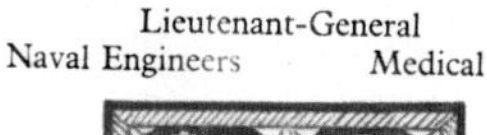

Line

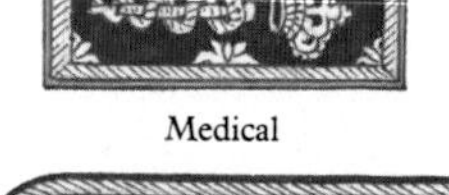

Medical

Admiral of Squad

Admiral of Division

Naval Engineers

Rear-Admiral

Commissariat

OFFICERS' RANK INSIGNIA

Capitano di Vascello

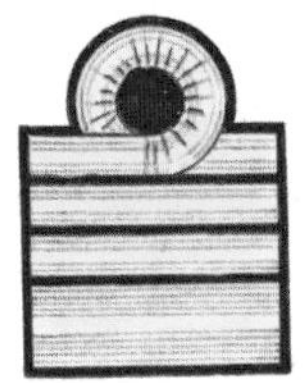

Capitano di Vascello

Capitano di Fregata

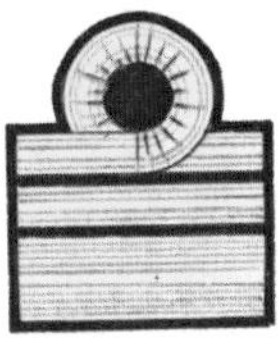

Capitano di Fregata

Capitano di Corvetta

Tenente di Vascello

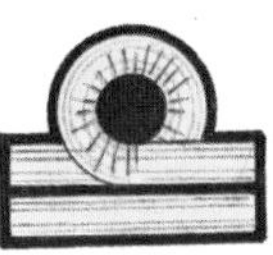

Sottotenente di Vascello

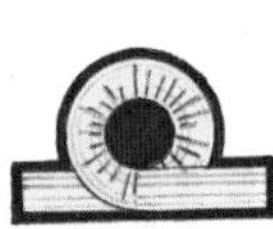

Guardiamarina

Senior Officers Line

Senior Officers Medical

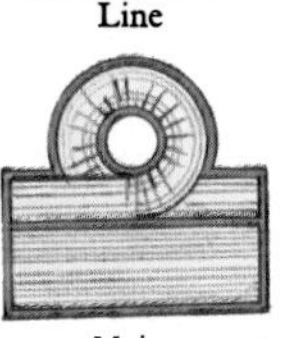

Major Medical

Capitano di Corvetta

1° Tenente di Vascello

Tenente di Vascello

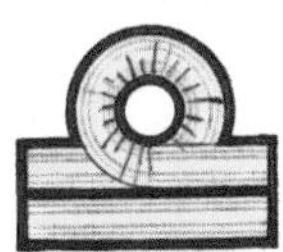

Lieutenant Naval Engineers

Junior Officers Line

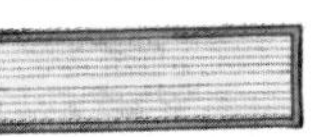

Junior Officers Medical

Mechanical Services

Technical Services

Accountancy Services

1° Sottotenente di Vascello

Sottotenente di Vascello

Guardiamarina

Directors of Music

ITALY

PETTY OFFICERS' RATE INSIGNIA AND TRADE BADGES

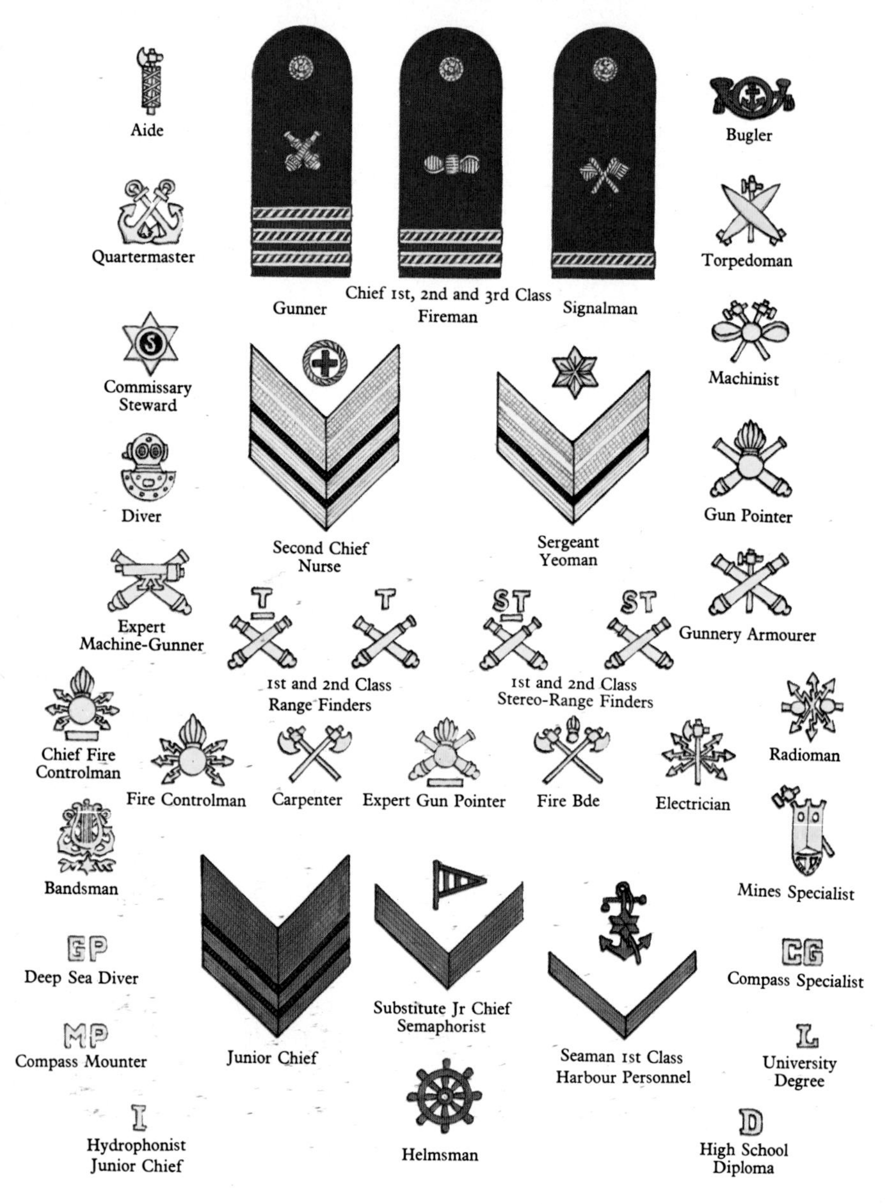

TRADE BADGES

Artificer Fireman Motors Specialist — Artificer Fireman Volunteer — Naval Motors Drafted — Artificer Fireman Volunteer — Engineering Drafted

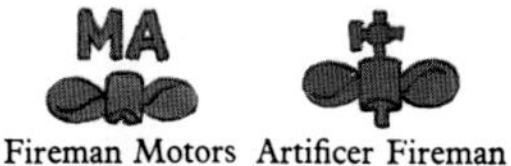

Submarine Personnel — Fireman Motors Specialist — Artificer Fireman — Fireman Engineer — Licensed Mounters

TS

Driver — Facing Instructor — School Title — P.T. Instructor — Volunteer

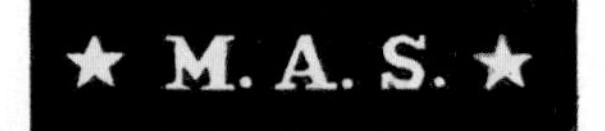

BADGES OF 'SAN MARCO' MARINES

O.R.s' Cap Badge

Sleeve Badge

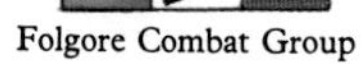

Folgore Combat Group

Officers' Collar Patch

O.R.s' Cuff Patch

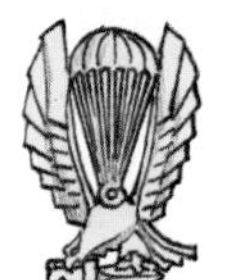
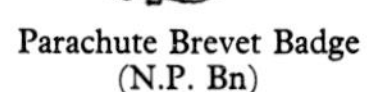

Parachute Brevet Badge (N.P. Bn)

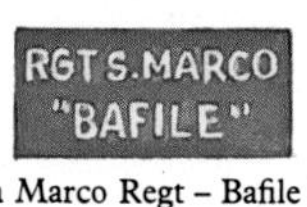

San Marco Regt – Bafile Bn

Officers' Collar Patch

NAVAL BADGES AND INSIGNIA OF THE ITALIAN SOCIAL REPUBLIC

Officers' Cap Badges

O.R.s' Cap Badge

Flag Officers

Admiral

Capitano di Corvetta

Sottotenente di Vascello

Anti-Submarine Group – La Spezia

Dredging Flotilla Venice

WAR NAVIGATION BADGES (2ND DEGREE)

Submarine Atlantic Base

Battle Ships

Cruisers

Torpedo Ships

Pilot Surface Assault Craft

Pilot Underwater Assault Craft

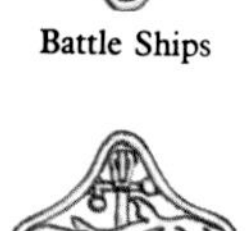

Submarines

Anti-Submarine Vessels

M.A.S.

Fulmine Bn

Assault Crafts

Auxiliary Ships

Hospital Ships

PLATE 38

NAVAL BADGES AND INSIGNIA OF THE ITALIAN SOCIAL REPUBLIC

Generals' Collar Badge

All Other Ranks' Collar Badge

Xth M.A.S. Infantry

San Marco – Military Police

Xth M.A.S. Infantry

San Marco

Training in Germany

San Marco – Artillery

Swimming Brevet

Lu po Bn

Barbarigo Bn

Adriatic Front

San Marco Reconnaissance

Para-Swimmers

Valanga Bn

Sagittario Bn

Xth M.A.S. Naval Assault

Artillery

Xth M.A.S. Infantry

Xth Flotilla M.A.S.

Xth Division M.A.S.

HEAD-DRESS INSIGNIA

Officers' Cap Badge (post-1941)

Officers' Cap Badge (pre-1941)

Officers' Cap Badge (embroidered)

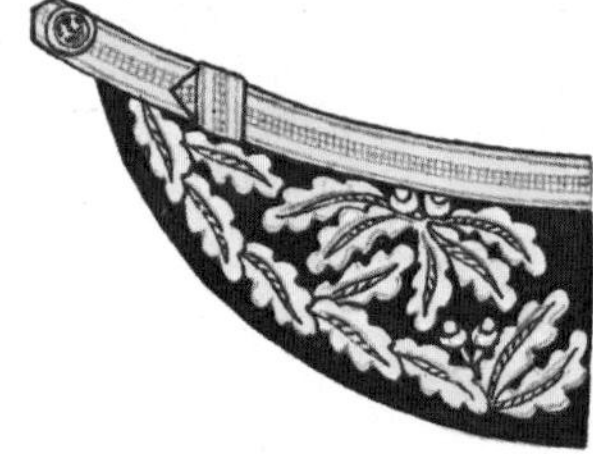

Flag Officers

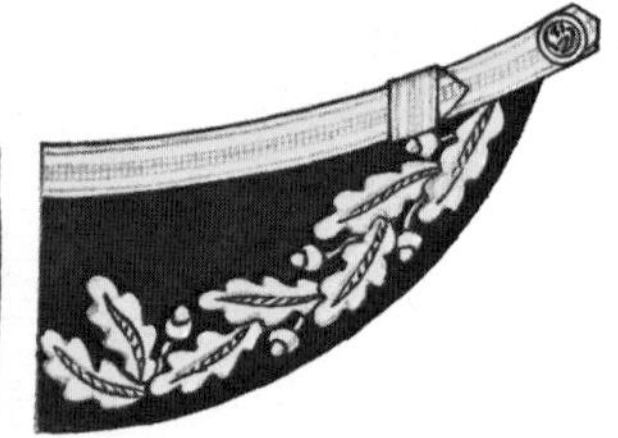

Captain and Commander

Officers' Garrison Cap

Nurse

Warrant Officers

U.S. Navy Aviators' Garrison Cap

Petty Officers

Midshipman

Warrant Officers' Pharmacist – Garrison Cap

Officers' Cap Badge U.S.C.G.

Officers' Cook and Steward

Officers' Steward

Surfman

Warrant Officers U.S.C.G.

Petty Officers U.S.C.G.

Cadet U.S.C.G.

Shore Establishment U.S.C.G.

OFFICERS' RANK AND CORPS INSIGNIA

Admiral of the Fleet

Admiral

Vice Admiral

Rear Admiral

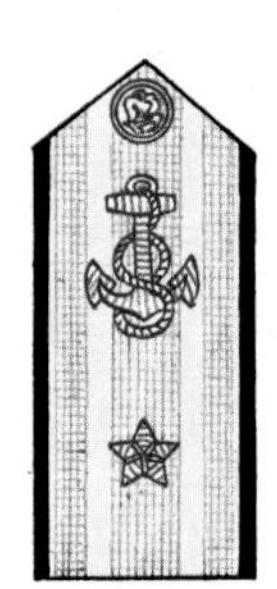
Commodore

Captain
Line

Chaplain
Jewish

Admiral
Line

Band

Lieutenant
Civil Engineering
Corps

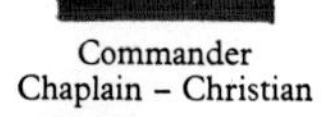
Commander
Chaplain – Christian

Hospital

Lieutenant Commander
Supply Corps

Lieutenant Commander
Dental Corps

Lieutenant (Junior Gr.)
Medical Corps

Ensign
Navy Nurse Corps

Ensign
U.S. Coast Guard

WARRANT OFFICERS' RANK AND CORPS INSIGNIA

Boatswain

Gunner

Carpenter

Ship's Clerk

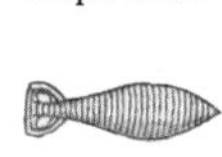
Torpedoman

Chief Warrant Officer
Aerographer

Warrant Officer
U.S.C.G. Pay Clerk

Radio Electrician

Machinist

Electrician

Photographer

Pharmacist

OFFICERS' MINIATURE RANK AND CORPS INSIGNIA

Admiral
of the Fleet

Admiral

Vice Admiral

Rear Admiral

Commodore

Captain

Commander

Lieutenant Commander

Lieutenant

Lieutenant
(Junior Grade)

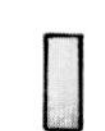
Ensign

Supply

Dental

Chaplain
Christian

Chaplain
Jewish

Medical

Civil Engineering

INSIGNIA FOR PETTY OFFICERS

Chief Petty Officer
Electrician's Mate
12 years with Good Conduct

Chief Petty Officer
Radioman
8 years

Chief Petty Officer
Turret Captain
4 years

Petty Officer 1st Class
Carpenter's Mate

Petty Officer 2nd Class
Signalman

Petty Officer 3rd Class
Quartermaster

CUFF MARKINGS

Construction
Battalions

Seaman/Fireman 1st Class

Minecraft
Personnel

Seaman/Fireman 2nd Class Apprentice Seaman/Fireman 3rd Class

CAP TALLIES

U.S. NAVY	U.S. COAST GUARD
U.S. Navy	U.S. Coast Guard

SPECIALITY MARKS

Aviation Pilot

Storekeeper

Boatswain's Mate, Coxwain

Chief Commissary Steward

Aviation Machinist's Mate

Torpedoman's Mate

Printer

Bugler

Parachute Rigger

Photographer's Mate

Aviation Metalsmith

Yeoman

Aviation Ordnanceman

Aviation Radioman

Aviation Electrician's Mate

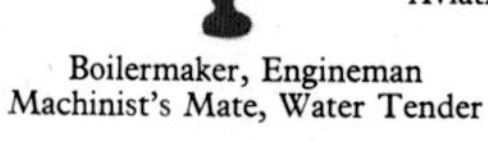
Boilermaker, Engineman
Machinist's Mate, Water Tender

Chief Officers' Steward or Cook

Motor Machinist's Mate

Aviation General Utility

Officers' Steward or Cook 1st Class

Officers' Steward or Cook 2nd Class

Aviation Carpenter's Mate

Radarman

Officers' Steward or Cook 3rd Class

Fire Controlman

Metalsmith, Molder
Shipfitter

Soundman

Musician

Gunner's Mate

Baker Cook

Hospital Apprentice
Pharmacist's Mate

Artificer

Aviation Aerographer's Mate

Mineman

Non-rigid Airship

DISTINGUISHING MARKS AND SPECIALIST RATINGS

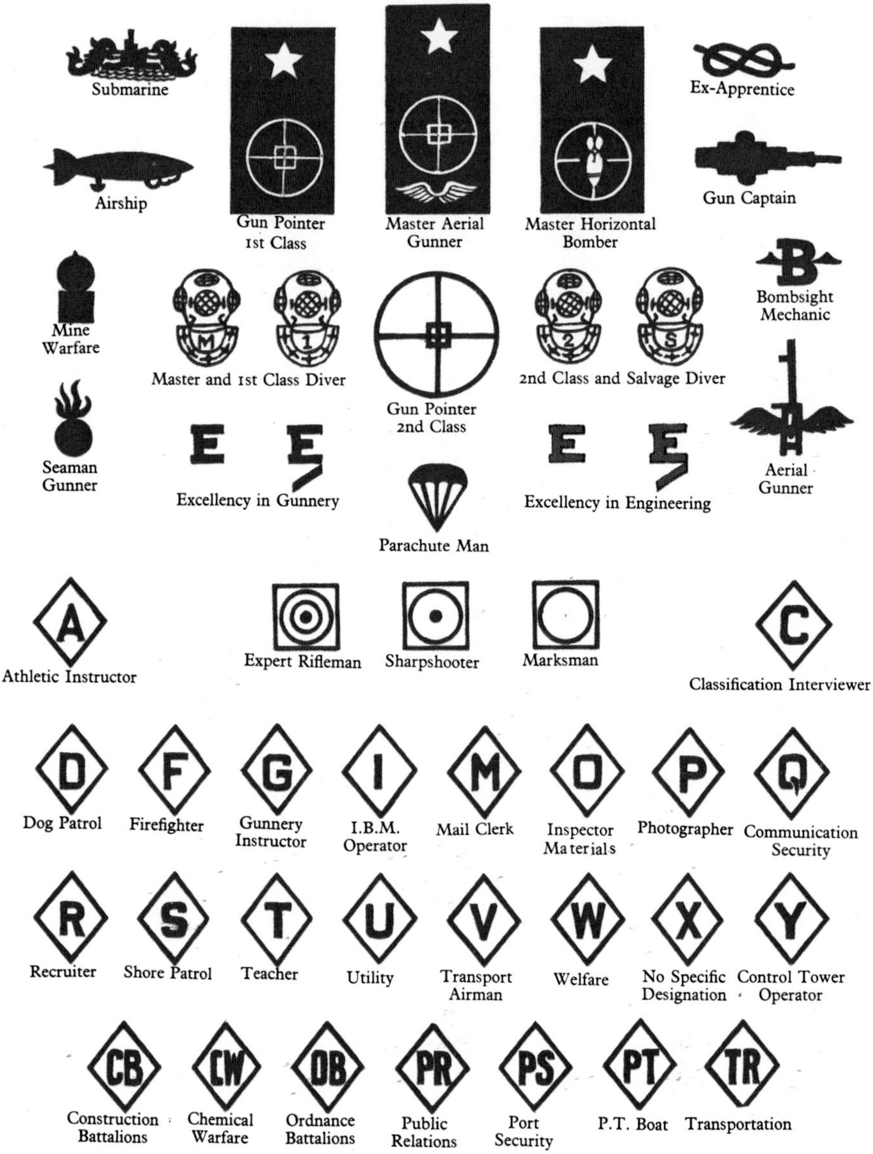

Submarine

Ex-Apprentice

Airship

Gun Captain

Gun Pointer 1st Class

Master Aerial Gunner

Master Horizontal Bomber

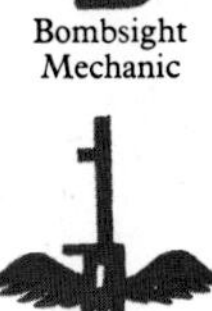

Bombsight Mechanic

Mine Warfare

Master and 1st Class Diver

2nd Class and Salvage Diver

Gun Pointer 2nd Class

Seaman Gunner

Excellency in Gunnery

Excellency in Engineering

Aerial Gunner

Parachute Man

Athletic Instructor

Expert Rifleman

Sharpshooter

Marksman

Classification Interviewer

Dog Patrol

Firefighter

Gunnery Instructor

I.B.M. Operator

Mail Clerk

Inspector Materials

Photographer

Communication Security

Recruiter

Shore Patrol

Teacher

Utility

Transport Airman

Welfare

No Specific Designation

Control Tower Operator

Construction Battalions

Chemical Warfare

Ordnance Battalions

Public Relations

Port Security

P.T. Boat

Transportation

PLATE 45

QUALIFICATION BADGES

Naval Aviator

Balloon Pilot

Aviation Observer

Submarine Officer

Submarine Surgeon

Submarine Combat Insignia

Flight Surgeon

Air Crew Member

Tactical Observer

Navigator

Radar Observer

MISCELLANEA

Shore Patrol

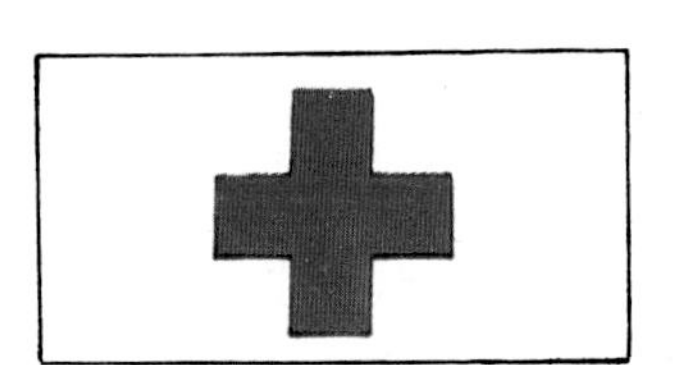
Geneva Cross

Amphibious Forces

Honorable Discharge

Seaman Guard

U.S.N. Officers

U.S.N. Enlisted Men

WAVES

U.S.N. Enlisted Men

U.S.M.C.

U.S.C.G.

U.S.M.C. HEAD-DRESS AND COLLAR, CORPS AND RANK INSIGNIA

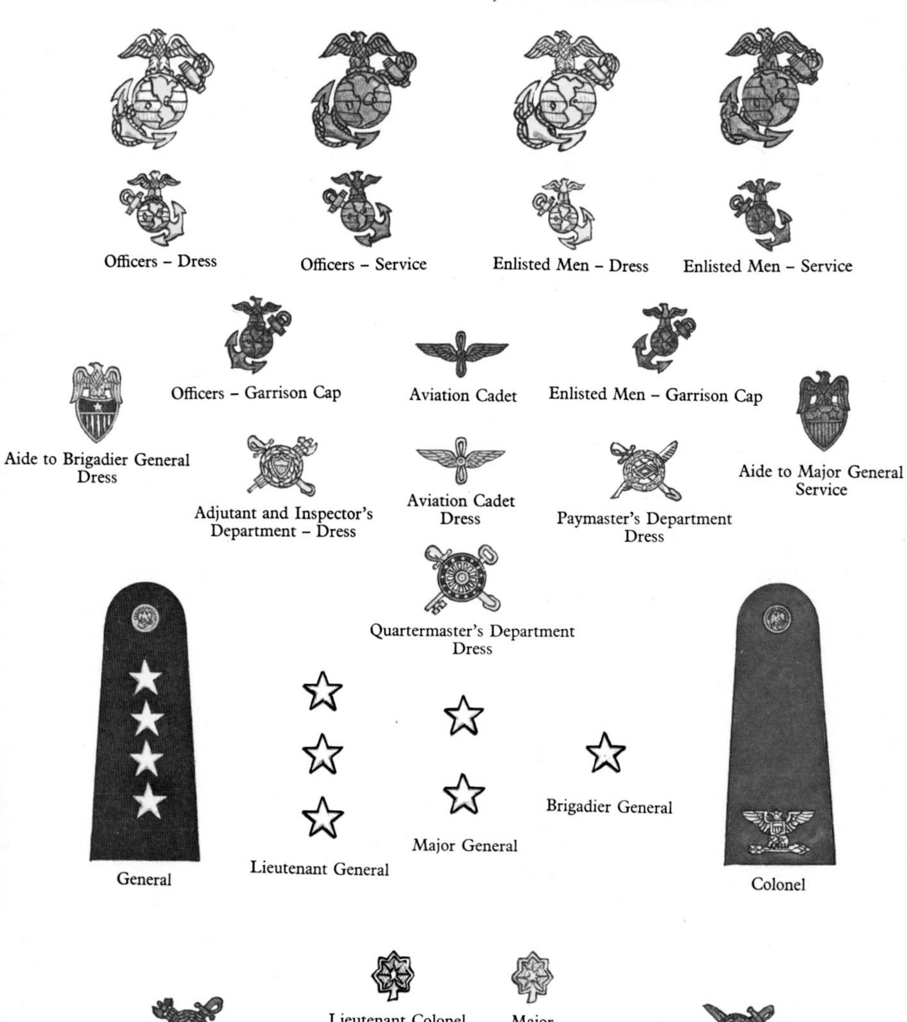

Officers – Dress

Officers – Service

Enlisted Men – Dress

Enlisted Men – Service

Officers – Garrison Cap

Aviation Cadet

Enlisted Men – Garrison Cap

Aide to Brigadier General Dress

Adjutant and Inspector's Department – Dress

Aviation Cadet Dress

Paymaster's Department Dress

Aide to Major General Service

Quartermaster's Department Dress

General

Lieutenant General

Major General

Brigadier General

Colonel

Lieutenant Colonel

Major

Adjutant and Inspector's Department – Service

Paymaster's Department Service

Captain

1st Lieutenant

2nd Lieutenant

U.S.M.C. WARRANT OFFICERS' RANK AND CORPS INSIGNIA

Marine Gunner
Dress

Chief
Warrant Officer

Chief Warrant Officer
Paymaster's Dept

Second Leader
Marine Band

Marine Gunner
Service

DISTINGUISHING MARKS

Gun Pointer 1st Class

Gun Pointer 2nd Class

Navy 'E'

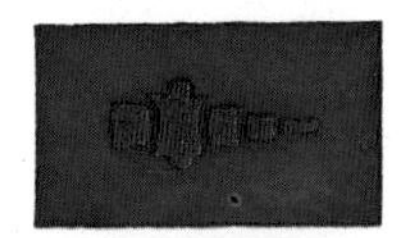

Gun Captain

SHOULDER SLEEVE INSIGNIA 1ST MARINE AMPHIBIOUS CORPS

Corps, Anti-Tank Bns,
155 Howitzer Bn

Artillery

Balloon Barrage Bns

Paratroopers

Defense Bns

Raiders

Service Supply

Aviation Engineers

U.S.M.C. N.C.O.s' RANK INSIGNIA

First Sergeant

1st Grade Line

Band Leader

1st Grade Staff

2nd Grade Line

2nd Grade Staff

3rd Grade Line

3rd Grade Staff

4th Grade

5th Grade

6th Grade

Musician P.F.C.

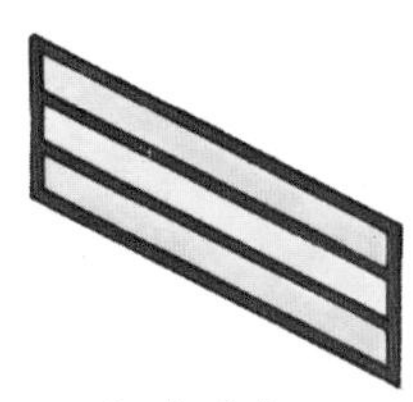
Service Stripes
12 years

Musician

PLATE 49

U.S.M.C. SHOULDER SLEEVE INSIGNIA – AMPHIBIOUS CORPS

3rd

5th

DIVISIONS

Marine Detachment Londonderry

1st

2nd (1st type)

2nd (2nd type)

3rd

4th

5th

6th

DEFENCE UNITS

13th Defense Bn

4th Marine Base Defense Air Wing

52nd Defense Bn

18th Defense Bn

Ship Detachments

51st Defense Bn

PLATE 50

U.S.M.C. SHOULDER SLEEVE INSIGNIA – FLEET MARINE FORCES

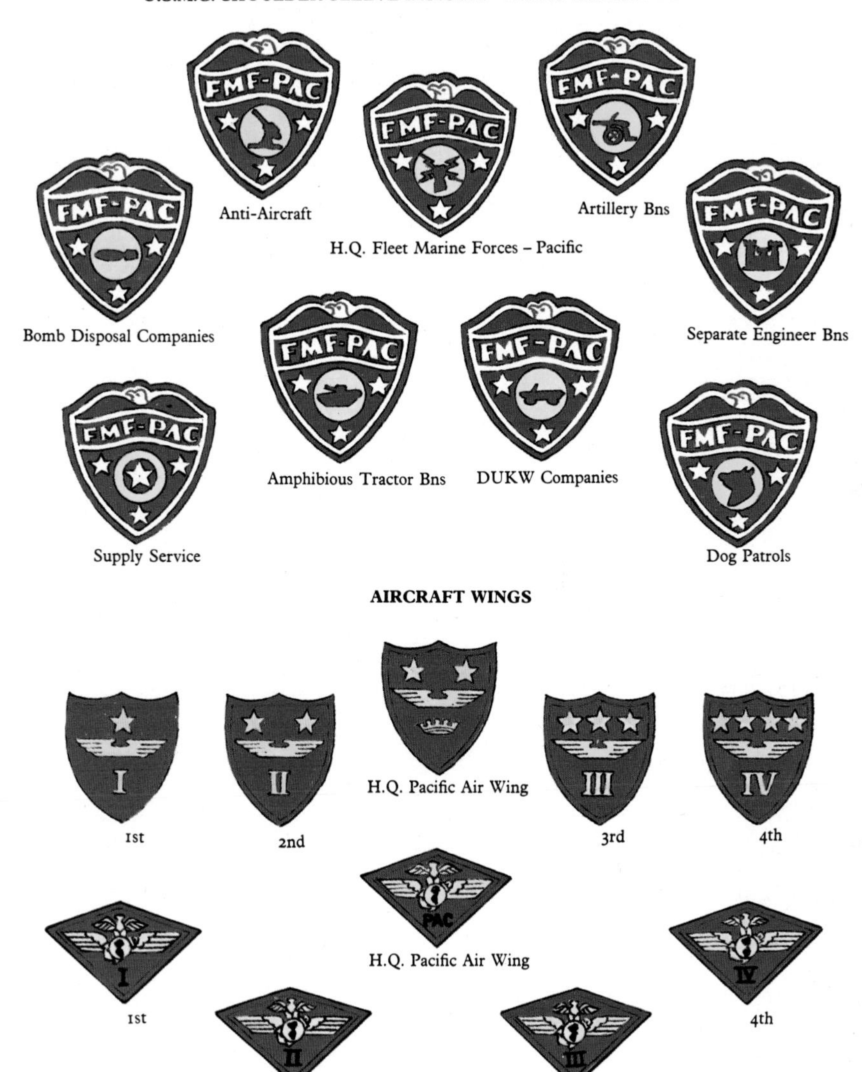

Anti-Aircraft

H.Q. Fleet Marine Forces – Pacific

Artillery Bns

Bomb Disposal Companies

Separate Engineer Bns

Amphibious Tractor Bns

DUKW Companies

Supply Service

Dog Patrols

AIRCRAFT WINGS

1st

2nd

H.Q. Pacific Air Wing

3rd

4th

H.Q. Pacific Air Wing

1st

4th

2nd

3rd

SUBSIDIARY SERVICES

Master
A.T.S.

Officers' Cap Badge
A.T.S.

Collar Badge

Officers' Cap Badge
M.S.

Lieutenant
M.S.

P.O.s' Cap Badge
Master at Arms
A.T.S.

A.T.S.

Collar Badge

Lapel Badge
Transportation Agent
A.T.S.

C.P.O.s' Cap Badge
M.S.

Wheelman
A.T.S.

Lapel Badge
Radioman
A.T.S.

Signalman
M.S.

P.O. 3rd Class
Storekeeper – M.S.

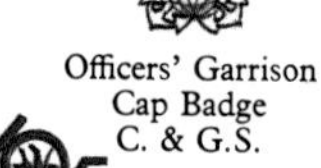

Officers' Garrison
Cap Badge
C. & G.S.

Electrician
C. & G.S.

Officers' Cap Badge
C. & G.S.

Mate
C. & G.S.

P.O. 1st Class
Oiler
C. & G.S.

Cap Badge
P.H.S.

Commander
C. & G.S.

Officers' Steward or Cook
Cap Badge – C. & G.S.

U.S. Cadet Nurse
Corps

Acting Assistant
Surgeon – P.H.S.

Cap Tally

Passed Assistant
Surgeon – P.H.S.

CAP BADGES

Midshipmen and Cadets
Line

Officers
Peaked Cap

Petty Officers
(embroidered)

Steel Helmet

All Ranks
Field Cap and Helmet
1st type

Steel Helmet

Seamen
White Cap

Petty Officers
(metal)

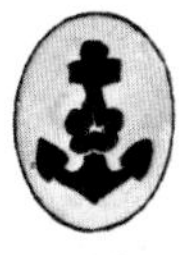

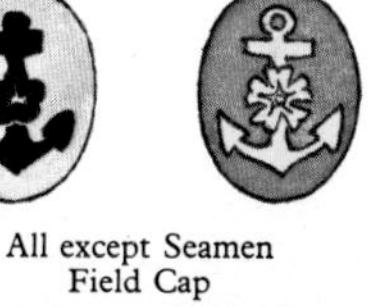

All except Seamen
Field Cap

Cap Tally

OFFICERS' RANK INSIGNIA

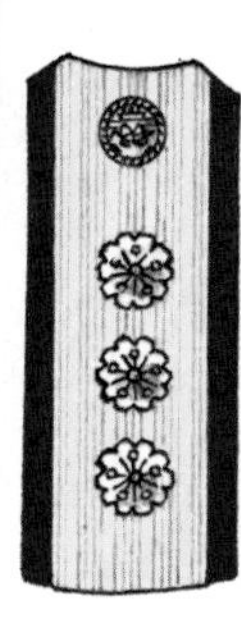

Admiral

Vice Admiral

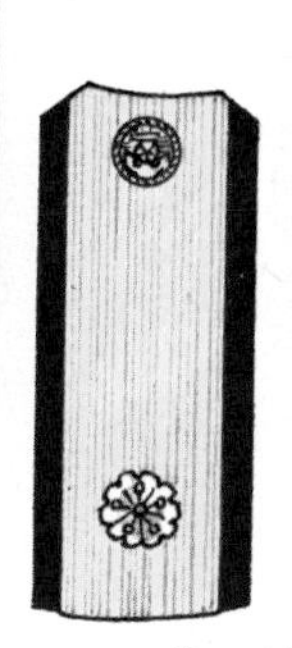

Rear Admiral

OFFICERS' RANK INSIGNIA

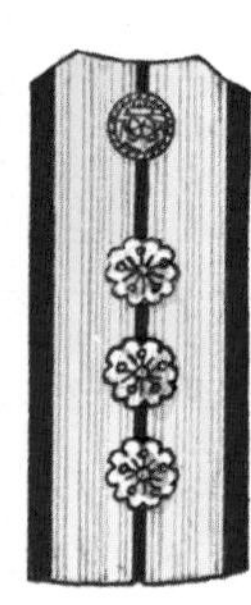

Commander
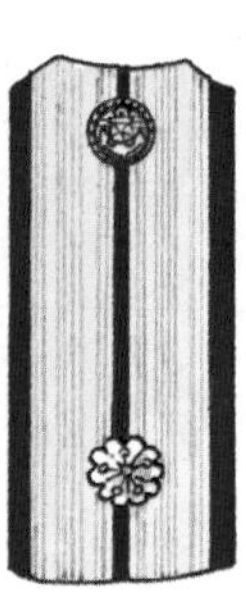

Captain

Lieutenant-Commander

Sub-Lieutenant

Lieutenant

Ensign

Cadet
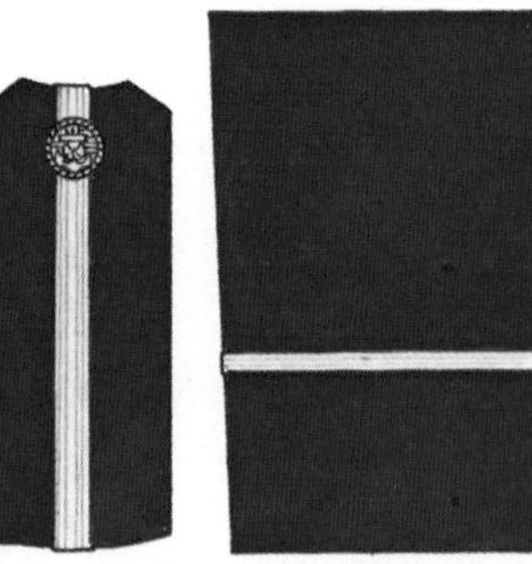

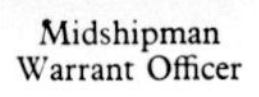

Midshipman
Warrant Officer

Midshipman

Warrant Officer

Cadet

RANK INSIGNIA – COLLAR PATCHES

Admiral

Vice Admiral

Rear Admiral

Captain

Commander

Lieutenant-Commander

Lieutenant

Sub-Lieutenant

Ensign

Midshipman

Cadet

Warrant Officer

RANK INSIGNIA – OFFICERS COMMISSIONED FROM THE RANKS

Lieutenant

Sub-Lieutenant

Ensign

Warrant Officer

JAPAN

PETTY OFFICERS' RATE BADGES (1ST TYPE)

Line
1st Class

Engineer
1st Class

Aviation
1st Class

Ordnance
1st Class

Administration
1st Class

Line
2nd Class

Engineer
2nd Class

Aviation
2nd Class

Ordnance
2nd Class

Administration
2nd Class

Line
3rd Class

Engineer
3rd Class

Aviation
3rd Class

Ordnance
3rd Class

Administration
3rd Class

SEAMEN'S RATE INSIGNIA

Line
1st Class

Engineer
1st Class

Aviation
1st Class

Ordnance
1st Class

Administration
1st Class

Line
2nd Class

Engineer
2nd Class

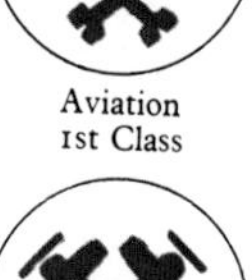
Aviation
2nd Class

Ordnance
2nd Class

Administration
2nd Class

Line
3rd Class

Engineer
3rd Class

Aviation
3rd Class

Ordnance
3rd Class

Administration
3rd Class

PLATE 56

PETTY OFFICERS' AND SEAMENS' RATE BADGES (1ST TYPE)

Musician
1st Class

Examples of various aviation badges

Musician
2nd Class

Musician
3rd Class

GOOD CONDUCT CHEVRONS (1ST TYPE)

Good Conduct according to duration of service

Excellent Conduct

Musician
1st Class

Musician
2nd Class

Musician
3rd Class

OTHER BADGES

Fighter Aircraft

Medical

Bomber Aircraft

Naval Collar Patch

Parachute Troops

Naval Aviation Collar Patch

JAPAN

RANK INSIGNIA – OFFICERS OF THE CORPS

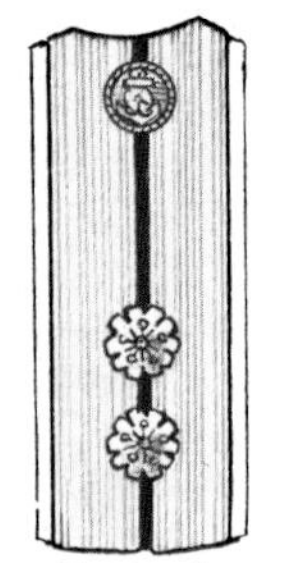
Commander
Paymaster

Captain
Construction

Ensign
Survey

Commander
Medical

Commander
Paymaster

Warrant Officer
Carpenter

Sub-Lieutenant
Engineer

Commander
Line

Commander
Justice

GOOD CONDUCT CHEVRONS, PETTY OFFICERS' AND SEAMENS' RATE INSIGNIA (2ND TYPE)

Good Conduct

Excellent Conduct

Special Training

P.O. 1st Class
Line

P.O. 2nd Class
Engineer

P.O. 3rd Class
Justice Clerk

Advanced Special
Training

Seaman 1st Class
Sick Berth

Seaman 2nd Class
Hydrographer

Seaman 3rd Class
Paymaster Clerk

PLATE 58

CAP AND RANK INSIGNIA

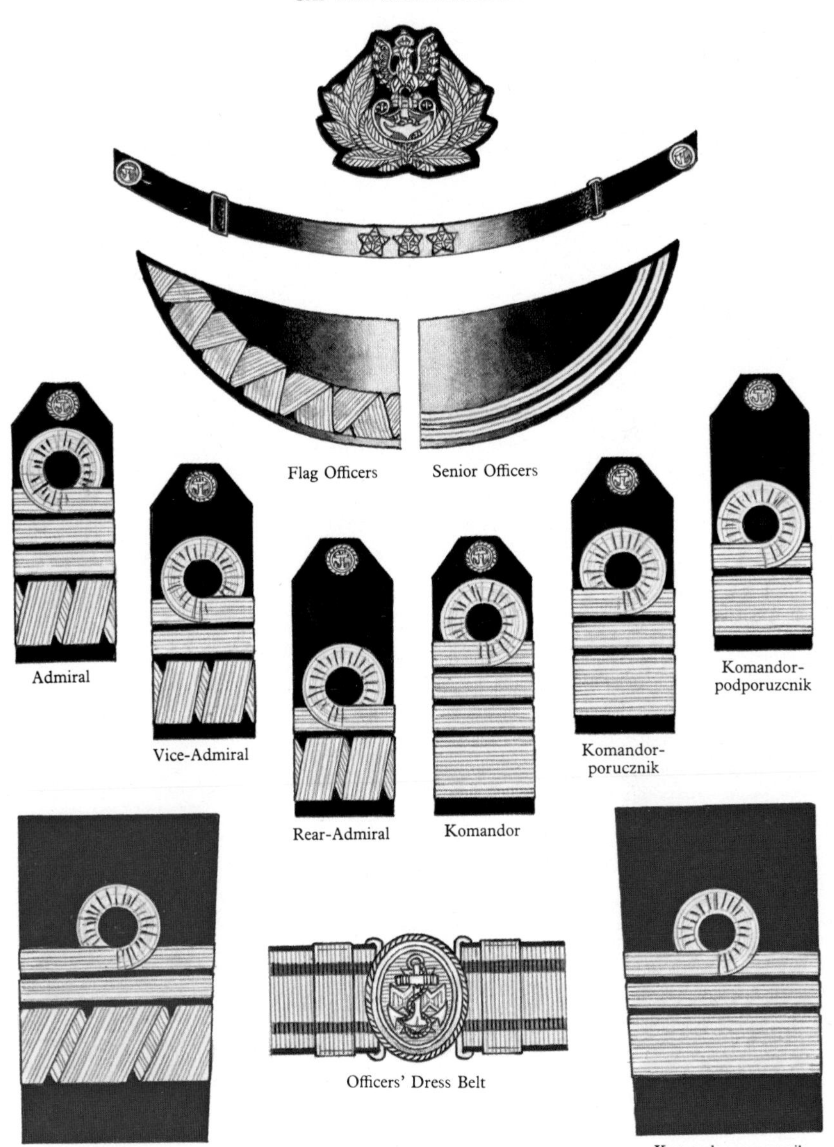

Flag Officers

Senior Officers

Admiral

Vice-Admiral

Rear-Admiral

Komandor

Komandor-porucznik

Komandor-podporuzcnik

Officers' Dress Belt

Vice-Admiral

Komandor-porucznik

POLAND

CAP AND RANK INSIGNIA

Porucznik

Junior Officers

Kapitan

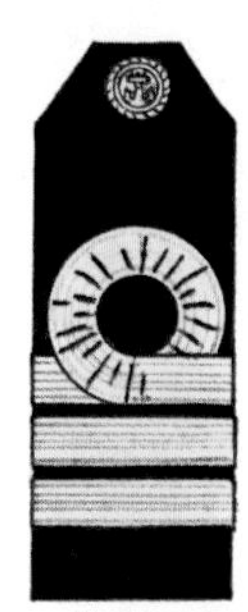

Kapitan

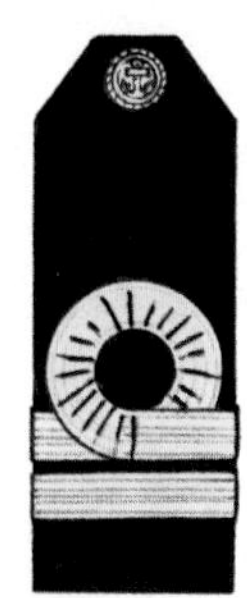

Porucznik

Podporucznik
Medical

Warrant Officer

Podporucznik
Administration

Chief Petty Officer
1st Class

Warrant Officer

P.O.s' Cap Badge

Chief Petty Officer 1st Class

CAP, RATE AND TRADE INSIGNIA

C.P.O. Reserve Cadet

Chief Petty Officer

C.P.O. Cadet

Helmsman

Chief Petty Officer

Mechanician

Signalman

Gunner

Electrician

Other Ratings' Cap Badges

Seaman

Petty Officer

Leading Seaman

Able Seaman

CAP TALLIES

MARYNARKA WOJENNA

O.R.P. GDYNIA.

TRADE BADGES

Range Finder Operator

Torpedo – Mineman

Writer

Plotter

Ordnance Artificer

Shipwright

Seaman Gunner

Carpenter

Photographer

Radio Telegraphist

Wireless Operator

Cook

Administrative Clerk

Stoker

Writer

Rifleman

Coxwain

Sick Berth Rating

Bandsman

Diver

CAP AND RANK INSIGNIA

Line

Engineering

Aviation

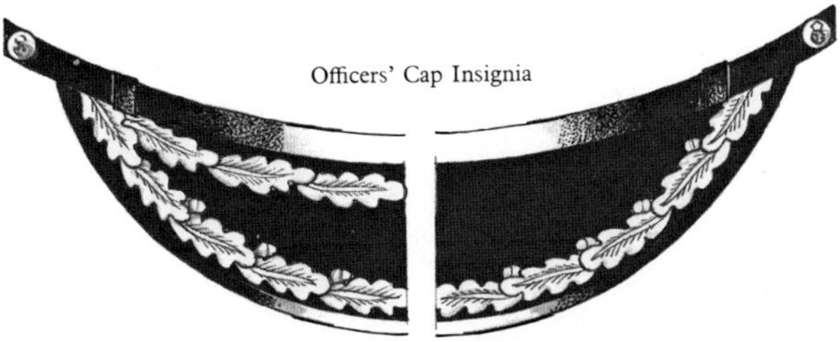

Officers' Cap Insignia

Flag Officers

Captain, Commander

Admiral

Medical

Administration

Vice-Admiral

Chaplains

Admiral

W.O.s and P.O.s

Yeoman

Musicians

Kapitein-Luitenant ter Zee

RANK INSIGNIA AND COLLAR BADGES

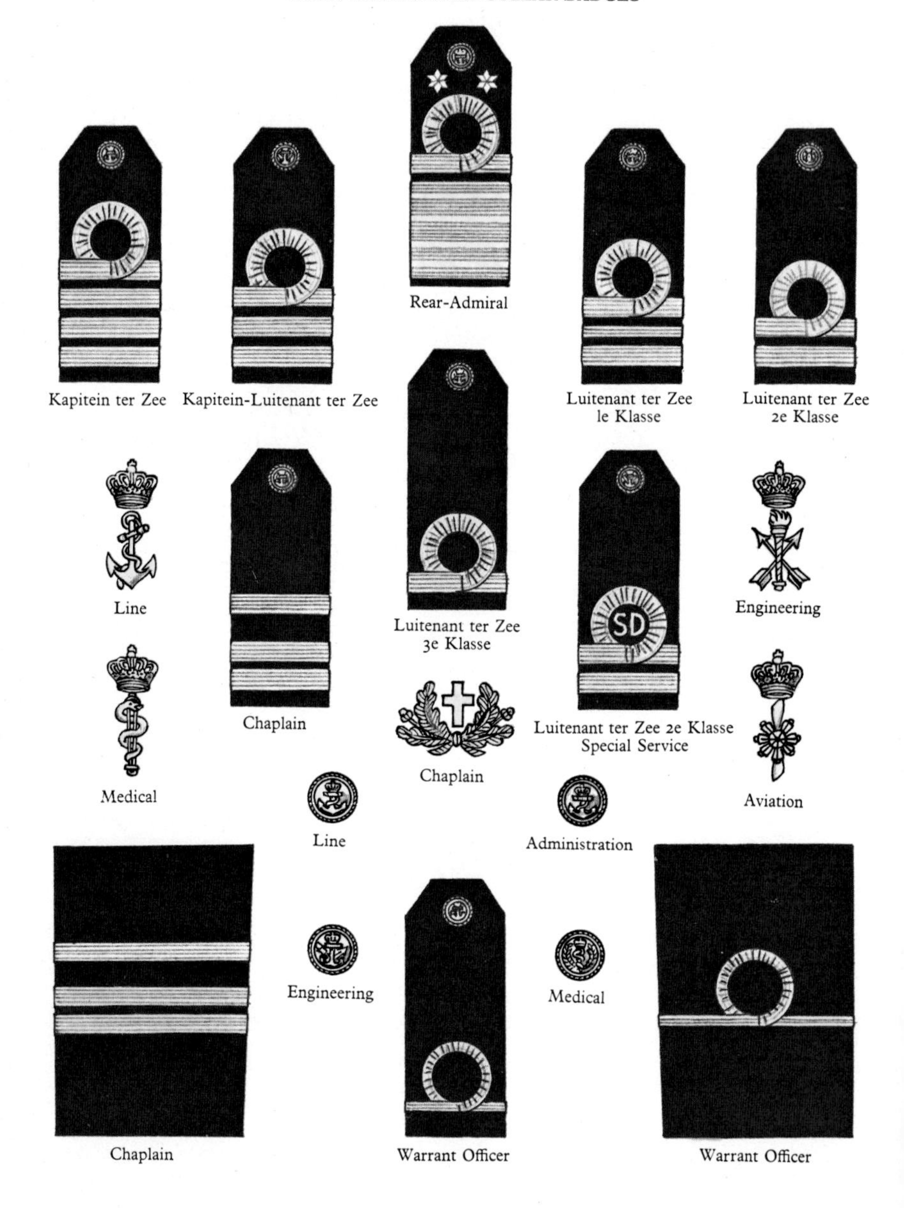

Kapitein ter Zee

Kapitein-Luitenant ter Zee

Rear-Admiral

Luitenant ter Zee le Klasse

Luitenant ter Zee 2e Klasse

Line

Medical

Chaplain

Luitenant ter Zee 3e Klasse

Chaplain

Luitenant ter Zee 2e Klasse Special Service

Engineering

Aviation

Line

Administration

Engineering

Medical

Chaplain

Warrant Officer

Warrant Officer

RATINGS' INSIGNIA

Chief Petty Officer

Petty Officer 1st Class

Leading Seaman
White for Yeoman Leading Seaman

WARRANT OFFICERS' AND PETTY OFFICERS' SPECIALITY BADGES

Boatswain

Ordnance Repairman

Signalman

Fire Controlman

Electrician

Nurse

Machinist

Telegraphist

Torpedoman

Aviation Repairman

Pilot

Musician

Steward, Cook

Yeoman

Storekeeper

Carpenter

KONINKLIJKE MARINE

Cap Tally

SPECIALITY AND TRADE BADGES

Signalman
Leading & Seaman
1st Class

Boatswain
Leading Seaman

Boatswain
Seaman 1st Class

Boatswain
Seaman 2nd Class

Telegraphist
Leading & Seaman
1st Class

Apprentice Torpedoman
3rd year

Aviation Repairman
Leading & Seaman 1st Class

Electrician
Leading
& Seaman
1st Class

Apprentice Carpenter
1st Class

Apprentice Fire
Controlman 2nd year

Machinist
Leading Seaman

Fireman
Leading Seaman

Fireman – Oiler

Fireman
1st Class

Fireman
2nd Class

Pilot
Leading & Seaman
1st Class
Apprentice

Yeoman, Steward,
Cook
Seaman 1st Class

Ordnance Repairman
Leading & Seaman 1st Class

Barber, Shoemaker,
Tailor
Seaman 1st Class

Nurse
Leading & Seaman
1st Class

Storekeeper
Leading & Seaman
1st Class

Musician
Leading Seaman

Musician
Aspirant

Musician
Apprentice

Mineman

Submarine Torpedoman

Sharpshooter
Rifle

Destroyer Torpedoman

Range Finder
Operator

Master Diver
1st Class

Master Diver
2nd Class

Gun Captain

Diver
1st Class

Diver
2nd Class

CAP AND RANK INSIGNIA

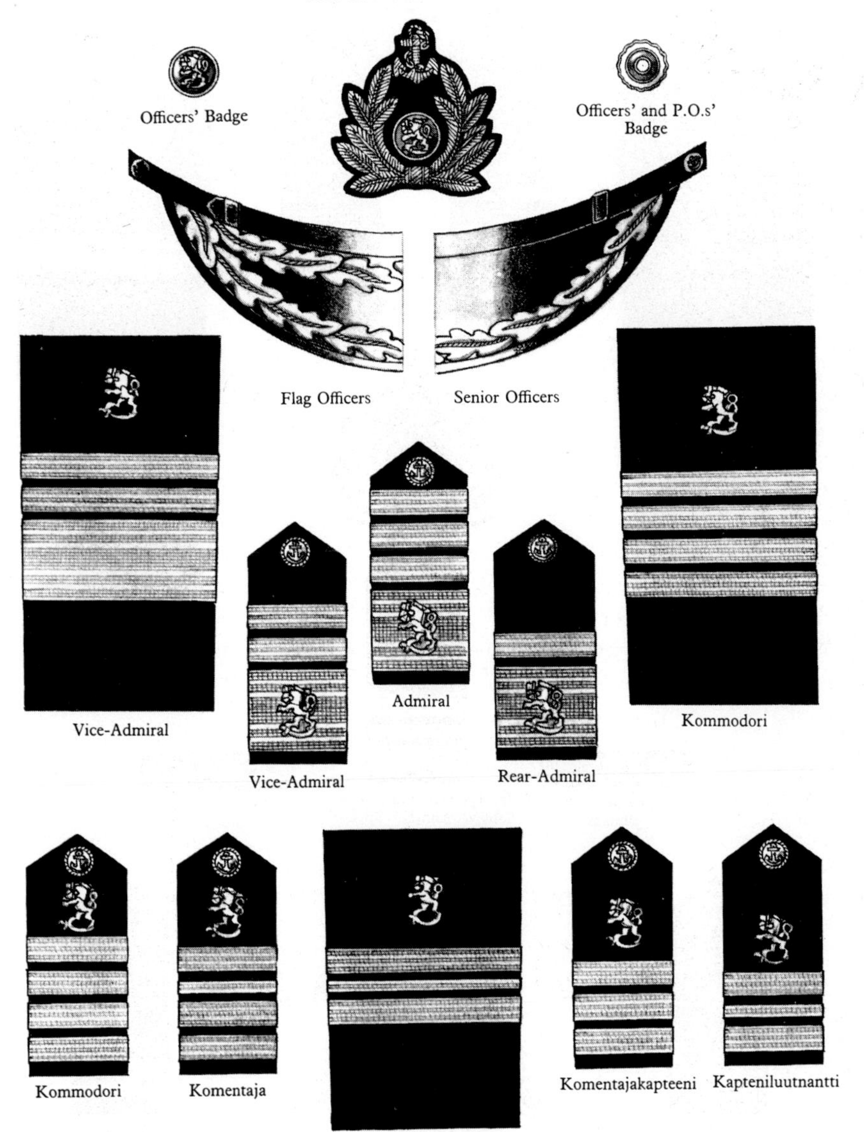

Kommodori Komentaja Kapteeniluutnantti Komentajakapteeni Kapteniluutnantti

CAP AND RANK INSIGNIA

Luutnantti

Aliluutnantti

Reservialiluutnantti
Reserve

Pastori
Chaplain

Shoulder Tab
Officers

Kapteeniluutnantti
Sotilasvirkamies – Specialist

Shoulder Tab
Specialists

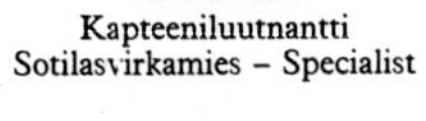

Flag Officers' Dress Belt

Luutnantti
Doctor

Officers

Specialists

Aliluutnantti
Musician

CADETS' CAP AND RANK INSIGNIA

Naval Academy Cadet

Navy Cadets

Cap Badge

Coast Artillery Cadets

Naval Academy (Coast Artillery) Cadet

Junior Sergeant Cadet
2nd year course – Navy

Cadet
1st year course – Navy

Sergeant Cadet
2nd year course – C.A.

MERISOTAKOULU

Master Navigator
Helmsman

Candidate

Cadet

Supply Master
Supplyman

Mine Master
Mineman

Master Nurse
Nurse

WARRANT OFFICERS' RANK INSIGNIA

W.O. 1st Class
Master Machinists

W.O. 2nd Class
Torpedo Master

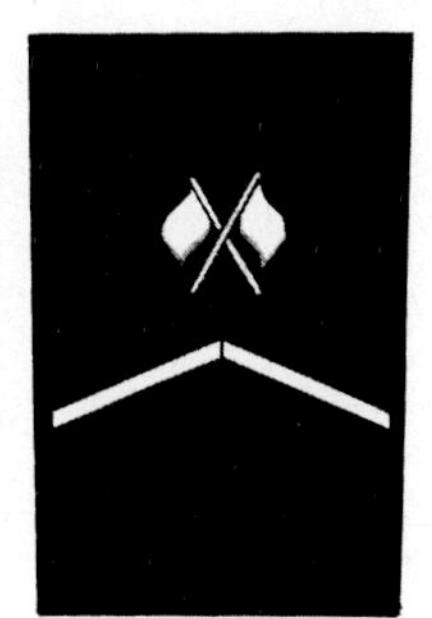

W.O. 3rd Class
Master Signaller

FINLAND

WARRANT OFFICERS' AND PETTY OFFICERS' INSIGNIA

Master Radioman
Radio Operator

Rifleman

W.O.s' Cap Badge

Master Electrician
Electrician

Band Master
Bandsman

P.O.s' Cap Badge

Master of Ordnance

Specialist P.O.s 'Cap Badge

PETTY OFFICERS' RATE INSIGNIA

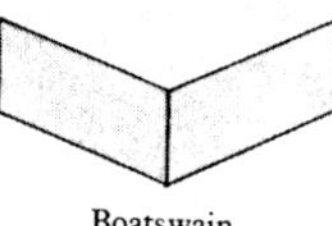
Boatswain

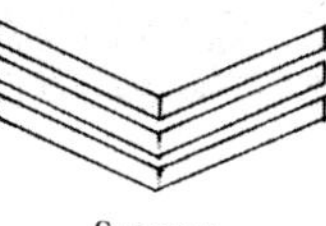
Sergeant

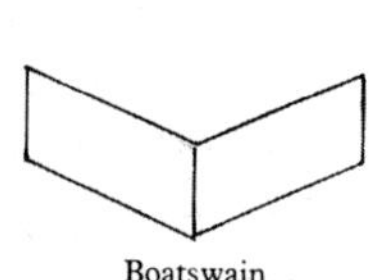
Boatswain
Specialist

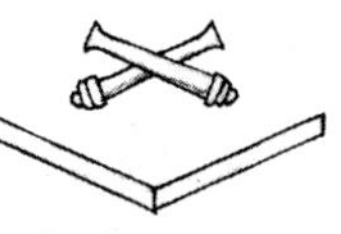
Leading Seaman
Gunner

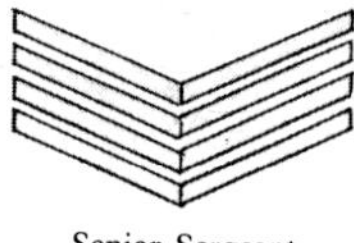
Senior Sergeant

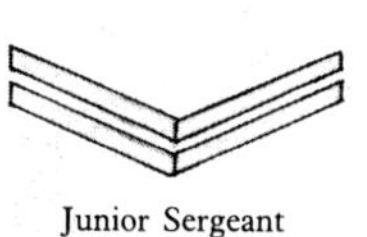
Junior Sergeant

Junior Sergeant
Conscript
Radio Operator

Seaman 1st Class

Seaman 2nd Class

Seaman 3rd Class

Leading Seaman
Conscript
Signalman

RANNIKKOLAIVASTO

Seaman's Cap Insignia

one sovereign could use the cypher of each sovereign under whom he had served.

The Honorary Chaplain to the King wore a special bronze badge, consisting of the Royal Cypher within an oval wreath, on the left side of the scarf in the conduct of religious services and on academic or ordinary clerical dress in other circumstances. A chaplain who had ceased to hold the appointment could still wear the special red cassock, but not the badge.

The chaplains' uniforms differed considerably from those of the naval officers, especially before the war, but the only relevant badges were the black Maltese crosses worn on the collar of the white tunic.

There were basically two types of buttons: flag officers and the Commodore 1st Class had a gilt raised button with a rope rim encircling a plain rim, within which was a wreath of laurel surrounding a foul anchor ensigned by the crown; the button of the other officers was the same but without the wreath. Both were made in three sizes: 37, 30 and 26 lines in button-maker's measures. Bronze buttons were used on the khaki uniform.

Cap badges for ratings, namely chief petty officers, were introduced in 1879, although engine room artificers had had the crown and anchor device since 1868. Seamen chief petty officers wore a gold and silver crown above a silver anchor, the latter in a gold ring, non-seamen had the whole badge in gold and the engine room artificers had a purple backing to the anchor, while that of the others was always black. In 1918, gold and silver badges were adopted for all.

The senior petty officers were allowed to wear peaked caps and jackets in 1920 and thus took on the badge previously used by the chief petty officers; the latter had a small gold laurel wreath added to theirs. The ring around the anchor was purely ornamental, often consisting of two cords, until, in 1970, a new order established that the Fleet Chief Petty Officer would wear two gold rings and the others one ring only.

The red cap badges for junior ratings originated in 1890, when the junior rates of many of the non-seamen branches obtained cap badges like those of the chief petty officers but embroidered in red.

There were cap badges embroidered in gold and silver, red thread, made of brass or painted red, as illustrated.

Plates 1, 2. R.N. Officers' Rank Insignia

The principal naval rank insignia consisted of rows of gold lace on the cuffs with the uppermost stripe curled into a circle.

Admirals and commodores were distinguished by a large lace stripe, 1¾ in

(44.5 mm) in width, with from one to four $\frac{9}{16}$ in (14 mm) stripes above it, the uppermost with a curl 2 in (51 mm) in diameter.

The Rear-Admiral and Commodore 1st Class had the same rows, with one large and one narrow stripe. The Commodore 2nd Class had the curl, 1¾ in (44.5 mm) in diameter, immediately above the large stripe.

The other officers used the $\frac{9}{16}$ in (14 mm) stripes, except for the Lieutenant-Commander who wore an additional ¼ in (6.5 mm) wide stripe in combination with two larger ones, as illustrated, all with the 1¾ in (44.5 mm) curl on top.

The Warrant Officer wore the narrowest stripe with curl as above. The space between the two rows of lace was ¼ in (6.5 mm) wide.

Only a few representative cuffs have been illustrated in order to save room whereas all the shoulder straps for each individual rank are shown because these are considerably smaller.

Shoulder straps were worn with greatcoat, watchcoat, white tunic and white mess jacket. All were made of blue cloth, except those of engineer, medical and accountant officers of flag rank, which were made of appropriate distinction cloth, with gold lace on top and a leather backing. The flag officers and the Commodore 1st Class had 2 in (51 mm) wide lace sewn along the shoulder straps, thus leaving a narrow piping of blue or other coloured distinction cloth exposed all around.

The shoulder straps were 5¼ in (133 mm) long and 2¼ in (57 mm) wide and had a button at the top and a leather tongue at the back.

Silver rank devices were placed on the gold lace as follows:

Rank	**Devices**
Admiral of the Fleet	The crown, the Royal Cypher and crossed batons surrounded by a wreath of laurel
Admiral	The crown, crossed sword and baton and three 8-pointed stars 1¼ in (32 mm) in diameter
Vice-Admiral	As above with two stars
Rear-Admiral	As above with one star 1¾ in (44.5 mm) in diameter
Commodore 1st Class	The crown, two small stars and an anchor with chain cable below

All the other officers and the Warrant Officer wore the stripes and curl, as on the cuffs, across their shoulder straps.

Executive officers had the stripes sewn directly onto cuffs and shoulder straps while non-executive officers were distinguished by a stripe, or stripes, of distinction cloth in conjuction with the rows of lace, i.e. the distinction cloth was used as backing to the stripes, below the single stripe, or on its own as a ⅛ in (3 mm) wide stripe in the case of midshipmen and cadets entitled to wear distinction cloth.

The following colours of distinction cloth were used:

Branch	Distinction Cloth
Engineer Officers	Purple
Medical Officers	Scarlet
Dental Officers	Orange
Accountant Officers	White
Instructor Officers Schoolmasters	Light blue
Shipwright Officers	Silver-grey
Wardmasters	Maroon
Electrical Officers	Dark green
Ordnance Officers	Dark blue

When serving afloat, Assistant Constructors of the Royal Corps of Naval Constructors and Electrical Engineering Officers wore the uniform prescribed for a lieutenant, the former with silver-grey distinction cloth, the latter with dark green distinction cloth between their stripes.

Khaki uniform could be worn, when ordered by the senior officer, instead of blue or white uniform, by officers employed ashore outside Great Britain; in this case stripes were displayed on the cuffs and distinction cloth, if necessary, as on the blue jacket, but gold lace was replaced by khaki braid of the same width. Blue shoulder straps with gold lace stripes were used with khaki battledress during the war.

Midshipmen of the Royal Navy wore, on each side of the collar, a white turnback of 2 in (51 mm) with a notched hole of white twist 1½ in (38 mm) long and a corresponding button, while the cadets had the notched hole and button only.

Plate 3. R.N.R. Officers' Rank Insignia

The Royal Naval Reserve was formed in 1859 and its cadre of officers was organised five years later. The latter wore the same uniforms as the officers of the Royal Navy but different insignia, which has undergone several changes and modifications since those early days. Their cap badges carried the initials 'RNR' above the anchor and waved gold braid stripes, until World War I when ordinary naval officers' cap badges were adopted and gold lace substituted for gold braid.

The stripes were one-half the width of those prescribed for officers of the Royal Navy, adapted in pairs to form two waved lines, one superimposed upon the other so that a section of blue cloth showed between the curves. A 6-pointed star, made of intersecting lace, replaced the curl.

The Commodore 2nd Class wore the large stripe straight and the Lieutenant-Commander wore the thin stripe straight but in combination with two pairs of waved stripes. The coloured cloth worn by non-executive officers did not fill the space between the two rows of lace but consisted of a narrow stripe only.

Midshipmen of the Royal Naval Reserve wore blue turnbacks and notched holes and the cadets blue notched holes on both sides of the collar.

Ratings used uniforms of the Royal Navy and the badges they were eligible to wear plus, since 1924, the initials 'RNR' on the left cuff.

Plate 4. R.N.V.R. Officers' Rank Insignia

The Royal Naval Volunteer Reserve was instituted in 1903 and its officers had the initials 'RNV' in the cap badge above the anchor and waved stripes of gold braid. As with the Royal Naval Reserve, the initials were abolished and gold lace replaced gold braid.

The waved stripes, ⅜ in (9.5 mm) wide, were worn parallel to each other and surmounted by a squarish, waved curl; the Commodore 2nd Class had his large stripe set straight below the curl and the Lieutenant-Commander wore a straight ⅛ in (3.2 mm) stripe between two waved ones.

Distinction cloth was placed in between the stripes; officers of the Special Branch wore distinction cloth of emerald green. By Admiralty order at 6 August 1942 the half stripe of the Lieutenant-Commander was to be waved instead of straight; by order on 6 May 1943 the half stripe on his shoulder straps was to be waved in the same way as the broad stripes.

Midshipmen and cadets of the Royal Naval Volunteer Reserve wore maroon turnbacks and notched holes of maroon twist. Chaplains, when officiating at naval, military and air force services, could wear the scarf authorised to be worn by chaplains of the Royal Navy with the addition of the letters 'RNVR' in gold, below the badge.

Ratings wore the above initials on the left cuff. In 1958 the Royal Naval Reserve and the Royal Naval Volunteer Reserve were amalgamated and the resulting organisation took over the title of the former.

Plate 5. R.N. Branch Officers' Rank Insignia

The civil branches of the Royal Navy have been mentioned already, in the introduction to this chapter and in the section dealing with officers' rank insignia.

The badges of the Fleet Air Arm have been dealt with in a previous volume dedicated to aviation insignia of World War 2. Only two examples have been illustrated in this plate: the gold and silver winged badge worn on the left forearm by naval pilots and the initial 'A', placed in the curl of the rank insignia, which identified personnel of the Air Branch.

Women's Royal Naval Service

The Women's Royal Naval Service was formed in November 1917 and its personnel became known as 'Wrens' because of the service's initials.

The organisation was disbanded after World War I and reformed in 1939 under the command of Mrs (afterwards Dame) Vera Laughton Mathews, who had the title of Director and initially wore four blue stripes on the cuffs, later the stripes equivalent to the male rank of Rear-Admiral. The first officers' ranks were given as Chief Officer, 1st Officer and 2nd Officer, the Superintendents having been separately recruited; 3rd Officers were appointed and in uniform by January 1940 and appeared in the Navy List for the first time in March 1940. The following were the officers' ranks of the W.R.N.S. compared with those of the Royal Navy:

W.R.N.S.		R.N.
Chief Commandant Director W.R.N.S.	both equivalent to	Rear-Admiral
Deputy Director		Commodore
Superintendent		Captain
Chief Officer		Commander
1st Officer		Lieutenant-Commander
2nd Officer		Lieutenant
3rd Officer		Sub-Lieutenant
Cadet (O.T.C. only)		Midshipman/Cadet R.N.

Chief Wrens were equivalent to Chief Petty Officer and wore the buttons on the cuffs, the rank of Petty Officer was adopted a little later in 1939 and was identified by blue crossed anchors on the left upper sleeve and the Leading Wren had a single blue anchor on the left sleeve.

The officers wore special cap badges on the tricorne hat; they were smaller than the male's badge and the 6-leaved wreath was embroidered in blue silk. Chiefs and petty officers used the tricorne hat also, with badges similar to their male counterparts but made of blue embroidery. Initially all ratings were issued with pull-on hats which were recalled in late 1942 and substituted by tricorne hats or round hats, according to rate.

The officers wore special blue stripes on the cuffs and shoulder straps, with a diamond in place of the curl. The large stripe of Chief Commandant and Director was 1¾ in (44.5 mm) in width, the normal, medium-sized stripe was ½ in (12.7 mm) and the additional narrow stripe of the 1st Officer was ¼ in (6.3 mm) in width.

At the outbreak of the war, Dr A. Genevieve Rewcastle was appointed to W.R.N.S. Headquarters as Surgeon & Agent and, in the early 1940s, she became W.R.N.S. Medical Superintendent, wearing the normal blue rank stripes on red distinction cloth. Later, however, she was entered as a Naval

Surgeon Lieutenant (on an equal footing with the male officers), wearing a Wrens' suit and tricorne hat, but with R.N.V.R. gold waved stripes on a red backing, and a gold Royal Navy cap badge. In due course she was promoted to Surgeon Lieutenant-Commander and was transferred from the staff of the Director W.R.N.S. to that of the Medical Director-General. Other women doctors were also entered as R.N.V.R. medical officers.

Shoulder straps with rank insignia were worn on the greatcoat and on tropical rig.

Wrens wore blue non-substantive badges, without additional crowns and stars, on all uniforms. The following were used during World War 2:

6-pointed star with:	
G in centre (Wrens only)	General duties: Net Defence, Boat's Crew, Laundrymaid, Messenger, Hall Porter, Postman, Steward (General) including Petty Officers' Messman and Night Porter
MT in centre	Despatch Rider, Motor Driver
C in centre	Cook
OC in centre	Officers' Cook
OS in centre	Officers' Steward, Wine Steward, Mess Caterer, Ward Room Attendant
W in centre	Writer, Mail Clerk, Degaussing Recorder, Chart and Book Corrector
Crossed flags	Communications: Visual Signaller, Coder, Teleprinter Operator, Radio-Telegraph Operator, Signal Distributing Office Watch-keeper, Switchboard Operator, Classifier
Winged lightning flash	Radar Operator (worn below crown by Chief Wrens entered before April 1942)
Dividers	Plotter, Bomb Range Marker, Chart Corrector
Crown:	
Within laurel wreath	Regulating Chief Wren
Without addition	Regulating P.O. Wren

Plates 6, 7, 8. Petty Officers' and Non-substantive Badges

The first rate badges were adopted in 1827 in the form of an anchor surmounted by the crown and an anchor alone for 1st Class and 2nd Class Petty Officers, respectively. These badges were cut out from white cloth and were sewn on the upper left sleeve.

Later the rates of Chief Petty Officer and Leading Seaman were added and the badges were changed as follows:

Chief Petty Officer	Crown and anchor surrounded by wreath
1st Petty Officer	Crown and crossed anchors
2nd Petty Officer	Crown and anchor
Leading Seaman	Anchor

The first non-substantive badge, for gunners, was introduced in 1860. Others followed and many developments and changes became necessary in order to avoid confusion between rate and speciality. In 1879 the chief petty officers obtained new uniforms, similar to those of the officers, with their own badge on the peaked cap which, as mentioned earlier, was changed in 1920 when senior petty officers were allowed to wear peaked caps as well.

By the outbreak of World War 2, the Chief Petty Officer was identified by his cap badge with wreath, three buttons on the cuffs and non-substantive badges on the collar of the jacket. The petty officers' rates were unified in 1913, when that of 2nd Class Petty Officer was abolished, but the crown and crossed anchors badge was retained and the Leading Seaman continued to wear the anchor.

Rate and non-substantive badges were red for wearing on blue uniforms, blue for white uniforms and embroidered in gold for the No. 1 uniform. Chief petty officers wore gold badges on the right forearm of the white tunic, above the three buttons.

The non-substantive badges were worn on the upper right sleeve end and consisted of a speciality device, combined or not with the crown, 6-pointed stars and letters of the alphabet. Since their introduction these badges have been constantly modified in accordance with technological developments; herewith follows a list of those used during World War 2:

Crossed guns/single gun:

Crossed—crown above, star below	Gunner's Mate
Crossed—star above, star below	Director Layer
Crossed—star above	Gunlayer (1935–39)
Crossed—star above, star and A below	Anti-aircraft Rating 1st Class
Crossed—star above, star and C below	Control Rating 1st Class
Crossed—star above, star and L below	Layer Rating 1st Class
Crossed—star above, star and P below	Patrol Service Gunnery Instructor
Crossed—star above, star and Q below	Quarters Rating 1st Class
Crossed—star above, star and R below	Radar Control Rating 1st Class
Crossed—star above, A below	Anti-aircraft Rating 2nd Class

Crossed—star above, C below	Control Rating 2nd Class
Crossed—star above, L below	Layer Rating 2nd Class
Crossed—star above, P below	Patrol Service Gunlayer
Crossed—star above, Q Below	Quarters Rating 2nd Class
Crossed—star above, R Below	Radar Control Rating 2nd Class
Crossed—star above, Q and DEMS below	Gunlayer, Defensively Equipped Merchant Ships
Crossed—BD below	Gunlayer, Boom Defence
Single—star above	C.P.O. Gunner
Single—star above, A below	Anti-aircraft Rating 3rd Class
Single—star above, C below	Control Rating 3rd Class
Single—star above, L below	Layer Rating 3rd Class
Single—star above, P below	Seaman Gunner Patrol Service
Single—star above, Q below	Quarters Rating 3rd Class
Single—star above, R below	Radar Control Rating 3rd Class
Single—star above, Q and DEMS below	Seaman Gunner, Defensively Equipped Merchant Ships
Single—BD below	Quarters Rating 3rd Class, Boom Defence

The gun was the first device to be adopted in 1860 and, at that time, looked like an old cannon; the modern version came into use in 1903. Since then, and after World War 2, many other badges not mentioned in this context have been used, starting with those depicting crossed guns or the single gun, both with crown and star above and one star below, and many others with different letters of the alphabet. In general, the use of letters became widespread during the war; before, they were rarely used to identify a specific trade or a service; such is the case of the 'SSS' which stands for Shore Signal Service.

The torpedo, initially crossed with a cannon, appeared in 1885 and on its own in 1903, in two versions: the crossed torpedoes and single torpedo badges as follows:

Crossed torpedoes/Single torpedo:

Crossed—crown above, star below	Torpedo Gunner's Mate
Crossed—crown above, wheel below	Torpedo Coxwain
Crossed—star above, star below	Leading Torpedoman (Low Power)
Crossed—star above	Leading Torpedoman
Crossed—star above, star and CM below	P.O., Controlled Mining
Crossed—star above, star and CMS below	P.O., Observation Mining
Crossed—star above, star and MS below	P.O., Wireman, Minesweeping

Crossed—star above, star and LC below	P.O., Wireman, Landing Craft
Crossed—star above, star and J below	P.O., Wireman, Cable Jointing
Crossed—star above, star and L below	P.O., Wireman
Crossed—star above, CM below	Leading Wireman, Controlled Mining
Crossed—star above, star and CMS below	Leading Wireman, Observation Mining
Crossed—star above, MS below	Leading Wireman, Minesweeping
Crossed—star above, LC below	Leading Wireman, Landing Craft
Crossed—star above, J below	Leading Wireman, Cable Jointing
Crossed—star above, L below	Leading Wireman
Single—star above	Seaman Torpedoman (1904–47), C.P.O. Torpedoman (1909–47)
Single—star above, CM below	Wireman, Controlled Mining
Single—star above, CMS below	Wireman, Observation Mining
Single—star above, MS below	Wireman, Minesweeping
Single—star above, LC below	Wireman, Landing Craft
Single—CM below	Watchkeeper, Controlled Mining
Single—BD below	Torpedo Rating, Boom Defence

Torpedo ratings, besides dealing with torpedoes, handled highly specialised electrical tasks; wiremen installed and maintained electrical equipment.

The crossed signalling flags and the ship's propeller were introduced in 1890. the highest rating of the former was the Chief Yeoman of Signals, who wore crown and star above and two stars below the crossed flags from 1909 to 1932.

Crossed flags:

Crown above, star below	Visual Signalman 1st Class
Crown above	Visual Signalman 2nd Class (C.P.O. and P.O.)
Crown above, SSS below	P.O., R.N. Shore Signal Service
Star above, two stars below	Visual Signalman 2nd Class (if below P.O.)
Star above, star below	Visual Signalman 3rd Class
Star above	Trained Operator (Visual Signalling)
Without addition	Signalman if not trained operator (Visual Signalling)
SSS below	Signalman, R.N. Shore Signal Service

BD below	Visual Signalman (Boom Defence)
LC below	Landing Craft Signalman
Star above, C below	Leading Coder (1940–41)
C below	Leading Coder (1941–48), Coder (1940–48)

3-bladed propeller:

Crown and star above, star below	Chief Motor Mechanic
Crown above, star below	Mechanician
Crown above	Stoker P.O.
Star above, star below	Motor Mechanic
Star above	Leading Stoker, Stoker 1st Class
Without addition	Stoker 2nd Class
FF below	Stoker, Fire-fighter

2-bladed propeller:

Crown and star above, star below	Chief Motor Mechanic
Star above, star below	Motor Mechanic

The 2-bladed propeller above differed from that used by ratings of naval aviation as the former was a ship's propeller while the latter was an aircraft's propeller.

Badges for wireless telegraphists were adopted in 1909 and the following were used during World War 2:

Winged lightning flash:

Crown above, star below	Wireless Telegraphist 1st Class
Crown above	Wireless Telegraphist 2nd Class if C.P.O., P.O.
Star above, two stars below	Wireless Telegraphist 2nd Class, if not C.P.O., P.O.
Star above, star below	Wireless Telegraphist 3rd Class
Star above	Wireless Telegraphist, Trained Operator
Without addition	Telegraphist, not Trained Operator
Crown and A above, M below	Radio Mechanic, Fleet Air Arm, if C.P.O.
Crown above, M below	Qualified Radio Mechanic, if C.P.O.
A above, M below	Radio Mechanic, Fleet Air Arm, if not C.P.O.
M below	Radio Mechanic
P below	Radar Plot Rating
R below	Radar Control Rating

Crown above, SWS below	P.O., Shore Wireless Service
SWS below	Telegraphist, Shore Wireless Service

The Shore Wireless Service, like the Shore Signal Service previously mentioned was a pre-war organisation; the other letters, 'A', 'M', 'P' and 'R' were introduced in 1944.

The red cross for sick berth ratings was adopted in 1885 and developed in the following badges by the early 1940s:

Red cross:

D above	Dental Surgery Attendant
DM above	Dental Mechanic
L above	Laboratory Attendant
M above	Masseur
O above	Operating Room Assistant
X above	X-ray Assistant
Without addition	Sick Berth Attendant

Crowns, stars and letters below the device were added after World War 2; earlier all ratings up to Chief Petty Officer used the same badge.

Crossed clubs:

Crown above, star below	Physical and Recreational Training Instructor 1st Class
Crown above	Physical and Recreational Training Instructor 2nd Class

Crossed axe and hammer:

Crown above	Chief Shipwright
Star above	Chief Blacksmith, Chief Plumber, Chief Painter, Chief Cooper
Without addition	All other Artisans

Gun over crossed axe and hammer:

Star above	Chief Armourer
Without addition	Armourer's Mate and Crew

Coil of rope below harpoon crossed with lightning:

Crown above	Submarine Detector Instructor
Star above, star below	Higher Submarine Detector
Without addition	Submarine Detector
Star above, star and S below	Harbour Defence Operator 1st Class
Star above, S below	Harbour Defence Operator 2nd Class

S below	Harbour Defence Operator 3rd Class

Crossed fid and marline spike:

Star above	Chief Sailmaker, Sailmaker
Without addition	Sailmaker's Mate, Fabric Worker

Crossed shackle and marline spike:

Star above, BD below	Chief Rigger, Rigger, Boom Defence
BD below	Rigger's Mate, Boom Defence

Cobweb and lightning flashes:

Crown above, star below	Radar Plot Instructor
Star above, star below	Radar Plot Rating 1st Class
Star above	Radar Plot Rating 2nd Class
Without addition	Radar Plot Rating 3rd Class

Dividers:

Without addition	Navigator's Yeoman

Camera:

Crown above	C.P.O. and P.O. Photographer
Star above	Leading Photographer
Without addition	Photographer

A new set of non-substantive badges, depicting a 6-pointed star with an initial in its centre, was introduced in 1932 and used until 1948. Later, others were added, with different letters, and crowns and stars were added to the basic devices for petty officers' rates.

6-pointed star with:

C in centre	Cook
OC in centre	Officers' Cook
OS in centre	Officers' Steward
S in centre	Supply Rating
W in centre	Writer

The officers' cooks and stewards wore plain 'OC' or 'OS' as a badge during World War 1.

Rangefinder:

Star above, star below	Rangetaker 1st Class

Sextant:

Without addition	Surveying Recorder

A set of four aviation badges appeared in 1935. The device was an aeroplane with straight wings which, in 1939, was changed to an aeroplane with swept wings and, in the same year, aviation mechanics and fitters obtained badges displaying propellers, as follows:

Aeroplane:

Crown above, star below	Rating Observer
Crown above	Acting Rating Observer
Star above, star below	Air Gunner 1st Class
Star above	Air Gunner 2nd Class
Without addition	Air Gunner 3rd Class, Naval Airman, General Duties

2-bladed aircraft propeller:

Crown above, A below	Air Mechanic (Airframes), C.P.O. and P.O.
Star above, A below	Air Mechanic (Airframes), Leading Rating
A below	Air Mechanic (Airframes), Other Ratings
Crown above, E below	Air Mechanic (Engines), C.P.O. and P.O.
Star above, E below	Air Mechanic (Engines), Leading Rating
E below	Air Mechanic (Engines), Other Ratings
Crown above, L below	Air Mechanic (Electrical), C.P.O. and P.O.
Star above, L below	Air Mechanic (Electrical), Leading Rating
L below	Air Mechanic (Electrical), Other Ratings
Crown above, O below	Air Mechanic (Ordnance), C.P.O. and P.O.
Star above, O below	Air Mechanic (Ordnance), Leading Rating
O below	Air Mechanic (Ordnance), Other Ratings
Without addition	Air Mechanic, Unclassified

4-bladed aircraft propeller:

Star above, A below	Air Fitter (Airframes), Leading Rating and above

A below	Air Fitter (Airframes) below Leading Rating
Star above, E below	Air Fitter (Engines) Leading Rating and above
E below	Air Fitter (Engines) below Leading Rating
Star above, L below	Air Fitter (Electrical) Leading Rating
L below	Air Fitter (Electrical) below Leading Rating
Star above, O below	Air Fitter (Ordnance) Leading Rating and above
O below	Air Fitter (Ordnance) below Leading Rating
Without addition	Air Fitter, Unclassified
Crown:	
Within laurel wreath	Master-at-Arms, C.P.O.
Without addition	Regulating P.O.
Crossed rifles:	
Without addition	Marksman
Diver's helmet:	
Without addition	Diver
Bugle:	
Without addition	Bugler
Bomb:	
Without addition	Bomb Disposal

The badge of Combined Operations was worn by personnel of the Royal Navy and of the Royal Marines, on a round background by the latter; it was worn on the right cuff of the naval ratings' uniform and on both upper sleeves of the khaki battledress. The last four badges listed were worn on the right cuff, with the exception of the Chief Petty Officer Diver, who wore the badge in the usual manner.

Rate and career in a speciality were unrelated and each speciality developed its own badges; therefore the crowns and stars on the badges of one speciality did not necessarily have the same meaning as they had in another. Many new badges appeared in the 1930s and 1940s until, eventually, in 1948, a process of reorganisation began with the aim of establishing some order among the non-substantive badges.

Only a few examples of these have been illustrated; however, at least one of each speciality listed is included.

Good conduct chevrons were adopted in 1849 for wearing on the left upper sleeve, on their own or under rate insignia of Petty Officer and below. There were gold, red and blue stripes according to uniform: one stripe for three years' service, two for eight and three for thirteen or more years of good service.

Plate 8. Cap Tallies

In peace-time the cap ribbon, or tally, identified the ship or establishment to which a sailor belonged, while during the war it displayed the initials 'H.M.S.' only, standing for 'His Majesty's Ship'.

The Commonwealth nations followed the same principal; thus, in war-time, their sailors displayed the initials 'H.M.S.' combined with national initials, except for the South Africans who had the initials 'S.A.' with a crowned anchor in the middle.

The uniforms and insignia of the Royal Navy were used throughout the Commonwealth, but buttons were different: the Canadians and Australians had their country's name across the centre and below the anchor, respectively; the buttons of the Indian Navy carried the Star of India as a background to the usual crowned anchor, and the South Africans buttons displayed the initials 'S.A.' and the crowned anchor, as on the tally.

The tallies were black with gold wire, later with yellow silk letters woven in the centre; the tally's ends were tied into a bow which naval regulations prescribed to be worn above the left ear while often the bow was worn, unofficially, above the left eye instead, and with a silver *3d*. piece placed into its centre in order to improve its appearance.

The five examples of ship's tallies illustrated were all worn by Stanley A. Statham, formerly Leading Torpedoman (Low Power). H.M.S. *Glorious* was an aircraft carrier, *Cossack* was a Tribal class destroyer, *Effingham* was a cruiser of the Hawkins Class, which was lost in 1940, *Neptune*, a one-stack cruiser of the Leander Class, lost in 1941.

The badge of the Royal Navy Youth Entries was worn on the upper sleeve of the uniform by Sea Cadets or personnel of the Home Guard and Air Training Corps and identified young men, aged 17 years, accepted by the navy and awaiting call-up at the age of 18 years.

Plate 9. Merchant Navy, Royal National Lifeboat Institution and H.M. Coastguard

A small number of insignia of these three organisations have been illustrated in order to prevent the reader from confusing them with those of the Royal

Navy. There were others as well because several steamships' companies had their own uniforms and badges.

The officers of the Merchant Navy displayed special rank insignia, i.e. stripes of gold lace combined with a diamond, and had special rank titles, which differed according to speciality. The Captain (Certified Master) wore four stripes, the two middle ones joined to form a diamond, the Chief Officer, 1st Officer, 2nd Officer and 3rd Officer wore respectively three stripes, two and a narrower stripe, two stripes and one stripe, all combined with the diamond. The uncertified Junior Officer had one stripe only, with a half diamond, i.e. the stripe was twisted to form a 'v' in the centre of the cuff.

Distinction cloth was displayed as illustrated, red for Surgeon, purple for Engineer and white for Purser.

The wireless officers wore waved stripes: the 1st Wireless Officer had two stripes and the diamond, while the 2nd and 3rd had two stripes and one respectively, without the diamond. Stewards were identified by one straight stripe below 6-pointed gold stars.

The officers of H.M. Coastguard wore from one to four stripes with curl on the cuffs; the Chief Inspector had the two outer stripes of gold lace and his deputy of silver, while all other stripes were made of black lace.

The Inspectors and Higher Grades and the District Officers wore the cap badge with oak wreath and had the visor of the peaked cap covered with blue cloth. Inspectors and Higher Grades had black oak leaves embroidered along the edge of the visor, the District Officers had a plain blue cloth visor and the others wore the smaller cap badge and black leather visor.

The Coxswain of the Royal National Lifeboat Institution was distinguished from the other ratings by his cap badge alone.

The Royal Marines

The Royal Marines trace their origins to the Duke of York and Albany's Maritime Regiment of Foot, otherwise known as the Admiral's Regiment, formed in 1664, and recruited largely from the Trained Bands of London. They were organised into a permanent corps in 1775, with 'Divisions' at Chatham, Portsmouth and Plymouth, under the control of the Board of Admiralty.

The Royal Marines provided detachments of small-arms men for duty on the upper decks of His Majesty's ships and landing parties, and in these roles they helped to protect and consolidate the empire for centuries.

During the French Wars they were present at every naval battle; nearly three thousand officers and men were at Trafalgar, whilst they also gained much experience and distinction in innumerable raiding and other amphibious operations. They were rewarded by the granting of the title 'Royal' in 1802.

Artillery companies were added to the Corps in 1804 to man a portion of the armament of the ship and, as their role in defence of ships subsided, they were redeployed in land operations; thus, after the Crimean War, they were divided into Blue Marines (Royal Marine Artillery) and Red Marines (Royal Marine Light Infantry).

These two branches were amalgamated in 1923 under the old title the Royal Marines.

During World War 2 they were called upon to perform a whole range of new tasks: formations for the defence of naval bases overseas, providing crews for landing crafts, beach control parties and armoured units for close support on the beaches, not to mention the well-known R.M. Commandos. All this in addition to their normal activities, such as the defence of ships, the forming of battalions, siege regiments and anti-aircraft units.

Plate 10. Badges of the Royal Marines

The badge of the Royal Marines is composed of the Royal Crest, which was initially displayed on the officers' shoulder belt plates in 1797, by the laurel wreath, which it is claimed was awarded to them after the battle of Belle-Île in 1761, and by the globe. The latter was granted by King George IV in 1827, when the Royal Marines claimed one hundred and six battle honours in campaigns all over the world for their new colours and received the globe instead.

Only one battle honour was selected for display; it commemorates the capture and defence of Gibraltar, the marines' proudest achievement. The motto *Per Mare Per Terram*, believed to have been used for the first time in 1775, means 'By Sea By Land' and truly describes their deployment. The anchor is often portrayed in the Royal Marines' Insignia to denote that the Corps is part of the Naval Service. It was first used by the marines in 1747.

The cap badges displayed the Royal Crest, the globe and the wreath; the collar badges the globe and wreath only; all were in two variants, for blue dress and khaki service dress uniforms.

The officers' dress cap badge had a silver globe with the continents above it painted in gold, the Royal Crest and wreath were made of gilt and the former was detached from the rest. The Warrant Officer and Quartermaster Sergeant also wore cap badges in two separate pieces but entirely finished in gilt. The Sergeants had gilt cap badges but in one piece, with the crest attached to the ends of the wreath and on the top of the globe; the other ranks had the same badge but made of brass.

The dress collar badges followed the pattern of the cap badge, therefore the officers' had the silver globe, those of the Warrant Officers, Quartermaster Sergeant and Sergeants were identical, i.e. made of gilt, and the collar badges of the other ranks were made of brass. Collar badges had shorter fittings at the back than cap badges.

The officers wore smaller collar badges on the lapels of the mess dress. The first badge illustrated, with the wreath joining on top, was used from 1897 to 1921; another badge, with a small bugle in between the ends of the wreath, was worn from 1921 to 1923 by officers of the Royal Marine Light Infantry and matched their cap badges, which carried the bugle instead of the Royal Crest. The other badge illustrated, with the wreath's ends parted, was used from 1923 to 1953, later followed by an anodised version.

Before the war, until 1939, a silver globe and embroidered wreath was worn by officers on the collar of the frock coat, while other ranks had collar badges embroidered in yellow thread on a red background for the collar of the blue tunic.

Bronze cap badges were worn on khaki caps and, again, there were two versions: with detached crest for officers, the Warrant Officer and Quartermaster Sergeant, and in a single piece for all other ranks. Black bakelite cap and collar badges were issued to the other ranks during World War 2.

The lyre was adopted in 1906 as a distinguishing badge for the personnel of the Naval School of Music. It was worn on cap badges in place of the Royal Crest and a vast array could be found: some badges were gilded, others made of brass with the lyre detached or attached either to the ends of the wreath or to the globe as well. The lyre was worn above the globe and laurels from 1921 to 1946 and was then replaced by the normal R.M. cap badge.

The officers wore the lyre on the collar with an additional scroll which carried the motto from 1921 to 1930, the other ranks had the plain lyre in brass or embroidered in yellow on red backing; the latter badge was abolished in 1939 when the wearing of blue dress was discontinued but the brass badge continued to be used until 1951 and by Boys Junior Musicians until 1970, later in an anodised version.

The 'RMB' titles, which come in small and large variations were also adopted in 1921; one type was made without the top bar across and has a full stop after the initials. The normal shoulder titles of the Royal Marines, with initials 'RM', were made in bronze and in brass, in small and large sizes.

The three divisional bands, at Chatham, Portsmouth and Plymouth, were granted special cap devices: the former received the silver Rose of York in 1902 as a reward for accompanying the Duke of Cornwall and York, the future King George V, on his tour of the colonies.

The band of the Portsmouth Division was granted the Prince of Wales's Plume in 1876 to commemorate the prince's visit to India and was worn until the amalgamation of the R.M.A. and R.M.L.I. in 1923. Later the badge was still worn by bandsmen at Deal until that band was dispersed in 1930. However, the band of the Royal Marine Artillery went with King George V to India for the Delhi Durbar and thus was awarded the King's Cypher on the ball of the grenade of the cap badge, a distinction which was retained by the band of the Portsmouth Division.

The Prince of Wales's Plume was also granted to the R.M.L.I. band of Plymouth in 1921 for going with the prince, later King Edward VIII, on his visit to Canada and Australia.

The band serving on the Royal Yacht, since 1925, wear a special shoulder flash which, in fact, reads 'Royal Yacht', and it is still worn today underneath an embroidered crown.

The officers wore rank insignia of army pattern, in gold or bronze according to type of uniforms, and shoulder titles.

The rank of Warrant Officer was instituted in 1943 and was identified by the initials 'WO' surrounded by a laurel wreath, as illustrated, on the shoulder straps. In April 1949 it was abolished and the warrant officers still in charge were upgraded to commissioned officers.

Other rank badges typical of the marines were those for quartermaster sergeant instructors: the Royal Crown within a laurel wreath above crossed guns for gunnery, above crossed rifles for musketry and above crossed clubs for the physical training instructors.

The Royal Marines, although a naval organisation, were basically a separate body, primarily where uniforms and insignia were concerned. The officers' rank distinction followed the army's pattern, but had a special rank of Captain-General, later taken by King George VI and at present by the Duke of Edinburgh. The non-commissioned officers used a mixture of army and navy badges, including some non-substantive badges, which worked out perfectly for their own purpose, and some extra badges of their own.

The King's Badge was adopted in March 1918, following King George V's inspection to R.M. Depot at Deal. It was granted to the best all-round marine in each King's Squad and he kept it throughout his service. At the same time the title of 'King's Squad' was given to each recruits' squad as it became in turn the senior squad in the Corps. The badge was worn on the right upper sleeve of all uniforms and therefore many variations are in existence: the Royal Cypher and surrounding laurel wreath in gold on dark blue, or red on dark blue, gold on red, gold on dark green, white on khaki or brown on summer drill background, according to uniform.

Plate 11. Badges of the Royal Marines

Formation signs were adopted during World War 2 for wearing on the upper sleeves of the battledress.

The Royal Marines Division was in existence from 1941 to 1943 and later the trident was used by the 116th R.M. Brigade, which was formed by the 27th, 28th and 30th R.M. battalions. The 117th R.M. Brigade (31st, 32nd and 33rd R.M. Bns) wore the foul anchor within an 8-pointed star in 1945.

The anchor, with a gold grenade superimposed, was used by the R.M. Engineers from 1940 to 1945 and by the personnel of the 34th Amphibian Support Regiment in 1945–46. A seahorse was the emblem of the 104th Training Brigade, which, in 1943, was redesignated R.M. Training Group.

The R.M. Siege Regiment used a grenade with protruding ball embroidered in red thread and 'T', 'U' and 'W' 4 in (102 mm) batteries of the R.M. Coast Artillery were distinguished by a small maroon triangle from 1941 to 1944.

Red figures cut out from felt and sewn on khaki background were worn on the shoulder straps during the war; an Arabic '7' was used by the 7th R.M. Battalion in 1941–42 and a Roman 'VII' in 1943–44 until March, when the battalion was converted to become the 48 R.M. Commando. The 9th R.M. Battalion used the Roman figure from 1941 until August 1943 when it became the 46 R.M. Commando. Other badges existed as well but only those of the 7th and 9th battalions are displayed at the Royal Marines Museum.

The 30th Assault Unit used the number '30', embroidered in light blue thread on a dark blue background, the 31st R.M. Battalion had a red '31' on khaki and the 33rd had a red '33' on a dark blue background. These badges were worn in the later months of the War.

The shoulder title of the Royal Marines was straight, with red lettering on a blue background, and was worn on battledress by all except commandos from 1943 to 1966. The woven pattern was issued and commandos wore it with the number above and 'COMMANDO' designation below, in three pieces attached together.

Unofficial badges were worn as well: some 'ROYAL MARINES' titles were red on ultramarine blue instead of dark blue, or with dark blue lettering on a red background. There were embroidered commandos' titles, often with the wording displaced, as for the example illustrated of a shoulder title of the 44 R.M. Commando. New curved titles were adopted by the commandos in 1946.

Royal Navy titles were curved, embroidered in white thread on a dark blue background. There were three; besides those illustrated, there was one which displayed only the designation 'COMMANDO'.

The triangular formation sign with the red dagger was used by the personnel of the Special Service Group in 1944–46 and, after the disbandment of the army commandos, it was worn by the 3rd R.M. Commando Brigade from 1946 to 1976 and later re-adopted by army personnel.

The Union of Socialist Soviet Republics

Peter the Great was the creator of the first Russian fleet and he engaged English technicians and naval officers with the purpose of extending Russian power across the seas. However, Russia was basically a land nation without direct access to the Atlantic and Mediterranean and hampered by lack of communications with its far east territories.

Eventually three main fleets developed: the Baltic Fleet, which could not get out from the Baltic Sea without the goodwill of the neighbouring countries; the Black Sea Fleet, trapped in that sea by Turkey, and the Far Eastern Fleet, based at Vladivostok, lost beyond Siberia and without much scope for deployment.

The latter was badly mauled during the Russo–Japanese War and later World War 1 and the successive Revolution obliterated the last vestiges of Russian naval power.

Slowly the fleet was reorganised, new ships were built, but not even during World War 2 was the Soviet Navy strong enough to achieve any outstanding success although, in fairness, the great battles fought by land armies on the Eastern Front minimised the valid cooperation given by the other services.

The insignia used after February 1943 are illustrated in this chapter dedicated to the Soviet Navy, as conventional naval insignia were worn previously by all ranks.

Plate 11. Cap and Rank Insignia

The officers of the Soviet Navy were divided into executive and non-executive officers: the former included those of the Line and Line Engineering, the latter the officers serving in all the other naval corps or services.

Line officers wore gold insignia, i.e. the cap badge and embroideries on the peaked cap's visor, cuff stripes, shoulder straps, buttons, etc. while the officers of the services had gold or silver insignia according to specific branch. Therefore there were gold or silver cap badges.

The badge depicted a foul anchor superimposed on a round, protruding cockade with black centre, surrounded by a laurel wreath, the whole ensigned by the 5-pointed red star with hammer and sickle in a white centre.

The flag officer's cap was fitted with a double cord and displayed two sprigs of laurel leaves on the peak, the Captains of 1st, 2nd and 3rd Rank had a black leather chin strap and one row of oak leaves on the peak. Cords and embroideries were of gold or silver, according to branch of service. Cap badges and embroideries were later made of metal, finished as an imitation of embroidery.

The flag officers' buttons depicted the emblem of the Soviet Union above crossed anchors while those of all other ranks carried the anchor alone.

Plates 12, 13. Officers' Rank Insignia

Executive and non-executive officers had different rank insignia and rank titles as the latter were designated by army titles.

They displayed rank insignia in the form of stripes below a 5-pointed star on the cuffs and by means of shoulder straps.

At the beginning of the war the officers wore conventional stripes of lace on the cuffs but new regulations published in February 1943 introduced shoulder straps of traditional Russian pattern, made of gold or silver lace according to corps, and shorter cuff stripes.

The shoulder straps were used by all officers on the dark jacket, tunic and greatcoat while cuff stripes were worn by officers of the Line and Line Engineering only. However, the officers of the other corps wore special trimmings on the cuffs of the dress jacket, in gold or silver according to the metal of their shoulder straps and with the same distinction cloth backing. Only shoulder straps were worn on the white tunic and on the greatcoat.

The cuff stripes of the service dress measured $3\frac{1}{8}$ in (80 mm) in length and those of the parade jacket $3\frac{15}{16}$ in (100 mm). The flag officers' and Captain 1st Rank's stripe was $1\frac{3}{16}$ in (30 mm) wide and the other two were $\frac{1}{2}$ in (12.7 mm) and $\frac{1}{4}$ in (6.5 mm) wide; the latter was worn combined with larger ones by the ranks of Captain-Lieutenant and Lieutenant. The stars above the stripes were embroidered in gold and measured 2 in (51 mm) in diameter for flag officers and $1\frac{3}{16}$ in (30 mm) for the other officers.

The trimmings on the cuffs of the corps officers' dress jacket identified class of rank: the generals wore three stripes and three double bars, the senior officers had two stripes and two double bars and junior officers had one stripe and one double bar only, in gold or silver according to corps.

The shoulder straps were the same as those used by the army and identified rank and branch of service. Officers of the Line and Line Engineering had gold ones with black piping and the latter were distinguished by the additional engineers' badge (crossed wrench and hammer). The flag officers (admirals) wore gold naval stars of rank on the shoulder straps while the generals of the corps had army type stars, as illustrated.

The shoulder straps of the flag officers were covered by gold or silver lace of admirals'/generals' pattern, with a zigzag design interwoven; the senior officers' gold or silver shoulder straps carried two longitudinal lines of coloured piping and those of the junior officers had one line of piping only. The button was always of the same metal as the lace while the rank stars of the generals and of the officers, and the corps badge, were made in the opposite metal, i.e. silver on gold and vice versa.

The following shoulder straps were used during the war:

Corps	**Lace**	**Piping**	**Badge**
Line	gold	black	—
Line Engineering	gold	black	Crossed wrench and hammer
Aviation	gold	light blue	—
Aviation Engineering	gold	light blue	Crossed wrench and hammer
Coastal Defence	gold	brown	—
Naval Constructions	silver	black	Crossed wrench and hammer
Supply	silver	red	—
Medical (with mil. training)	silver	red/green	Serpent and cup

The silver shoulder straps of the medical officers had green piping embodied and red piping around the outer edges.

The officers of auxiliary services were identified by narrow shoulder straps, $\frac{3}{16}$ in (4.5 mm) wide for a general and $\frac{5}{32}$ in (4 mm) for other officers, as admirals'/generals' shoulder straps were always slightly wider than those of the others.

The following were in existence:

Corps	**Lace**	**Piping**	**Badge**
Medical (without mil. training)	silver	red	Gold serpent and cup
Veterinary	silver	red	Silver serpent and cup
Administration	silver	red	—
Legal	silver	red	Shield on crossed swords

The Guards' badge was instituted on 28 March 1942 as an award for units of the armed forces which had gained particular distinction in battle. The badge was made of brass and enamel.

Plate 14. Cap and Rate Insignia

Midshipmen and chief petty officers wore uniforms of officers' type, the former with officers' cap badge and the latter with their own badge, depicting a foul anchor ensigned by the red star and surrounded by a rope. All the other ratings had sailors' uniforms with a sailors' cap with tally and red star. Petty officers with more than 5 years' service were entitled to wear the peaked cap with the red star at the front.

The black cap tallies carried the name of a fleet, for instance 'BLACK SEA FLEET' or the name of a ship's crew, for instance 'THE GLORIOUS'; the tally illustrated reads 'RED CAUCASUS'. Ratings serving on ships awarded Guards' attribute wore tallies with orange stripes, inspired by the old order of bravery of St George.

In 1943 the rate badges were transferred from the sleeves on to the shoulder straps and consisted of yellow lace stripes, as illustrated. Letters of the cyrillic alphabet were attached to the outer ends of the shoulder straps to identify the wearer's unit or organisation.

Circular trade badges were worn on the upper sleeves: the trade's devices were embroidered in red and the actual badges, of the same colour as the uniform on which they were intended to be worn, had a red edging. The Boatswain had an anchor, the Helmsman a steering wheel, the Gunner crossed guns, etc.

The leather belt of the ratings carried a brass buckle with the star and hammer and sickle within, superimposed upon an anchor.

Marines wore a gold foul anchor on the left upper sleeve and aviators wore the winged badges illustrated in previous volumes.

Denmark

The Danish Navy was founded by King Hans in 1500 and, due to the insular configuration of Denmark, the fleet played a dominant role in the history and development of the nation.

Its greatest victory was won at the battle of the Bay of Koege in 1677 against the Swedish Navy and other successful engagements took place in the Great Northern War, during the period between 1701 and 1720.

The Battle of Copenhagen is widely known because it was fought against the British fleet under the command of Admiral Nelson. The last important engagement occurred in 1864, when the Danish Navy won against a combined Austro–Prussian force.

Plate 15. Officers' Cap and Rank Insignia

The insignia worn during World War 2 followed the rules established by the regulations published in 1937 and were used until 1951 when drastic changes took place. No shoulder straps were used by the Danish Navy until 1951 and the flag officers' insignia and other badges were altered then too.

Flag officers, senior officers and junior officers wore different cap badges; all had the crown above an oval red-white-red Danish cockade with the foul anchor superimposed but the surrounding oak leaves wreath was different for each class of rank. The flag officers' wreath was somewhat larger than that of the senior officers, although both had twelve leaves, while the junior officers' wreath had ten leaves only.

Rank was identified by gold lace stripes on the cuffs. Flag officers used stripes $1\frac{1}{8}$ in (28 mm) in width, in combination with $\frac{9}{16}$ in (14 mm) stripes, with the top one twisted in a round curl.

The other executive officers wore rows of $\frac{9}{16}$ in (14 mm) lace in combination with narrower ones, with the curl; the officers of three special branches were identified by devices in the curl and the officers of the corps had stripes on distinction cloth backing, with the corps emblem in place of the curl.

The initial 'R' superimposed upon an anchor was the device for the officers of the Reserve, the initial 'F' ('Flyver') identified an officer of Aviation and 'K' ('Kyst') an officer of the Coast Artillery.

In 1951 the same cap badge was introduced for all officers, from admiral to sub-lieutenant, new flag officers' rank insignia of British pattern were adopted, together with ornaments of gold oak leaves on the peaked cap's visor.

Plate 16. Officers' Rank Insignia

The officers of the corps included naval engineers, supply officers and medical officers, who had different rank titles: 'Maskinmester', 'Intendant' and 'Laege', respectively.

The executive officers and the officers of the corps had not the same hierarchy of rank: the engineers and intendants, for instance, had an intermediate rank between Sub-Lieutenant of 1st and of 2nd Grade, in the form of one medium and one narrow gold stripe, but did not use the rank identified by two medium and two narrow stripes. The top rank they could reach was 'Stabsmaskinmester' and 'Stabsintendant', respectively, which corresponded to the executive rank of Commander-Captain.

The medical officers reached the rank of 'Stabslaege' with four medium stripes but did not use the rank corresponding to Commander-Captain, nor the intermediate rank of the engineers and intendants mentioned above.

The officers of the corps could be identified as follows:

Corps	Badge	Distinction Cloth
Naval Engineers	Anchor and propeller	Crimson
Supply	Anchor and caduceus	White
Medical	Anchor and Aesculapius staff	Poppy red

The corps badges were embroidered in gold wire. The distinction cloth was shown in between the stripes, or below a single stripe. The following is a comparative scheme of ranks:

Executive Officers	Naval Engineers	Supply Officers	Medical Officers
Commander	—	—	Staff Doctor
Commander-Captain	Staff Machinist-Master	Staff Intendant	—
		—	
Captain (two ranks)	—		Senior Doctor (two ranks)
	Machinist-Master 1st Grade	Senior Intendant	
Captain-Lieutenant	Machinist-Master 2nd Grade	Intendant 1st Grade	Senior Doctor 2nd Grade
Sub-Lieutenant 1st Grade	Machinist-Master 3rd Grade	Intendant 2nd Grade	Asst Doctor over 3 years service
—	Junior Machinist-Master 1st/2nd Grade over 3 years service	Asst Intendant over 3 years service	—

Executive Officers	Naval Engineers	Supply Officers	Medical Officers
Sub-Lieutenant 2nd Grade	Junior Machinist-Master 2nd Grade under 3 years service	Asst Intendant under 3 years service	Asst Doctor under 3 years service

Midshipmen's, Cadets' and Chief Petty Officers' Insignia

Midshipmen, cadets and chief petty officers wore the same cap badge: the crown above the oval cockade with foul anchor superimposed, surrounded by a wreath of four oak leaves, the whole embroidered in gold.

Midshipmen and cadets wore a $\frac{9}{32}$ in (7 mm) wide stripe of gold lace on the cuffs, with the curl for 'A' Class and without the curl for ordinary midshipmen and cadets.

The chief petty officers used a different type of gold lace stripe $\frac{13}{32}$ in (10 mm) in width, $3\frac{1}{2}$ in (90 mm) in length; the stripes were placed at $\frac{7}{32}$ in (5 mm) from each other, the lowest at $2\frac{3}{4}$ in (70 mm) from the sleeve's edge in the case of C.P.O. 1st Grade, at $3\frac{5}{16}$ in (85 mm) for C.P.O. 2nd Grade and at $3\frac{15}{16}$ in (100 mm) for the 3rd Grade. They wore golden metal corps badges on the collar of the jacket.

Plate 17. Petty Officers' and Seamen's Insignia

The cap badge for petty officers was made of brass, in two pieces: the crown and anchor, and the wreath, and was placed on the peaked cap above a round silk cockade.

The chevrons were $\frac{9}{16}$ in (14 mm) wide and $3\frac{1}{2}$ in (90 mm) long on the side and were sewn at $\frac{9}{32}$ in (7 mm) from each other. Yellow chevrons were used on blue uniform and blue chevrons on white uniform.

There were petty officers of 1st and 2nd Class with three and two chevrons respectively; a single chevron insignia existed as well and was worn by the Reservist Leader of the fire brigade at naval bases.

Cap tallies with the name of ships were used from 1909 until about 1932 and were then replaced by the 'KGL. MARINE', i.e. 'Royal Navy' type for all. The tally was $1\frac{1}{8}$ in (28 mm) wide and the letters were $\frac{15}{32}$ in (12 mm) high; on its right side there was a red-white-red Dannebrøg cockade and on the left the tally was knotted into a bow.

Trade Badges

Conscripted able-bodied seamen wore a red crown above the anchor on both upper sleeves, while qualified tradesmen wore yellow badges woven on black silk, as illustrated.

Germany

The 'Kriegsmarine' of the Third Reich traced its origins to the small fleet of Prussia but most of these ships were ceded to Sweden in 1815. A new programme of naval development started in 1835 but, after the Danish–German War of 1848–50, most ships were sold.

In 1853 Prussia acquired what is now the port of Wilhelmshaven from the State of Oldenburg, and Kiel in 1865 after another war against Denmark.

The Prime Minister Otto von Bismarck's ambition was to unite all German States into one realm with a powerful army and navy and the first obvious step to achieve the latter was to secure the best harbours available.

By the time of the Franco–Prussian War, the North German Federation had thirty-seven warships, which included three armoured frigates, but the real rise of the fleet coincided with the rule of Emperor Wilhelm II; his navy became one of the strongest in the world and the construction of the Kiel Canal, between the Baltic and the North Sea, became a factor of great strategic importance.

Squadrons went to Africa and China; in 1897 the naval personnel numbered twenty-three thousand and sixty-five thousand by the outbreak of World War 1.

The Treaty of Versailles reduced drastically the strength of the German Navy and, by 1935, a naval treaty between Britain and Germany limited the latter's navy to 35 per cent of the strength of the Royal Navy.

This treaty was repudiated before the outbreak of World War 2. The uniforms of the 'Kriegsmarine' were derived from those of the 'Reichsmarine', which in turn were developed from the uniforms of the 'Kaiserliche Marine'.

Plate 18. Cap and Rank Insignia

The officers, warrant officers and midshipmen used the same cap badges. The eagle and cockade with wreath were worn on the peaked cap; the former was usually made of gilded brass although embroidered badges were used as well, especially towards the end of the War. The black, white and red national cockade was trimmed with gold wire and the wreath, of twelve oak leaves and four acorns, was embroidered in gold.

A smaller embroidered eagle and the cockade alone were worn on the front of the navy blue side cap by officers, warrant officers and midshipmen, whilst the other ratings had machine embroidered badges, a yellow eagle and a plain black, white and red cockade. Metal badges were worn on the ratings' hat, above the tally.

All officers had the cap's visor covered with blue cloth and bound with black leather on which flag officers displayed gold oak leaves in two rows, senior naval officers (Captain, Commander and Lieutenant-Commander) one row only of oak leaves and junior officers a gold waved rim. In 1963, these embroideries were adopted by the 'Bundeswehr'. Gold piping on the side cap denoted officer's rank.

Rank was shown by means of cuff stripes and shoulder cords in the usual naval fashion; however, as it was generally difficult for army personnel to identify naval ranks, naval officers who worked with the army often wore shoulder straps on the blue jacket as well.

The German officers had their stripes higher on the sleeves than did British or American officers. Flag officers wore a large gold lace stripe, combined with from one to four medium stripes above it, and shoulder cords formed by two gold and one silver plaited stripes of braid, with silver 4-pointed stars, or pips, to identify each individual rank.

As usual with German military tradition, the lowest rank in each specific class did not wear the pip, the Great Admiral had crossed batons on the shoulder cords instead of pips and, like the General Admiral, wore one broad and four medium stripes on the cuffs. The rank of Commodore was seldom used: he wore a single large gold stripe on the cuffs and shoulder cords, as for a Captain.

The cloth backing to the shoulder cords of all officers of the active list, regardless of branch, matched in colour the uniform on which they had to be worn.

Plate 19. Officers' Rank Insignia

Executive officers or officers of the Line wore a 5-pointed star above the cuff stripes and no device on the shoulder cords, while those of the other branches were identified by embroidered badges on the cuffs, in place of the star and by metal badges on the shoulder cords. The flag officers' badges were made of silver and those of the other officers of gilded brass, to match the metal of the pips. The following were the branches and corresponding badges:

Branch	**Badge**
Line	Star
Engineering	Cogwheel
Medical	Aesculapius staff
Ordnance	Crossed cannons
Defensive Ordnance	Mine
Coast Artillery	Winged grenade

Branch	Badge
Communications	Lightning
Technical Communications	Cogwheel above lightning
Torpedo Technician	Torpedo above cogwheel
Administration	Winged caduceus
Intendance	As above on gold bar
Legal	Sword above gold bar

The last two branches were organised in 1944 from officers formerly belonging to the service of Administrative Officials. Their badges had a gold bar below, $\frac{19}{32}$ in × $\frac{7}{32}$ in (15 mm × 5 mm) in size, made of lace. Reserve officers wore two small gold oak leaves below the branch badge.

The shoulder cords were basically the same as those of the army; those for senior and junior officers were made of silver braid, plaited for the former and straight for the latter, with buttons, pips and badges of gilded brass.

Plate 20. Breast Insignia

All ranks of the German Navy wore the national insignia, the eagle, on the right breast of the uniform and, therefore, of course, there were innumerable variations in relation to style and manufacture. Basically, the officers wore gold embroidered eagles on blue uniforms and gilded badges with a pin at the back on white uniforms; the ratings' badges were silk woven or machine embroidered in yellow cotton, on a navy blue background.

These badges were considerably larger than those worn on the cap.

Chaplains' Badges

The chaplains were classed as Administrative Officials with officers' status but without a definite rank and therefore without conventional rank insignia.

They wore a silver cap badge, with the Roman Cross in between the eagle and the cockade, silver breast insignia and silver buttons. Their collar patches were embroidered in silver and depicted the cross above two oak leaves and acorns on a violet background.

Midshipmen's and Chief Petty Officers' Rate Insignia

The midshipmen wore silver shoulder cords which could be described as 'half' shoulder cords, because they were made with only one double strand of silver braid turned back around the button hole. The Senior Midshipman wore two silver pips, the ordinary Midshipman none and branch badges of officer's type were added between the pips or on the plain cords by the non-executive midshipmen. The gold star, or branch badges were shown on the cuffs as illustrated.

Ratings graduated in their own particular department and initially wore the round badges illustrated on Plate 22; on achieving Petty Officers' rate they changed to the badges on Plate 21, with additional anchor, and eventually graduated to wearing shoulder straps, with small departmental badges made of brass.

The shoulder straps were made of blue cloth, edged by gold lace of special naval pattern and carried silver pips according to rate and the departmental badge.

The various departmental rates developed independently one from another, each with different titles, and equivalent rates were not necessarily represented by the same number of pips, nor were the pips placed in the same position.

Plate 21. Petty Officers' Badges

The petty officers wore, on the left upper sleeve, the departmental badge combined with an anchor, except for those of the Line who wore the anchor alone and the Boatswain who had crossed anchors.

The senior petty officers had a small chevron below the badge and the Candidate Officer had two chevrons, one smaller than the other.

These badges were embroidered in yellow silk on a dark blue background for use on blue uniforms, or in medium blue silk or wool on white for white uniforms. Brass badges were worn on the 'Uberzieher', i.e. the short overcoat, and on the parade jacket, with two rows of buttons at the front and the buttons on the cuff tabs.

Chief petty officers wore officers' type uniform, while the petty officers wore sailors' uniforms, naval hat with tally, jumper and, in cold weather, the short overcoat mentioned above.

On 1 December 1939 medium blue collar patches were adopted for wearing on the overcoat, with one gold stripe for petty officers and two for senior petty officers.

The cap tally usually displayed the type and name of the ship or organisation to which a sailor was attached, but all were replaced by the 'KRIEGSMARINE' (Navy of War) tally illustrated. In 1940 the side cap was introduced as a more practical type of head-dress, in variations and with different badges according to rate.

Plate 22. Departmental Badges

The departmental badges, in yellow on dark blue or blue on white, according to type of uniform, were worn on the left upper sleeve above eventual chevrons.

All except two accord with the badges illustrated in the previous plates; the device of the Line department for seamen was the star, as for the officers' branch, and the badge of the admirals' staff had no counterpart among those of higher ratings.

Seamen's Rate Badges

The chevrons of the seamen identified rate and long service at the same time. Those of the two upper ranks were made of plaited gold braid and the others of gold lace of naval pattern, and were adopted in 1936, although their designations were subsequently modified in 1938 and in 1940.

A smaller silver lace chevron or stripe below these ratings' badges denoted that the wearer was respectively awaiting promotion to petty officer's rate or in training for promotion.

Plate 23. War Awards and Clasps

Eight badges were introduced during World War 2 as a reward for individuals or crews who had achieved special merits in action; all were worn on the left breast.

The Submarines' War Badge was adopted in January 1918 and re-instituted in October 1939 for crews who had been engaged in at least two operational sorties, or one particularly successful sorty.

The Destroyers' War Badge was instituted in June 1940 and was also awarded to crews of motor torpedo boats until May 1941, when the E-Boats received their own award; the badge of the latter had initially a silver central device and, later, from January 1943 onward, the central part was made of grey metal and the boat protruded well out of the oak wreath frame, as illustrated.

Personnel of minesweepers, anti-submarine and escort vessels were granted a badge, in August 1940, that was awarded for participation in three operational sorties, or one that was particularly successful.

The auxiliary cruisers were, in fact, armed merchant ships and their crews obtained badges in April 1941; a special badge with diamonds was awarded for exceptional merit.

The High Seas Fleet War Badge was instituted in April 1941 to reward crews of battleships and cruisers for 13 weeks of active service at sea, or single successful actions. A higher award with diamonds existed as well.

Individuals usually could obtain a badge for having been wounded in action or if their ship was sunk in action.

The Coast Artillery War Badge was instituted in June 1941 and was awarded on the basis of points gained for spotting, detecting and shooting down enemy aircraft, eight being the requisite number.

All the badges above were oval in shape and all followed a basic pattern: they carried the German Eagle on top, a central device which identified the award and an oval frame of gold oak leaves and acorns. The Blockade Runners' Badge was different because it was round in shape and was made of black metal, except for the eagle and the chain around the badge, which were silver. It was instituted in April 1941 for crews of German merchant vessels who succeeded in bringing their ships back home or scuttled them to avoid enemy capture, who managed to get back home after their ship was sunk or who were wounded as a result of enemy action.

As German submariners performed great deeds of valour, year after year, throughout the war, Grand Admiral Doenitz instituted a Submarine War Badge with diamonds which was awarded to submarines' commanders for exceptional merit and, in May 1944, the Submarine Combat Clasp started to be issued to crews. The first clasp was made of bronze and a second one, of silver, was instituted in the following November and later a gilt clasp as well, but the latter probably was never awarded.

The Naval Combat Clasp was created in November 1944, in one single bronze version, as an additional reward for those who already possessed a naval war badge. All naval personnel were eligible except submariners, who had their own clasps. It was awarded to individuals who fulfilled a further five times the conditions required for obtaining a war badge and was worn above the ribbon bars.

The Small Fighting Means ('Kleinkampfmittel') was a new naval branch created in the autumn of 1943 and, as its title suggests, it consisted of frogmen, manned torpedoes and midget submarines, etc. deployed in unconventional naval warfare.

A sawfish was the emblem of this new branch and, therefore, when on 30 November 1944 war badges were instituted, the sawfish became their main device. The badge of the first four classes was worn on the right upper sleeve and consisted of the emblem embroidered in gold or yellow on a blue circular patch, as illustrated. The 7th Class badge was given after 2 months' service in the branch, the 6th Class was awarded for participation in one combat action, the 5th in two and so on. A bronze clasp was awarded for five actions, silver clasp for seven actions and gilt clasp, the 1st Class, for ten or more combat actions. The clasps were worn above ribbon bars, or above the left breast pocket.

Cadets' Badges

The cadets wore sailors' uniform and were distinguished from their shipmates by the badges they had on the left sleeve, in place of the departmental insignia.

The badge depicted the emblem of the officers' branch for which the cadet was training, surrounded by an oval frame, the whole in gold on blue or blue on a white background.

The badge of Defensive Ordnance was the last to be adopted, possibly in 1940.

Plates 24, 25. Trade Badges

The trade badge was worn on the left sleeve, below rate insignia. Some incorporated small chevrons, which in some cases denoted seniority of specialisation, grade or class of specialisation or attendance at specific courses.

Two small oak leaves and one acorn below the emblem identified a specialist of the Reserve.

In August 1940 a new set of trade badges was adopted and the previous ones were abolished; the following were the new badges:

Grenade with one, two or three chevrons below—for 3rd, 2nd and 1st Gun Leader, respectively.

Winged grenade—for A.A. Gunner and Observer; with one or two chevrons below for 2nd and 1st Gun Leader, respectively.

Rangefinder—for Range Taker; with one chevron below for holder of A.A. certificate and with two chevrons for Range Taker training for petty officers' rate.

Torpedo with one or two chevrons below—for 3rd and 2nd Torpedo Specialist, respectively.

Mine with one chevron below—for Mines Specialist.

Diver's helmet with one, two or three chevrons below—for Ship Diver, Torpedo Diver and Submarine Diver, respectively.

Arrow pointing down with one and two chevrons below—for Underwater Detector Specialists with Seamen's and Petty Officers' Course, respectively.

Arrow pointing up and with one chevron below—Unqualified and Qualified A.A. Detector Listener; with two chevrons below for A.A. Searchlights Specialist Leader.

Wheel with electric sparks and with one or two chevrons below—for Coastal Electrician and Electrotechnician of 3rd and 2nd course, respectively.

3-bladed propeller with one and two chevrons below—for Motor Engineer of 3rd and 2nd Course, respectively.

Grenade ball with three flames, and with two chevrons below—for Coast Artillery Gun Leader, apprentice and specialist, respectively.

Grenade ball with three flames and wings—for A.A. Coast Artillery Gun Leader.

Circle with two converging arrows, and with chevron below—for Armourer Specialist in general and of Artillery, Coastal and A.A. Gunnery.

Two chevrons, the uppermost with a curl—for Drummers and Pipers. Only four of these new badges have been illustrated in the last row of trade badges because they differed from the previous ones; all the others, or at least the main emblems, were the same as those of the old badges.

Bandmasters

Bandmaster and music directors wore officers' uniforms but with special rank insignia, stripes with curl and lyre in the curl on the cuffs and different shoulder cords, which incorporated strands of blue braid, as illustrated.

In 1940 the stripes with curl were abolished and bandmasters were allowed to use the straight gold stripes below the branch badge like all the other naval officers.

The following were their ranks and the corresponding ranks for officers of the Line:

Bandmasters	**Line**
Musikmeister	Leutnant z.S.
Obermusikmeister	Oberleutnant z.S.
Stabsmusikmeister	Kapitänleutnant
Musikinspizient	Korvettenkapitän
Obermusikinspizient	Fregattenkapitän

Plate 26. Badges for Field Grey Uniforms

Naval detachments that served on land, for instance on coastal defence, wore field grey uniforms of army pattern; later in the war the navy raised many battalions and larger formations specifically for land warfare and their personnel used army uniforms as well.

The admirals initially did not wear field grey uniforms and only a few used it later, therefore some items of their dress, for instance the colour of their collar patches, greatcoats' lapels and trousers' stripes are still in controversy; probably it was ultramarine, cornflower or middle blue.

The officers wore on the peaked cap gold naval badges, the wreath embroidered on dark bluish-green felt, gold or silver chin strap cords for admirals and other officers, respectively, and plain black leather visors. The side, or field, cap carried the same badges as the one made of blue cloth, but with badges embroidered on a dark bluish green background. Similarly, all breast eagles were embroidered or woven on dark bluish-green cloth.

The same colour was used as a backing to the silver double bars worn by the officers on the collar, officers' shoulder cords and ratings' shoulder straps.

The admirals' shoulder cords, made of two gold and one silver strand of braid as usual, were placed on a medium blue cloth background but, apart from the background, the cords, rank insignia and button were the same as those used on the blue uniform.

The ratings' insignia were different, as illustrated, because the 'field grey' navy had more rates than the 'blue' navy. During the late stages of the War field grey shoulder straps were issued to the ratings, as the quality of uniforms progressively deteriorated.

The badges illustrated are typical of the 'field grey' navy, although normal branch badges were used as well, for instance doctors wore the Aesculapius staff, etc. Other devices were often worn in combination with branch badges or on their own: the initials 'N' for 'Nordsee', 'O' for 'Ostsee' and Roman or Arabic numbers, all made of brass.

Plate 27. Officials' Insignia

The Officials ('Marinebeamten') were individuals, employed in administrative roles at ministries and other offices connected with the navy, who wore naval uniforms and had rank distinctions equivalent to those of the active service.

The major difference between the personnel of the active list and of the 'Marinebeamten' was that the latter wore all insignia and buttons of silver.

Officials with officers' status wore chin strap cords, in gold for flag ranks and silver for the others, on the peaked cap, instead of embroideries on the visor, which was made of black leather. They had silver lace stripes on the cuffs below the Administrative Officials' badge, the German Eagle, combined with the branch devices of specific administration.

All these oval-shaped badges have been illustrated; usually three devices identified an official with a university degree while two or one branch devices were worn by those with lesser qualifications. Eight devices were in existence in 1939 and two more were added to the active list: Intendance and Legal, with personnel drawn from the Administrative Officials.

Officials' shoulder cords and pips were the same as those of the navy but were placed on underlay of different colours, as in the following list:

Branch	**Colour**
Supreme Command of the Navy	Dark blue
Administrative Officials, Pharmacists, Non-technical Teachers of Naval Schools	Cornflower blue
Legal Officials	Crimson
Technicians, Ship's Pilots	Black

Senior ratings wore special cords made of plaited strands of blue and white braid, with the eagle, branch device and one or two pips according to rate, the whole on arm-of-service colour underlay.

Also the officials used field grey uniforms with insignia, in this case on a dark bluish-green background, as already described in the section dealing with naval field grey uniforms.

The designation 'Sonderführer' means 'Special Leader' and referred to specialists with particular qualifications, but without naval training, who served in the navy. Those ranking as officers had small gold foul anchors on the collar and ratings wore the anchor attached to the blue collar patches, below the gold braid.

France

Until the period of the late Consulate there was no uniformity of naval dress; crewmen especially wore what was provided by their officers or were left to their own resources. The first uniforms appeared in 1804 and were, at least for the sailors, rather austere, in complete contrast with those worn a few years later during the period of the Empire. These uniforms were magnificent but had no naval character whatsoever.

The Restoration suppressed all the luxury and the sailors' dress was left once again to the discretion of their commanders until the 1820s, when at least some garments were issued especially to the sailors. The outlook of the 'matelot' began to appear under the reign of Louis Philippe; the sailors were issued with a straw hat ornamented by a ribbon which displayed the name of the ship in gold letters. The collar with three white stripes, the predecessor of the modern one, appeared at that time also.

The woollen tuft on top of the hat was introduced during the period of the Second Empire and was red and white at that time, but it was only in the period of the Third Republic that naval uniforms began to assume the practical features of the modern dress.

The process of modernisation was, however, rather slow; for instance, summer uniforms were officially adopted only in 1929 and special uniforms and utility garments appeared later, in the 1930s.

Plate 28. Flag Officers' Cap and Rank Insignia

The cap badge of the flag officers was embroidered in gold on dark blue cloth and consisted of a wreath of ten laurel leaves with a plain foul anchor for the officers of the corps, an anchor with additional wings and lightnings for executive flag officers.

Special gold embroideries on the cap band distinguished the flag officers from the other officers and, at the same time, identified their rank and corps. Small 5-pointed stars were displayed at the front and the type of embroidery also identified rank, as follows: the Admiral of the Fleet, Admiral and Vice-Admiral of Squadron had an additional stripe of silver braid along the top of the cap band, the Vice-Admiral used the same embroidery as the upper ranks but without the silver braid and the Rear-Admiral had a plainer type of embroidery.

Flag officers of the executive branch ('Officiers de marine') were called admirais while those of the other corps were called generals.

The embroidery of the former depicted oak leaves and acorns while the generals had their own distinctive embroideries, according to corps, full embroideries for the top ranking generals and a plainer pattern for the lower rank, as mentioned above. The embroidery of the medical officers, pharmacists and chemists, for instance, depicted laurel leaves and snakes, commissaries had oak and vine leaves, engineers of naval artillery had olive leaves and crossed cannons above anchors and engineers of hydrography had plain olive leaves.

Gold chin strap cords were worn by admirals and generals on the peaked cap. They also used another cap for duties on board ship: it had a plain cap band, leather chin strap and an oval-shaped badge at the front which displayed the rank stars.

Rank insignia in the form of stars were worn on the cuffs and on the shoulder straps; the latter were edged with a gold stripe and carried a foul anchor and the stars were on the outer ends.

Plain rectangular shoulder tabs embroidered in gold were worn on the blue jacket; four patterns existed, according to class of rank.

The rank of Admiral of the Fleet was created for Admiral Darlan on 6 June 1939 and remained in existence until his death in 1942. He wore two stars above three on the embroidered cap band while, on the cuffs and shoulder straps, one star was always placed above the other four, as illustrated.

The officers of the corps could usually graduate to two flag ranks, although pharmacists, for example, could attain only one. Their rank titles were preceded by the corps' name, for instance:

'Médecin Général de 1ère Classe'	Medical—Vice-Admiral
'Commissaire Général de 1ère Classe'	Commissariat—Vice-Admiral
'Pharmacien Général de 2ème Classe'	Pharmacy—Rear-Admiral

The officers of the Fleet Equipage (Officiers des Équipages de la Flotte') did not reach flag rank as their top rank was 'Officier en Chef des Équipages de la Flotte' which corresponded to the executive rank of 'Capitaine de Frégate'. Musicians graduated up to the rank of 'Chef de Musique Principal', i.e. 'Capitaine de Corvette'.

Plate 29. Officers' Cap and Rank Insignia

The cap badge of the officers below flag rank had only eight leaves in the wreath and the foul anchor in its centre. They displayed their rank in the form of lace stripes on the cap band and on the cuffs, and on the shoulder straps.

The executive officers had their stripes attached to the sleeve, or dark blue shoulder straps, while the officers of corps had the stripes on coloured backing which protruded $3\frac{15}{16}$in (100mm) above and below the stripes and wore coloured shoulder straps without the anchor.

The following coloured velvet backings were used:

Corps	Colour
Directors of Music	Blue-grey
Mechanical Officers	Violet
Interpreters and Naval Cypher Officers	Ultramarine
Naval Engineers of various specialities	Black
Commissariat	Otter brown
Medical	Crimson
Chemists and Pharmacists	Light green
Hydrographical Professors	Light violet
Recruiting and Administrative Staff	Ash grey

The officers of the Fleet Equipage were specialists who had been commissioned from the ranks and were distinguished by a rectangular patch with button on the cuffs and shoulder straps.

Rank titles varied as shown in the following scheme:

Executive Branch	Fleet Équipage	Corps
Capitaine de Vaisseau	—	en Chef de 1ère Classe
Capitaine de Frégate	en Chef	en Chef
Capitaine de Corvette	Principal	Principal
Lieutenant de Vaisseau	de 1ère Classe	de 1ère Classe
Enseigne de Vaisseau de 1ère Classe	de 2ème Classe	de 2ème Classe
Enseigne de Vaisseau de 2ème Classe	—	de 3ème Classe

The designation of the officers' corps was placed before the rank titles, as for example 'Médecin de 1ère classe' in the case of a Doctor. Officers of the Fleet Equipage had 'Officier' in front of their rank title.

Plate 30. Cap and Rate Insignia

The insignia of midshipmen, petty officers, quartermasters, etc. have been illustrated in this plate.

A foul anchor surrounded by a wreath of two laurel leaves only was the cap badge of the Midshipman and of the ratings who were entitled to wear the peaked cap. The gold badge was used by personnel of the Fleet Equipage, musicians, firemen, signalmen and harbour personnel, while the red badge was used by musicians, firemen, signalmen and harbour personnel only.

The Midshipman, the senior petty officers and others, while wearing special uniform, wore gold cap badges; the Midshipman, Chief and 1st Petty Officer and the Petty Officer had also a gold stripe of lace around the cap band.

All wore rate insignia on the cuffs and, down to 2nd Petty Officer, on the shoulder straps as well; lower ratings had stripes on the cuffs only.

The Midshipman's stripe was gold and blue and, like the stripes of the Chief and 1st Petty Officer, was worn straight, horizontally. The Petty Officer and 2nd Petty Officer used lace of special pattern, in the form of chevrons on the shoulder straps and oblique stripes on cuffs. The large stripe was $\frac{7}{8}$ in (22 mm) in width, the narrow one $\frac{15}{32}$ in (12 mm) and the narrow stripes were placed at a distance of $\frac{5}{64}$ in (2 mm) from each other, with the lower end at $3\frac{1}{2}$ in (90 mm) from the bottom edge of the sleeve, the higher end at $7\frac{1}{16}$ in (180 mm).

The Quartermaster ('Quartier-Maître de Maistrance') qualified at the 'École de Maistrance' and wore a gold and blue stripe on the cuffs. The junior quartermasters had three or two red stripes according to class and the Qualified Seaman a single large one.

The junior ratings wore a special badge on the left breast of the summer vest; it depicted a blue anchor surrounded by a blue rectangular frame and with blue stripes at the bottom which identified rate class.

Plate 31. Cap, Rate and Speciality (on collar) Insignia

Some specialists were entitled to different insignia: tailors wore stripes of gold and red lace, yeomen wore gold stripes on the upper sleeves and buglers were identified by an additional stripe sewn along the edge of the sleeves, as illustrated.

The gold foul anchor was worn by junior ratings on the blue hat, above the tally, but not on the white hat of the summer uniform. A larger anchor $2\frac{9}{16}$ in (65 mm) in width, cut out from red cloth, was worn on the left side of the blue cap used by naval mechanics and drivers. The same badge was also worn on both sides of the collar of coats and overcoats by junior ratings of the Fleet Equipage.

All the other badges were worn in pairs on the collar of jackets and tunics, in gold or red according to the colour of the cap badge and of the rate insignia. Musicians had the lyre on the shoulder straps as well. The personnel of the Naval Police wore army type uniforms with all their insignia and buttons of silver. They were distinguished by the wearing of silver anchors on the kepi and on the collar of the tunic.

Speciality and Other Badges

Naval aviators wore speciality badges made of metal on the right breast. All consisted of a silver anchor superimposed on to a rope, gold wings and a 5-pointed star for aircraft personnel or wings and a steering wheel for airship or balloon personnel.

The specialities of the aircraft crew included mechanics, telegraphists, machine-gunners, bombardiers and observers.

Physical Training Instructors of the navy wore the same badge as the instructors of the army, in gold or silver according to rank. The badge was pinned on the left side of the breast.

After 1940, France continued to fight together with the Allies and the new French Navy was designated 'Forces Navales Françaises Libres' and adopted the Cross of Lorraine as their emblem.

The officers wore, on the breast, an enamelled, diamond-shaped badge; the sailors had a plainer badge, embroidered in blue, white and red, with gold edges.

A number of enamelled badges were used by personnel of some vessels, of which one has been illustrated: it was the badge of the torpedo boat *Combattante* and depicts the French cockerel and the Cross of Lorraine.

Plate 32. Speciality Insignia (on sleeves)

The junior ratings of the Fleet Equipage wore crossed anchors, cut out from red cloth, on the right sleeve, while speciality insignia were worn on the left sleeve. Holders of a superior certificate had a gold embroidered 5-pointed star, with the top point downwards, on both sleeves above the rate stripes.

The submarines had crossed torpedoes and lightnings, $2\frac{3}{4}$ in (70 mm) wide, embroidered in gold or red thread. The fusiliers were marines embarked on ships and wore the flaming grenade in gold, silver or red, according to rate and qualification.

The radio-telegraphist on coastal duty held a temporary brevet of General Service and wore a red badge, while those on permanent duty of General Service had the gold badge.

The crossed cannons of the Gun Aimer and his proficiency star were made of red cloth, in contrast to the other badges which were embroidered. The proficiency stars were placed at $1\frac{3}{16}$ in (30 mm) above the speciality badge.

The cap tallies used before the war displayed the name of the ship or of a corps to which an individual could be assigned, later the tallies of the Free French Navy carried the initials 'F.N.F.L.' only.

Italy

The Italian Royal Navy was derived from the Sardinian Navy, which traced its origins to a single galley that Amedeus V, County of Savoy, had built in 1287 for sailing on the Lake of Geneva. By 1316 a fleet of four galleys patrolled the lake and, after 1388, when Nice was taken over by the County of Savoy, an access was gained to the Mediterranean, and more galleys were built there as a defence against pirates.

The first major battle in which Savoy's vessels participated was fought at Lepanto in October 1571, against the Turks. At that time a ship's crew was composed of the officers of the upper stern, the leading seamen, embarked soldiers and the crew 'at the oars'.

By the beginning of the eighteenth century, the fleet was divided into two squadrons, galleys and sailships and a battalion of permanent marines was assigned to the former, contrary to the previous rule of embarking any unit on foot when necessary. However, two regiments called 'La Marina' were formed previously but fought on land with the French Army. A third one was raised in 1714 and, a few years later, absorbed the battalion of marines mentioned above; one battalion was deployed on land duties and the other on ships.

Eventually, in 1798, the regiment became part of the French Army, it was disbanded in 1800 and re-formed in 1814 as an infantry regiment. Meanwhile, another battalion of marines was formed in Sardinia, but it was only after the Restoration and the acquisition of Genoa and the region of Liguria that the growth of the navy became in earnest.

The period of Victor Emmanuel II's rule (1849–78) was the most eventful in respect of naval expansion as, due to its process of unification, Italy became a seafaring nation, because of its geographical position in the centre of the Mediterranean sea.

The Royal Decree of 17 November 1860 established the Italian Royal Navy, born by the amalgamation of the Sardinian, Borbonic and Sicilian, Tuscan and Papal navies. The whole service was restructured and, through subsequent reorganisations, it became the modern Italian Royal Navy of the twentieth century.

Plate 33. Head-dress Insignia

Officers, chiefs and senior petty officers wore the peaked cap with gold embroidered naval badge: the corps' badge on an oval background called a 'shield', surrounded by six laurel leaves, the whole ensigned by the crown.

There were three types of badges, according to rank:

1. For Great Admiral, with Royal Crown with gold cushion and purple base.
2. For flag officers with the rank of Admiral of Army (Fleet) and Admiral of Squad in Command of Army, with Royal Crown with purple cushion and base.
3. For all other ranks, with Royal Crown with blue cushion and base.

The central badge and the distinction cloth of the shield varied according to corps:

Corps	Badge	Distinction Cloth
Line	Foul anchor	Blue velvet
Naval Engineers	Roman helmet, axe and hammer superimposed on anchor	Crimson velvet
Naval Ordnance	Sword superimposed on anchor	Avana brown felt
Doctors	Red cross superimposed on anchor	White felt
Chemists–Pharmacists	Aesculapius staff	Green felt
Commissariat	Star superimposed on anchor	Purple felt
Port Captaincy	Foul anchor	Grey-green felt

The above were the basic corps but special badges and distinction cloths were used by the following as well:

Chaplains	Gold cross superimposed on anchor	Violet silk
Mechanical Engineers	3-bladed propeller superimposed on anchor	Crimson velvet

The latter were officers serving in the Temporary Role for Machinist Officers, an offspring of the Naval Engineers.

The corps that, for the sake of brevity, has been termed 'Line' included all the executive officers of the General Staff (Stato Maggiore (di Vascello)) and of the Royal Corps of Maritime Crews ('Corpo Reale Equipaggi Marittimi').

The Medical Corps was subdivided into a Medical Role, i.e. doctors, and Pharmacists' Role, composed of chemists and pharmacists.

The personnel of the Naval Ordnance used another corps' badge also which depicted a crossed cannon and torpedo with lightnings at the sides.

All the corps' badges were made of brass.

The officers and chiefs displayed rank insignia on the cap band. Flag officers had a gold embroidered 'greca', the traditional emblem of Italian admirals and generals, surmounted by gold stripes of braid, numbered according to rank.

Senior officers wore one large gold lace stripe with one to three narrower ones above, according to rank, and junior officers had only the narrow stripes around the cap band. Two or more stripes were woven in one piece with black (Line) or coloured intervals on the outer edgings, according to corps.

The chiefs had one stripe only on the cap, regardless of class; their stripe was made of gold lace and blue silk. The other senior petty officers entitled to wear the peaked cap had a plain cap band.

The officers' insignia on the cap corresponded with the rank badges they wore on the cuffs.

Plate 34. Flag Officers' Rank Insignia

The officers of the line had naval rank titles while those of the other corps had army titles. As usual, in an effort to avoid confusion, the officers' rank titles have been left in the original language and the flag officers' titles have been translated literally into English. The Italian admirals were in command of 'armate', 'squadre' and 'divisioni', as the fleet was subdivided in this manner, and, therefore, in this context, these terms are purely nautical.

Shoulder straps were worn, as usual, on white jackets and overcoats, shoulder tabs and cuff stripes on blue jackets. Gold stripes all around the cuffs were displayed on the pre-war dress frock coat only.

The flag officers' shoulder straps were made of gold lace and carried a gold embroidered border, the crown, corps badge and rank insignia in the form of 5-pointed stars; those of the Admiral of Squad in Command of Army had a small crown embroidered in gold wire on blue velvet above the stars and just below the corps badge. All shoulder straps were piped with appropriate distinction cloth, lined at the back with white cloth, and were attached to the jacket by means of a tongue and a gilt button with screw fitting.

The flag officers' shoulder tabs measured $3\frac{3}{16}$ in × $1\frac{3}{8}$ in (80 mm × 35 mm) in size; they were made of navy blue felt, lined with white cloth, with coloured piping, as on the shoulder straps, and carried a gold embroidered outer border or frame, the crown and the corps badge. The following badges and distinction cloth were used on shoulder straps and tabs:

Corps	Badge	Distinction Cloth
Line (S.M.)	Foul anchor	Blue felt
Line (C.R.E.M.)	Foul anchor	Black velvet
Naval Engineers	Roman helmet, axe and hammer surrounded by a wreath	Crimson velvet

Corps	Badge	Distinction Cloth
Naval Ordnance	Sword superimposed on anchor	Avana brown felt
Doctors	Aesculapius staff	Light blue felt
Chemists–Pharmacists	Aesculapius staff	Green felt
Commissariat	Gold laurel wreath	Purple felt
Port Captaincy	Foul anchor	Grey-green felt

The generals of the naval ordnance wore the badge alone, without the wreath, on the shoulder tabs.

The type of crown, in relation to the cushion and base, matched the crown of the cap badge, as in the previous plate.

The main rank insignia were worn on the cuffs, at $3\frac{1}{2}$ in (90 mm) from the bottom of the sleeve and consisted of the 'greca' and stripes, 3 in (75 mm) in length, the latter surmounted by a round curl, the whole embroidered in gold. The admirals' badges were embroidered on navy blue cloth, those of the generals of corps were also embroidered on navy blue but their stripes and curls were edged in corps' colour.

The officers and senior petty officers who served on submarines wore a special brass badge on the breast; it depicted a dolphin, surrounded by a wreath and ensigned by the crown.

Plate 35. Officers' Rank Insignia

The shoulder straps of the officers were made of navy blue cloth and were similar in shape and size to those of the flag officers. Senior officers' straps had a gold embroidered border stripe, the crown and rank stars, and those of the junior officers had the crown and stars only. First lieutenants had a small embroidered bar on the outer end of their shoulder straps. No corps' badges were worn on the shoulder straps, but the crown alone, for all.

The shoulder tabs of the senior officers were 3 in × 1 in (75 mm × 25 mm) in size, with coloured piping, gold embroidered border and central rope on dark blue background. Junior officers' tabs consisted of a stripe of gold lace, sewn above a patch of distinction cloth which protruded all around the gold lace.

Gold lace stripes were displayed on the cuffs: the senior officers had a large stripe, $\frac{25}{32}$ in (20 mm) wide, and from one to three narrower ones $\frac{15}{32}$ in (12 mm), the top one with the curl; the junior officers had the narrow stripes only. Stripes and curl were sewn on navy blue cloth or distinction cloth, according to corps.

Until 1936 the specialist officers used rank stripes without the curl. They were usually commissioned from the ranks due to long service and high performance in specialised tasks.

Plate 36. Petty Officers' Rate Insignia and Trade Badges

The rate of Chief ('capo'). in three Classes, corresponded to the army rank of Warrant Officer and therefore the chiefs had officers' type uniform and special stripes on the shoulder straps, together with a speciality badge embroidered in gold.

The next two ratings, the Second Chief and Sergeant, were identified by chevrons, one large and two narrow, one large and one narrow, woven in one piece with blue intervals, with a gold speciality badge on top.

The Junior Chief, Substitute Junior Chief and Seaman 1st Class had red woven chevrons, one large and two narrow in the case of the former, a medium one $\frac{5}{16}$ in (8 mm) for the substitute and a narrow chevron $\frac{7}{32}$ in (5 mm) for the Seaman 1st Class. Red badges were used with red chevrons, or on their own in order to identify the seaman's trade.

The conscripted seaman wore a plain red embroidered anchor on both upper sleeves, others graduated to a red trade badge, to red chevrons and later to petty officers' gold chevrons and gold badges.

The red badges were rather small, the largest on average about $1\frac{3}{8}$ in (35 mm) in width and the gold ones were smaller still. Sailors with a university degree or high school diploma were automatically eligible for the 'L' (Laurea) or 'D' (Diploma) badges, respectively. Buglers did not qualify for petty officers' rate and therefore only the red badge existed.

Plate 37. Trade Badges

Although trade badges were usually embroidered in red cotton, in the case of volunteers with specific trades, as illustrated, gold letters were worn above the usual trade badge. Lower ratings embarked on submarines wore a special badge on the left upper sleeve: it depicted the usual submariners' dolphin in a circle inscribed 'SOMMERGIBILI' $1\frac{25}{32}$ in (45 mm) in diameter, the whole in white metal.

The volunteer second chiefs and conscripted seamen who re-enlisted for the period of 1 year were allowed to wear a $1\frac{9}{16}$ in (40 mm) gold or red stripe, respectively, on both lower sleeves below the volunteer's badge, the Savoy Knot.

Cap Tallies

A vast array of Italian naval cap tallies can still be found, all woven in yellow silk on a black ribbon and a selection have been illustrated.

The first tally is the war-time pattern worn by all ships' personnel, the translation of which reads 'Royal Navy'. Others were worn in the same period, or earlier: ★REGIE NAVI★ (Royal Ships), ★M.A.S.★ (Motoscafo Anti-

Sommergibile—Anti-Submarine Motor Boat), *SILURANTI* (Motor Torpedo Boats), *R.CAPITANERIA DI PORTO* (Royal Port Captaincy), *R.GUARDIA DI FINANZA* (Royal Customs Guard), etc. Before the war there were cap tallies with the name of the ships, like for instance *R.N.BIXIO* and *R.N.ANDREA DORIA*, in which case 'R.N.' stands for 'Regia Nave', i.e. 'royal ship'. There were others, like for example *R.CT.NULLO* and *R.CT. FOLGORE*, or *R.SOMM. BALILLA* which identified the type of vessel, 'CT' for 'Cacciatorpediniera' and 'SOMM.' for 'Sommergibile'.

The third tally 'NINO BIXIO' represents the pattern worn during World War 1. Some tallies have chevron-like devices on one or both ends which do not identify rank but are purely ornamental and, at the same time, prevent the tally from unthreading.

Badges of 'SAN MARCO' Marines

The 'San Marco' Regiment derived from the marines of long standing history and other units that fought during World War 1. The former, the 'Reggimento Marina' were formed initially by the 'Monfalcone', 'Grado' and 'Caorle' battalions but, in April 1918, the first battalion was named after Lieutenant-Commander Bafile, and another battalion was formed as well, the 'Golametto'.

The 'Raggruppamento Marina' consisted of naval artillery units deployed on land or on pontoons along the coast.

These two formations were amalgamated in August 1919 into the 'Reggimento San Marco' as, during the late stages of that war, both were deployed on the river Piave and Adriatic coast in the defence of Venice, St Mark's city. The Lion of St Mark badge was introduced at that time, embroidered in gold on red collar patches for officers and petty officers and in yellow cotton on red cuff patches for the other ratings.

Marines were issued with grey-green uniforms of army pattern during World War 1 but retained their badges and naval rank titles, although the officers and senior ratings wore army type rank insignia. The same rules of dress were confirmed after the war: the officers wore grey-green service dress, with peaked cap of naval pattern, shoulder tabs instead of shoulder straps, brown leather Sam Browne belt and black riding boots. Junior ratings and seamen wore the basic naval uniform but made of grey-green cloth and with trousers tucked into puttees; in 1936 their naval hat with tally was replaced by a grey-green beret with a brass Lion of St Mark on a red patch as cap badge. They wore trade badges embroidered in black on a grey-green background on the upper sleeves, on their own or above black chevrons. Seamen without specific specialisation wore the foul anchor.

The officers (and senior petty officers) wore collar patches like the one illustrated at the bottom left of this plate: the Lion of St Mark was embroidered in gold and the star was made of white metal. Initially the patch was sewn at the front of the stand collar and therefore the lions were embroidered horizontally, facing the stars and the opening of the collar. Later, after 1934, when jackets with lapels were adopted, smaller lions were embroidered on the top of the patch, as illustrated. The bottom of the collar patch fitted the bottom of the collar, thus patches with pointed bottom ends were made for pointed collars, as for instance the collar of the British battledress. The cuff patches' device was initially embroidered in yellow wool, later in cotton, or rayon. Junior chiefs had an additional gold stripe sewn at the bottom of their cuff patches.

A special embroidered or metal badge was worn on the left upper sleeve by all personnel of the Swimmers–Parachutists Battalion ('Battaglione Nuotatori Paracadutisti'—N.P.Bn) of the Royal Navy and was used later by the navy of the Social Republic, until it was replaced by another badge.

The Armistice of 8 September 1943 led to the formation of two Italian navies, one in the south which carried on the traditions of the old Royal Navy and another one in the north, as part of the armed forces of the Italian Social Republic.

The badges of the former did not change. The Combat Group 'Folgore' was formed on 24 September 1944 as part of the new Italian armed forces and subsequently took part in the Italian Campaign on the Allies' side. It was constituted by a regiment of parachutists, the 'San Marco' regiment of marines and an artillery regiment.

All the personnel of combat groups wore a similar formation sign, the green-white-red colours with the combat group's emblem in the centre; in the case of the 'Folgore' a lightning' as 'folgore' means 'lightning' in Italian.

All personnel wore British battledress, the marines with dark blue beret with naval cap badge for officers and senior petty officers, and a small brass anchor for other ratings and seamen. They had collar or cuff patches according to rank, as before, until 1945, when cuff patches were adopted for officers as well, instead of collar patches.

The regiment was divided into three battalions, named 'Bafile', 'Grado', and 'Caorle' and a shoulder title of the former exists, embroidered in gold wire; it is not known if the other battalions had shoulder titles as well.

Plate 38. Naval Badges and Insignia of the Italian Social Republic

Northern Italy became a republic after the Armistice, thus crowns and royal emblems were deleted accordingly. In the case of the navy, the crown was cut off from badges, shoulder straps and tabs; later new ones were made with the

Republican Eagle in place of the crown on cap badges and the anchor alone embroidered in the centre of shoulder straps and tabs. Three cap badges have been illustrated, one with the crown cut off, the regulations badge with eagle on the left and a smaller one, possibly for the beret, with incorrect leaves in the wreath.

The national emblem, the white star, was replaced on the collar by the 'gladio', a Roman sword superimposed on a round wreath, and eventually new dress regulations were published, which prescribed chin strap cords for officers and some other Germanic features. However, the personnel as a whole kept on wearing their old uniforms with the new badges which, in any case, except for the lack of royal emblems and the new Republican Eagle, were the same as before.

On 27 May 1944 a set of nine badges was introduced to reward long and distinguished service in war-time: bronze badges (1st Degree) were awarded for 18 months of embarkation, or 1,000 hours of navigation at sea including participation in at least one war engagement. Silver badges (2nd Degree) required 30 months of embarkation or 3,000 hours of navigation and three war engagements, and gold badges (3rd Degree) were given for 48 months of embarkation or 5,000 hours at sea and six war engagements. A set of silver badges only has been illustrated.

As, by then, the naval contingent had become ineffectual, new units of marines were created for fighting on land and their personnel wore grey-green uniforms.

A number of badges, for wearing on the breast or on the left upper sleeve were introduced during this period and have been illustrated in this and the following plate.

Plate 39. Naval Badges and Insignia of the Italian Social Republic

The 3rd Division of Marine Infantry 'San Marco' was formed in March 1944 from units of an Italian grenadiers division in training at Grafenwöhr, Germany. The latter was originally raised in December 1943 from a mixed personnel, mainly Italian sailors picked up in the Aegean and Black Shirts that were in Greece at the time of the Armistice. Others later joined up, mainly ex-marines and sailors.

Meanwhile another unit, which existed before the Armistice, the Xth Flotilla M.A.S., was strengthened in Italy and eventually became a division. The initials 'M.A.S.' stand for 'Motoscafo Anti-Sommergibile', i.e. Anti-Submarine Motor Boat.

The men of both units wore similar uniforms: a grey-green beret with brass anchor at the front, a grey-green jacket originally used by parachutists, virtually a 'sahariana' without collar and lapels, and long, baggy trousers tucked into the boots. Officers and petty officers usually wore riding breeches with boots or puttees. However, the personnel of many units were issued with normal infantry uniforms because of lack of supplies.

All wore naval cap badges and marines' type of collar patches, of different colours, as illustrated. A new Lion of St Mark was adopted during the period of the Social Republic: the badge was made of brass and had a tablet at the base with the motto *iterum rudit leo*, i.e. 'The Lion Still Roars', but, contrary to the previous badge, the lion held a closed book, perhaps an omen of the impending disaster.

All ranks who had completed a period of training in Germany were entitled to wear a special badge on the right breast, on the pocket or above it. Artillery personnel of the 'San Marco' Division had the anchor above crossed cannons on the upper sleeves.

Personnel of the reconnaissance unit of the 'San Marco' wore a special white metal cap badge which depicted a flaming grenade above crossed Roman swords, and special black collar patches with a white skull in place of the Lion of St Mark.

Exactly the same cap badge, the foul anchor in brass, was worn during this period by the marines of the King in the South and by those of Mussolini in the North.

The United States of America

The importance of sea power became apparent to the American public during the Civil War when both the Northern and Southern forces attempted to blockade each other's main ports and coastline. The first major engagement between ironclad ships took place during that conflict.

More experience was gained during the war against Spain which was followed by a period of territorial expansion in which the U.S. Navy played a major role. The opening of the Panama Canal led to a great strategic improvement as the Atlantic and Pacific fleets could communicate and support each other directly through the canal.

An American battle squadron operated with the British Grand Fleet during World War I and innumerable destroyers and submarine chasers of the U.S. Navy gave valid aid to the Allies' cause.

The insignia of the U.S. Navy and of the U.S. Coast Guard have been grouped together as these two organisations wore the same uniforms and the same type of badges. During peace-time, the Coast Guard comes under the Secretary of the Treasury while, in war-time, since 1799, it has been under the direction of the Secretary of the Navy.

Plate 40. Cap Head-dress Insignia

As a general rule, the naval peaked cap matched in colour the rest of the uniform, except for the white cover, which could be worn with the white or with the blue uniform. The cap band was black, to match the background of the cap badge, the visor was made of black leather, covered with blue cloth in the case of senior officers entitled to gold leaves, the chin strap of the officers and warrant officers was made of gold braid while the chief petty officers, officers' cooks and stewards had plain leather chin straps.

There were two types of gold embroideries for the peaked cap's visor: with a double row of gold oak leaves and acorns for flag officers and a single row for the ranks of Captain and Commander; after 1 January 1944, the visor's embroideries were used only on formal occasions, otherwise the plain visor was worn by all. At the same time, a black braid chin strap was introduced for everyday use and the gold one was relegated to formal wear, although, in fact, the black chin strap never turned out to be very popular. Later, the use of the visor's embroideries and gold chin strap became optional.

All naval officers, down to Chief Warrant Officer, wore the same cap badge, which could be found in metal or embroidered versions; initially, until May

1941, the eagle faced to its left, later to its right, towards the wearer's sword arm, the correct heraldic position of honour.

The Warrant Officer's cap badge depicted two crossed foul anchors, the Midshipman wore one gold anchor and the petty officers had the initials 'U.S.N.' in silver superimposed upon the anchor. Officers' cooks and stewards had the initials alone, in brass.

The U.S. Coast Guard had different cap badges, with the United States Shield in prominence, superimposed on the anchors of the warrant officers and petty officers and in the centre of the cap badge worn by Shore Establishment personnel. U.S.C.G. cadets wore the foul anchor in gold ensigned by a silver star and the officers' stewards the initials alone. Most surfmen eventually adopted the cap device of the Shore Establishment but the former badge, illustrated, still remained in use.

The U.S.C.G. officers wore a large American Eagle, with the shield on its chest clutching a horizontal foul anchor.

The nurse's peaked cap was adopted in 1942 for wearing with street uniform: it displayed a left collar badge at the front, above the cap band. The nurse's white cap had a 1½ in (38 mm) black velvet band across the front on which gold lace rank stripes were displayed. The Superintendent of the Navy Nurse Corps, Sue Dauser, became Captain in March 1943 and, together with the administrative commanders, did not wear the white uniform cap but displayed rank by cuff stripes and shoulder straps, in accordance with navy regulations.

Bandsmen wore a special badge on the peaked cap of the dress uniform, which has not been illustrated; it depicted a gold silk or rayon embroidered lyre superimposed upon an anchor. The cap had a red and gold cap band.

The garrison cap could be used by commissioned officers, warrant officers and by chief petty officers and matched the colour of the rest of the uniform; therefore there were blue, white, light khaki, green (winter khaki) and grey garrison caps, with miniature rank insignia on the right side and small cap device on the left for officers, corps devices on both sides for warrant officers and small cap device on the left side only for the Chief Petty officer.

Naval aviators and observers wore miniature aviation wings on the left side of the garrison cap until the spring of 1943 and later changed to the ordinary small naval badges.

Plate 41. Officers' Rank and Corps Insignia

The officers' rank and corps' insignia were usually combined, on the cuffs of the sleeves, shoulder straps and on the khaki shirt's collar.

Cuff stripes are the conventional naval officers' rank distinction and were shown in gold on dress and blue service coats, in black on overcoats and green winter working aviation coats, with the black Line star in the latter case; corps devices were not worn on the overcoat.

The overcoat carried cuff stripes and shoulder straps, except for the winter aviation working overcoat and raincoats, which showed no rank insignia.

The same type of stripes was applied on the sleeves and on the shoulder straps. At the beginning of World War 2, the stripes were worn all around the cuff but later they were placed on the outside only, from seam to seam and, from 1 January 1944, only the shorter stripes were permitted on service dress.

Flag officers were distinguished by gold lace stripes 2 in (50 mm) in width, combined on the sleeves with ½ in (13 mm) stripes and with silver anchor and stars upon the stripe on the shoulder straps. A narrower stripe, ¼ in (6.5 mm) wide, was worn in combination with larger ones by the Lieutenant Commander and Lieutenant (Junior Grade), and the narrow stripe on its own by the Aviation Cadet, although later during the war the latter started to wear the Line star instead of the stripe.

Shoulder straps were 2⅜ in (60 mm) in width, covered with navy blue or black cloth according to uniform, with stripes and badges, as illustrated. When grey working uniforms were introduced, new slate grey shoulder straps were adopted which carried black lace stripes, black embroidered 5-pointed star or corps devices, black anchor and rank stars for the flag officers.

The rank of Admiral of the Fleet was introduced on 14 December 1944; the rank of Commodore, but not its pay grade, was suspended from 1899 to April 1943 and, during World War 2, there were two graduations of the Rear Admiral's rank: the Rear Admiral of the upper half received the pay of his rank while that of the lower half was on the pay grade of the Commodore.

The Line Officer was qualified in all respects for command at sea of a specified ship or class of ship while a Staff Officer belonged to a corps and wore the corps badge instead of the 5-pointed star. Flag officers not of the Line wore a minature corps badge upon the shank of the anchor on the shoulder straps and the corps badge above the cuff stripes, in place of the star. Flag officers of the U.S. Coast Guard had the shield upon the anchor.

The following were the corps and their respective badges:

Corps	**Badge**
Medical	Silver acorn and gold oak leaf
Dental	Gold oak leaf and two silver acorns
Supply	A sprig of three oak leaves with three acorns in gold
Chaplain { Christian	Inclined, gold Roman Cross
Chaplain { Jewish	Gold Star of David above the Tablets of the Law
Civil Engineering	Two gold sprigs of two live oak leaves and a silver acorn

Corps	Badge
Nurse	Gold foul anchor with oak leaf, acorn and silver initials superimposed
Band	Gold lyre

The U.S. Coast Guard was not a corps but a service in its own right with the Coast Guard Shield as its badge, in gold for officers and warrant officers, silver for the Chief Petty Officer and in white or dark blue according to uniform, for the enlisted men. Chief petty officers and enlisted men wore the shield on the right forearm of the jumper.

Nurses wore their badge on the collar and, as we have seen already, on the cap as well.

The corps badges, also called sleeve markings, were always embroidered when worn on the sleeves while those for the shoulder straps could be embroidered or made of metal. Smaller badges, about five-eighths the size of those mentioned above, were worn on the left side of the collar of the khaki shirt and, together with rank insignia for the shirt's collar, are illustrated on Plate 42.

Plate 42. Warrant Officers' Rank and Corps Insignia

The Chief Warrant Officer and Warrant Officer were distinguished by large and narrow broken stripes, respectively; i.e. gold stripes with intermittent blue segments. They had the corps badge above the stripe and on the collar of the khaki shirt and some had special rank titles: for instance, the Chief Warrant Officer who wore the crossed anchors device was known as Chief Boatswain, the Chief Gunner wore the bursting cannon grenade, and so on.

The following were the corps and their respective badges:

Corps	Badge
Boatswain	Crossed foul anchors
Gunner	Bursting cannon grenade
Carpenter	Carpenter's square
Ship's Clerk	Crossed quill pens
Torpedoman	Torpedo
Radio Electrician	Four zigzag rays of lightning
Machinist	3-bladed propeller
Electrician	Globe
Photographer	Camera
Pharmacist	Caduceus
Aerographer	Circle divided by an arrow
Pay Clerk	A sprig of three oak leaves

The warrant officers of the U.S. Coast Guard wore, on the sleeves and on the shoulder straps, the shield and the corps badge as illustrated.

Officers' Miniature Rank and Corps Insignia

Naval officers wore U.S. Army/Marine Corps type of rank insignia on the garrison cap and on the shirt collar of the khaki summer working uniform. These badges were smaller than those worn on the shoulder straps by personnel of the other two services and were attached by means of a pin; admirals' stars, when more than one, were attached one to the other. Officers of the Line had rank insignia on both sides of the collar while Officers of the Corps wore the rank insignia on the right side and a minature corps insignia on the left side of the collar.

All miniature corps badges were made of metal and were about five-eighths of the size of those used on the sleeves and shoulder straps. The officers' badges were made of gold metal.

The warrant officers wore their corps badges on the collar of the khaki summer shirt: the Chief Warrant Officer had silver badges, the Warrant Officer gold ones, made of plain metal and not intended to imitate embroidery. A version of the photographer's badge shows a front view of a camera.

Plate 43. Insignia for Petty Officers

The rating badge consisted basically of the eagle, chevrons, arc and speciality mark. The eagle and speciality mark were white and the chevrons and arc were red on a navy blue background for blue uniform, while all the devices were navy blue on a white background for wear on white uniform. Navy blue badges on slate grey were used on grey uniforms.

The Chief Petty Officer and Petty Officer with no less than 12 years' service, holding three consecutive good conduct awards or equivalent outstanding record, were entitled to gold chevrons and silver embroidered eagle and speciality mark on blue uniform. The Chief Petty Officer who did not qualify for gold chevrons wore the usual white and red insignia or, optionally, silver embroidered eagle and speciality mark, but always red chevrons and arc. The chief petty officers wore officers' type uniform while petty officers had sailors' uniform.

The personnel of the Seaman Branch had the rate badge on the upper right sleeve and those of the other branches on the left. Branch was identified by a stripe of braid $\frac{23}{64}$ in (9 mm) in width sewn all around the seam between the sleeve and the shoulder of the jumper; Seaman Branch was shown by a stripe along the right shoulder, white for blue jumper and blue for white jumper, while the other branches, commonly known as Fireman Branch, displayed a red stripe on the left shoulder, regardless of the colour of the jumper.

Initially the eagle of the rate insignia faced to its left; thus the eagle of those who wore the badge on the left arm faced backward, but during the war it was decided that the eagle should always face forward of the wearer, regardless of its position on the uniform.

Service stripes, each representing 4 years of service were worn on the left forearm by those entitled. They were red for blue uniform and blue for white uniform. Three consecutive good conduct awards entitled the holder to gold service stripes on blue uniform.

Cuff Markings

The newly recruited sailor usually became an Apprentice Seaman and wore a single white stripe on both cuffs of the jumper; later he graduated to Seaman 2nd Class with two stripes, or Fireman 3rd Class, retaining in this case the single stripe, in accordance with his branch mark, i.e. Seaman Branch if he had a white stripe along the right shoulder seam, Fireman if he had a red one on the left shoulder. The cuff stripes were 7/32 in (5 mm) in width and the double and treble cuff markings were joined together by vertical stripes; the whole insignia was about 4¾ in (120 mm) long.

Two coloured shoulder sleeve insignia complete this plate, that of the Construction Battalions, nicknamed 'Seebees', and of the Minecraft Personnel.

Plate 44. Cap Tallies

Petty officers and non-rated enlisted men wore two types of cloth head-dress, the navy blue nicknamed 'Donald Duck' cap and the white hat with folded-up brim.

The former displayed a black tally with 'U.S. NAVY' or 'U.S. COAST GUARD' titles, according to service, while the latter did not show any insignia.

Speciality Marks

These badges have been illustrated in navy blue on a white background, as worn as part of rating insignia or on their own on the white uniform.

Speciality marks were introduced in 1841, starting with the crossed anchors of the Boatswain; many marks later disappeared or were changed to a new design following the development of tasks and specialisations on ships. The marks illustrated are those in use during World War 2. Many others were adopted later, during the last 30 years.

Marks whose title included the word 'Mate' indicated that the career in the speciality advanced up to the rank of Warrant Officer; thus the rating assisted his warrant officer in that particular job.

The badges were dark blue for white uniforms and of white or silver embroidery for blue uniform, except for the red cross of the Hospital Apprentice—Pharmacist Mate, which was red for all uniforms.

Most marks, and the job they represented, are self explanatory but some brief additional notes could still help the reader to understand better this rather difficult subject.

There was no Boatswain's Mate 3rd Class as this rate was known by the title of Coxswain; duties included the steering of ships and handling of boats, with knowledge of signals, charting of compass courses, directing salvage operations, etc. The Quartermasters' duties included the steering of ships, signalling by semaphore or blinker searchlight, etc. general navigation, the taking of soundings, the use of the rangefinder—a variety of jobs which had nothing in common with those of the army counterpart.

Aerographers dealt with meteorological observation and the Fire Controlman, who wore the gun's rangefinder as his badge, controlled the firing of the ship's gun. The Soundman's badge depicted earphones with an arrow across. The Chief Commissary Steward was always a Chief Petty Officer and his lower ratings were Baker and Cook, whose badge was the crescent moon with horizontal stripes below. The rate of Chief Officers' Steward or Cook was adopted in 1942; the rate badges of the Messman Branch, later redesignated Steward Branch, have been illustrated as worn on blue uniform.

Plate 45. Distinguishing Marks and Specialist Ratings

Distinguishing marks identified special qualifications attained by non-rated men or ratings, but in addition to the qualifications shown by the speciality mark.

Although distinguishing marks were usually worn above or below the elbow on either sleeve, the positioning was specified in each case. The Ex-Apprentice badge, for instance, was worn by the Chief Petty Officer below the rating badge and by the petty officers on the breast of the jumper, below the loop that held the neckerchief.

As usual the badge was white for blue uniform and blue for white uniform except the 'E' for Excellence in Engineering which was always red. Second and further awards of an 'E' in gunnery or engineering were identified by one or more small bars under the original badge.

Many badges illustrated as speciality marks were initially used as distinguishing marks by non-rated enlisted men. These are the following which are not shown again for lack of space:

Qualification	Badge
Quartermaster	Ship's wheel
Storekeeper	Crossed keys
Signalman	Crossed flags
Radioman	Lightning sparks

Qualification	Badge
Boilermaker	3-bladed propeller
Electrician's Mate	Globe
Gunner's Mate	Crossed cannons
Musician	Lyre
Yeoman	Crossed quill pens
Torpedoman's Mate	Torpedo
Aerographer's Mate	Circle divided by an arrow
Gun Range Finder Operator	Rangefinder

The Fire Controlman and the Gun Range Finder Operator wore the same badge but the former's was a speciality mark and the latter's a distinguishing mark.

The specialist ratings and their corresponding specialities were introduced during the war and all depicted letters of the alphabet, about ⅝ in (16 mm) in height, enclosed in a diamond-shaped frame; specialists were eligible for ratings.

The letter 'I' stood for International Business Machine Operator, later changed to Punched-card Accounting Machine Operator. The initials 'PT' identified the PTC Motor Torpedo Boats' specialists. In 1943, the frame was dropped from the badge of the Construction Battalions.

Initially about a dozen specialists' badges were adopted, followed by more and more until, eventually, even an 'X' badge appeared for individuals who had no specific qualification.

Many of these badges, as well as speciality and distinguishing marks, were used also by the U.S. Coast Guard.

Plate 46. Qualification Badges

The Naval Aviator wings were adopted at the beginning of 1919 and were used during World War 2 by pilots of the U.S. Navy, Marine Corps and Coast Guard. The Aviation Observer badge appeared in 1922 as a one-winged device, which, in 1927, developed into the Balloon Observer badge which was later redesignated Balloon Pilot badge. The wings of the Naval Aviation Observer were finally introduced in 1929.

The Flight Surgeon badge was the next to be introduced, followed, in 1944, by the Air Crew Insignia, with stars above it in a scroll, to show the number of engagements in which the wearer had taken part, namely air combat, action against enemy ships or fortified positions on the ground. No more than three stars could be applied on to the badge which, incidentally, could be used by officers and enlisted men not eligible for other aviation wings.

The badges of the Tactical Observer, Navigator and Radar Observer were adopted later during the war. Smaller wings, about half the size of the normal ones, were worn by officers on the evening dress and white mess jacket.

There were three types of submarine badges: for officers, for surgeons and the Combat Insignia. The latter was awarded to officers and men who completed one or more missions in which the submarine sank at least one enemy vessel or accomplished a combat mission of equal importance. The officers wore it below their ribbons.

A badge similar to that of the submarine's officers, but embroidered, was worn by enlisted men as a distinguishing mark on the right forearm.

Miscellanea

Personnel on Shore Patrol duty wore a navy blue armlet, $3\frac{15}{16}$ in (100 mm) wide, with large yellow 'SP' initials on the upper sleeve opposite the rating badge. The Geneva Cross armlet was always worn on the right upper arm.

The Honorable Discharge badge depicted the American Eagle in a circle, the whole embroidered in yellow on cloth matching the colour of the uniform, and was worn on the right breast.

The shoulder sleeve insignia of Amphibious Forces, depicting the inter-allied emblem of combined operation, in gold on red background for the navy, was worn on the upper left sleeve, below the shoulder seam.

Women members of the Women's Reserve of the U.S. Naval Reserve were known as W.A.V.E.S. while members of the Women's Reserve of the U.S. Coast Guard Reserve were called S.P.A.R.S. Officers of both organisations wore the male officers' cap badge on their distinctive hats while the enlisted women had naval or Coast Guard tallies instead.

Naval female officers had special collar badges depicting a white anchor on a blue propeller, the whole on a navy blue circular background. The Shore Establishment device was worn on both sides of the collar by S.P.A.R.S.; officers and enlisted women wore the Coast Guard Shield on the sleeves according to usual custom.

Both W.A.V.E.S. and S.P.A.R.S. officers wore rank stripes of 'reserve' blue instead of gold on the sleeves but no shoulder boards and both used distinctive shoulder bags of the same pattern.

The personnel of the U.S. Marine Corps Women's Reserve wore the same badges as their male counterparts and brown leather shoulder bags of special pattern.

Gilt buttons were used by officers and warrant officers of the U.S. Navy; they depicted the eagle perched on the shaft of the anchor encircled by thirteen stars. Large black buttons displaying the foul anchor were used by enlisted men on the overcoat and smaller ones with 'NAVY' above the anchor were worn on the dungarees. The officers' cooks and stewards had small black buttons, the anchor without rope, on the jacket of the blue uniform and the same type of button, but smaller, was worn by all enlisted men on the trousers.

The Coast Guards' button for officers and warrant officers had a straight eagle perched on top of the anchor and a laurel and oak leaves wreath. Enlisted men used black U.S. Navy buttons.

Marines had gilt and bronze buttons according to uniform; the button displayed the eagle perched on top of the anchor, with the thirteen stars placed around the top half of the button's edge.

Plate 47. U.S.M.C. Head-dress and Collar, Corps and Rank Insignia

The emblem of the U.S. Marine Corps, adopted in 1868, displayed the American Eagle above the globe, which is superimposed upon a foul anchor, with a scroll above the whole device that depicts the corps motto *Semper Fidelis*.

The latter scroll is not shown on insignia worn on uniform. Large badges made of metal were worn on the peaked cap, smaller ones on the garrison cap and on the collar. The officers' large badge had a separate rope, in imitation of a real rope, which was twisted in place around the anchor, while the rope of the enlisted men's badges was struck as part of the badge and therefore the spaces between the anchor and the rope were not cut out.

The badges used by officers on the blue and the white dress caps were made of silver and gilt, enlisted men's dress cap badges were made of brass, while the badges used on service dress, by both officers and enlisted men, were made of bronze, differing by their rope, as mentioned above.

The badge used on the garrison cap and on the collar had no rope at all; the former were always made of bronze while the collar badges matched the cap badge, i.e. with variations in silver and gilt, brass and bronze, according to type of uniform. Collar badges were worn in pairs with the anchors facing inward; the garrison cap badge was worn on the left side of the cap with its centre at $1\frac{31}{32}$ in (50 mm) from the front.

Aviation cadets wore a winged propeller in bronze or silver and gilt but, eventually, their training was taken on by the U.S. Navy, thus they came to wear naval uniforms and became part of the U.S.M.C. on receiving commission.

All officers had a cross-shaped ornament made of braid on the top of the peaked cap; the braid matched the colour of the cap. The permanent staff officers of departments and the aides-de-camp used special badges on the lapels of the service jacket and behind the U.S.M.C. device on the standing collar of the blue and the white tunic.

Service dress badges were made of bronze, while the badges for blue or white uniforms were made of silver and gilt and, except for the badge of the Adjutant and Inspector's Department, they had a coloured enamel finish.

The insignia of the Adjutant and Inspector's Department depicted a shield surrounded by a laurel wreath upon a sword crossed with fasces; the same badge was worn on the right and on the left side of the collar, while the following other badges were worn in pairs.

The badge of the Paymasters' Department depicted a sprig of oak leaves on a red tablet, encircled by an oak leaves wreath superimposed upon a sword crossed with a quill pen. A wheel with thirteen spokes and thirteen stars on a blue enamelled rim, superimposed on crossed sword and key, was the badge of the Quartermasters' Department.

The Aides-de-Camp wore, on the collar, the eagle above the shield, with one or more stars on the latter according to the number of stars of the general whom the officer was supposed to aid.

The officers of the Marine Corps used rank insignia of army type: generals had silver stars, the Colonel an eagle, the Lieutenant Colonel and Major silver or gold oak leaves, respectively, and the company officers displayed rectangular metal bars, the 2nd Lieutenant one only, made of gold.

In 1942 the Commandant of the Marine Corps was upgraded to the rank of Lieutenant General and later to the rank of General, with four stars.

Shoulder straps of jackets, tunics and overcoats of the U.S.M.C. differed from those of the other services in so far as they had rounded ends instead of pointed ends, as illustrated.

Plate 48. U.S.M.C. Warrant Officers' Rank and Corps Insignia

The U.S. Marine Corps had two warrant officers who wore departmental badges like the officers, plus the gunner's grenade and the lyre of the Second Leader of the Marine Band.

The commissioned Chief Warrant Officer, later redesignated Commissioned Warrant Officer was known simply as 'Chief' and wore as rank insignia a gold bar with a blue band across its centre. Departmental chiefs had special titles: Chief Marine Gunner, Chief Pay Clerk, Chief Quartermaster Clerk and the chief of the Adjutant and Inspector's Department was known as Chief Quartermaster Clerk (A. and I.) to distinguish him from the chief of the Quartermasters' Department.

Chief warrant officers wore the Marine Corps badge and departmental chief warrant officers and gunners wore their appropriate badge as well on the collar of jackets and tunics and rank insignia on the shoulder straps, as did the officers. However, on the overcoat and raincoat, they had the departmental device or the grenade as well as the rank insignia on both shoulder straps.

The Warrant Officer wore only the departmental device in lieu of rank insignia on the shoulder straps. The 2nd Leader of the Marine Band wore a silver lyre on all uniforms while all the other chiefs and warrant officers had bronze badges on service uniform and 'dress' badges on blue and on white uniforms. The Leader of the Marine Band was an officer.

Miniature rank insignia, departmental badges, the grenade and the lyre were worn on the collar of the khaki summer shirt in accordance with usual custom.

Distinguishing Marks

Four naval distinguishing marks could be awarded to marines and were worn on the right forearm of dress blue and service uniforms, centred between the elbow and the bottom of the sleeve, except for the 'E', which was placed at 2½ in (63 mm) above the bottom edge of the sleeve.

The badges were red on blue or khaki cloth background, according to uniform.

Shoulder Sleeve Insignia—1st Marine Amphibious Corps

Cloth patches were seldom granted to the marines and, in March 1943 only, the Commandant of the Marine Corps authorised the wearing of a limited number of shoulder sleeve insignia, starting with the insignia of the 1st Division; others were adopted later.

The 1st Marine Amphibious Corps was identified by a rather large blue patch in the shape of a square shield, depicting the constellation of the Southern Cross and a red diamond in the centre which identified the deployment or specialisation of its wearer.

The plain red diamond was used by anti-tank units, the 6⅛ in (155 mm) Howitzer Battalion and all corps personnel, except those who were part of the following units which had special badges in the diamond:

Units	Badge
Balloon Barrage Battalions	Captive balloon
Defence Battalions	Anti-aircraft gun
Paratroopers	Open parachute
Raiders	Skull
Service & Supply	5-pointed star

Later, artillerymen were granted the crossed cannons in the diamond.

All shoulder patches were worn on the upper left sleeve, below the shoulder seam.

Plate 49. U.S.M.C. N.C.O.s' Rank Insignia

The U.S. marines used three types of chevrons: gold on a red background for the dress blue uniform, green (dark khaki) on red for the green winter uniform and black on light khaki for the summer shirt.

The non-commissioned officers of the Line had chevrons joined by arcs while those of the Staff had theirs joined by ties, i.e. straight stripes.

The marine advanced into the Line or Staff careers by becoming a Private 1st Class (6th Grade) but only when he reached the 3rd Grade rank did the arc or tie identify the branch to which he belonged. Aviation N.C.O.s wore ties under their chevrons as aviation was one of the specialisations of Staff.

The branches were: Line, Music, Signals and Radio, Quartermaster, Paymaster, Aviation and Mess.

The lozenge within the First Sergeant's badge was adopted during World War 2, while the badge with three chevrons and three arcs was worn by the Sergeant Major and Master Gunnery Sergeant (1st Grade Line). The First Sergeant was quoted as the leading man in his company while the other two were experts in their own trades: the Sergeant Major in drills, regulations, billeting and administration and the Master Gunnery Sergeant in arms and ordnance.

The 1st Grade Staff covered the ranks of Master Technical, Quartermaster and Paymaster Sergeant and there were no rank insignia with the lozenge in the Staff branches. The Gunnery Sergeant (2nd Grade Line) wore three chevrons and two arcs while the Technical Sergeant, Drum Major and Supply Sergeant (2nd Grade Staff) had three chevrons and two ties. The Platoon Sergeant (3rd Grade Line) and the Staff Sergeant (3rd Grade Staff) wore three chevrons and one arc, or tie, respectively. The Sergeant (4th Grade), Corporal (5th Grade) and Private 1st Class (6th Grade) wore three, two and one chevron, and the Private (7th Grade) had no rank insignia at all.

There were five grades of musician: Principal Musician with rank insignia corresponding to the 2nd Grade; 1st, 2nd, 3rd Class Musician and Private 1st Class, all with the lyre below the chevrons. Later the whole system was changed with the creation of the rank of Band Leader, wearing three chevrons, three arcs and the lyre, and of Musician with one chevron, one arc and the lyre.

Until September 1942 chevrons were worn on both upper sleeves, later on the left sleeve alone.

Service stripes, each corresponding to 4 years of service, were worn on the outer part of the forearm of the left sleeve in colours matching the colour of the chevrons.

Plate 50. U.S.M.C. Shoulder Sleeve Insignia—Amphibious Corps

The first corps patch to be adopted for the Amphibious Corps, Pacific Fleet, later became the insignia of the 5th Marine Amphibious Corps, and the three stars on the badge stand for the rank insignia of a Lieutenant General, a corps commander.

The patch of the 3rd Marine amphibious Corps depicted the mythological sea monster Leviathan of the Scriptures, below the corps' number in Roman figures. The head of an alligator below three white stars was the emblem of the 5th Corps, formerly Amphibious Corps, as already mentioned.

Divisions

The 'Guadalcanal Blaze' of the 1st Marine Division was the first divisional insignia adopted during World War 2 and was designed by Lieutenant Colonel M. B. Twining, U.S.M.C., who served in the division as operations officer at Guadalcanal. Appropriately the badge depicts the figure '1', inscribed 'Guadalcanal', upon the constellation of the Southern Cross, on a blue background.

The patch of the 2nd Marine Division followed in style that of the former, with a figure '2', in the form of a snake, inscribed with the same battle honour. This badge was superseded by another pattern, showing a hand holding a torch and the Southern Cross, the whole on an arrowhead-shaped red background.

A 3-pointed star device on an equilateral curvilinear red triangle became the badge of the 3rd Marine Division and the figure '4', on a red diamond, the badge of the 4th Marine Division. The 5th Marine Division's badge displayed a blue arrowhead which symbolises the marines' role of relentless attack, upon a 'V', which stands for Victory and for its numerical designation, the whole on a red shield. Three battle honours were shown in the badge of the 6th Marine Division: 'Melanesia' referred to the islands northeast of Australia; 'Micronesia' to the islands of the West Pacific, including the Marianas, Carolinas, Marshall, Palao and Gilbert Islands, and the battle honour 'Orient' was selected because the 4th Marine Regiment, lost in Bataan and later reactivated as part of the 6th Division, came from China, and in anticipation that the final stages of the war would be fought in the Orient.

The marines serving in Londonderry, Northern Ireland, adopted a patch which combined the Marine Corps emblem and the Irish shamrock, a fine badge which however remained unofficial and was eventually discarded.

Defence Units

The defense battalions were deployed as anti-aircraft units: the 13th Defense Battalion's patch carried a seahorse while the other three battalions' badges displayed emblems symbolic of their deployment, a sword upon wings in the case of the 18th and anti-aircraft guns for the other two.

There were two variants of the Ship Detachments' patch: with blue or with black anchor under the seahorse.

The patch of the 4th Marine Base Defense Air Wing showed the figure '4' above an eagle poised to drop a bomb. The unit was formed in August 1942 and, in November 1944, it joined the 4th Aircraft Wing.

Plate 51. U.S.M.C. Shoulder Sleeve Insignia—Fleet Marine Forces

Some rather large shield-shaped patches, embroidered in yellow and white on a red background, were used by the Fleet Marine Forces. The central device identified the assignment of the wearer, i.e. a fist holding four lightnings for headquarters, an anti-aircraft gun for anti-aircraft personnel, a field gun for artillery, etc.

Aircraft Wings

Aviation personnel wore special patches based on the design of the aircraft fuselage insignia, with yellow stars, wings and a Roman number below, which refers to the wing's number. The headquarters' emblem displayed a Spanish crown, which stands for California where it was organised.

Later these shield-shaped badges were replaced by kite-shaped ones, somehow simplified in their symbolism: all depicted a winged Marine Corps emblem with the unit's designation below.

Plate 52. Subsidiary Services

The personnel of some subsidiary services which, incidentally had little or nothing in common with the U.S. Navy, wore navy-blue uniforms and used insignia of naval type; it may be useful therefore to show at least some specimens of their badges.

The Army Transport Service was redesignated during the war as Army Transportation Corps Vessels and was supervised by the Water Division of Transportation Corps, Army Service Forces. It shared its badges with another subsidiary organisation, the Harbor Boat Service. Their personnel had special rank designation identified on uniform by gold, silver or lustrous black stripes, often on branch colours, according to rank or speciality on the cuffs and shoulder marks. Port officials had white braid on white uniforms and brown on khaki uniforms.

The officers' cap badge depicted the American Eagle with enamelled shield on the breast, perched on crossed anchors. The Marine Superintentent and Superintending Engineer wore, on the collar, the initials 'A.T.S.' upon the ship's steering wheel with thirteen stars on the rim; the other officers wore the initials only in gold, the stewards only in silver. The following branch badges were worn on the lapels

Badge	Designation of Task
Foul anchor in gold	Marine Superintendent, Master, Chief Stevedore, Deck Officers, A.T.S. and Master, Mate, Pilot, H.B.S.

Designation of Task	Badge
3-bladed propeller in gold	Superintending Engineer, Engineering Officers, A.T.S. and Chief and Assistant Engineer, H.B.S.
Insignia of Transportation Corps in gold	Transportation Agent
Crossed quill pens in gold	Clerks on piers and on transports
Five lightnings in gold	Radioman, civilian
Crescent in silver	Steward

Personnel of the A.T.S. and H.B.S. had the initials above the foul anchor on their gold buttons, stewards wore silver buttons.

The petty officers wore, on the peaked cap, a branch badge or the designation of task surrounded by a wreath, as follows:

Badge	Task
Crossed anchors	Boatswain
Crossed batons	Master at Arms and Assistant
Crossed axes	Carpenter
Ship's steering wheel with stars on blue enamel rim	Wheelman
3-bladed propeller	Machinist, Refrigerating Engineer, Deck Engineer, Chief Electrician, Plumber, Boilermaker, Water Tender and their Assistants

and the following designation of task in place of the badge: Yeoman, Storekeeper, Assistant Storekeeper, Baggagemaster, Porter, Watchman and Barber.

Ratings wore from one to three red chevrons above the red branch badge on a blue background, as illustrated.

U.S. Maritime Service

The insignia of the Maritime Service followed the U.S. Navy pattern and its personnel used the rank insignia and rank-rate designation of the navy. The officers graduated up to the rank of Vice Admiral and wore gold lace stripes on the cuffs and shoulder marks below corps devices, surrounded by a gold wreath. The device, or emblem, of Line was the foul anchor; the others were the same as those of the U.S. Navy, for Supply, Hospital Corps, Radio Electrician and Chaplains.

The warrant officers used navy devices as well, all except those of Gunner,

Torpedoman and Aerographer and, like their officers, wore them enclosed in a wreath.

The petty officers had red chevrons and speciality marks of naval type below a red anchor combined with the initials 'USMS'.

U.S. Coast and Geodetic Survey

The emblem of this organisation depicted a silver globe with a gold triangle in its centre, which suggests the triangulation methods used in geodetic surveys.

It was worn by all commissioned officers above the rank stripes on the cuffs and shoulder marks, with the exception of the commandant, a Rear Admiral, who had the device superimposed upon a foul anchor on his shoulder marks, and the device alone on the cuffs.

Civil service ships' officers graduated as Chief Engineer, Surgeon, Mate or Deck Officer and wore a 3-bladed propeller, the naval hospital device or binoculars respectively, instead of the globe and triangle. The Deck Officer had no insignia.

Ratings wore chevrons like naval ratings except that the eagle of the U.S.C. & G.S. was perched on the top segment of a globe; chief petty officers with 12 years' meritorious service had gold chevrons and arc. The following speciality badges were used:

Speciality	**Badge**
Boatswain	Foul anchor
Yeoman	Crossed quill pens
Carpenter	Axe
Radio Technician	Lightnings
Oiler	3-bladed propeller
Coxwain	Fouled arrow
Electrician	Armature
Quartermaster	Steering wheel
Master at Arms	Shield
Pharmacist	Red cross
Officers' Steward or Cook	Crescent

The cap badges of officers and Chief Petty Officer have been illustrated; the latter is similar to the badge worn by the Rear Admiral on the shoulder marks. The officers' stewards and cooks wore on the cap the initials 'US' above 'C&GS' and, like their counterparts of the navy, had bars instead of chevrons as rate insignia.

Petty officers and seamen wore the white hat or blue cap, the latter with the tally illustrated.

U.S. Public Health Service

The emblem of this organisation is a winged caduceus superimposed on a horizontal foul anchor, the former signifying medicine and the latter a sailor in distress.

This emblem was part of the cap badge and on its own was worn on the garrison cap, above rank stripes on cuffs and shoulder marks and as a lapel badge on olive drab army type uniforms. The rank titles of the Public Health Service corresponded with those of the army and navy medical corps and were displayed in naval style on uniforms or in army style on olive drab uniforms, according to assignment.

The P.H.S.'s emblem was used as a corps device, as follows:

Corps	**Badge**
Medical and Engineer Officers	The emblem
Acting Assistant Surgeon	With additional 'A'
Dental Officers	With additional 'D'
Scientific Officer	With additional 'S'

Additional badges were worn above the corps badges by:

Intern at Marine Hospitals	Aesculapius staff
Pharmacist	Winged caduceus
Administrative Assistant	Crossed key and pen
Chaplain	Roman Cross

Cadet nurses in training wore a special grey uniform with beret and displayed a special shoulder sleeve insignia on the left upper arm.

Japan

The Japanese started to organise a modern fleet in the middle of the last century with the help of Dutch experts, as initially they had bought some ships from Holland. Later, British expertise and influence took over and, by 1894, the Japanese defeated the Chinese fleet. The Russo-Japanese War of 1904–05 marked another Japanese success and, later, the advance continued into China.

All was made possible by the raising of a powerful and efficient navy. The first major modernisation of uniforms took place in 1884 and, although many changes took place later, those first dress regulations established the standards of uniforms and badges for the next 50 years.

Uniforms became more practical, and insignia less decorative, as the Imperial Japanese Navy became progressively more engaged farther and farther from its homeland.

Plate 53. Cap Badges

The officers wore, on the peaked cap, a gold anchor in a ring surrounded by a gold wreath, the whole ensigned by a silver cherry blossom; the petty officers wore the cherry blossom superimposed upon the anchor with an oval gold edge around it and the midshipmen had a gold foul anchor alone.

The cherry blossom upon the anchor was worn by officers and ratings, except seamen, on the field cap; the latter wore a plain anchor. There were several variations of both these badges as the colour of the emblem and its background changed according to the colour of the cap. Some badges were embroidered in gold, others in yellow or blue thread, others woven in silk.

The cap tally of the sailors had swallow's tail-shaped ends and a yellow anchor on both sides.

Plates 53, 54 and 55. Officers' Rank Insignia

The naval officers had the same rank titles as the officers of the army, the former's title was preceded by the term 'Kaigun' (Navy) and the latter's by 'Rikugun' (Army) in order to distinguish between the services.

Rank distinction was shown in the form of gold lace stripes with curl on the cuffs of the blue dress uniform and overcoat, black lace stripes on the service dress tunic and, in the latter's case, additional collar patches. The service dress tunic had black lace trimmings along the top and front edge of the collar, the front and skirt and on the pockets.

The flag officers had two large stripes with one, two or three medium stripes above, the uppermost with the curl, and the other officers used medium stripes; the Lieutenant-Commander's and Sub-Lieutenant's combined with a narrow one (which, on its own, was used by midshipmen and cadets), the former with the curl and the latter without it.

Only some examples of cuff stripes are shown, but all the shoulder straps for each rank have been illustrated.

Shoulder straps were intended for use on the white tunic but were often worn on blue and khaki tunics as well. They were shaped in a particular manner, typical of all Japanese epaulettes and shoulder straps and carried gold lace stripes, which distinguished class of rank, and silver cherry blossoms to identify individual ranks.

The Midshipman wore the stripe of the junior officers' class without the cherry blossom device and the Cadet had a gold anchor on plain blue shoulder straps.

The collar patches were made of navy blue cloth, with gold stripes and silver cherry blossoms, as on the shoulder straps, and were worn on the blue service uniform, khaki jackets and shirts.

Only cherry blossom devices were worn on the collar of the cape and identified class of rank: three cherry blossoms were worn by flag officers, two by senior officers and one by junior officers.

Officers who were commissioned from the ranks were identified by different badges, as illustrated; they could graduate to the rank of Lieutenant and had three gold cherry blossoms below the usual navy cuff stripes. They had silver cherry blossoms on the shoulder straps but above a narrower gold lace stripe, of warrant officer's width.

The rank insignia of non-executive officers have been illustrated on Plate 58. The corps were identified by coloured distinction cloth placed as a background to the cuff stripes, on both sides of the gold lace on the shoulder straps and as longitudinal piping on the collar patches. Midshipmen and cadets of the corps wore a coloured anchor on the cap.

The following were the corps and their corresponding colours:

Corps	**Colour**
Engineers	Violet
Ship and Engine Constructors	Brown
Ordnance Constructors	Purple-brown
Medical	Red
Legal	Pale green
Paymasters	White
Survey Officers	Black
Aviation Officers and Hydrographers	Light blue
Chief Carpenters (Warrant Officer)	Green
Bandmaster (Warrant Officer)	Grey-blue

During the course of the war, gold or dark blue stripes, according to the colour of the cap badge, were adopted for wear on the field cap, all around its base, below the badge. These stripes identified class of rank: three stripes for flag officers, two for senior officers and one for junior officers.

Cuff stripes of reduced version were adopted as well, for practical reasons. The stripes and curl were sewn on a square patch of dark blue cloth and, as such, could be worn on the breast or on the upper sleeve of special field uniforms or overalls.

In January 1944, the conventional rank insignia on the cuffs were changed to three, two or one narrow gold stripes without curl, according to class of rank, with three, two or one gold cherry blossoms below, according to rank.

Plate 56, 57. Petty Officers' and Seamen's Rate Badges (1st type)

Petty officers and seamen at first wore their rate and corps devices combined on the upper sleeves. The badges were round in shape and displayed red devices on dark blue background for wear on blue uniform, blue devices on white for white uniform.

The petty officers were identified by a wreath on the badges; the Petty Officer 1st Class and Seaman 1st Class wore crossed corps devices ensigned by a cherry blossom, those of 2nd Class wore crossed devices without the cherry blossom and those of 3rd Class had a single corps device in the badge.

The design of several badges was modified during the war, as for instance the device of the Aviation Corps, illustrated, and new ones were added.

Red or blue Good Conduct chevrons, according to uniform, were worn above the badge; chevrons with a small cherry blossom at the apex identified Excellent Conduct.

Midshipmen and cadets of the navy wore the anchor on the collar and, later, a winged cherry blossom was adopted instead for those of the naval aviation.

Plate 58. Good Conduct Chevrons, Petty Officers' and Seamen's Rate Insignia (2nd Type)

The second pattern of rate badges was yellow and only the background was changed to match the colour of the uniform. All displayed an anchor, on its own for seamen and surrounded by a wreath for petty officers, ensigned by a cherry blossom in corps colour. Three, two or one yellow bar above the cherry blossom identified the specific class of rating, although the rates' titles by then had been altered to include the Seaman 2nd Class who wore the anchor and cherry blossom without any bar.

Later, the definitive graduation included the Leading Seaman, who wore three bars, the Superior Seaman with two, the Seaman 1st Class with one bar, and the Seaman 2nd Class.

Ratings of the Line had yellow cherry blossom in the badge while those of the other corps used the colours previously listed. The badge was worn on the right upper sleeve, below eventual Good or Excellent Conduct chevrons, as before, but now yellow. A larger cherry blossom device, in two versions, as illustrated, was worn on the left upper sleeve by those who had attained special training qualifications.

Poland

The modern Polish Navy was created after World War 1 but it has a long history that goes back to the years before the partitions of the eighteenth century. Danzig became a naval base in the mid-sixteenth century and its ships destroyed a Swedish squadron in 1627; later, King Władysław IV strengthened the navy and constructed a fortified base on the Hel Peninsula.

However, Poland was mainly engaged in land warfare due to its geographical position in the centre of Europe; thus it never became a sea-faring power and never had colonies overseas.

After World War 1, Poland became the possessor of a narrow strip of land on the Baltic and a naval base was constructed at Gdynia, and became active in 1924. In the following years, Poland had some ships built in France but, by the late 1930s, it had its own arsenal and shipyard at Gdynia, where minesweepers were built and later two destroyers laid down.

On 28 August 1939, on the basis of an agreement between the Polish Naval Staff and the British Admiralty, three Polish destroyers, *Grom*, *Błyskawica* and *Burza*, left Gdynia and arrived in Britain, where they were met by the destroyer H.M.S. *Wallace*, on 1 September, on the first day of the war.

Plate 59. Cap and Rank Insignia

The first naval dress regulations, the Order No. 5 dated 18 January 1919, prescribed infantry type of uniforms with light blue and white piping and additional foul anchor on cap badges and shoulder straps.

At that time, many sailors came to the Polish Navy after having served in foreign navies, namely the Austrian, Russian and German Navy, and still wore foreign uniforms. Due to lack of supplies, they probably continued to wear those uniforms but with Polish insignia.

The first comprehensive dress regulations which introduced dark blue and white uniforms appeared in 1920 and were subsequently modified by several orders, the last one dated 9 December 1936.

The officers' blue and white caps had a gold and silver embroidered badge, black leather chin strap and visor which displayed the wearer's rank in the form of gold stars applied on to the former and stripes on the visor. The flag officers had a 'zigzag', the senior officers a double stripe and the junior officers a single stripe.

Officers wore gold lace stripes on the cuffs of the blue jacket and the same stripes on the shoulder straps of the white jacket and overcoat. The flag officers used large gold lace stripes, twisted to form a zigzag, surmounted by one, two or three narrow stripes with curl, according to rank. The senior officers had the large stripe, straight, in place of the zigzag and the junior officers wore the narrow stripes alone.

The dress belt was made of leather, covered on the outside by gold lace with two woven blue stripes and lined on the inside by navy blue velvet. A plain black leather belt could be used with the same buckle, which displayed the same emblem present on the buttons.

Plate 60. Cap and Rank Insignia

Gold metal stars could be fixed directly on to the chin strap or were embroidered in gold wire on a small patch of black cloth, and slipped on the chin strap.

Distinction cloth identified the naval branches and was worn as a backing to the officers' rank stripes, showing in between the stripes or below the one stripe rank. The following were the branches of the Polish Navy and their distinguishing colours:

Branch	Distinction Cloth
Line	—
Medical	Cherry red
Legal	Raspberry red
Technical	Green
Administration	Brown
River/Coastal	Light blue
Band	White

Doctors, advocates of the Legal Branch, musicians and administrative officers usually came from the army as they did not need training for executive naval command.

The officer cadets wore officers' uniforms and the chief petty officers' peaked cap and were eligible to ratings' chevrons and stripes but not to trade badges. They were distinguished by a gold metal badge, depicting a 5-pointed star surrounded by a laurel wreath which was later abolished.

Reserve officer cadets used piping of white and red twisted cords as their own distinction: ratings of 'A' category used it around the cuffs of the blue jacket and as piping to the shoulder straps, and those of 'B' category at a distance of $\frac{13}{32}$ in (10 mm) all around their stripes on the upper left sleeve.

The Warrant Officer and chief petty officers ('B' Category) wore gold chevrons, $\frac{15}{32}$ in (12 mm) in width, the former above a $\frac{9}{32}$ in (7 mm) stripe on both cuffs; chevrons and stripe were sewn on a backing of red felt which protruded all around the edges.

The Warrant Officer used the officers' type of cap badge while the others had their own pattern: a silver embroidered eagle with gold crown, perched on a blue 'Amazon' shield with a gold foul anchor in its centre, the whole on an oval felt background.

The Chief Petty Officer ('Bosman') was promoted to Chief Petty Officer 1st Class ('Starszy Bosman'—Senior Boatswain) after 6 years of service with good conduct.

Plate 61. Cap, Rate and Trade Insignia

Warrant and chief petty officers wore the gold trade badge on the left upper sleeve at 2$\frac{3}{8}$–2$\frac{3}{4}$ in (60–70 mm) below the shoulder seam; the trade badge was not worn on the white jacket, nor on the work jacket.

The 'SP' initials stand for 'Szkoła Podchorążych' and, like the badge of the reserve cadets, was made of brass; both were similar to the cadets' badges of the army but the latter were made of white metal instead.

The junior ratings ('A' Category) wore a metal badge on the sailor's hat, at the front above the tally: the eagle and shield were made of white metal and the anchor of brass.

Rate was identified by one, two or three gold stripes on the left upper sleeve, at 1$\frac{3}{16}$ in (30 mm) below the trade badge or, when lacking the trade badge, at 1$\frac{31}{32}$–6$\frac{5}{16}$ in (150–160 mm) below the shoulder seam. The stripes were sewn on a red backing, like those of the senior ratings.

Plate 62. Cap Tallies and Trade Badges

The tallies were made of black silk and displayed the ship's name or the general title 'Marynarka Wojenna' in yellow letters.

The trade badges were self-explanatory, in red on a navy blue background. The first set of badges was adopted in 1920 and included crossed signallers' flags, crossed cannons, a flaming grenade, etc. others were added and modified later in accordance with the development of the service and progress of modern specialisations. Non-qualified seamen wore a plain foul anchor.

The Free Polish Navy in Great Britain

The three Polish destroyers in British ports were joined by the submarines *Wilk* and *Orzel* and, later, the training ships *Wilia* and *Iskra* turned up at Casablanca. In May 1940, the Royal Navy ceded H.M.S. *Garland* to the Polish Navy: the ship, then in Malta, retained its name but its initials 'H.M.S.' were changed to 'O.R.P.' ('Okret Rzeczypospolitej Polskiej'—Ship of the Polish Republic).

A new navy was slowly built on this modest basis and Polish vessels validly participated in war operations in the Atlantic and Mediterranean.

The old uniforms and insignia continued to be worn in Britain; new ones were tailored locally and the first amendments to the dress regulations were published in 1941. By the Order No. 5 of 27 October, Paragraph 53, the rings of gold lace previously placed all around the cuffs were replaced by stripes on the outside of the cuffs and the rate insignia of the cadets were changed to stripes on the cuffs, which identified 1st, 2nd or 3rd Year Course.

In April 1942, the Warrant Officer's insignia was replaced by a gold lace stripe ¼ in (6.3 mm) in width, with curl, worn on both cuffs. The Petty Officer was allowed to wear the cap and uniform previously strictly reserved for the chief petty officers.

A new Polish naval service composed of women was organised in April 1943, on the basis of the British 'Wrens' and with similar uniforms.

In November 1943, the naval staff dealt with the chaplains: the new regulations specified that they should wear officers' uniforms without rank stripes, with the Roman Cross in gold on the collar and shoulder straps, and one or two stripes on the visor of the peaked cap, according to rank. Chaplains were identified by their clerical collar.

The officers of Commissariat were given white distinction cloth in March 1944 and, in November, the branches of Naval Aviation and Coastal Defence were formed within the Navy. The personnel of the latter wore khaki army uniforms with a blue beret, blue shoulder straps with foul anchor, naval cap badges and army pattern rank insignia but in gold. The Coastal Defence was subdivided into three branches: Line, Technical and administration. All wore blue collar patches in two shapes: for officers' service dress and ratings' battledress, as the patches had to match the different shapes of the collar. The collar patches had coloured piping at the top, as follows:

Branch	**Colour**
Line	White
Technical	Dark green
Administration	Brown

The very last amendments to the dress regulations were published in September 1945 and dealt with the Coastal Defence and Naval Aviation. The officers of the latter were ordered to wear an 'L' ('Lotnictwo') inside the curl of their rank stripes.

Netherlands

Only since 1815, when the Netherlands became a kingdom, can one speak of the Royal Netherlands Navy, although the history of the Dutch Navy goes back to the early thirteenth century. During the latter part of the sixteenth and the beginning of the seventeenth century, sea battles took place between Dutch and Spanish fleets. Some famous battles were those of Zuider Zee (1573), the Armada (1588), Sluys (1603), Gibraltar (1607), the Slaak (1631) and the Downs (1639).

After the Eighty Years' War was concluded by the Treaty of Westphalia, by which the independence of the Republic of the United Provinces was recognised, the Dutch neglected their navy, with the result that, during the First Anglo–Dutch War, the latter were beaten and the Low Countries had to concur with the Treaty of Westminster, which proved inconclusive.

In the second half of the seventeenth century Dutch naval power was restored in all waters which were important to commerce; in the Baltic and its approaches, in the North Sea, in the Mediterranean and in the Caribbean, Dutch ships-of-war came into action when commercial interests had to be defended. Some famous battles were the Four Days' Battle (1666), Chatham (1667), Sole Bay (1672), Schooneveld (1673), Texel (1673), Oland (1676), Beachy Head (1690) and La Hogue (1692).

Great admirals like Tromp, De Ruyter, Kortenaer, Banckert, Evertsen and many others led their fleets to victory.

The eighteenth century saw the decline of Dutch sea power until 1780 when the Fourth Anglo-Dutch war broke out. During this war, which lasted four years, the battle of Doggerbank (1781) was fought.

In 1795, the Batavian Republic was proclaimed and, once again, Dutch and English ships met at sea and, at Camperdown (1797), one of the bloodiest naval battles was fought. In 1806 the Republic became the Kingdom of Holland with the brother of Napoleon, Louis, as king. In 1810 this kingdom was incorporated into the French Empire and, after the defeat of Napoleon, the Netherlands became a kingdom, in 1815.

During the nineteenth century and the beginning of the twentieth the Royal Netherlands Navy was mainly employed in the pacification of the Dutch colonies in the Far East and the suppression of piracy. During World War 1, its main task was the maintenance of neutrality and it was not until the outbreak of World War 2 that the Royal Netherlands Navy was again involved in combat, and suffered severe losses.

Plate 63. Cap and Rank Insignia

The officers of the various corps of the Royal Netherlands Navy were identified by badges rather than by corps colours. The cap badge of all except chaplains consisted of a wreath of twelve oak leaves and acorns ensigned by the crown, with the corps' emblem in the centre: the chaplains' badge had no crown and its wreath had eight oak leaves only. All wreaths had six acorns.

The following were the corps, their emblems and type of embroidery:

Corps	Emblem	Embroidery
Line	Foul anchor	Gold
Administration	Foul anchor	Silver
Engineering	Torch above crossed arrows	Gold
Medical	Aesculapius staff	Gold
Aviation	Aircraft engine above propeller	Gold
Chaplains	Roman Cross	Gold

Flag officers wore peaked caps with two rows of oak leaves and acorns on the visor, the captain and commander had one row only along the edge. All the other officers, the chaplains, warrant and petty officers had plain black leather visors.

The Warrant Officer and Petty Officer wore the crown and anchor on the cap, in silver for Yeomen and gold for all others; musicians had the lyre below the crown, the whole in gold.

Officers and warrant officers displayed rank insignia on the cuffs or on the shoulder straps, according to uniform. The flag officers displayed one large and one medium stripe of gold lace, the latter with the curl, and their individual rank was identified by small 6-pointed silver stars placed as shown in the illustrations.

Plate 64. Rank Insignia and Collar Badges

Administrative officers wore silver lace stripes, all the others gold stripes. Chaplains were restricted to one rank only ('Vloot Geestelijke') with two gold stripes and a separate silver one above; they did not have a curl but, contrary to all the other officers, they wore their badge on the shoulder straps.

The officers of the Special Service ('Officieren voor Speciale Diensten') had the initials 'SD' in the curl and could rank up to Captain only; they were reserve officers who were enlisted for special duties.

The collar badges worn on the blue jacket were the same as the corps emblem of the cap badges, except for the chaplains who wore the usual cross surrounded by a wreath with four oak leaves and two acorns, the same badge as on the shoulder straps.

The personnel serving in line and aviation, and the chaplains, had the same gold buttons with crown above the anchor; administration had the same buttons but made of silver; engineers had the crowned anchor superimposed upon crossed torch and arrow and medical personnel's buttons displayed the crown above the Aesculapius staff surrounded by an oak wreath. The buttons of the latter two were made of gold, in accordance with the general rules.

The Warrant Officer was identified by a narrow stripe with curl worn on the cuffs or shoulder straps, of gold or silver as usual.

Plate 65. Ratings' Insignia

The three ratings of the Royal Netherlands Navy wore chevrons on the cuffs of the blue jacket, the Chief Petty Officer and Petty Officer had two gold chevrons and one respectively; the Leading Seaman wore two yellow chevrons, or white ones in the case of a Yeoman Leading Seaman, on the cuffs of the overcoat.

The Chief and Petty Officer wore special patches with small chevrons, as above, on the collar of the white and khaki tropical tunic, while the Leading Seaman had one inverted 'V' chevron on the upper sleeves of the jumper or tropical uniform.

Warrant Officers' and Petty Officers' Speciality Badges

The warrant and petty officers wore speciality insignia of gold on the left sleeve of the blue uniform.

The Warrant Officer of most specialities was called 'Opper' plus his speciality title, but the Warrant Officers' Machinist was known as 'Adjudant-onderofficier-machinist' and a pilot as 'Adjudant-onderofficier-vlieger'.

The Chief Petty Officer Boatswain's title was 'Schipper' and all the others were known by their speciality title preceded by the word 'Majoor'.

The Petty Officer Boatswain was called 'Bootsman'; the others had their speciality title preceded by 'Sergeant.'

All the badges illustrated were made of gold wire, except the crown of the Yeoman which was made of silver.

The traditional Dutch cap tally displayed the title 'Royal Navy' in gothic script and was later replaced by another one, illustrated, with the title in block letters, yellow on black silk.

Plate 66. Speciality and Trade Badges

Speciality badges, in gold for leading seamen and red for seamen, were worn on the left upper sleeve of the blue uniform but not on tropical uniform; on the jumper of the white summer uniform no badges, except the chevron, were worn by leading seamen.

Bar exceptions, gold badges were used by the Leading Seaman and Seaman 1st Class, red ones by Seaman 2nd Class and apprentices.

Examples of speciality badges have been illustrated but there were more: there were four variations of badges for Torpedoman, Aviation Repairman, Electrician and Fire Controlman, a gold badge for Leading Seaman and Seaman 1st Class, a red badge with two small bars below for the 3rd Year Apprentice, with one bar for the 2nd Year Apprentice and the red badge without any bar for the 1st Year Apprentice. Carpenters wore a gold badge, a red one with bar and another without a bar.

The trade badge was worn on the right upper sleeve of the blue uniform. Beside those illustrated, red crossed flags were used by signallers, crossed flags and lightning by telegraphists, crossed guns by gunners and gold crossed guns were awarded to the Marksman Gunner. The last two rows of badges illustrated were trade badges; those above were speciality badges.

Finland

Many Finns served in the Swedish Navy during the period when Finland belonged to Sweden, from the twelfth century to 1809, and later in the Russian Navy. No less than three hundred became officers and seventy of them reached the rank of rear-admiral and above during the latter period.

After the Russo–Swedish War of 1808–09, Finland became part of the Russian Empire as an autonomous grand duchy, retaining its own laws and institutions, and even some national defence forces which included small naval units called Sea Equipage.

Finland became an independent republic on 6 December 1917 as a result of the Russian Revolution and, after the War of Independence fought by government troops against Russian and Finnish Reds, the Finnish Navy was established in the summer of 1918. The ships were those that the Russians had left behind and the officers were Finns who had served in the Russian Navy and some German naval experts.

In the 1920s, British naval experts were employed in reorganising and planning a new ship-building programme, which was carried out in the next decade.

During the Winter War (December 1939–March 1940) the Finnish Navy consisted of the following units: the Helsinki Naval Base, the Turku Naval Base and the Coastal Fleet, but operations were restricted by the severe weather from the beginning of January onwards, when the whole Baltic Sea was frozen.

After the Germans had started Operation 'Barbarossa' Finland became involved in another war against the U.S.S.R., which ended with the Armistice of Moscow, in September 1944. The Peace Treaty was finally signed in Paris on 10 February 1947.

Plate 67. Cap and Rank Insignia

The first official naval uniforms were introduced in 1919 and followed the international naval pattern with some Russian and German features.

The executive officers' cap badge depicted the gold Finnish Lion on a round, protruding red enamel background, on a gold base. On the peaked cap (lippalakki') this badge was centred between two sprays of gold embroidered laurel leaves, below a gold anchor. The white-blue-white cockade, in brass and enamel, was used by cadets of the Reserve, warrant and petty officers, and also by officers, and a painted version of this badge was worn by seamen.

Two rows of gold oak leaves on the peaked cap's visor identified flag officers and one row senior officers, from the rank of Kommodori to Komentajakapteeni.

The Finnish Lion was always worn in conjunction with the rank stripes by all executive officers, usually above the stripes but, in the case of the flag officers' shoulder straps, it was worn superimposed upon the wide stripe, as illustrated. The stripes were made of gold lace, 1 of $1\frac{5}{8}$ in (40 mm) in width for flag officers, $\frac{19}{32}$ in (15 mm) and $\frac{7}{32}$ in (5 mm) the narrower stripes.

Shoulder straps were used on the white uniform, overcoat and fur coat while, on all other uniforms, rank insignia was displayed on the cuffs.

Plate 68. Cap and Rank Insignia

Non-executive officers wore the same uniform as executive officers but had an additional stripe, or stripes of distinction cloth with the rows of gold lace on the cuffs and shoulder straps. The distinction cloth filled the interval, or intervals between two or more stripes or it was placed below a single stripe. The branches were identified as follows:

Branch	**Distinction Cloth**
Executive Officers	None
Engineer Officers	Violet
Medical Officers	Red
Musicians	Blue

The officers of the Reserve wore special stripes, of gold lace but adapted to a zigzag pattern, until the summer of 1940 when this distinction was abolished.

Only one rank of Chaplain existed and was identified by a cross above a large stripe placed on the cuffs and shoulder straps.

Specialist officers were distinguished by silver insignia and by a 6-pointed star worn in conjunction with their rank stripes, instead of the Finnish Lion. They had silver embroidered cap badges, silver stripes, silver shoulder tabs, buttons, etc.

The shoulder tabs or epaulettes, according to order of dress, were worn on the frock coat in use before the war. The dress belt is another item that was abolished during the war: the flag officers' belt was made of gold lace and carried a design of oak leaves and acorns, the officers' belt had horizontal alternate gold and blue stripes and the warrant officers had a plain cloth belt. However, the buckle and fittings could be attached to a leather belt as well, which was worn on service dress in lieu of a Sam Browne belt.

Plate 69. Cadets' Cap and Rank Insignia

The cadets of the regular navy wore, on the peaked cap, the officers' Finnish Lion above four gold embroidered laurel leaves, the whole badge edged by a thin blue cord. Basically they wore officers' uniforms while the cadets of the Reserve had seamen's uniforms and therefore seamen's head-dress, with their own cap tally and petty officers' cockade made of metal and enamel.

The former had special shoulder straps for full dress. These straps had rounded inner ends, were edged with gold lace and carried the Naval Academy's badge on the outer ends and an anchor or crossed cannons in the centre, which identified navy or coast artillery branch, respectively.

The anchor or the crossed cannons devices were also worn on the left upper sleeve, together with chevrons; inverted 'V' chevrons on the top to identify progress of training and 'V' chevrons below that showed the cadet's rank, as they attained petty officers' rank while at the Academy.

Reserve officer cadets were eligible to two ranks only, Candidate and Cadet, which were identified by two, or one, upper chevrons worn above the 'RUK' badge ('Reserviupseerikoula'—Reserve Officers' School).

Warrant Officers' Rank Insignia

The warrant officers wore officers' uniforms with badges of their own pattern. They were divided into three classes and displayed rank insignia in the form of inverted 'V' chevrons, $\frac{9}{32}$ in (7 mm) in width, on both cuffs of the jacket. Above the apex of the chevrons they had the speciality badge, embroidered in gold. Speciality badges were also worn on the shoulder straps, which were of officers' pattern but made of plain cloth.

All these badges have been illustrated in this and the following plate; the 'Master' rank title was used by the warrant officers while the plain title of speciality refers to the ratings.

Plate 70. Warrant Officers' and Petty Officers' Insignia

The warrant officers' cap badge consisted of the white-blue-white enamelled cockade centred between a gold embroidered anchor and a four-leaf laurel spray, the whole edged by a blue cord.

The naval petty officers had the same cockade below a gold metal anchor, placed on an oval background edged by a gold cord. The specialist petty officers wore only a white metal anchor surrounded by a silver cord.

Petty Officers' Rate Insignia

The petty officers wore gold chevrons (silver for specialists) on the left upper sleeve and, except for the top and bottom ranks, they had army titles divided into three grades: Senior Sergeant, Sergeant and Junior Sergeant. The boatswains had wide chevrons, while the other ratings had narrow ones, $\frac{9}{32}$ in (7 mm) in width, with gold speciality badges above them.

There were three classes of seamen identified by blue anchors and blue bars. The petty officer candidate wore a plain white bar.

Conscripted seamen were also eligible for ratings but their badges were red: initially one horizontal red bar, two red bars and, later, an individual could attain one or two red chevrons and speciality badges made of red felt.

All seamen and conscripted petty officers wore the sailor's hat with silk tally and a tin badge painted white and blue.